The Principles of Teaching and Learning

First Edition

Dr. Mohamed Bataineh, Dr. Majedah Abu Al-Rub, and Dr. Adel T. Al-Bataineh

The World Islamic Sciences and Education University
Yarmouk University
Illinois State University

cognella®

SAN DIEGO

Bassim Hamadeh, CEO and Publisher
Angela Schultz, Senior Field Acquisitions Editor
Susana Christie, Senior Developmental Editor
Alisa Munoz, Project Editor
Abbey Hastings, Production Editor
Jess Estrella, Senior Graphic Designer
Greg Isales, Licensing Coordinator
Natalie Piccotti, Director of Marketing
Kassie Graves, Senior Vice President of Editorial
Jamie Giganti, Director of Academic Publishing

Cover: Copyright © 2016 iStockphoto LP/smartboy10.

Printed in the United States of America.

3970 Sorrento Valley Blvd., Ste. 500, San Diego, CA 92121

BRIEF CONTENTS

DETAILED CONTENTS

Preface

This book is based on the idea that preservice and inservice teachers can acquire certain skills and knowledge that will help them become more caring and effective educators. Because this educational era emphasizes factors such as accountability, technology integration, reflective thinking, standards, and performance-based instruction, you will find, incorporated into the content and the structure of the text itself, teaching principles central to each of these factors. For example, each chapter begins with an introduction that outlines the rationale for the reading and a set of suggested learning outcomes, and each one ends with discussion questions. You will also find comprehensive information that covers the theoretical foundations and the historical development of education. The book provides teachers with the foundational knowledge to understand student learning and equips them with practical skills and tools that are necessary to prepare curriculum, plan instruction, assess students, and manage the classroom environment effectively.

While there is much of value in the performance-based movement, the teaching and learning processes are not as precise or clear-cut as some proponents of the movement imply. A teacher's success depends to a large degree on the success of his or her students. To help students succeed, teachers must not only develop a range of pedagogical skills; they must also develop the personal characteristics conducive to effective teaching. A good teacher must, for example, be accepting of individual differences and opinions, be fair with students, and be receptive to new ideas. Characteristics such as these are as crucial to good teaching as any of the skills and procedures about to be presented. We are confident that this book will provide you with research based and common-sense foundations and skills to help you in your learning and teaching journey.

The book covers twelve chapters that focus on the following topics:

- Educational Philosophies and Why You Need One
- Why the Schools Are as They Are
- Learning Theories and Instructional Models
- Selecting Instructional Units
- Classifying and Using Precise Instructional Objectives
- Whole-Class Instructional Activities

- Small-Group and Individualized Instructional Activities
- Planning Daily Lessons
- Principles of Preparing and Administering Tests
- Student Assessment and Teacher Evaluation
- Classroom Management
- Educational Technology

Each chapter includes a brief introduction, learning outcomes, a list of key terms, people and ideas, discussion questions, and references. Through these resources, the readers are encouraged to discuss, analyze, and debate issues that relate to learning and teaching. The authors hope that this book will contribute to the advancement of knowledge in the areas of learning and teaching.

Acknowledgments

We gratefully acknowledge the time, effort, and ideas that others contributed to this book. Dr. Michael A. Lorber, Professor Emeritus of Education at Illinois State University, kindly provided us the initial incentive and encouragement to publish the book. His expertise, support and guidance throughout the last two decades have been invaluable for our professional and personal development. Moreover, we express our deepest gratitude to Mrs. Ellen Jane Lorber for her friendship, encouragement, and support. Her insights about education have been valuable in developing this book.

Our appreciation also goes to all of our students who provided us with valuable comments and many of the insights that found their way into this text.

We also would like to convey our thanks and gratefulness to our parents, *El haj* Tawfig Ahamed Al-Bataineh and *El Hajeh* Meriam Mansour Al-Bataineh, for their love, support, encouragement, and their lifelong self-sacrifices.

Finally, this book is dedicated to five amazing children: Emma, Benjamin, William, Steven, and Adam.

CHAPTER 1

Educational Philosophies and Why You Need One

INTRODUCTION

What would you say if a prospective employer asked you for your philosophy of education, or whether you agreed or disagreed, philosophically, with No Child Left Behind? If you were to say something such as, "Well, I want to help all students learn," or "well, it sounds reasonable," the prospective employer might very well put you into the category of applicants who want to teach but who have not thought deeply about the profession or their place in it. You can do better.

This chapter is intended to familiarize you with some of the most influential schools of thought concerning education. Further, this information will help you to better understand the premises that underlie the proposals that people make for changing what is taught and how it is taught.

LEARNING OUTCOMES

You will be able, in writing, to:

1. Create a comparison chart, perhaps a Venn diagram, depicting the common and unique characteristics of perennialism, essentialism, progressivism, and existentialism.
2. After identifying two philosophies of education, orally describe two student evaluation techniques that are more commonly used with one than with the other.
3. Based on your experiences, select the educational philosophy that seems most appropriate to you and describe two reasons why that philosophy seems more appropriate than each of the others.

WHAT IS A PHILOSOPHY OF EDUCATION?

Educational philosophies represent basic theories and viewpoints that eventually acquire labels such as Perennialism, Essentialism, Progressivism, and Existentialism. **John Dewey**, one of America's greatest educational theorists, warned against 'isms. He said that "in spite of itself, any movement that thinks and acts in terms of an 'ism becomes so involved in reaction against other 'isms that it is unwittingly controlled by them."[1] Nonetheless, the 'isms are alive and well and understanding them will help you make more informed choices.

When educational philosophies in their "pure" forms are discussed, the differences among them seem clear. However, when these philosophies are applied in school settings, compromises are often made and some of the differences disappear. Further, most philosophies have at least one goal in common, the production of educated people who can live happy and productive lives. The problem is that *educated*, *happy*, and *productive* mean different things to different people. Still further, many educators are eclectic; they pick and choose elements from different philosophies as they develop their own. You are likely to do the same, but the task will be easier if you first know something of four basic philosophies.

A WORD OF ADVICE

Educational philosophies are usually stated with great conviction and are often supported with strong, cause-effect arguments. You might, therefore, want to consider the following advice offered by Gautama **Buddha** (563?–483? BC):

> Believe nothing because a so-called wise man said it.
>
> Believe nothing because a belief is generally held.
>
> Believe nothing because it is written in ancient books.
>
> Believe nothing because it is said to be of divine origin.
>
> Believe nothing because someone else believes it.
>
> Believe only what you yourself judge to be true.

Note: What you believe may not actually be true, but your belief will guide your actions, nonetheless. Choose your beliefs carefully.

LEARNING FROM THE ANCIENT GREEKS

Virtually all philosophies of western education are rooted in ancient Greek thought, so pulling back the curtain of history just a little will shed a great deal of light on today's controversies in education. As you read, keep in mind that when we are talking about the ancient Greeks, we are talking about a relatively small number of people. For example,

Sparta, at its height in the fifth century BC, had a population of about 250,000, of which about 25,000 were full citizens.[2] At about the same time, **Athens** had a population of about 335,000, of which about 35,000 were full citizens.[3] What is said about education in ancient Greece pertained only to full citizens. The other ninety percent of the population, the females, foreigners, serfs, and slaves, were excluded, partially or altogether, from formal education.

The numbers are relevant because, although ancient Greece is often cited as the source of democracy, when it came to education, it was not so democratic. The Greeks saw education as necessary, but only for the children of citizens. Educating all the children of all the people is an idea born in the New England colonies. With a system educating about fifty-five million K–12 students in public and private schools (estimated as for Fall 2007),[4] student diversity and sheer logistics become problems of a magnitude never encountered by smaller societies then or now.

A look at the views of the Elder Sophists, Socrates, Plato, and Aristotle, will help expose the roots of modern educational philosophies. Much of their thinking is still valid today.

The Elder Sophists—The First Professional Teachers

The Elder Sophists were a group of itinerant teachers who, at about 450 BC, went from city-state to city-state operating "as freelance teachers in competition with each other, accepting fees for their work."[5] Since success in ancient Greece depended largely on one's ability to speak in public, the Sophists met the needs of their students by specializing in the teaching of rhetoric, "the art of oratory, especially the persuasive use of language to influence the thoughts and actions of listeners."[6] Despite this, it should be noted that the Sophists' ideal was the **polymath**, a person expert in all areas of knowledge.

The idea of meeting students' needs was evidently a good one. **Protagoras**, the best known of the Elder Sophists, was "able to charge 10,000 drachmas for a two- or three-year course of instruction at a time when one drachma was a skilled worker's daily wage. By 350 BC, however, the price of such a course had fallen to about 1,000 drachmas."[7]

Protagoras had some ideas that are clearly parts of modern philosophies. For example, Plato attributes to him the idea that "Of all things, the measure is Man."[8] This is the root of the modern philosophy of **existentialism** and of "situation ethics," or the idea that what is right is dependent on time, place, and circumstance. His view, "Art without practice, and practice without art, are nothing,"[9] is central to progressivist thinking. He also believed that "all men were capable of intelligent, socially responsible self-rule, but that they could not achieve their potential without education."[10] The idea that all children can learn is accepted in all philosophies today. **Gorgias**, with his idea that nothing (absolute) exists, also helped lay the foundation for existentialism.

Until the time of the Sophists (the fifth century BC), instruction had been mostly tutorial. The Sophists, however, modified the tutorial system and taught groups of students rather than individuals. "It was the first recorded instance of mass instruction."[11]

It is likely that the Sophists introduced the technique of analysis in teaching. "By analyzing exemplary models of writing and speaking, they formulated rules for effective writing and speaking. They also combined theory and application. First, the Sophists taught their students the rules (theory) of the spoken and written word. Then they prepared a model speech for them to copy, analyze, discuss, and present in actual spoken practice. … Because the Sophists' procedures were inherently systematic, the student always knew what was of expected of him, how he might achieve his goals, and how well he was progressing."[12] Most educators today still think that these are sound pedagogical practices. The way the Elder Sophists taught helps explain why they are often regarded as the first professional teachers.

Socrates—Knowledge Is Inborn; Questioning Can Draw It Out

Socrates (c. 470–399 BC) believed that knowledge was good in and of itself, that the main purposes of education were to guide and motivate moral conduct, and that much knowledge was inborn and could be drawn out by skillful questioning.

The questioning technique used by Socrates, which came to be called the **Socratic Method**, required that each question lead to a definite point and that the questioner build only on the facts students already knew. If the student had to collect data in order to reach a new conclusion, the teacher had strayed from Socrates's model.[13] The Socratic Method is typically easier to use with younger people because we tend to make assumptions about what people know based on their age and, therefore, ask questions that are inappropriate to the Socratic Method. For a brief, but cogent summary of the Socratic Method, read an article published by Life Lessons. The URL is: https://lifelessons.co/critical-thinking/socratic-method/.

Keep in mind what happened to Socrates. When his educational views and practices conflicted enough with those thought to be proper by the city administrators, they sentenced him to death. We are kinder today, but if your educational views and practices differ enough from those thought to be proper by the teachers and administrators in your school, you might not be rehired after your first year.

Plato—The Ideal World of Ideas; Learn by Thinking

Plato (c. 427–347 BC) contributed many ideas still revered today. For example, he believed that the world we see is illusory and that the real world exists as pure "Forms" or "Ideas" that never change. He also believed that education should concern itself with helping people comprehend these never-changing Truths. The idea of eternal Truths is central to most religions and to the twentieth century philosophy of perennialism, which has its roots in idealism.

Plato was among the first to formally recognize individual differences. In *The Republic*, Plato described how social harmony could be achieved in an ideal society by requiring all citizens to begin formal education, but allowing those least able or least inclined to profit from instruction to leave. They would become menial workers. Those who could profit from more instruction would continue with military training and would become the warriors and guardians of the state. The most able, the intellectual elite, would go on to further study and become the philosopher-kings who would rule. This awareness of, and concern for, individual differences is important to progressivism. We also see the roots of a tracked educational system and the resulting stratified society.

Aristotle—World Ruled by Natural Laws; Learn by Experience

Aristotle (c. 384–322 BC) said the following:

> Education should be regulated by law and should be an affair of state. … Since there is a single end for the city as a whole, it is evident that education must necessarily be one and the same for all … but at present there is a dispute concerning its tasks. Not everyone conceives that the young should learn the same things either with a view to virtue or with a view to the best way of life, nor is it evident whether it is more appropriate that it be with a view to the mind or with a view to the character of the soul. Investigation on the basis of the education that is current yields confusion, and it is not at all clear whether one should have training in things useful for life, things contributing to virtue, or extraordinary things; for all of these have obtained some judges (supporters). Concerning the things relating to virtue, nothing is agreed. Indeed, to start with, not everyone honors the same virtues, so it is reasonable to expect them to differ as well in regard to the training in it.[14]

Aristotle (c. 384–322 BC) agreed with most other ancient Greeks that the state's welfare depended on an educated citizenry and that the state should take an active role in guiding education. As you will see in the following chapters, Congress has taken an active interest in, and has heavily influenced, education in the United States. Aristotle was also one of the first people to articulate the disagreements about the purposes of education. Those disagreements continue to this day.

The thinking of Plato and Aristotle concerning education differed in at least one respect. Plato believed that thought, pure cognition, was the major tool of learning and that knowledge was its own reward. Aristotle believed that little or nothing was in the mind other than what got there through the senses. **John Locke** (1632–1704) echoed that idea when he said that the mind was a **tabula rasa**, a blank tablet, on which all that we know is written via our experiences.[15] Aristotle also saw knowledge as having more utilitarian purposes than did Plato.

Aristotle's interest in examining new things and in scientific investigation was well known to his students. One of them, Alexander the Great, remembered his teacher's interest and sent to him a steady stream of plants, animals, and artifacts as he went about conquering most of the world known at that time. This concern for scientific investigation is central to essentialism and to progressivism.

As a point of information, it was Aristotle who introduced the idea of syllogistic reasoning in *Prior Analytics*. Such reasoning consists of a major premise accepted as true. This is followed by a minor premise, also accepted as true, which is followed by a conclusion that must be true if the major and minor premises are true. The following is the most common example of a syllogism:

Major premise: All men are mortal.

Minor premise: Socrates is a man.

Conclusion: Socrates is mortal.

Plato and Aristotle also believed that the mind was made of separate powers or "faculties" such as memory, judgment, and reasoning, and that these faculties could be strengthened by rigorous mental exercise.[16] This **faculty theory** was not disproved until Edward L. Thorndike's study in 1922–23.

"TRADITIONAL" PHILOSOPHIES—PERENNIALISM AND ESSENTIALISM

Of all the educational philosophies that could be explored, four—Perennialism, Essentialism, Progressivism, and Existentialism—seem to be most pervasive. We will look first at Perennialism because it focuses on the **seven liberal arts** (grammar, rhetoric, logic, arithmetic, geometry, music, and astronomy). These subjects have been the foundation of Western education since the Middle Ages (from about 500–1500), and to a large extent, they still dominate the secondary curriculum.

Perennialism (Roots in Idealism)

Perennialism reflects Plato's belief that Truth (with a capital "T" to denote its eternal nature) and values are absolute, timeless, and universal. The goal of education should be to help all students discover and understand these Truths, and the study of humanity's accumulated knowledge is the best way to accomplish this goal. Perennialists are sometimes accused of advocating a separate-subjects curriculum, but the Truths sought cut across time, place, and the subject-matter lines that educators establish to manage instruction. Viewed from this perspective, perennialism seems very much concerned with curricular integration or as it is sometimes called, interdisciplinary studies. It does not, however, rely greatly upon tests as measures of achievement and is not, in that respect, congruent with the expectations of the No Child Left Behind (NCLB) Act. The work of Robert Hutchins and Mortimer Adler will help further delineate the basic tenets of Perennialism.

Robert M. Hutchins (1899–1977) was thirty years old when he became president of the University of Chicago, where he served for twenty-two years (1929–1951). His views are often associated with perennialism. He wrote:

> One purpose of education is to draw out the elements of our common human nature. These elements are the same in any time or place. The notion of educating a man to live in any particular time or place, to adjust him to any particular environment, is therefore foreign to a true conception of education.[17]
>
> If education is rightly understood, it will be understood as the cultivation of the intellect. The cultivation of the intellect is the same good for all men in all societies.[18]

Hutchins also believed that schools are called upon to teach too much. Many educators agreed with him then, and many more would agree now. What follows is a listing of some of the functions that have been assigned to, or assumed by, the schools. Many of these had once been the primary responsibility of the home, church, or workplace, while others emerged from concerns at the state and federal levels.

1640–1900	Basic reading, writing, and arithmetic. Transmission of values and knowledge associated with a democratic society (includes history of the United States and our form of governance)
1900–1930	(Due to immigration of Europeans to America in the early 1900s) Nutrition Immunization Health
1930s	Vocational Education Practical Arts Physical Education School Lunch Programs
1950s	Sex Education introduced (topics escalating through the 1990s) Foreign Languages (strengthened) Driver Education Safety Education (strengthened in succeeding decades)

1960s	Consumer Education
	Career Education
	Peace Education
	Leisure/Recreational Education
	Early Childhood Education/Pre-School programs for at risk children
1970s	Drug and Alcohol Abuse Education
	Parent Education
	Character Education/Values Clarification
	Special Education (mandated by the federal government)
	School breakfast programs added
1980s	Bilingual Education
	Global Education
	Ethnic Education
	English as a Second Language
	Multicultural Education
	Full-Day Kindergarten
	After school programs for children of working parents
	Stranger/Danger—Sexual Abuse Prevention Education
	Child Abuse Monitoring (legal requirement for teachers)
	Keyboarding and computer literacy
1990s	HIV/AIDS Education
	Death Education
	Geography (re-emergence as a separate subject)
	Inclusion of special education students
2000s	"Volunteer" service
	Increased emphasis on high-stakes testing
	Accountability
	Online Instruction

The problem here is not the value of the topics. The problem is that teachers who were prepared to teach in particular disciplines are not well prepared to provide meaningful instruction in many of these other areas. As new topics were added, the function of schools became less clear and teachers less sure of what was expected of them. Hutchins seems to have made a good point. Further, neither the school day nor the school year has been lengthened to accommodate the new inclusions. As **Alfred North Whitehead** noted:

> Lack of time is the rock upon which the fairest educational schemes are wrecked. It has wrecked the scheme which our fathers constructed to meet the growing demand for the introduction of modern ideas. They simply increased the number of subjects taught.[19]

With the Perennialist conviction that much of our cultural heritage was already written and was available for study, Hutchins, working with another educator with Perennialist views, **Mortimer J. Adler** (1902–2001), compiled and edited the fifty-four volumes of ***Great Books of the Western World***. Published by Encyclopedia Britannica in 1952, these volumes contained the Bible and the works of people such as Homer (*Odyssey, Iliad*), Archimedes, Galileo, Shakespeare, Spinoza, Huygens, Sir Isaac Newton, Leibnitz, John Locke, and many others.

Adler took the principles of Perennialism (and some principles of progressivism) and put them into practice first at the high school level and then K–12, with the **Paideia** (py-dee-a) Project. A basic premise of the project, and one that Adler credits to John Dewey, is that if democracy is to succeed then all children must be given the same educational opportunities, the same quantity of public education, and the same quality of education.[20] Adler quotes Hutchins's statement that "the best education for the best, is the best education for all."[21] As might be expected, this position raised questions by those concerned with individual differences.

Adler argued that in order to provide the general and liberal education he saw as necessary for all students, "all sidetracks, specialized courses, or elective choices must be eliminated. Allowing them will always lead a certain number of students to voluntarily downgrade their own education."[22] The curricular model he advocated was laid out in three columns and is shown in Table 1.1. The three columns do not correspond to separate courses, nor is one kind of teaching and learning necessarily confined to any one class.

Table 1.1 Curricular Model for the Paideia Project

Goals	Acquisition of Knowledge	Development of Intellectual Skills—Skills of Learning	Enlarged Understanding of Ideas and Values
	by means of	*by means of*	*by means of*
Means	Didactic Instruction, Lectures, Responses, Textbooks, and other aids	Coaching, Exercises, and Supervised Practice	Maieutic or Socratic Questioning and Active Participation
	in the three areas of of subject matter	*in the operations of*	*in the*
Areas, Operations, and Activities	Fine Arts; Mathematics and Natural Sciences; History, Geography, and Social Studies	Reading, Writing, Speaking, Listening, Calculating, Problem Solving, Observing, Measuring, Estimating, Exercising Critical Judgment	Discussion of books (not textbooks) and other works of art and involvement in artistic activities, for example, music, drama, and visual arts

Adler, Mortimer J., *The Paideia project, An Educational Manifesto* (New York: Macmillan Publishing, 1982, p. 23).[23]

Distinguishing Characteristics of Perennialism in Its "Pure" Form

1. Has its roots in Idealism—perfection exists only in the world of ideas and can be best studied via cognition alone.
2. The role of education is to help students understand perennial Truths, rather than to meet contemporary, often transitory, needs.
3. To accomplish this goal a single curriculum should exist for all students.
4. The curriculum should consist of the most general and abstract subjects such as philosophy and logic, since they cut across time, place, and circumstance, but it should emphasize the integration of that knowledge.
5. The curriculum should include the study of original sources such as the *Great Books*.
6. The interests of students are of little consequence of designing and implementing the curriculum.

Points of Contention

1. The role of education should be broader than simply cultivating the intellect and studying ideas of the past. Focusing on the past does not prepare students for today or tomorrow as effectively as focusing on modern scientific studies and the changing state of knowledge.
2. Curricular choices must exist to accommodate differences in abilities and interests among students and students should help determine what they will learn.
3. Focusing on the past does not prepare student for today or tomorrow as effectively as focusing on modern scientific studies and the changing state of knowledge.

Essentialism (Roots in Realism)

Essentialism is the philosophy that underlies virtually all of today's secondary school curriculums and, when people speak of the "traditional" curriculum, what they typically mean is an essentialist curriculum. One of the main goals of essentialists is to pass on to each new generation of learners the cultural and historical heritage, beginning with a strong foundation in the "basics." It is primarily subject-centered, and it sees the teacher as a master of a particular subject field.[24]

Growth of Subject Separation in Teacher Education

The interrelatedness of knowledge began to be lost as more knowledge became available and people began to specialize. In 1439, William **Byngham** founded one of the first schools of education, **Godhouse College** in England.[25] Although students in the school were already teachers, Byngham started the idea of student teaching and it is also likely that he advocated that students learn subject-matter as separate disciplines. Later, in 1684, Jean **Baptiste de la Salle** founded another school of education at Rheims, France. Baptiste de la Salle was among the first to organize subject matter to facilitate group instruction and to advocate the orderly promotion of students from one unit of subject material to another.[26] These early schools of education became known as **normal schools** because they set the norm or standard for good teaching practices. The idea of breaking knowledge into disciplines and dealing with each discipline separately became the norm and it continues to dominate education today. Regardless of its advantages, this approach does little to convey to students the interrelatedness of knowledge.

There are, however, two less frequently mentioned characteristics that make essentialism seem "right" to so many. One characteristic is that essentialism emphasizes clear, measurable goals. One of those goals is to help students acquire a common and strong knowledge base (English, math, social studies, and science) that they can use to make judgments, deal with the world, and solve problems. Using this knowledge base, students can move on to new discoveries and perhaps develop new solutions to existing problems. Students can build on what others have learned and experienced. They do not have to learn by trial and error (i.e., discovery learning). The fact that some students might not recognize the value of this approach is of little concern to essentialists. They believe that students, because of their lack of experience, are not aware of what they need to know. Therefore, they should trust their elders and apply themselves to the prescribed studies.

A second characteristic is that essentialists believe that competition is inherent in the human species and is a driving force in virtually all human endeavors. They accept that people compete with each other for power, status, goods, and services and that nations do the same. Essentialists seek to prepare students, and the country, to compete successfully in the global economy. Cooperative learning is not excluded, but neither is it a major characteristic of essentialism. For these reasons, supporters of the No Child Left Behind Act are likely to see essentialism as an excellent educational philosophy.

One way to visualize an essentialist curriculum is to think of a hallway with rooms on each side. Each room is labeled with a content area such as math, history, or English. Students are required to spend time in each room and, after doing that, they can return to rooms of their choice and spend more time there. Sound like your high school experience? The words of three essentialists will give you a fairly good idea of that philosophy.

William S. Bagley (1874–1946)

> Gripping and enduring interests frequently grow out of learning efforts that are not intrinsically appealing or attractive.

The control, direction, and guidance of the immature by the mature is inherent in the prolonged period of infancy or necessary dependence peculiar to the human species.

While the capacity for self-discipline should be the goal, imposed discipline is a necessary means to this end.[27]

Arthur Bestor (1908–1994)

The curriculum should consist essentially of disciplined study in five great areas: (1) command of the mother tongue and the systematic study of grammar, literature, and writing; (2) mathematics; (3) sciences; (4) history; and (5) foreign language.[28]

Liberal education is designed to produce self-reliance. It expects a man to use his general intelligence to solve particular problems. Vocational and "life-adjustment" programs, on the other hand, breed servile dependence.[29]

Concern with the personal problems of adolescents has grown so excessive as to push into the background what should be the school's central concern, the intellectual development of its students.[30]

Hyman G. Rickover (1900–1986)—Father of the Nuclear Navy

For all children, the educational process must be one of collecting factual knowledge to the limit of their absorptive capacity. Recreation, manual or clerical training, etiquette, and similar know-how have little effect on the mind itself and it is with the mind that the school must solely concern itself. The poorer a child's natural endowments, the more does he need to have his mind trained. ... To acquire such knowledge, fact upon fact, takes time and effort. Nothing can really make it fun.[31]

Distinguishing Characteristics of Essentialism in Its "Pure" Form

1. Has its roots in realism—focus on the practical.
2. The roles of education are to perpetuate the culture and to teach students the knowledge, skills, and values needed to become contributing members of society.
3. To accomplish its goals, the subject-centered curriculum should focus first on teaching that which is known and then on helping students build on that knowledge to explore the unknown, particularly via scientific investigation.

4. Non-academic subjects such as vocational courses, physical education, and the fine arts should be minimized in, or excluded from, the curriculum.
5. Progress in education should be measurable at the end of some reasonable time frame, and one useful tool in this measurement is the standardized test.

Points of Contention

1. The role of education should be to introduce students to, and help them acquire, the skills and understandings needed to appreciate all aspects of life. Since life includes cognitive and physical activities, creative endeavors, and recreational endeavors, the curriculum should include all of these things.
2. A separate-subjects curriculum fragments knowledge whereas the intent of a curriculum should be to help students integrate knowledge.
3. It is better to focus on the process of learning rather than on learning specific content.
4. Education should be a life-long endeavor and efforts to "measure" it, particularly via tests, are misguided.

"NONTRADITIONAL PHILOSOPHIES"—PROGRESSIVISM AND EXISTENTIALISM
Progressivism (Roots in Pragmatism)

Progressivism is the philosophy most often cited in contrast to perennialism and essentialism. Most progressivists believe that the curriculum should be more student-centered than subject-centered, more focused on activities than on passive learning, and more aimed at long-term rather than short-term goals. Most progressives also believe that since knowledge is continually changing and expanding it is more important to learn *how* to think than to learn *what* to think.

John Dewey (1859–1952)

John Dewey is perhaps the most often cited progressivist. He had an abiding faith in the link between an educated citizenry and the flourishing of democracy and thought that schools should be a place where students could learn the skills needed to live in a democratic society. He believed that students had an innate desire to know and grow, and that the best way to capitalize on those desires was to give students tasks and materials they saw as relevant to their own needs. Even though he was a biologist by training, he believed that the curriculum should be interdisciplinary. Students would learn elements of math, science, and English, etc., as they needed those elements to do certain things and solve relevant problems. Further, he saw cooperation and standards established for individuals as more beneficial than competition and standards established for groups.

As early as 1938, Dewey saw that some educators, such as **William Kilpatrick** (1871–1965), had taken some of his ideas, such as the project method, well beyond his intent. From that point forward he spent a good deal of time pointing out that he did NOT agree with those who wanted to "make little or nothing of organized subject-matter ... or to proceed as if any form of direction or guidance by adults was an invasion of individual freedom."[32] With respect to the project method, often cited as a hallmark of progressivism, Dewey said, "I do not urge it as the sole way out of educational confusion, not even in the elementary school, though I think experimentation with it is desirable in college and secondary school."[33] They may help you judge for yourself what Dewey advocated.

One of progressivism's most distinguishing characteristics, and one that clearly differentiates it from perennialism and essentialism, is the view that the curriculum should be **student-centered** rather than **subject-centered**. In thinking about student-centered versus subject-centered curricula, consider the characteristics of the whole K–12 curriculum, not just the secondary curriculum. When viewed from this perspective, it becomes clear that there is a gradual shifting from student-centeredness at the lower levels to subject-centeredness at the higher levels. The shift may not be as linear as depicted in Figure1.1, but the gradual change in emphasis is evident in all K–12 curriculums.

There are sound reasons for the change in emphasis. When students are young, they need the kind of nurturing, structure, and consistency that a single teacher in a self-contained classroom can provide. Their need to learn how to act in a group and to master fundamental skills is greater than their need for learning about particular subject-matter in-depth. Teachers can more easily plan lessons that cut across subject-area lines because the students are with them for a whole day, not for just an hour. For example, a first-grade teacher can use an interdisciplinary approach when teaching about seasons by having

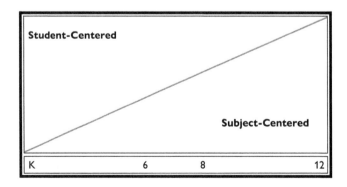

Figure 1.1 The Focus of K-12 Curriculum

students draw seasonal pictures, write seasonal stories, and think about how seasons affect us and the world around us.

As students move through the grade levels, they are typically able to profit from increasingly detailed knowledge. To provide this knowledge and guide student learning, teachers need to be increasingly knowledgeable about particular subjects. This, in turn, results in departmentalization and a subject-centered curriculum. These factors make curricular integration easier at the elementary level than at the secondary level.

Theodore R. Sizer (1932–2009)

Since the 1970s, Theodore Sizer has been working to reform and restructure schools, largely along progressivist lines. In 1984, he published *Horace's Compromise: The Dilemma of the American High School*,[34] in which a fictional teacher, Horace Smith, explains what he believes is wrong with today's high schools and suggests ways the schools might be restructured and improved. In 1984, Sizer launched a movement known as the Coalition of Essential Schools at Brown University, in Rhode Island.[35] The Coalition for Essential Schools is still at Brown, but Dr. Sizer retired in 1997.

In 1992, Sizer authored a sequel to Horace's Compromise, entitled *Horace's School: Redesigning the American High School*.[36] In *Horace's School*, Horace Smith has been appointed Chair of a committee whose charge is to review the purposes and practices of the fictitious Franklin High School. In portraying the committee meetings, Sizer's arguments are sometimes hard to follow. For example, he argues that one indicator of the need to reform schools is the poor performance of United States students in comparison to students internationally.[37] Shortly thereafter, however, he raises the valid question of whether the tests are appropriate measures of learning.[38] What is left unexplained is why, if the tests are inappropriate measures, their results should be considered at all.

In true progressivist fashion, Sizer has Horace arguing that when it comes to high school diplomas, "no one should be left out."[39] He also argues that students should be directly involved in all aspects of school life: "Students who eat meals at school should help prepare them."[40] Ideas such as this have been tried, but they failed. For example, in 1916, educators in Gary, Indiana, implemented what came to be called the **Gary Plan**. Among other features, students did much of the work of the school. They ordered and distributed lunchroom supplies, kept accounts, and did some of the maintenance and repair work in the school. Unfortunately, the students required so much adult checking and supervision, and the time required so detracted from academic pursuits, that the plan was soon abandoned.[41]

All ideas about educational reform ultimately come down to what it is that students are expected to know and be able to do. Aristotle noted the lack of agreement in his day and we have the same lack of agreement today. Each group of reformers is simply one more group that thinks that the current emphasis is wrong and that it should be something else. No matter how things change, it is a good idea to keep in mind that teachers can only do so much. In trying to do one thing, they must, because of time restrictions, do less of something else. For example, in X amount of time, content breadth must come at the expense of content depth. Loading more expectations on teachers will reduce, not increase, the effectiveness of schools. Sizer made this point by arguing that less is more (i.e., less breadth, more depth).

The most recent variant of progressivism is **constructivism**. Constructivists focus on two of progressivism's main points: having students try to solve complex problems and using cooperative learning strategies. However, in doing this, constructivism suffers from one of the same problems that plagues progressivism; namely, it is more time-consuming than direct instruction. Students spend considerable time learning things on their own that they could be taught more quickly via direct instruction. The progressives and constructivists argue that having small groups of students learn things on their own has greater long-term value to the students than accomplishing a task more quickly.

Adherents of No Child Left Behind (NCLB) are ambivalent here. Progressivists and constructivists certainly want all students to obtain and be able to use practical knowledge. However, their main interest is in helping students learn how to learn and how to work cooperatively. These elements are not mentioned in the NCLB Act and are not tested in most state-mandated tests. You can see why some people have mixed feelings about progressivism.

Differentiating Characteristics of Progressivism

1. Roots in pragmatism—learn by doing.
2. The role of education is to prepare students to live in a democratic society.
3. The curriculum should be interdisciplinary and structured so that students work at solving relevant problems and find it necessary to acquire certain skills and understandings in order to solve those problems. Students should learn how to think rather than what to think.
4. Textbooks, memorization, and other traditional tools and techniques should be replaced, as much as possible, with actual experiences and problem-solving.

Points of Contention

1. The main goals of education should be to pass on the cultural and historical heritage of the society and to prepare people to compete successfully in life and in the job market.

2. A subject-centered curriculum allows teachers to develop the expertise needed to help students learn in-depth. Time spent trying to integrate knowledge must come at the expense of time spent acquiring more knowledge.

3. While the application of knowledge is critical, students cannot apply what they do not know. Learning via trial and error is costly in terms of instruction time. Direct instruction saves time by helping students profit from what others learned by trial and error.

4. Progressivism ignores the basic competitive nature of our society and tends to sacrifice high standards for good feelings.

Existentialism

Existentialism is built on Protagoras's idea that man is the measure of all things. It takes the position that all people are unique individuals and that each person must define, and find, happiness for themselves. **Jean-Paul Sarte** (1905–1980) argued this same point persuasively in *Being and Nothingness,* published in France in 1943. Noted existentialist **Ivan Illich** maintained in *Deschooling Society*[42] that we did not need schools at all. He believed that education should take place throughout society, not just in school buildings. In 1921, **A. S. Neill**, another existentialist, started a boarding school in Suffolk, England. The name of the school was Summerhill, and it had a maximum enrollment of about fifty students aged five through fifteen, most of whom were children of wealthy Americans. In his book *Summerhill*, Neill describes his existentialist views and the operating philosophy of Summerhill.

> My view is that a child is innately wise and realistic. If left to himself without adult suggestion of any kind, he will develop as far as he is capable of developing. … We set out to make a school in which we should allow children freedom to be themselves. In order to do this, we had to renounce all discipline, all direction, all suggestion, all moral training, all religious instruction.[43]

Another educator with existentialist views is **John Holt,** who wrote, "Learning is not everything, and certainly one piece of learning is as good as another. … In short, the school should be a great smorgasbord of intellectual, artistic, creative, and athletic activities, from which each child could take whatever he wanted, and as much as he wanted, or as little."[44]

Differentiating Characteristics

1. Each person should have the freedom and the responsibility to choose what, when, and how to learn.

2. Any planned curriculum will, by definition, infringe on the freedom of individuals to make choices.

Points of Contention

1. Learners are not aware of what they do not know and therefore cannot make wise choices about what to learn.
2. Society as a whole is often called upon to help individuals deal with the consequences of poor choices so it has a vested interest in doing what it can to teach people how to make wise choices.

Reconstructionism (Also Known as Postmodernism)

Reconstructionism is a contemporary philosophy that focuses on the reconstruction of experiences and knowledge. According to reconstructionism education is considered as a creative self-learning process in which the emphasis is on helping the learner construct knowledge. Similar to progressivism, the focus is on providing the learner with problems and activities to solve problems. The learning activities take into consideration students' interests, abilities, and backgrounds.[45]

SUMMARY

Since the time of the ancient Greeks, people have debated what students should learn and why they should learn it. The debate continues today with the different positions reflecting different philosophies of education.

Perennialists tend to focus on acquiring knowledge for its own sake. They consider knowledge as eternal truths. Essentialists see the value in acquiring knowledge for its own sake as well; however, knowledge serves as a practical tool to generate more knowledge. They also see education as serving a more utilitarian purpose—the furthering of the interests of the state. Both philosophies tend to see education as subject-centered and tend to favor a core of subjects that are required of everyone. Strong advocates of No Child Left Behind are very often essentialists.

Progressivists, along with their more recent cousins, the constructivists, tend to see education as student-centered and are more concerned with process, particularly with problem-solving, than with content. Progressivists and constructivists, more than perennialists and essentialists, tend to see great value in group work and in hands-on learning.

Existentialism remains a fringe philosophy. Few people are willing to grant students the kind of freedoms advocated by existentialists for fear that our cultural heritage would be lost and that students would be ill prepared to take their places as productive members of society.

Reconstructionism (known also as postmodernism) is a student-centered philosophy that emphasizes reconstructing or rewriting experiences. Also, the focus is helping the learner construct his/her own knowledge based on their own unique learning styles, interests and abilities. The main contention with this philosophy is the challenge that teachers face in providing individualized instruction to larger groups of students. Such efforts would require a lot of creativity, ingenuity, and the understanding and knowledge of how learners develop and learn.

KEY TERMS, PEOPLE, AND IDEAS

Philosophy

Educational Philosophy

Elder Sophists, 450 BC—First Professional
  Teachers—Rhetoric

Socrates—Socratic Method—Inborn
  Knowledge

Plato—Truth through thought—Individual
  Differences—Faculty Theory

Aristotle—Learn via the senses—
  Syllogistic Reasoning

John Locke—Tabula Rasa (Blank Sheet), 1690

Perennialism—Hutchins, Adler

Essentialism—Bagley, Bestor, Rickover

Progressivism—Dewey, Sizer

Constructivism

Gary Plan

Student-centered, Subject-centered

Existentialism—Illich, Holt

QUESTIONS FOR CONSIDERATION

1. Why, in the light of the current focus on high stakes testing, is the idea of educational philosophies either moot or useful?
2. To the extent to which the task of helping students pass tests and prepare for vocations can be separated from the task of helping students understand and deal with the world around them, which task seems more important to you, and why?

ENDNOTES

1 John Dewey, *Experience and Education* (New York: Collier Cooks, 1938), 6.

2 Joseph Swain and William H. Armstrong, *The Peoples of the Ancient World* (New York: Harper and Row, 1959), 191.

3 Marvin Perry, *A History of the World* (Boston: Houghton Mifflin, 1985), 69.

4 Fast Facts: Enrollment trends, Retrieved May 4, 2020 from http://nces.ed.gov/fastfacts/display.asp?id=65.

5 Paul Saettler *The Evolution of American Educational Technology* (Englewood: Libraries Unlimited, 1990), 24.

6   William Morris (ed.). *The American Heritage Dictionary of the English Language* (Boston: Houghton Mifflin Co., 1970), 1114.

7   Saettler, *The Evolution of American Educational Technology*, 48.

8   From Plato's dialogue entitled "Protagoras," as cited in Walter Kaufman (ed.), *Philosophic Classics: Thales to St. Thomas* (Englewood Cliffs: Prentice-Hall, 1961), 72.

9   Kaufman, 73.

10   Saettler, *The Evolution of American Educational Technology*, 25.

11   Saettler, *The Evolution of American Educational Technology*, 24.

12   Saettler, *The Evolution of American Educational Technology*, 25–26.

13   Saettler, *The Evolution of American Educational Technology*, 26.

14   Aristotle (384–322 BC)—*The Politics*, Book 8, Chs 1 and 2, trans. by Carnes Lord. (Chicago: The University of Chicago Press, 1984), 229–30.

15   John Locke, "Essay Concerning Humane Understanding," (1690). In John Locke, *Encyclopedia Britannica* 14 (Chicago: Encyclopedia Britannica, Inc., 1960), 274.

16   William C. Morse, and G. Max Wingo, *Psychology and Teaching*, 2nd ed. (Chicago: Scott, Foresman, 1962), 242.

17   Rober M. Hutchins, *The Higher Learning in America* (New Haven: Yale University Press, 1936), 66.

18   Hutchins, *The Higher Learning in America*, 67.

19   Alfred North Whitehead, *Essays in Science and Philosophy* (New York: Philosophical Library, 1947), 176.

20   Mortimer J. Adler, *The Paideia Project: An Educational Manifesto* (New York: Macmillan Publishing, 1982), 4.

21   Adler, 6.

22   Adler, 21.

23   Adler, 23.

24   Arthur K. Ellis, John J. Cogan, and Kenneth R. Howey, *The Foundations of Education* (Englewood Cliffs: Prentice-Hall, 1981), 85–86.

25   J. A. Johnson, H. W. Collins, V. L. Dupuis, and J. N. Johansen, *Introduction to the Foundations of American Education* (Boston: Allyn and Bacon, 1979).

26   J. Mulhern, *A History of Education*, 2nd ed. (New York: The Ronald Press, 1959), 407.

27   William C. Bagley, "The Case for Essentialism in Education," *NEA Journal* 30, no. 7 (1941): 201–02. In Ellis, Cogan, and Howey, 88–89.

28   Arthur Bestor, *The Restoration of Learning* (New York: Knopf, 1956), 48-49. In Tanner and Tanner, 7.

29   Bestor, *The Restoration of Learning*, 79. In Tanner and Tanner, 395.

30   Bestor, *The Restoration of Learning*, 120. In Ornstein and Hunkins, 45.

31 Hyman G. Rickover, "European vs. American Secondary Schools," *Phi Delta Kappan*, 40 (November 1958): 61. In Tanner and Tanner, 110.

32 John Dewey, *Experience and Education* (New York, Collier Books, 1938), 22.

33 John Dewey, *The Way Out of Educational Confusion* (Cambridge: Harvard University Press, 1931), 36. In Arthur G. Wirth, *John Dewy as Educator* (New York: University Press of America, 1989), 212.

34 Theodore R. Sizer, *Horace's Compromise: The Dilemma of the American High School* (Boston: Houghton Mifflin, 1984).

35 Coalition of Essential Schools, Box 1969, Brown University, Providence, Rhode Island 02912.

36 Theodore R. Sizer, *Horace's School: Redesigning the American High School,* (Boston: Houghton Mifflin, 1992).

37 Sizer, *Horace's School,* 109.

38 Sizer, *Horace's School,* 110–11.

39 Sizer, *Horace's School,* 117.

40 Sizer, *Horace's School,* 123.

41 Abraham Flexner and Frank Bachman, *The Gary Schools* (New York: General Education Board, 1918). In Tanner and Tanner, 2nd ed., 285–86.

42 Ivan Illich, *Deschooling Society* (New York: Harper and Row, 1971).

43 A. S. Neill, *Summerhill* (New York: Hart Publishing, 1960), 4.

44 John Holt, *How Children Fail* (New York: Dell, 1964), 177–80. In Tanner and Tanner, 2nd ed., 139.

45 Allan Ornstein, "Philosophy as a Basis for Curriculum Decisions," in A. C. Ornestein, E. F. Pajak, and S. B. Ornstein (eds.), *Contemporary Issues in Curriculum* (Boston: Pearson, 2011), 7.

CHAPTER 2

Why the Schools Are as They Are

INTRODUCTION

Have you ever heard of the "golden rule"? No, not that one—the one that relates to economics and says, "He who has the gold makes the rules"? Well, politicians have, and they have used it to help shape what you will teach and how you will teach it. Their interest in education is spurred, at least in part, by continual concerns about the effectiveness of our schools.

This chapter will, first, present evidence concerning the effectiveness of schools. You can compare this evidence with that presented by critics of education and then reach your own conclusions. The chapter will then examine, in chronological order, a few of the ideas and ideals that seem central to most secondary schools in the United States and that account for the high degree of curricular consistency. Many of these ideas and ideals were expressed in national legislation and in reports and studies of national renown. This information will help you better understand the legislation and reports that have helped shape education in the United States.

LEARNING OUTCOMES

You will be able, in writing, to:

1. Describe the provisions of at least two federal legislative acts that directly affected education.
2. Take a position for or against the continuation and/or increase in the federal government's influence in education and cite at least two facts to support your position.

3. Take a position for or against the idea that performance, rather than time under instruction, should be used to measure education in the United States and support that position with at least two cause-effect arguments.
4. Use cause-effect reasoning to explain at least two strengths and two weaknesses that you see in the No Child Left Behind Act.

THE EFFECTIVENESS OF OUR SCHOOLS

The news could be better. First, educators sometimes make it difficult to find the facts. For example, using data provided by the schools, the National Center for Educational Statistics (NCES) reported that the dropout rate in 1960 was about 27 percent, but compared with about 9.9 percent in 2003.[1] That decline is good news, if it is real. However, Nathan Thornburgh, in an article titled "Dropout Nation," argues that studies by independent researchers show that nationally, the 2005 high school dropout rate is closer to 30 percent overall and closer to 50 for Latinos and African Americans.[2] His arguments are compelling, especially when he explains how schools have manipulated dropout rate figures to make them appear lower than they actually are.

To complicate matters still more, in an article titled "Accurately Assessing High School Graduation Rates,"[3] Mishel and Roy argue that many estimates of dropout rates are based on "flawed analyses of inadequate data." In their analysis of the data, Mishel and Roy found that the current dropout rate is most likely about 14 percent.

There is deep concern over the dropout problem, primarily because of the serious effects of dropping out of school. In one study it was found that:

1. High school dropouts are 72 percent more likely than graduates to be unemployed.
2. Dropouts make up about half of the heads of households on welfare.
3. About 75 percent of prison inmates never earned a high school diploma.
4. About 77 percent of state prison inmates who do not complete high school or earn a general equivalency diploma return to prison.[4]

Clearly, when data provided by schools is contradicted by data provided by private investigators, the credibility of the school data is called into question. The provisions of the NCLB Act are helping to ensure that the data provided by public schools is more accurate than in the past.

Second, the mean scores on the SAT (formerly known as the Scholastic Aptitude Test), as seen in Table 2.1, show a significant drop over the ten-year period.[5]

Table 2.1 Group Mean SAT Scores 2006–2016 for College-Bound Seniors

Year	Critical Reading			Mathematics			Writing		
	Male	Female	Total	Male	Female	Total	Male	Female	Total
2006	505	502	503	536	502	518	491	502	497
2007	503	500	501	532	499	514	487	499	493
2008	502	499	500	532	499	514	486	499	493
2009	502	497	499	533	498	514	485	498	492
2010	502	498	500	533	499	515	485	497	491
2011	500	495	497	531	500	514	482	496	489
2012	498	493	496	532	499	514	481	494	488
2013	499	494	496	531	499	514	482	493	488
2014	499	495	497	530	499	513	481	492	487
2015	497	493	495	527	496	511	478	490	484
2016	495	493	494	524	494	508	475	487	482

Mean scores on the ACT are similar to the SAT means in that they show a net loss since 2012. The SAT total scores dropped fifteen points between 2006 and 2016. As shown in Table 2.2, the ACT scores dropped one composite score between 2012 and 2019. [6]

Third, the public does not rate public schools highly. Gallup historical trend data between 2006 and 2018 shows a lack of satisfaction with public education. In 2019 and 2020, Americans' satisfaction with the quality of public education is slightly higher than

Table 2.2 Average ACT Scores 2012–2019 for Total Group

Year	# of Test Takers	English	Math	Reading	Science	Writing	Composite
2012	1,666,017	20.5	21.1	21.3	20.9	7.1	21.1
2013	1,799,243	20.2	20.9	21.1	20.7	7	20.9
2014	1,845,787	20.3	20.9	21.3	20.8	7.1	21.0
2015	1,924,436	20.4	20.8	21.4	20.9	6.9	21.0
2016	2,090,342	20.1	20.6	21.3	20.8	19.3*	20.8
2017	2,030,038	20.3	20.7	21.4	21.0	6.5	21.0
2018	1,914,817	20.2	20.5	21.3	20.8	—*	20.8
2019	1,782,820	20.1	20.3	21.2	20.6	—*	20.9

*2016 Writing results are based on ACT Writing from September 2015 to August 2016, when the test was scored on a scale of 1–36.

**As of 2018, ACT seems to no longer provide information about writing score averages (except indirectly through ELA scores).

previous years. In 2020, the data shows that 50 percent of Americans are satisfied with the quality of K–12 education while 48 percent of Americans are dissatisfied with K–12 education quality in the United States. The average dissatisfaction in the quality of K–12 education since 2006 is 50.77 percent, while the average satisfaction in the quality of K–12 education is 45.22 percent. The results since 1996 are shown in Figure 2.1.[7]

While the responses made it clear that the more people know about a school, the more likely they are to think well of its performance, the ratings are not encouraging.

With effectiveness of our schools being called into question, how to make them more effective has become a political, as well as a pedagogical, issue, but that is not new. Although the US

Constitution makes no mention of education—that was deliberately left in the hands of the states—

the government has a long history of involvement in education.

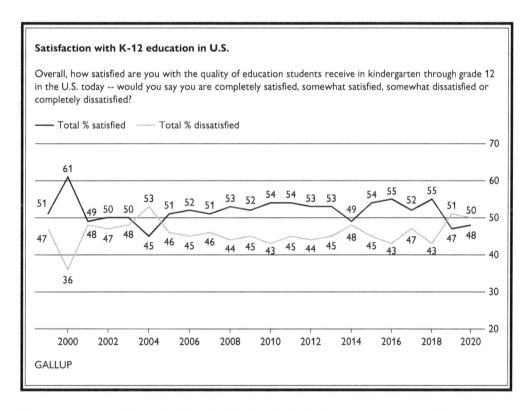

Figure 2.1 Gallup Polls 2006–2020 Satisfaction With K–12 Education in the United States

FROM PILGRIMS TO PROGRESSIVES—SOME MILESTONES
How and Why Secondary Schools Were Established
The Boston Latin Grammar School

The first secondary school in the New World, was established by the village of Boston, in the Massachusetts Bay Colony in 1635. The main purpose of the Latin Grammar School was to prepare students to go on to colleges and universities, so it followed a subject-centered, liberal arts curriculum. That curriculum became the standard model for secondary schools.

Harvard University

The first university in the New World was established in 1636 so that students could continue their education here rather than having to go back to England or Europe. It mainly prepared religious leaders, lawyers, and doctors.

When the "lower" schools were established later, they accepted, as one of their main roles, the preparation of students for secondary schools. To do this, they followed essentially the same subject-centered, liberal arts curriculum. A look at a typical K–12 curriculum today will show that for the most part, the initial power structure is still with us. When colleges change their entrance requirements, high schools change their curriculums to prepare their graduates to meet those requirements. Those changes, in turn, prompt changes in the K–8 curriculum. As a point of information, junior high schools first appeared in 1909 in Berkeley, California and Columbus, Ohio and typically include grades 7-9, although there are many variations. True to the pattern, they used the expectations of high schools in their districts as a guide in developing their curricular offerings.

The State's Interest in Education—Educating All the Children at Public Expense
The "Old Deluder Satan" law

The "Old Deluder Satan" law was passed by the General Court of the Massachusetts Bay Colony in 1647:

> It being one chief project of the old deluder, Satan: to keep men from the knowledge of the Scriptures ... it is therefore ordered that every township in this jurisdiction, after the Lord hath increased your number to 50 householders, shall then forthwith appoint one within their town to teach all such children as shall resort to him to write and read ... and it is further ordered, that where any town shall increase to the number of 100 families or householders, they shall set up a grammar school, the master thereof being able to instruct youth so far as shall be fitted for the university.[8]

The law established two precedents that are still with us. Although the law stipulates only that townships educate "all such children as resort to him," for all practical purposes it came to mean that all the children of all the people should be educated. This is noteworthy because until this time, societies had restricted formal education either to males, to citizens, or to children of the wealthy or powerful. A second precedent was that the state had the right to pass laws concerning education including curricular focus, attendance, and public support. The public support precedent was challenged in 1872, when some citizens in Kalamazoo, Michigan, challenged the right of the city to use taxes to support secondary education. The issue was settled when the Supreme Court of Michigan ruled that the City of Kalamazoo had the right to establish, and support by taxation, schools at any level.[9]

College Preparation versus General Education

The Academy

Benjamin Franklin argued in 1751 that schools should prepare students for vocations as well as for college, and suggested that the first **Academy**, the model for later comprehensive high schools, be started in Philadelphia. In addition to the courses required for college preparation, such as mathematics, Greek, Latin, and philosophy, the Academy offered courses in vocational areas such as carpentry, surveying, and bookkeeping. Part of that academy became the University of Pennsylvania. While comprehensive high schools are now the most common type of high school, their curriculums are still centered on preparation for college. The reason is as follows.

Since colonial times, higher education has been seen as the surest way to a "good life." While not all students go on to college, most parents hope that their children will, and in 2005, just over 68.6 percent of all high school graduates did enroll in two or four-year colleges immediately after graduation.[10] It seems reasonable to assume that as long as parents see a college education as a goal for their children, high schools will continue to make preparation for college a central part of their curriculums.

First Federal Action Concerning Education

Land Ordinance of 1785

The **Land Ordinance of 1785** specified that land in the Northwest Territories (the present states of Ohio, Indiana, Illinois, Michigan, Wisconsin, and parts of Minnesota) be surveyed into townships six miles on a side; that each township be divided into thirty-six sections, each containing 640 acres; and that one section in each township, or the proceeds from the sale of it, be used for public education.[11] This act marks the beginning of federal involvement in education and it also establishes the precedent for federal aid to education.

Vocational Education Emerges

The Morrill Land Grant Act of 1862

The **Morrill Land Grant Act**, signed into law by President Lincoln in 1862, granted public lands to the states for the specific purpose of providing for the foundation and maintenance of colleges, "where the leading object shall be, without excluding other scientific and classical studies, and including military tactics, to teach such branches of learning as are related to agriculture and the mechanical arts ... in order to promote the liberal and practical education of the industrial classes in the several pursuits and professions of life.[12]

Today, there is a land-grant university in each state with the universities of California, Illinois, Wisconsin, Purdue, the Massachusetts Institute of Technology, Cornell, Michigan State, Ohio State and Pennsylvania State being among the largest.[13] The act marked the first time that Congress specified curricular content. Vocational education became a legitimate part of the curriculum for higher education and the long dominance of the Perennialist philosophy was directly challenged. In time, vocational education was included in the curriculums of most secondary schools.

Essentialism and Instructional Time

Committee of Ten Report, 1893

Officially titled the Committee on Secondary School Studies, the Committee of Ten Report was released in 1893 to (1) try to bring order to the diverse secondary education programs, (2) reconcile the demands of those who saw high school in terms of preparation for college with those who saw high school as preparation for the world of work, and (3) increase articulation between high schools and colleges. Men such as Charles Eliot, chair of the committee, heavily influenced its deliberations. Eliot was president of Harvard University and, as did most of his peers, had attended schools with predominantly perennialist curriculums.

The report began with the premise that while not all students went on to college, all students would benefit from studying the same subjects. The Committee then considered nine subjects: (1) Latin; (2) Greek; (3) English; (4) other modern languages; (5) mathematics; (6) physics, astronomy, and chemistry; (7) natural history (biology, including botany, zoology, and physiology); (8) history, civil government, and political economy; and (9) geography (physical geography, geology, and meteorology). It concluded that these subjects were equally valuable if well taught. It did not consider the subjects of art, music, physical education, and vocational education because these subjects were not required for admission to college.[14] The inclusion of "modern" subjects such as physiology and geology, and the exclusion of art, music, physical education and vocational education; are characteristic of essentialism.

The Committee also recommended that all pupils who studied a given subject study it in the same way and to the same extent, and it exemplified its thinking by proposing four high school programs: Classical, Latin Scientific, Modern Languages, and English. The Modern Languages and English programs did not require Latin, so they were considered by the committee to be inferior.[15] For each program, the Committee proposed specific courses and, of importance here, a specific number of class periods per week for each subject. This last element had the effect of formally equating learning with time under instruction rather than with competence.

Time Under Instruction and the Carnegie Unit
Committee on College Entrance Requirements
The **Committee on College Entrance Requirements** recommended in 1895 that high schools assign credits for various subjects in order to systematize the college admission process. The ideas of specifying a given number of instructional periods per week, and of assigning credits to subjects for the purpose of college admission, were brought together in 1906.

The Carnegie Unit
The Carnegie Foundation for the Advancement of Teaching recommended in 1906 a way of standardizing measures of instructional time. It recommended that instructional time be divided into "units," and it defined a unit as satisfactory completion of a subject that met five days per week, a minimum of forty minutes per period, and a minimum of 120 clock hours for the school year.[16] This became the **Carnegie Unit**.

Education was, and to a large degree still is, assessed in terms of instructional time, with learner competence being assumed on the basis of a passing grade. However, many states now require that, in order to graduate from high school, students not only accumulate a specific number of Carnegie Units but also demonstrate specific competencies such as passing a constitution test and/or a consumer science test. Since the passage of the No Child Left Behind Act (2002), competencies are becoming increasingly important.

A switch to assessing education fully on the basis of learner competencies rather than time under instruction would require the broad acceptance of specific competencies (remember Aristotle's observation about the lack of agreement about goals of education during his time), a new basis for paying teachers, and a new basis for funding schools. Such changes will not be made easily.

In addition to establishing time, rather than competence, as the measure of education, the various committee reports at the beginning of the 1900s had other long-lasting effects. One was to perpetuate traditional subjects and methods. This included not only organizing curriculums on the basis of separate subjects, but also the idea that student interests were of little importance. Further, the use of whole-class instruction was established as standard rather than individualized or small-group instruction.

The Smith-Hughes Act

The **Smith-Hughes Act**, which passed in 1917 provided federal aid for education in vocational areas such as home economics, agricultural, trade, and industrial subjects in high schools. It accomplished this goal, and, in addition, it strengthened the role of the federal government in establishing curricular goals for the country as a whole. The National Education Association (NEA), which is now the largest teacher organization in the United States, was not wholly supportive of this legislation. It pointed out that the establishment of vocational education as an alternative to the traditional curriculum might have the effect of establishing a two-tracked system with the vocational track always seen as inferior to the college preparatory track.

Commission on the Reorganization of Secondary Education

The **Commission on the Reorganization of Secondary Education** issued in 1918 a report that said, in essence, that "Secondary education should be determined by the needs of the society to be served, the character of the individuals to be educated, and the knowledge of the educational theory and practice available." The Commission saw the main purpose of secondary schools as giving "flesh and blood reality to the ideal of democracy." To help do this, the Commission listed seven **"Cardinal Principles of Secondary Education."** In summary, those principles called for secondary school curriculums to include

1. *Health*—Good health habits need to be taught and encouraged by the school. The community and school should cooperate in fulfilling the health needs of all youngsters and adults.
2. *Command of fundamental processes*—The secondary school should accept a responsibility for continuing to teach and polish the basic tools of learning, such as arithmetical computation, reading, and writing that were begun in the elementary school.
3. *Worthy home membership*—Schools should give students an understanding of the interrelationships of the family in order for the give-and-take to be a healthy, happy affair. Proper adjustment as a family member will lead to proper acceptance of responsibility as a family leader later in life.
4. *Vocation*—The secondary school should teach students to appreciate all vocations. The basic skills of a variety of vocations should be made available to students who have the need or desire for them.

5. *Citizenship*—The students' basic commitment to proper citizenship must be fostered and strengthened during the adolescent years. The secondary school needs to assume this responsibility not only in the social sciences classes but in all subjects.

6. *Proper use of leisure time*—The students should be provided opportunities while in secondary school to expand the available possibilities of leisure time. (The Commission felt that using leisure time properly would enrich the total personality.)

7. *Ethical character*—The secondary school should organize its activities and personal relationships to reflect good ethical character, both to serve as an exemplar and to involve the student in a series of activities that will provide opportunities to make ethically correct decisions.[17]

Where to draw the line in balancing the progressivist goals exemplified in the Cardinal Principles, against the more traditional goals of preparing students for college, remains a major point of contention. Time and money are two of the limiting factors.

Discrediting the "Faculty" Theory
Edward L. Thorndike

Edward L. Thorndike (1874–1949) conducted a study in 1924 that did much to discredit the **"faculty" theory**. One of the ideas that persisted since ancient Greek times was that the mind consisted of specific "faculties" which, like muscles, could be developed by specific exercises, such as the study of particular subjects. It was largely because this idea was accepted so widely and for so long that subjects such as Greek and Latin remained in the secondary curriculum. Thorndike, using a sample of 8,564 students, compared gains in general intelligence (as reflected by intelligence quotient [IQ] scores) of students who studied English, history, geometry, and Latin with those who studied English, history, geometry, and shop work. If the faculty theory was valid, students who studied Latin should have scored higher than those who studied shop work. They did not. Thorndike concluded that "the expectation of any large difference in general improvement of the mind from one study rather than another seems doomed to disappointment."[18]

It should be noted that while Thorndike's study discredited the "faculty" theory, it is true that the more you work in a particular area the more skilled you become in it. For example, if you practice playing the piano or playing tennis regularly, you will become a better pianist or tennis player. You may never become a great pianist or a great tennis player, but you will improve. Some reasons for this are that, over time, you learn new techniques, you learn how to eliminate small mistakes, and you learn how to do things more efficiently.

The Eight-Year Study—1933–1941

The **Eight-Year Study** was commissioned by the Progressive Education Association (which adopted its name from the progressive branch of the Republican political party). It is included here primarily because it is still considered one of the most carefully conducted long-term studies in education, and seeing the research methodology that was followed will give you a yardstick against which to judge other research studies in education.

After a yearlong study in 1933, the Progressive Education Association identified a number of weaknesses in the secondary schools. Today, critics of education claim that many of these weaknesses still exist:

1. did not have a clear-cut, definite, central purpose;
2. failed to give students a sincere appreciation of their heritage as American citizens;
3. did not prepare students adequately for the responsibilities of community life;
4. seldom challenged the student of first-rate ability to work up to the level of his intellectual powers;
5. neither knew their students well nor guided them wisely;
6. seldom provided opportunities for students to release or develop their creative energies;
7. had curriculums far removed from the real concerns of youth;
8. taught subjects that had lost much of their vitality and significance; and
9. had principals and teachers laboring earnestly, often sacrificially, but usually without any comprehensive evaluation of the results of their work.[19]

The progressivists wanted to know how students who went to high schools with "progressive" curriculums would compare, after four years of college, with students who had gone to high schools with "traditional" curriculums. To find out, the Progressive Education Association (PEA) persuaded more than three hundred colleges and universities to release thirty secondary schools from the restrictions of college entrance requirements. The graduates of these high schools would not have to meet Carnegie Unit requirements for college entrance (120 clock hours in a subject during a school year with 16 units in specific subject areas required for graduation).

A commission appointed by the PEA selected the thirty public and private secondary schools, large and small, urban and rural, and coast-to-coast, on the basis of their willingness to implement a "progressive" curriculum. Each graduate of one of the thirty schools was matched with a graduate of a "traditional" high school (who had therefore met the usual college entrance requirements) on the basis of age, sex, race, scholastic aptitude scores, home and community background, and interests. This matching was done by the colleges and resulted in 1,475 matched pairs of subjects. The results of the study were published in 1942, and showed among other things that graduates of the thirty schools

1. earned a slightly higher total grade average;
2. earned higher grade averages in all subject fields except foreign languages;
3. received slightly more academic honors each year;
4. were more often judged to possess a high degree of intellectual curiosity and drive;
5. were more often judged to be precise, systematic, and objective in their thinking; and
6. more often demonstrated a high degree of resourcefulness in meeting new situations.[20]

With such promising results from a carefully controlled longitudinal study, one would expect a flood of proposals for developing more progressive curriculums. It did not happen. In 1942, the country was embroiled in World War II. Attention was focused on Germany and Japan, not on America's public schools. The results of the Eight-Year study were largely ignored.

The study did have its critics and at least one of their points is difficult to ignore. Despite the careful matching and tracking of the students, it was virtually impossible for the investigators to document the specific commonalties of the "Progressive" curriculums implemented by the schools. Some schools said their curriculum was "experimental" while others simply said theirs was "non-traditional." This problem meant that the study's findings could not be easily generalized. There was no single "Progressive" curriculum that could be credited with the success of the students so there was nothing that could easily replace the existing "traditional" curriculums.

The results of the Eight-Year Study did have some impact. An increasing number of educators accepted the Commission's conclusions that: (1) "success in the college of liberal arts does not depend upon the study of certain subjects for a certain period in high school, and (2) there are many different kinds of experience by which students may prepare themselves for successful work in college."[21] Further, some educators began to seriously consider alternatives to traditional content and methods. They were, for example, willing to look at content with respect to its relevance, or lack of relevance, to students—something of little concern to traditionalists. Some were also willing to replace textbooks, to one extent or another, with instructional materials that they, themselves, developed or organized. Still others began to de-emphasize rote memorization and to increase active student participation. The Eight-Year study did have an effect, but primarily for those who already accepted at least some Progressivist ideas.

In comparison to the activities in education from 1890 through the 1930s, the 1940s, and 1950s were relatively quiet. High school curriculums remained largely conservative and traditional with occasional experiments with Progressive ideas. After the end of World War 2, and resumption of a more normal life in the United States, education once again became a focus of attention.

POST–WORLD WAR II TO THE PRESENT
The Supreme Court—Separate Is Not Equal
Brown v. Board of Education of Topeka
In 1954 the US Supreme Court, in **Brown v. Board of Education of Topeka**, over-turned *Plessey v. Ferguson* (1896), and ruled that separate schools for blacks and whites were inherently unequal. The ruling set in motion massive efforts at school integration including the allocation of millions of dollars for school bussing. Whether the money spent on bussing could have been used in better ways is debatable. What is less debatable is that, as the number of students being bussed increased, (1) the size of schools increased (in part, to minimize bussing costs); (2) the intimacy of neighborhood schools where teachers, parents, and students knew each other fairly well was greatly reduced, and (3) fewer students were able to take advantage of time before and after school to get extra help from teachers. As is often the case, the solution to one problem caused other problems.

Research done by the Civil Rights Project at Harvard University shows, unfortunately, that in some areas of the country, particularly in the South, many of the desegregation gains made in the years immediately following *Brown v. Board of Education of Topeka* are being reversed. Breslow, Wexler, and Collins explained that "in the wake of the Brown decision, the percentage of black students in majority white southern schools went from zero to a peak of 43.5 percent in 1988. But those changes have reversed in recent years, with data from UCLA's Civil Rights Project showing that by 2011 that figure was back to 23.2 percent, just below where it stood in 1968."[22]

Sputnik and the National Defense Education Act
On October 4, 1957 the Soviet Union launched **Sputnik**, the first artificial Earth satellite. This was the time of the Cold War between the United States and the Soviet Union, so the launching, and the telemetry beeps every ninety-eight minutes as the satellite passed overhead, did not sit well with the American public. Politicians were quick to argue that the United States was in danger of losing its technological edge.

The Great Society and Compensatory Education
The **National Defense Education Act** (NDEA) was passed in 1958. It authorized three major things. First, it provided millions of dollars for the development of new programs

in math and science and, later, in foreign languages. Second, it caused many people who had embraced Progressivist ideas to change their minds and return to the subject-centered, Essentialist curriculum, which they saw as more rigorous and more accountable. Third, it relegated the Fine Arts to a peripheral position in the curriculum and, in so doing, strengthened the feeling that many Americans already had—that schools should focus on practical and immediate needs. The view of education as a broad enlightening endeavor, something to be valued for itself, was diminished.

The Elementary and Secondary Education Act was passed in 1965. It was part of President Lyndon B. Johnson's Great Society program. As part of that program, Congress allocated $1.3 billion to improve education for poor and minority children. Chief among these compensatory education programs was, and is, the **Head Start** program. This program was designed to provide special help for children aged three to five who were poor and disadvantaged. It is mentioned here to demonstrate a point.

In 1968, Westinghouse Learning Corp., under contract with the United States Office of Economic Opportunity, conducted a national-level evaluation of the Head Start program. It concluded that "Head Start children did not differ significantly in the elementary grades on most intellectual and socioemotional variables from their peers who had not enrolled in the program."[23] In 1985, there was a second national-level study, this one included in the Child Support Report (CSR) The results of this study were more positive than those of the earlier study, but the conclusion was that any gains children might make in the Head Start program were short-term and "washed out" by the end of the first or second grade unless the individual attention that was provided in Head Start was continued (McKey et al.).[24] It should be noted that, despite evidence that the Head Start program is not effective in promoting significant academic achievement, it is politically popular and each year receives millions dollars that many believe might be spent more wisely. Political expediency sometimes supersedes empirical data. It should be noted that the No Child Left Behind Act (2002) is the latest reauthorization of the 1965 Elementary and Secondary Education Act.

The **Bilingual Act** was authorized in 1968 and required that schools take steps to help non-English-speaking students learn. In most cases this meant providing these students with extra help in learning English and many teachers were trained to teach English as a Second Language (ESL). Generally, the goal of ESL programs is to help students move from their native language to Standard English as quickly as possible.

The **Education for All Handicapped Children Act** (Public Law 94-142) became law in 1975. It became a law because some states, finding that educating the handicapped was expensive, wanted to limit the opportunities they had to provide to children with disabilities. PL 94-142 required that public schools (1) evaluate the status of students with special needs at least once each year, (2) develop an Individualized Educational

Plan (IEP) for every handicapped student, and (3) place each handicapped student in the least restrictive environment (which means that, whenever possible, students should be placed in the classrooms in which they would normally be placed if they were not disabled). This law was strengthened in 1986, by passage of Amendment 99-457, which extends the rights and protections provided in PL 94-142 to disabled children three to five years of age.

Since the term Individual Education Program or Plan will be used throughout this text, it will be useful to briefly explain one point here. That point is the part of an IEP that specifies annual goals. The law says, "These are goals that the child can reasonably accomplish in a year. The goals are broken down into short-term objectives or benchmarks. Goals may be academic, address social or behavioral needs, relate to physical needs, or address other educational needs. The goals must be measurable-meaning that it must be possible to measure whether the student has achieved the goals."[25] The point that causes confusion is whether meeting the goals of an IEP equates with meeting course objectives or high school graduation requirements.

If a student's special needs can be met by modifying instructional procedures (e.g., providing more time for an assignment, providing large-print materials, or providing taped rather than printed material); there is little question that use of the IEP will not interfere with the student's achievement of the course objectives. However, if a course objective calls for a competence that the student cannot perform, and for which a suitable alternative cannot be found, a problem arises. For example, if a required competence was to make an oral presentation to a group, a student with a severe stuttering problem would be unlikely to do that satisfactorily. While an IEP might include an analogous activity such as making a videotaped presentation, that activity is not the same as making the presentation to the group. In cases such as this, a student might receive credit for meeting the requirements of the IEP, but he or she might not receive credit for meeting the course requirements. This would then lead to questions about whether the student met all graduation requirements. The question is still open and is most often decided on a case-by-case basis. However, the increasing pressures of the No Child Left Behind Act are prompting many educators to increasingly assign course grades based the extent to which students demonstrated the competencies required in the course.

The significance of PL 94–142 and PL 99–457 is three-fold. First, it demonstrates, once again, strong federal involvement in education. Second, the mandating of Individualized Education Plans means that teachers need to think about the extent to which the content, instructional procedures and experiences of their courses might be modified to accommodate students with special needs. Third, the fact that teachers might have severely disabled students in their classrooms raises questions about their preparation for dealing with severely handicapped students and the extent of their legal liability. Solving one problem sometimes causes others.

The Commission's Report, *A Nation at Risk*

The commission's report, ***A Nation at Risk,*** was released in 1983 by the **National Commission on Excellence in Education**, which was formed by then–United States Secretary of Education Terrell H. Bell, who had asked that the quality of education in the United States be investigated. By the end of the 1970s, the economies of countries such as Japan, West Germany, and Korea—countries that the United States had helped rebuild after World War II and the Korean War—were strong and getting stronger. American businessmen complained that American workers were not as well prepared as their counterparts in Europe and Asia. The commission's report, *A Nation at Risk*, seemed to support the fears of the businessmen. Among other findings, the commission found the following.

1. International comparisons of student achievement completed a decade earlier revealed that on nineteen academic tests, American students were never first or second and, in comparison with other industrialized nations, were last seven times.

2. Some twenty-three million American adults are functionally illiterate according to the simplest tests of everyday reading, writing, and comprehension.

3. About thirteen percent of all seventeen-year-old children in the United States can be considered functionally illiterate. Functional illiteracy among minority youth may run as high as forty percent.

4. Average achievement of high school students on most standardized tests is now lower than 26 years ago when Sputnik was launched.

5. School achievement for over half the population of gifted students does not match their tested ability.

6. The College Board's Scholastic Aptitude Tests (SAT) demonstrate a virtual unbroken decline from 1963 to 1980. Average verbal scores fell over fifty points and average mathematics scores dropped nearly forty points.

7. Both the number and proportion of students demonstrating superior achievement on the SATs (those with scores of 650 or higher) have also dramatically declined.

8. Many seventeen-year-old children do not possess the "higher-order" intellectual skills we should expect of them. Nearly forty percent cannot draw inferences from written material, only twenty percent can write a persuasive essay, and only one-third can solve a mathematics problem requiring several steps.

9. Business and military leaders complain that they are required to spend millions of dollars on costly remedial education and training programs in such basic

skills as reading, writing, spelling, and computation. The Department of the Navy, for example, reported to the commission that one-quarter of its recent recruits cannot read at the ninth-grade level, the minimum needed to understand written safety instructions. Without remedial work they cannot even begin, much less complete, the sophisticated training essential in much of the modern military.[26]

The commission also found that while "the public understands the primary importance of education as the foundation for a satisfying life, an enlightened and civil society, a strong economy, and a secure nation," it "has no patience with undemanding and superfluous high school offerings."[27]

"Secondary school curricula have been homogenized, diluted, and diffused to the point that they no longer have a central purpose. In effect, we have a cafeteria-style curriculum in which appetizers and desserts can easily be mistaken for the main course." It added that "this curricular smorgasbord, combined with extensive student choice, explains a great deal about where we find ourselves today."[28]

In light of its findings, the commission made five broad recommendations that were followed by detailed explanations. The first three were as follows.

1. State and local high school graduation requirements be strengthened and that, at a minimum, all students seeking a diploma be required to lay the foundation in the Five New Basics by taking the following curriculum during their four years of high school: (a) four years of English; (b) three years of mathematics; (c) three years of science; (d) three years of social studies; and (e) one-half year of computer science. For the college-bound, two years of foreign language in high school are strongly recommended in addition to those taken earlier.
2. Schools, colleges, and universities adopt more rigorous and measurable standards; higher expectations for academic performance and student conduct; and four-year colleges and universities raise their admission requirements.
3. Significantly more time be devoted to learning the New Basics. This will require more effective use of the existing school day, a longer school day, or a lengthened school year.

The fourth recommendation had to do with teachers and teacher preparation. It called for higher standards for teachers, eleven-month contracts, financial incentives to attract outstanding students to the teaching profession, and greater involvement by teachers in planning programs. The fifth recommendation had to do with leadership and fiscal support. Among other things, it said, "The Federal Government has *the primary responsibility* to identify the national interest in education."[29]

The Nation at Risk report profoundly affected education in the United States. Many high schools adopted the "New Basics" and adjusted their curriculums accordingly. Many elective subjects were deleted, and time and resources reallocated to subjects in the New Basics. In the subject areas themselves, courses such as Pre-Algebra, Consumer Math, and Ecology were deleted and additional sections of Algebra, Geometry, Trigonometry, Biology, Chemistry, and Physics were provided. High school curriculums became increasingly subject-centered and academically oriented (i.e., Essentialist), and they remain mostly that way today.

In *The Manufactured Crisis* (1995), David Berliner and Bruce Biddle, both of whom are nationally respected researchers, provide data rebutting key contentions of the *Nation at Risk* report. Some of those contentions follow.

1. Student achievement nationwide has recently fallen across the nation (pages 13–35),
2. College-student performance had recently declined in America (pages 35–41),
3. Students are dumber today than they used to be; student intelligence is determined only by inheritance; and student intelligence is largely fixed before students enter school (pages 41–51),
4. American schools fail in comparative studies of student achievement (pages 51–63)
5. America spends a lot more money on education than other countries (pages 66–70), and
6. Money is not related to school achievement.[30]

Since these contentions are still believed by many people, and debated by many others, it is suggested that you read *The Manufactured Crisis* for yourself and reach your own conclusions.

National Education Goals for the Year 2000

The **National Education Goals for the Year 2000** were released in 1989. The document was adopted by the nation's fifty governors and President George H. W. Bush that spelled out specific national educational goals. One of those goals named five school subjects-English, mathematics, science, history, and geography—for which challenging national achievement standards should be established.[31] This in turn, paved the way for federal funding of the development of those standards. The standards were developed, were soon adopted or adapted by state Boards of Education and became the basis for many statewide achievement tests. Many people believe that they are also paving the way toward a national curriculum.

America 2000

President George H. W. Bush released in 1991 *America 2000, An Education Strategy*; his vision of what education should be like by the year 2000. Six goals were central:

1. All children in America will start school ready to learn.
2. The high school graduation rate will increase to at least 90 percent.
3. American students will leave grades four, eight, and twelve having demonstrated competency in challenging subject matter including English, mathematics, science, history, and geography; and every school in America will ensure that all students learn to use their minds, so they may be prepared for responsible citizenship, further learning, and productive employment in our modern economy.
4. United States students will be first in the world in science and mathematics achievement.
5. Every adult American will be literate and will possess the knowledge and skills necessary to compete in a global economy and exercise the rights and responsibilities of citizenship.
6. Every school in America will be free of drugs and violence and will offer a disciplined environment conducive to learning.[32]

The goals for *America 2000* were far broader than those of earlier goal statements. However, as its predecessors, *America 2000* focused primarily on traditional academic subjects. Further, conspicuous by their absence in *A Nation at Risk* and *America 2000* are recommendations concerning the fine arts, physical education, vocational education, or any of the many other topics and subjects that various groups would like to see in the curriculum. Clearly, this does not please everyone, so the debate about what students should learn and why they should learn it continues. However, there is now one difference.

Both *A Nation at Risk* and *America 2000* focus on American students as a group, reaching higher standards. Since we are talking about millions of students, we are now seeing an increased dependence on the use of standardized tests to determine if students are meeting those higher standards. This, in turn, is changing the focus from what students are taught, to what they are able to do. This means there is likely to be an increased emphasis on relatively short-term, measurable, goals. Being able to specify meaningful and measurable goals will be crucial to your success in the classroom, but it is also triggering concerns about the long-term purposes of education.

The No Child Left Behind Act (NCLB)

The **No Child Left Behind Act** (NCLB) is the most recent the reauthorization of the Elementary and Secondary School Act (1965). It was signed into law (Public Law 107-110) by President George W. Bush on January 8, 2002.

The NCLB Act provided millions of federal dollars for education, but in return for these dollars, schools were required to meet certain requirements. The first of these was that schools publicly report the achievement of their students on standardized tests in aggregate and by subgroups. Since the 1954 *Brown v. Board of Education of Topeka* decision, educators have worked hard to desegregate schools and to de-emphasize racial and ethnic differences. With the NCLB requirement that scores be reported by subgroups, educators are required to group students by race and ethnicity. Not only is this likely to re-ignite problems related to segregation but it is also increasingly difficult to do. For example, because of the growing number of mixed marriages, not all students are clearly black or white, Hispanic or non-Hispanic, so simply trying to classify students is time-consuming and difficult.

Second, NCLB requires that all students be tested. Given the mobility of our student population, this requirement entails its own problems. For example, if a student transfers to a school a week before tests are administered, should he or she be tested? To not test the student violates the NCLB requirement, but the new student's test performance would unfairly reflect upon the instruction provided by teachers in that school. States have now been given some flexibility in solving this problem. For example, in June 2005, states received permission to move the beginning date for determination of a full academic year from September 30 to May 1. This change allows schools with summer programs to provide those additional resources to children who need help in reading and/or math. Test results of students enrolled in the district by May 1 but who move from school to school in that district between May 1 and the testing date will be reflected only in the District Report Card and not the individual School Report Card.[33]

Another requirement is that ninety-five percent of all students in each subgroup meet the school's adequate yearly progress (AYP) goal. This requirement raised another problem. Some schools, because of poor funding, the makeup of the student body, and other factors often beyond the control of the teachers, are finding it difficult to meet these goals. However, if they fail to meet them, they lose federal dollars. Ironically, these are the schools that most often need more, not less, funding.

Given the difficulties many schools are having in helping all students reach annual yearly progress (AYP) goals as specified in NCLB legislation, the Department of Education has gradually allowed school districts greater flexibility. For example, in the original NCLB act, school districts that failed to meet their AYP goals for two consecutive years had to allow students to transfer to schools that were meeting their AYP goals. If a district failed to meet its AYP goals for a third consecutive year, it had to offer free tutoring to its students. In July of 2006, the Dept. of Education allowed qualifying districts to offer free tutoring after the second year and to defer the transfers to the third year. The change was made because it was found that many parents preferred having their children tutored where they were rather than transferring their children to a different school.[34]

It is interesting to note that while the *Nation at Risk* report, the National Education Goals for the year 2000, America 2000: An Education Strategy, and the No Child Left Behind Act all call for higher student performance standards, they all focus on what the schools and teachers should do. None focus on, or even mention, the responsibilities of parents and students.

American Recovery and Reinvestment Act of 2009 (ARRA)— Race to the Top Program

During his first term in office, President Obama signed into law the American Recovery and Reinvestment Act of 2009 (ARRA). According to Race to the Top Program Executive Summary,

> [ARRA is] historic legislation designed to stimulate the economy, support job creation, and invest in critical sectors historic legislation designed to stimulate the economy, support job creation, and invest in critical sectors, including education. The ARRA lays the foundation for education reform by supporting investments in innovative strategies that are most likely to lead to improved results for students, long-term gains in school and school system capacity, and increased productivity and effectiveness.[35]

Part of the ARRA legislation is a grant fund that was intended to provide the States with a $4.35 billion grant fund titled Race to the Top (RTTT).

> [RTTT] is a competitive grant program designed to encourage and reward States that are creating the conditions for education innovation and reform; achieving significant improvement in student outcomes, including making substantial gains in student achievement, closing achievement gaps, improving high school graduation rates, and ensuring student preparation for success in college and careers; and implementing ambitious plans in four core education reform areas:
>
> • *Adopting standards and assessments that prepare students to succeed in college and the workplace and to compete in the global economy;*
> • *Building data systems that measure student growth and success, and inform teachers and principals about how they can improve instruction;*
> • *Recruiting, developing, rewarding, and retaining effective teachers and principals, especially where they are needed most; and*
> • *Turning around our lowest-achieving schools.*
>
> Race to the Top will reward States that have demonstrated success in raising student achievement and have the best plans to accelerate their reforms in

the future. These States will offer models for others to follow and will spread the best reform ideas across their States, and across the country.[36]

SUMMARY

Over the years, federal legislation and national reports have been important in shaping education in the United States. Even before the Constitution was written, some colonists had passed laws providing for the education of all the children of all the people and providing public funding for this purpose. In establishing the secondary school first, the colonists unintentionally established a curricular power structure that remains with us today. In that structure, the entrance requirements of colleges and universities largely dictate what courses the secondary schools will offer. This, in turn, largely dictates what is taught in grades K–8. This structure is unlikely to change as long as most parents want their children to have the opportunity to attend college.

The trail of legislation, studies, and reports indicates that the nation, as a whole, is primarily interested in having schools educate all students and produce citizens who can help the nation compete successfully in the global economy. Most often these interests result in support for subject-centered, academically oriented, essentialist, curriculums that focus on relatively short-term, measurable objectives. The progressive idea of an integrated (cross-disciplinary) curriculum focusing on problem-solving and including a wide range of "non-academic" options is still alive, but it is usually seen as less practical than essentialist curriculums, particularly at the high school level. It is also interesting to note that in all of the reports and legislation discussed, including the No Child Left Behind Act and Race to the Top program, much is said about the responsibilities of government and teachers, but nothing is said about the responsibilities of parents and students.

KEY TERMS, PEOPLE, AND IDEAS

1635: Boston Latin Grammar School—First secondary school

1636: Harvard

1647: Old Deluder Satan Law

1872: Kalamazoo, Michigan—Tax money can be used for secondary education

1751: Benjamin Franklin—First Academy—Prototype for comprehensive high schools

1785: Land Ordinance—First federal action concerning education

1862: Morrill Land Grant Act—Established land-grant colleges that included agriculture and the mechanical arts

1893: Committee of Ten Report—Essentialism and instructional time

1906: Carnegie Unit—One class, five days a week, forty minutes per period, 120 clock hours per year

1917: Smith-Hughes Act—First federal aid for secondary vocational education

1918: Commission on the Reorganization of Secondary Ed.—Seven Cardinal Principles

1924: Edward L. Thorndike—Discredited the "Faculty" Theory

1933: The Eight-Year Study, 1933–1942

1954: *Brown v. Board of Education of Topeka*—Separate is inherently unequal

1957: Sputnik I, Oct. 4, 1957—First human-made satellite

1958: National Defense Education Act (NDEA) —Massive federal funding for math and science

1965: Lyndon Johnson, Great Society, Compensatory Education—Project Head Start

1975: Education for All Handicapped Children Act (Public Law 94–142)

1983: *A Nation at Risk*—Back to basics, higher standards

1991: America 2000

2002: No Child Left Behind Act (Public Law 107–110)

2009: Race to the Top (American Recovery and Reinvestment Act of 2009 (ARRA)

QUESTIONS FOR CONSIDERATION

1. Do you agree or disagree with the idea that all students should meet the same academic standards as reflected on standardized tests? Why?
2. To what extent do you agree or disagree with the idea of a national curriculum? Why?

ENDNOTES

1   Fast Facts: Dropout Rates. Retrieved April 2, 2020, from http://nces.ed.gov/fastfacts/display.asp?id=16.

2   Nathan Thornburgh, "Dropout Nation," *Time* 167, no. 16 (April 17 2006): 32.

3   Lawrence Mishel and Roy Joydeep, "Accurately Assessing High School Graduation Rates," *Phi Delta Kappan* 88, no. 4 (Dec. 2006): 287–92.

4   Data gathered by Joyce Fritch and included in Phyliss Coulter, "Dropping the Dropout Rate," *The Pantagraph*, Sunday, Feb. 27, 2005, 1, Bloomington, IL.

5   CollegeBoard SAT 2006 College Bound Seniors. Retrieved April 15, 2020, from https://reports.collegeboard.org/pdf/total-group-2016.pdf.

6   PrepScholar: Average ACT Score for 2019, 2018, 2017, 2016, and Earlier Years. Retrieved April 20 from https://blog.prepscholar.com/average-act-score-for-2015-2014-2013-and-earlier-years.

7   Gallup Historical Trend Polls 2006–2020 Satisfaction With K–12 Education in the US. Retrieved October 17, 2020 from https://news.gallup.com/poll/1612/Education.aspx.

8   Wayne Dumas, and Weldon Beckner, *Introduction to Secondary Education* (Scranton: International Textbook Co., 1968), 5–6.

9   Dumas and Beckner, *Intro to Secondary Education*, 27.

10   US Bureau of Labor Statistics: Economic New Release: College Enrollment and Work Activity of Recent High School and College Graduate Summary. Retrieved May 1, 2020 from http://www.bls.gov/news.release/hsgec.nr0.htm.

11   Daniel J. Boorstin, and Brooks Mather Kelley, *A History of the United States* (Lexington: Ginn and Co., 1981), 101.

12   "Morrill, Justin Smith," *Encyclopedia Britannica 15* (Chicago: Encyclopedia Britannica, 1960), 820.

13   "Land-Grant Colleges," *Encyclopedia Britannica* 13 (Chicago: Encyclopedia Britannica, 1960), 648B.

14   Daniel Tanner and Laurel N. Tanner, *Curriculum Development*, 2nd. ed. (New York: Macmillan, 1980), 233.

15   Tanner and Tanner, *Curriculum Development*, 233–34.

16   Peter Oliva, *Developing the Curriculum*, 2nd ed. (Glenview: Scott, Foresman and Co., 1988), 319.

17   Commission on Reorganization of Secondary Education, Cardinal Principles of Secondary Education, Bulletin No. 35 (Washington, DC, United States Government Printing Office, 1918), 5–10. In Tanner and Tanner, 275–76.

18   Edward Thorndike, "Mental Discipline in High School Studies," *Journal of Educational Psychology* 15 (January 1924), 98.

19   Wilford M. Aiken, *Adventure in American Education, Volume I: The Story of the Eight-Year Study* (New York: Harper & Brothers, 1942), 4–10.

20   Wilford M. Aiken, *The Story of the Eight-Year Study with Conclusions and Recommendations (Adventure in American Education), (Harper & Brothers (January 1, 1942),* 111–12.

21   Aiken, 117.

22   J. M. Breslow, E. Wexler, and R. Collins, The Return of School Segregation in Eight Charts. *Frontline PBS, 2014. Retrieved May 5, 2020 from* https://www.pbs.org/wgbh/frontline/article/the-return-of-school-segregation-in-eight-charts/.

23   Marvin C. Alkin, ed., "Compensatory Education," *Encyclopedia of Educational Research*, Vol. 1, (New York: Macmillan, 1992), 208.

24   McKey, R. H., Condelli, L., Granson, H., Barrett, B., McConkey, C., & Plantz, M. (1985, June). The impact of Head Start on children. Families and communities. (Final report of the Head Start Evaluation, Synthesis and Utilization Project). Washington, D. C.: CSR, Inc.

25   US Department of Education: "A Guide to the Individualized Education Program." Retrieved May 10, 2020 from https://www2.ed.gov/parents/needs/speced/iepguide/index.html.

26   Commission on Excellence in Education, *A Nation at Risk* (Washington, D.C.: United States Government Printing Office, 1983), 8–9.

27   *Nation at Risk*, 17.

28   *Nation at Risk*, 18.

29   *Nation at Risk*, 32–33.

30   David C. Berliner and Bruce J. Biddle, *The Manufactured Crisis* (New York: Addison-Wesley Pub., 1995).

31   Govinfo: 20 USC 5812 - National Education Goals. Retrieved May 15, 2020 from https://www.govinfo.gov/content/pkg/USCODE-2015-title20/pdf/USCODE-2015-title20-chap68-subchapI-sec5812.pdf.

32   America 2000, An Education Strategy (Washington, DC: United States Government Printing Office, 1991), 19.

33   US Department of Education. No Child Left Behind Act of 2001: Retrieved May 20, 2020 from https://www2.ed.gov/nclb/landing.jhtml & https://www2.ed.gov/policy/elsec/leg/blueprint/publicationtoc.html.

34   US Department of Education. No Child Left Behind Act of 2001. Retrieved May 30, 2020 from https://www2.ed.gov/nclb/landing.jhtml.

35   US Department of Education. Race to the Top Program Executive Summary (2009), 2. Retrieved June 1, 2020 from https://www2.ed.gov/programs/racetothetop/executive-summary.pdf.

36   US Department of Education. Race to the Top Program Executive Summary, 2. Retrieved June 1, 2020 from https://www2.ed.gov/programs/racetothetop/executive-summary.pdf.

Figure Credit

CHAPTER 3

Learning Theories and Instructional Models

INTRODUCTION

Do you know how we learn or store memories such as math facts, events, a hug, or the taste of mom's apple pie? Do not feel bad if you do not know; no one else knows either. Nonetheless, teachers are charged with helping students learn, so it is to our advantage to examine some of the best researched learning theories and instructional models. The examination will reveal some of the strengths and weaknesses of each theory and model, giving you a better idea of how and why the theories and models differ.

LEARNING OUTCOMES

You will be able to do the following in writing:

1. Explain at least one distinguishing characteristic of behaviorism, Field theories, cognitive theory, and multiple intelligences.
2. Given a specific instructional task (such as teaching students the stages of the water cycle, or how to defend a point of view), explain whether principles of behaviorism, field theory, or cognitive theory would be most applicable, and use cause–effect reasoning and examples to explain your answer.
3. Explain the purpose of each of the four stages common to virtually all instructional models.
4. Explain one strength and one inherent weakness of the systems approach.

LEARNING THEORIES

By definition, a theory is "a system of assumptions, accepted principles, and rules of procedure devised to analyze, predict, or otherwise explain the nature or behavior of a specified set of phenomena."[1] As you read, keep in mind that all learning theories attempt to explain how people learn. However, researchers are just beginning to explore the intricacies of the human mind. Each of the theories may be partly or wholly correct or incorrect; we simply do not know.

Behaviorism

In its simplest form, behaviorism holds that by appropriately manipulating the environment, all living things can be made to behave in designated ways. For example, the direction an amoeba takes can be manipulated by placing it between two lines of salt. The amoebae will avoid the salt. **Ivan Pavlov** (1849–1936) demonstrated that dogs could be conditioned to salivate at the sound of a bell.[2] When you are driving and see a red light, do you stop? You probably do, without much thought. That kind of action demonstrates one of the key principles of behaviorism, namely, that humans, like all other living things, can be conditioned to behave in designated ways.

    John B. Watson (1878–1958) was one of the first psychologists to describe behaviorism as a unique aspect of psychology. His article, "Psychology as the Behaviorist Views It," published in 1913,[3] is regarded by some as the formal beginning of behaviorism. He was so convinced of the effectiveness of behaviorism that he said,

> Give me a dozen healthy infants, well-formed, and my own specified world to bring them up in, and I'll guarantee to take any one at random and train him to become any type of specialist I might select—doctor, lawyer, artist, and yes, even beggarman and thief, regardless of his talents, … abilities, vocations, and race.[4]

    The work of behaviorists such as **Edward L. Thorndike** (1874–1949)[5] and **B(urrhus) F(rederic) Skinner** (1904–1990)[6] did much to promote behaviorism during the 1940s and 1950s. Behaviorism was widely accepted by educators for a number of reasons. First, it was clearly demonstrable. You do not need an advanced degree to recognize that people can be induced to behave in particular ways by the use of appropriate rewards or the threat or use of punishment. As we get older, the rewards change from smiles and hugs to gold stars and A's on report cards and later, to important titles and salary increases. The principle remains the same. We have learned that to get certain rewards, we must exhibit certain behaviors, and to the extent that we want the rewards, we willingly modify our behavior accordingly.

A second reason many teachers apply behavioristic principles is that it puts them in control. The teacher determines what is to be learned and what the standards of behavior will be, and it is the teacher who manages the reward system to bring about the desired learning and behaviors. Behaviorism typically requires an external locus of control, and in schools, that locus of control is, most often, the teacher.

Behaviorism also assumes that learners are inherently neutral and passive, but we know that students, at least when they are young, are inherently curious and active. Nonetheless, in an era when classroom control is a major concern of teachers, it is understandable why many teachers adopt behavioristic strategies.

A third reason for the continued strength of behaviorism is that it has been shown to be effective in many applications, especially in programmed instruction. Behaviorists found that some complex behaviors could be learned more easily by breaking them into smaller, less complex segments and helping students learn the segments sequentially. Learning in this fashion is analogous to building a structure by adding brick after brick until the structure is completed. In education, for example, we first teach letters and simple words, then how to combine words into sentences, sentences into paragraphs, and finally, paragraphs into whole essays, reports, and other documents. This idea of dividing complex information or tasks into simpler, less complex units is particularly evident in tutorials and in drill and practice computer-assisted instruction programs.

Most behaviorists would agree that students come to school with different backgrounds, abilities, and interests. However, they would say that through the appropriate structuring of the information and skills to be learned and the appropriate use of incentives, these students can be taught the same things and will leave the educational process much more alike than when they began. A diagram of this viewpoint might look like Figure 3.1.

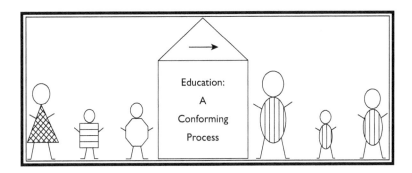

Figure 3.1 Behavioristic View

Problems with Behaviorism

Behaviorism has its critics. They point out that when the teacher provides an external locus of control, students are deprived of the opportunity to think for themselves. In fact, in many situations students are unaware that their behavior is being manipulated. The critics go on to argue that if we want citizens who can think for themselves and control their own behavior, we need to help them develop those skills in school and that behaviorism does not lend itself well to those goals.

Critics also point out that while principles of behaviorism may be effective in helping students learn factual information, sequences of events, and discreet facts, it is less effective in fostering creativity or the ability to solve problems. While students are in school, it is useful for them to have command of a large database of facts, figures, names, and places. However, unless that database is developed with an eye toward how, or whether, students will use that information after graduation, much of the information remains unused and is eventually forgotten. Clearly, behaviorism has its strengths and weaknesses.

Gestalt Theory

In the early 1900s, a group of German psychologists (**Max Wertheimer** [1880–1943], **Kurt Koffka** [1886–1941], and **Wolfgang Kohler** [1887–1967]) argued that learning takes place "when the individual sees the overall pattern (or gestalt) in a situation and changes his behavior accordingly. Thus, the learner responds as a whole organism and not automatically, or mechanically, through specific reflexes."[7] **Gestaltism** holds that the whole is more than the sum of the parts and that the learning process may indeed be more complex than suggested by the behaviorists. However, the behaviorists were more able than the gestaltists to dramatically demonstrate the efficacy of their principles, so for many years behaviorism was the most commonly accepted learning theory.

In the classroom, gestaltists are likely to spend more time than behaviorists in helping students assimilate ideas. This very often takes the form of helping students move from acquiring specific facts to seeing how they contribute to broader generalizations.

Cognitive Field Theory

Field theories were an outgrowth of gestaltism. Like the gestaltists, **Kurt Lewin** (1890–1947) believed that human activity was the result of complex psychological factors rather than simple environmental factors. He refined the broad view of gestaltism by arguing that regardless of how the teacher presents information, students perceive and interpret that information on the basis of their own experiences, needs, and abilities—their own **perceptual or cognitive fields**.[8]

A visit to any high school will quickly verify that students do, in fact, have widely different backgrounds, interests, and abilities. Unlike the behaviorists, however, the field

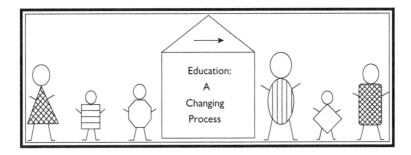

Figure 3.2 Cognitive Field Theorist View

theorists did not think that schooling would make all students alike. To the extent that their theory is correct, students would come to school with widely different backgrounds, abilities, and interests, but differences in cognitive fields would work against uniformity among the exiting students. A diagram of this viewpoint might look like Figure 3.2.

While both perceptual and cognitive fields come from the student's past experiences, they are different. A student's perceptual field is built on the input from his or her senses. For example, most students have seen blue objects and can visualize the color blue. Someone who was born blind cannot. His or her perceptual field is different. Similarly, while most students know what a subway is, a student from a developing country might not. Using a subway as an example of something would be meaningless for that student because it would not be part of his or her cognitive field.

Cognitive Psychology

Cognitive theory focuses on how learners acquire information and how they use that information to deal with new experiences and situations. Although **cognitive psychology** did not emerge as a separate branch of psychology until the early 1960s, it has deep roots. For example, **John Dewey**, in describing the educational practices typical of his day, said they could "be compared to inscribing records upon a passive phonograph disk to result in giving back what has been inscribed when the proper button is pressed in recitation or examination."[9] He certainly did not equate memorization with learning. He held that learning, and particularly reflective thinking, took place only under certain conditions.

> They are first that the pupil have a genuine situation of experience—that there be a continuous activity in which he is interested for its own sake; secondly, that a genuine problem develop within this situation as a stimulus to thought; third, that he possess the information to make the observations needed to deal with it; fourth, that suggested solutions occur to him which

he shall be responsible for developing in an orderly way; fifth, that he may have the opportunity and occasion to test his ideas by application, to make their meaning clear and to discover for himself their validity.[10]

In contrast to the behaviorist's brick-upon-brick view of learning, Dewey saw learning as adding ingredients to a stew. As more ingredients were added and the stew was continually stirred to integrate the new ingredients, the stew, or knowledge base, became richer and richer. This view of the way the mind works is consistent with recent research concerning the mind. In "Beyond the Brain," James Shreeve cites research that demonstrates that the brain is able to store and integrate pieces of information in ways far beyond the capabilities of our most advanced computers. The database built by the mind cannot be explained by using the brick-upon-brick analogy; the stew analogy seems closer to the mark even though how the mind works is still poorly understood.[11]

Jean Piaget (1896–1980) was another early cognitive theorist. Piaget is perhaps best known for his description of how the human intellect develops in phases.

Phase One	Sensory-motor (birth to about age 2)
Phase Two	Preoperational (about ages 2–7)
	A. Preconceptual thought (about ages 2–4)
	B. Intuitive thought (about ages 4–7)
Phase Three	Concrete operations (about ages 7–11)
Phase Four	Formal operations (about age 11 onward)[12]

Because of the ages they span, these phases are most relevant to preschool and elementary school students and their teachers. However, one of the key points underlying the phases is relevant to secondary-school teachers and is central to cognitive theory.

If cognitive psychologists are correct, cognitive development takes place as a consequence of the interaction of learners with their environment. Neither maturation alone, nor instruction alone, is sufficient; interaction is necessary. John Dewey explained this view when he defined education as "that reconstruction of experience which adds to the meaning of experience and which increases ability to direct the course of subsequent experience."[13]

To the extent that the cognitive theory is correct, teachers can maximize the learning potential of their students if they structure situations in which students must solve new problems. It is while thinking about these new experiences that learners assimilate new information and reorganize their knowledge base. The theory holds that people learn best if they are challenged to use information and skills.

Multiple Intelligences

Howard E. Gardner (b. 1943) is a Professor of Cognition and Education at Harvard Graduate School of Education. He is the co-director of Harvard's Project Zero, where he is studying how to design performance-based assessments, education for understanding, and the use of multiple intelligences to achieve more personalized curriculum, instruction, and assessment. He is the author of eighteen books and several hundred articles. In 1983, he challenged our ideas about intelligence in his book, entitled *Frames of Mind: The theory of multiple intelligences*. In this book, Howard Gardner proposed that humans possess multiple types of intelligence.[14]

According to Garner's theory, there are nine intelligences that enable people to perceive and understand new information. These intelligences are:

1. **Linguistic Intelligence**: the capacity to use language to express what's on your mind and to understand other people. Any kind of writer, orator, speaker, lawyer, or other person for whom language is an important stock in trade has great linguistic intelligence.

2. **Logical/Mathematical Intelligence**: the capacity to understand the underlying principles of some kind of causal system, the way a scientist or a logician does, or to manipulate numbers, quantities, and operations, the way a mathematician does.

3. **Musical Rhythmic Intelligence**: the capacity to think in music—to be able to hear patterns, recognize them, and perhaps manipulate them. People who have strong musical intelligence don't just remember music easily; they can't get it out of their minds because it is so omnipresent.

4. **Bodily/Kinesthetic Intelligence**: the capacity to use your whole body or parts of your body (your hands, your fingers, your arms) to solve a problem, make something, or put on some kind of production. The most evident examples are people in athletics or the performing arts, particularly dancing or acting.

5. **Spatial Intelligence**: the ability to represent the spatial world internally in your mind, the way a sailor or airplane pilot navigates the large spatial world or the way a chess player or sculptor represents a more circumscribed spatial world. Spatial intelligence can be used in the arts or the sciences.

6. **Naturalist Intelligence**: the ability to discriminate among living things (plants, animals) and sensitivity to other features of the natural world (clouds, rock configurations). This ability was clearly of value in our evolutionary past as hunters, gatherers, and farmers; it continues to be central in such roles as botanist or chef.

7. **Intrapersonal Intelligence**: having an understanding of yourself; knowing who you are, what you can do, what you want to do, how you react to things, which

things to avoid, and which things to gravitate toward. We are drawn to people who have a good understanding of themselves. They tend to know what they can and cannot do and know where to go if they need help.

8. **Interpersonal Intelligence**: the ability to understand other people. It's an ability we all need, but it is especially important for teachers, clinicians, salespersons, or politicians—anybody who deals with other people.

9. **Existential Intelligence**: the ability and proclivity to pose (and ponder) questions about life, death, and ultimate realities.[15]

Comparison of Learning Theories

A comparison of these theories will highlight some of their respective strengths and weaknesses. Behaviorism views the learning process in a very mechanical way: Find the right system of rewards, present the information in appropriate blocks, and learning will occur. The validity of the theory can be seen when its principles are followed to help students learn basic facts and information, particularly via programmed instruction. Those techniques, however, do little to foster the development of problem-solving skills, creativity, or self-control.

Field theories focus on the importance of each student's background, interests, and abilities, but they offer little practical help to teachers who may have twenty to thirty students in a class and who are expected to help each of those students achieve the same objectives by the end of the year. Teachers often try to use individual or group projects in the attempt to accommodate individual differences, but the attempts typically fall short of the goal. To a large extent, mass education as we know it requires that individuals subordinate much of their individuality to "the system." Field theorists would like the system to adapt to individual differences.

The cognitive theory makes it clear that students learn most effectively when they are challenged to solve problems and deal with new situations. One of its weaknesses is that it does little to explain how students acquire basic knowledge in the first place. Using information and skills to learn more, to solve problems, and to deal with life, are admirable goals and should be incorporated into every teacher's objectives. However, students must *have* information before they can use it or reorganize it.

The theory of multiple intelligences does not limit the intelligences to nine intelligences; there may be many more. While we all possess most of these intelligences, they are not equally strong. Rather, we may experience learning best with two or three of our intelligences. Since we all have nine (or more) intelligences, we may choose to use those that are most comfortable for us.

No single theory seems to adequately explain all the complexities of learning, nor does anyone offer principles that are useful in all situations. Researchers are still hard

Table 3.1 Theory Comparison Table

Theory	Major Voice(s)	Strengths	Weaknesses
Behaviorism	Watson, J. B. Thorndike, E. L. Skinner, B. F.	Mechanistic and prescriptive. Learning is facilitated by dividing tasks into small steps. Knowledge base is built fact upon fact.	Fails to deal with complex interactions that transform facts into useful knowledge.
Gestalt Theory	Wertheimer, M. Koffka, K. Kohler, W.	The whole is greater than the sum of the parts. Learning is complex, not mechanistic.	Many of the factors that affect learning are unique to the individual, so finding instructional techniques effective with many students is difficult.
Cognitive Field	Lewin, K.	Acknowledges that perceptual and cognitive fields affect each student's learning.	Same as above.
Cognitive Psychology	Dewey, J. Piaget, J.	Learning seen as continually adding ingredients to a stew to enrich it. Applying information helps embed it in the knowledge base.	Time spent helping students assimilate information is not available for the acquisition of new information.
Multiple Intelligences	Gardner, H.	Multiple intelligences may contribute to differences in learning styles.	It is difficult to accommodate different "intelligences" or learning styles in a single classroom.

at work trying to learn how we learn. The wise teacher will not be too quick to adopt or reject any one theory. See Table 3.1 for a Theory Comparison Table.

INSTRUCTIONAL MODELS

Instructional models describe, sometimes graphically, various instructional strategies. They are useful because they help educators visualize those strategies as a series of steps, see how the steps fit together, and analyze the strengths and weaknesses of each step. Some models are more complex than others, but each can be effective for specific purposes.

As useful as the following models are, keep in mind that they deal only with the teaching part of the teaching-learning process. The teaching part is open to examination because it is politically acceptable to hold teachers accountable for their actions while, at the same time, ignoring the fact that parents and students also have major roles in the teaching-learning process. Nonetheless, the models are likely to help you think about your responsibilities in helping students learn.

The Military Model

Whether it is true or not, the military is often credited with having a clear, easy-to-follow, instructional model: (1) tell them what you are going to tell them, (2) tell them, (3) tell them what you told them, and (4) test them. The model clearly adheres to the advice offered by **William of Ockham**, that "Entities should not be multiplied unnecessarily," (known as **Ockham's razor**) and its more modern version, the **KISS** principle (Keep It Simple, Stupid).[16] More importantly, the model incorporates steps that contribute to student learning. For example, it calls for a preview or overview of new information. A preview can help students create a mental framework that, in turn, can help them organize information as they receive it and to remember it later. You will note that each chapter in this book includes a rationale and sample objectives. The purpose of both is to give the reader a clear idea of what the chapter concerns and some things that they should be able to do after reading the chapter.

The model also calls for direct instruction. Direct instruction is teacher controlled, highly structured, and exemplified by the use of lectures and other teacher-directed techniques. Information is presented systematically, in small segments, and feedback concerning learning progress is continually provided. After surveying twenty years of research, **Levin** and **Ornstein** found that this kind of instruction is indeed effective.[17] The model also calls for the review of information to help students focus on main points and properly organize them in their minds. Finally, it calls for a determination of whether students have mastered, to an acceptable degree, the appropriate information and skills.

In many situations this model works quite well. However, its critics point out, first, that the model fails to recognize or provide for individual differences, and those differences might affect the capacity or willingness of students to benefit from the instruction. Critics also point out that the model does not provide for student involvement or for the development of self-control on the part of the students.

The Systems Approach

The systems approach is rooted in the Industrial Revolution and behaviorism. During the early 1900s, the Industrial Revolution was at its height and American industry was the envy of the world. One of the keystones of the Industrial Revolution was the idea of taking a complex task, such as building an automobile, and dividing it into a series of smaller, less complex tasks, such as building frames, body parts, and engines. Since this idea worked so well for industry, some educators thought it might also work well in schools.

One educator (and behaviorist), **Franklin Bobbitt** (1876–1956), went so far as to directly compare education and manufacturing. He said that "education is a shaping process as much as the manufacture of steel rails."[18] Some people agree and others disagree.

The second root, behaviorism, held that learning was largely a mechanical process. Students could be taught if they were presented with information that had been systematically arranged in small units and if the teacher (or machine) appropriately manipulated the reward system. The industrial model and behaviorism complemented each other, and this encouraged educators to adapt these ideas for use in education.

At the heart of most systems models are four key steps: (1) the specification of instructional objectives, (2) preassessment of students to determine their beginning abilities relative to the objectives, (3) instructional activities intended to help students achieve the objectives, and (4) evaluation in order to determine whether students have achieved the objectives.

These steps are not very different from the steps taken to achieve any goal. For example, when you get up in the morning you have to decide what to wear so you consciously or unconsciously specify an objective—typically, to dress appropriately for some activity. Next, you consciously or unconsciously assess your current dress and determine that your pajamas or nightgown are not likely to be appropriate. Then you do something to achieve the objective: you select and put on the clothes that you think will be appropriate. Finally, you engage in the planned activity and, if you were dressed appropriately for it, you achieved your objective.

The General Model of Instruction (GMI)
Since the steps are so basic to achieving any goal, it is surprising that it was not until 1970 that they were formally depicted as parts of instructional models. It was then that **Robert Kibler, Larry Barker**, and **David Miles**, in *Behavioral Objectives and Instruction*, depicted these four stages in the General Model of Instruction (GMI) shown in Figure 3.3.[19]

The Goal-Referenced Instructional Model
In the same year, **W. James Popham** and **Eva Baker**, in *Systematic Instruction*,[20] published a similar model, the Goal-Referenced Instructional Model shown in Figure 3.4.

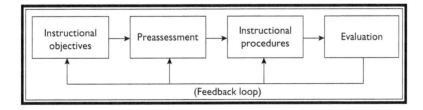

Figure 3.3 The General Model of Instruction

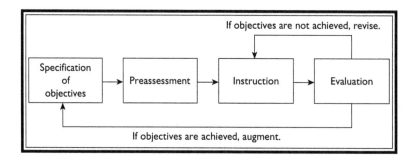

Figure 3.4 Goal-Referenced Instructional Model

In addition to the four basic steps, each model also includes a feedback loop that shows what follows evaluation. In the GMI, the loop indicates that once the objective has been achieved, the whole process is repeated with a new objective. If the objective was not achieved, the upward arrows under each step indicate that the teacher should examine that step, see if there is a problem in it and, if so, fix the problem. In the Goal-Referenced Instructional Model, the top loop goes only to the instruction step, implying that if students do not achieve the objective, the problem lies in that step and remedial instruction needs to be provided. Once the objective is achieved, the learner moves on to the next objective.

The Logical Instructional Model (LIM)

The Logical Instructional Model (LIM) depicts the same four stages as the preceding models, but it depicts them vertically and more importantly, it expands the preassessment step as shown in Figure 3.5. Since preassessment is such an important part of both the Logical Instructional Model (featured next) and the ASSURE model, it will be discussed immediately after depicting these two models.

ASSURE

The ASSURE model[21] is interesting for a number of reasons. One is that it makes use of an acronym to help students remember a process. The acronym, ASSURE, represents the following steps.

A	Analyze the learners (Same as Preassessment in the preceding models)
S	State objectives
S	Select media and materials (Included in the Instruction step of the preceding models)
U	Utilize materials (Included in the Instruction step of the preceding models)
R	Require Learner Performance (Refers to having students practice skills and use information. Ideally it would be included in the Instruction step of the preceding models.)
E	Evaluate

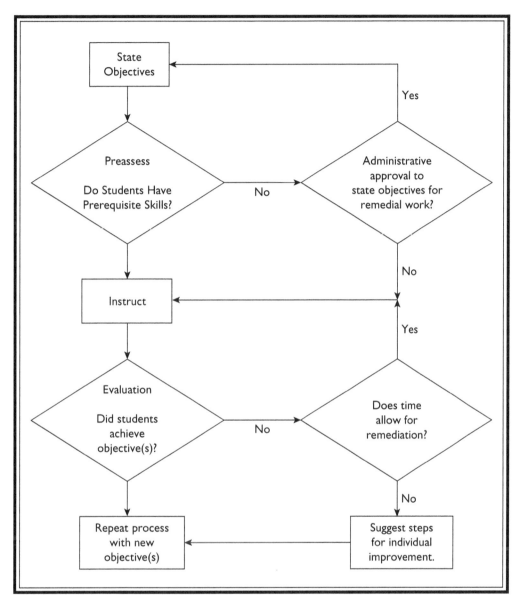

Figure 3.5 Logical Instructional Model

Preassessment

The Logical Instructional Model and the ASSURE model highlight the importance of preassessment. By calling for the analysis of students first, the ASSURE model, indicates that the objectives and instruction that follow should take into account the abilities and interests of the students. What is meant here is that the general type of *prospective* students—freshmen or seniors, general versus advanced placement, poor or rich—should be considered. If a teacher waited until the class actually met for the first time before doing this kind of preassessment, weeks of pre-school planning time would be lost.

However, once students are actually in the classroom, it is a good idea to determine the extent to which expected prerequisite skills are present. You could simply assume that students will have the prerequisite skills, but remember that you can divide the word "assume" into ass-u-me, making an ass of you and me. In this case, if your assumption is wrong it could make for a very unpleasant year for you and your students.

Rather than making an assumption about students' mastery of prerequisite skills, a wise teacher would construct a preassessment instrument. Such an instrument would call for the recollection and application of some of the key information and skills that you consider prerequisite to beginning instruction in your class. The test should not be long nor should it be part of the students' grades. Ideally, the test will verify that the students have the prerequisite skills and, as the LIM indicates, you can move on with your instructional plans. However, the test may demonstrate that many students do not have the necessary prerequisites. In this case, you have a problem and you should NOT try to solve it yourself.

Preassessment is also important if you have students with special needs. In such cases you are likely to be asked to work with a special education teacher to develop and/or implement an **individualized education plan** (IEP).

The Teacher's Role

As a teacher, you are part of a faculty that is trying to implement a school-wide curriculum. The principal is responsible for the overall implementation of that curriculum. If your preassessment reveals that a significant number of your students do not have the prerequisite knowledge or skills, you should take that information to the principal or to your department chair, depending on the administrative organization of the school, and together decide on a course of action. For example, you may believe that you should provide whatever remedial instruction is necessary to enable students to understand and benefit from new information. You want to start from where the students are and take them as far as they can go in the time available. That position is reasonable and the principal or department chair may agree with it.

You may, however, believe that students who get credit for your course should achieve the objectives normally associated with that course. You could point out that once the credit is on the transcript, future teachers, prospective employers, and anyone else who sees that transcript will assume that it is truthful and you want no part in providing false or misleading information for any reason. This position is also reasonable and the principal or department chair may agree with it.

Clearly, a strong case can be built for either position, but it is recommended that you get administrative approval before making a decision. If you arbitrarily decided to provide remedial instruction, it is not likely that you would have time to complete the rest of the planned instruction. At the end of the year, your colleagues and the principal could justifiably argue that because you did not teach what you were supposed to teach, your students are now unprepared to take the next course (assuming there is a sequence) and that your arbitrary action weakened the whole curriculum.

On the other hand, if you decided to ignore the students' deficiencies and go forward with the planned instruction, it is likely that many students would do poorly or fail. Parents would complain to you, the principal, or school board members, and your teaching ability might well be questioned.

The wisest course of action would be to take the results of your preassessment test to the principal or your department chair and discuss the options. If the principal or chair agrees that providing remedial instruction is appropriate and recognizes that doing so might keep you from completing the planned program, he or she can explain any lack of progress to critics. Similarly, if the principal or department chair agrees that following the existing syllabus is the appropriate thing to do, then he or she can explain that course of action to parents or other critics. The principal or department chair will typically know more about the curriculum and about the feelings of the faculty, the student body, and the community, than you, a new teacher. It would be wise to avail yourself of that knowledge. Further, bringing preassessment results to the principal or department chair for discussion is likely to add to your image as a professional. Not everyone thinks about preassessment or takes the time to do it.

Things to Think about concerning Instructional Models

There is no doubt that all instructional models help teachers divide instruction into steps and analyze the steps as well as the whole. However, there are at least two other points that you should consider. First, as you already saw, instructional models deal with only part of the teaching-learning process, the teachers' part. The models imply that if the students do not learn, there is something wrong with the instructional system and that if the teacher tinkers enough with the system, the students will learn. That may not be so.

Second, the feedback loops indicate that if students have not achieved the objective, remedial instruction should be provided. However, if the teacher has carefully planned instruction to help students achieve a year-long sequence of objectives, little if any time will be available for remediation. Time is always a critical variable.

Time and achievement are two variables central to the teaching-learning process. Public schools keep time stable and allow achievement to vary. We conduct classes for

X days (typically 180–185), and then attempt to grade students on how much progress they made during that time. In doing this, we make the assumption that like horses at the beginning of a race, all students begin at the same point. Preassessment can determine the extent to which the assumption is valid.

If achievement was held stable and time was allowed to vary, we might be able to engage in mastery learning. With enough time, we could probably help virtually all students master particular information and skills, but even then, student cooperation would be needed.

SUMMARY

Learning theories attempt to explain how people learn. Behaviorism holds that the behavior of all living things can be manipulated by controlling environmental variables. In teaching, this translates into dividing complex tasks or behaviors into smaller, simpler units, organizing the units in some logical order, and then arranging a reward system so that students are rewarded as they master each unit. Behaviorist principles are evident in our use of praise, gold stars, and grades to reward students. Behaviorists also tend to see the development of the mind in terms of building a cathedral, brick upon brick. Critics of behaviorism, including John Dewey, tend to see the development of the mind in terms of continually enriching a stew by adding new ingredients and continually stirring the mix. The most recent research seems to support the stew analogy.

Gestaltism holds that learning results from a complex interaction of knowledge, emotions, and environmental factors. These factors combine to help the learner see an overall pattern in a situation and this, in turn, brings about the behavior change or learning.

Field theory is an outgrowth of gestaltism. It holds that learners perceive and interpret the world around them on the basis of their existing knowledge and experiences—their cognitive fields. In this view, what specific students learn in any given situation is largely determined by the background, skills, and intents that they bring to the situation.

Multiple intelligences holds that learners possess nine types of intelligence. These intelligences enable them to perceive and understand new information.

Instructional models help teachers analyze the instructional process by dividing it into discrete steps. Most models include four basic steps: (1) the specification of instructional objectives, (2) preassessment of students to determine their beginning abilities relative to the objectives, (3) instructional activities intended to help students achieve the objectives, and (4) evaluation in order to determine whether students have achieved the objectives.

Preassessment is particularly important because it helps determine if students have the knowledge and skills needed to benefit from the intended instruction. Decisions about what to do if students do not have the prerequisites should be made in conjunction with the principal.

It is important to keep in mind that instructional models deal with instruction. The assumption is that if the teacher follows the steps of the model, students will learn. That assumption ignores the responsibilities of the learner. It is also important to keep in mind that instructional models do not deal with time as a variable.

The General Model of Instruction, the Goal-Referenced Instructional Model, and the Logical Instructional Model all include feedback loops. These loops call for remediation when needed, but instructional plans typically allow little, if any, time for remediation.

The ASSURE model would have teachers analyze their students before specifying instructional objectives and making instructional plans. While it is possible to make some generalizations about incoming students, teachers typically must be ready to start teaching on the first day and cannot afford to give up weeks of pre-school preparation time.

KEY TERMS, PEOPLE, AND IDEAS

Behaviorism, Pavlov, Watson, B. F. Skinner

Gestalt Theory: Overall pattern—the whole is more than the sum of the parts

Cognitive Field: Past Experiences affect interpretations of current events

Cognitive Theory: Learning is more than accumulating isolated facts

Multiple Intelligences: Humans possess many types of intelligences.

Instructional Models: Only the teaching part of the teaching-learning process

Military Model

Ockham's Razor: KISS

Systems Approach

General Model of Instruction (GMI)

Goal-Referenced Instructional Model

Logical Instructional Model (LIM)

ASSURE

Preassessment

Anecdotal Records

Check with principal before making curricular changes

Time and Achievement as two variables (time usually held constant)

QUESTIONS FOR CONSIDERATION

1. To what extent do you agree or disagree with the idea that behaviorism is "hardwired" into the human psyche?
2. Going from objectives, to preassessment, to instruction, and then to assessment is a clear and reasonable approach to planning, but does it stifle creativity?

ENDNOTES

1   William Morris, ed., *The American Heritage Dictionary* (Boston: American Heritage Pub. Co. and Houghton Mifflin Co., 1970), 1335.

2   Ivan Pavlov, *Conditioned Reflexes: An Investigation of Physiological Activity of the Cerebral Cortex* trans. G. V. Anrep (London: Oxford University Press, 1927).

3   John B. Watson, "Psychology as the Behaviorist Views It," *Psychology Review* 20 (March 1913), 158–77.

4   John B. Watson, "What the Nursery Has to Say about Instincts," in *Psychologies of 1925, ed.* C. A. Murchinson (Worcester: Clark University Press, 1926), 10. In Ornstein and Hunkins, 2nd ed., 110.

5   Edward L. Thorndike, *The Psychology of Learning, Vol. II: Educational Psychology* (New York: Teachers College, 1913).

6   B. F. Skinner, *Science and Human Behavior* (New York: Macmillan, Inc., 1953).

7   Paul Saettler, *The Evolution of American Educational Technology* (Englewood: Libraries Unlimited, Inc., 1990), 84.

8   Kurt Lewin, *Field Theory in Social Science* (New York: Harper and Row, 1951).

9   John Dewey, "Need for a Philosophy of Education," *The New Era in Home and School* 15 (November, 1934), 212. In Tanner and Tanner, 2nd ed., 117.

10   John Dewey, *Democracy and Education* (New York: Macmillan, 1916), 102. In Tanner and Tanner, 2nd ed., 11.

11   James Shreeve, "Beyond the Brain," *National Geographic* 207, 3 (March 2005): 2–31.

12   Jean Piaget, *Psychology of Intelligence* (New York: Harcourt, Brace and World, 1950).

13   John Dewey, *Democracy and Education* 89–90. In Tanner and Tanner, 2nd ed., 187.

14   Howard Gardner, Hobbs Research of Cognition and Education, Harvard Graduate School of Education, The 30th anniversary introduction to *Frames of Mind*. Retrieved June 4, 2020 from https://howardgardner.com/multiple-intelligences/.

15   K. Davis, J. Christodoulou, S. Seider, and H. Gardner, The Theory of Multiple Intelligences, Retrieved June 10, 2020 from https://howardgardner01.files.wordpress.com/2012/06/443-davis-christodoulou-seider-mi-article.pdf.

16   William of Ockham (1285?–1349?), Quodlibeta, in Margaret Miner and Hugh Rawson, Dictionary of Quotations, 2nd. ed. (New York: Signet/Penguin Books, 1964), 373.

17   Daniel U. Levine and Allan C. Ornstein, "Research on Classroom and School Effectiveness and Its Implications for Improving Big City Schools," *Urban Review* (July 1989), 81–95; Allan C. Ornstein and Daniel U. Levine, "Urban School Effectiveness and Improvement," *Illinois School Research and Development* (Spring 1991), 111–17.

18   Franklin Bobbitt, "The Supervision of City Schools: Some General Principles of Management Applied to the Problems of City Schools," *Twelfth Yearbook of the National Society for the Study of Education, Part I* (Bloomington, Illinois: Bloomington, IL: Public School Publication, 1913), 11.

19   Robert J. Kibler, Larry L. Barker, and David T. Miles, *Behavioral Objectives and Instruction* (Boston: Allyn and Bacon, 1970), 13.

20   W. James Popham and Eva Baker, *Systematic Instruction* (Englewood Cliffs: Prentice-Hall, 1970), 13–18.

21   Robert Heinich, Michael Molenda, and James D. Russell, *Instructional Media*, 4th ed. (New York: Macmillan, 1993), 34–37.

Figure Credit

Fig. 3.4: Adapted from W. James Popham and Eva L. Baker, *Systematic Instruction*, p. 17. Copyright © 1970 by Prentice Hall.

CHAPTER 4

Selecting Instructional Units

INTRODUCTION

Have you heard the expression, "Go west, young man"? That expression was common during the gold rush years because men got rich by going to the gold field. As a goal statement, "go west, young man" was not bad, but as are many goal statements, it was broad. To implement it, one had to make it more specific (e.g., go west and find gold). Many educational goals are, like "go west, young man," well intentioned, but are too broad to help you plan effective instruction. This chapter is intended to familiarize you with a variety of broad educational goals and to help you learn how to convert them into clear, concise, and easily understood instructional objectives.

LEARNING OUTCOMES

You will be able to do the following in writing:

1. Use cause-effect reasoning to explain why you believe that state-mandated learning standards do or do not conflict with the idea of providing for individual differences.
2. Correctly label at least eighty percent of a set of instructional objectives as (a) lacking an observable terminal behavior, (b) lacking a minimum acceptable standard, (c) lacking both an observable behavior and a minimum acceptable standard, or (d) acceptable as written.
3. Rewrite a set of poorly written instructional objectives so that at least eighty percent of them include observable terminal behaviors (identified with an underline) and minimum acceptable standards (identified with a double underline).

4. Given a "twenty-first-century" educational goal such as "knowing more about the world," use cause-effect reasoning to explain how you might help students achieve that goal in your own classroom.

BROAD GOALS

Virtually everyone agrees on broad goals such as peace on earth, good will toward men (and women), helping students become critical thinkers and problem-solvers, and to paraphrase Boyd Bode, preparing them to live good lives in a good society.[1] It is when the discussion focuses on what you should be doing with *your* students, in *your* classroom that disagreements arise.

The Seven Cardinal Principles

Among the best-known broad goals in education are the Seven Cardinal Principles: (1) health, (2) command of the fundamentals, (3) worthy home membership, (4) vocation, (5) citizenship, (6) leisure, and (7) ethical character. There is no doubt that these goals were well intended, but there is also no doubt that there were, and are, major differences of opinion about the amount of instructional time (if any) that should be devoted to each. If time and resources were unlimited, perhaps teachers could focus on all these areas. However, time and resources are limited so choices need to be made.

Tyler's Rationale

In 1949, **Ralph W. Tyler**, the director of research for the Eight-Year Study, wrote *Basic Principles of Curriculum and Instruction*.[2] In this work he listed four fundamental questions that he believed educators should address in establishing goals:

1. What educational purposes should the school seek to attain?
2. What educational experiences can be provided that are likely to attain those purposes?
3. How can these educational experiences be effectively organized?
4. How can we determine whether these purposes are being attained?[3]

He also described three sources of ideas for educational objectives. They may turn out to be one of your greatest aids in deciding what to teach.

1. Suggestions from subject specialists
2. Studies of the learners themselves
3. Studies of contemporary life outside the school.[4]

If one considers the sources that Tyler suggests, it becomes clear that he had a good point. Generally, people would rather be successful than unsuccessful. Every student would rather get A's than C's or D's, and every teacher would like to help make students' lives happier and more productive. Why then are so many students and teachers less successful than they would like to be? The reason may well be that sometimes neither the teachers nor the students see the utility or relevance of the information to be taught or learned. If the utility or relevance of the information is not clear, it is difficult to be enthusiastic about teaching or learning it. Tyler's three sources can help educators select general objectives wisely.

Subject-Area Specialist
National Groups and Councils
During the 1980s and 1990s, many national content area councils developed standards specifying what K–12 students should know and be able to do in their respective areas. Most standards developed by state boards of education reflect those content area standards. However, most standards do not include observable behaviors or minimum acceptable standards, so they cannot be used as written to assess students. One of the best and most comprehensive sets of national standards is *Principles and Standards for School Mathematics*, published in 2000 by the National Council of Teachers of Mathematics. *Principles and Standards* lists a number of skills and concepts that K–12 students should master. For example, under Number and Operations Standard for Grades 9–12, the standard is, "Understand numbers, ways of representing numbers, relationships among numbers, and number systems." Two of the expectations for this standard are to "develop a deeper understanding of very large and very small numbers and of various representations of them," and "compare and contrast the properties of numbers and number systems, including the rational and real numbers, and understand complex numbers as solutions to quadratic equations that do not have real solutions." *Principles and Standards* goes on to provide examples of problems that might be given to students to help them develop these skills. It should be noted that one of the objectives of *Principles and Standards* is to focus on concepts and skills that have practical applications. The URL for *Principles and Standards* is http://www.nctm.org/standards/content .aspx?id=16909.

Geography also has an excellent set of K–12 standards. In 1994, the National Geographic Society published *Geography for Life*, a set of eighteen standards divided into six main areas. Here is an example of a standard and an area: Seeing the World in Spatial Terms: How to use maps and other geographic representations, tools, and technologies to acquire, process, and report information from a spatial perspective.

The standards document provides examples of skills and learning opportunities for each area and for each grade category. For example, students in grade eight who are performing "at standard" would be able to do things such as, "relate the content of geography

to life experiences," and "apply the principles of geography to solving social and environmental problems."[5]

Further, the National Geographic Society also provides lesson plans, including well-stated instructional objectives relevant to the standards. The URL for
the geography standards is https://www.nationalgeographic.org/education/
resource-library/?q=&page=1&per_page=25.

Standards such as these can assist teachers in two ways. First, the standards give
teachers in each subject area a common framework for curriculum development. In the
long term, this is likely to lead to greater uniformity in curricular scope and sequence
nationwide. In the short term, subject area standards can suggest practical ideas for
instructional units.

Second, by acquiring the standards from a variety of subject areas, teachers will be
more able to see connections between their subject area and others. This will facilitate
efforts to develop cross-disciplinary units and in a larger sense, curricular integration.
Information about national standards in the arts, civics and government, foreign languages, geography, history, mathematics, and science is available from the respective
national organizations.

The emphasis on content area standards is widely accepted in the twenty-first century. In addition to the development of state learning standards for K–12 subject areas,
the majority of the states have adopted the Common Core State Standards initiative.
According to the Common Core State Standards Initiative website:

> The Common Core State Standards Initiative is a state-led effort coordinated
> by the National Governors Association Center for Best Practices (NGA
> Center) and the Council of Chief State School Officers (CCSSO). The stan-
> dards were developed in collaboration with teachers, school administrators,
> and experts, to provide a clear and consistent framework to prepare our chil-
> dren for college and the workforce …
>
> The standards are informed by the highest, most effective models from
> states across the country and countries around the world, and they provide
> teachers and parents with a common understanding of what students are
> expected to learn. Consistent standards will provide appropriate benchmarks
> for all students, regardless of where they live.
>
> These standards define the knowledge and skills students should have
> within their K–12 education careers so that they will graduate high school
> able to succeed in entry-level, credit-bearing academic college courses and in
> workforce training programs.

The standards

- are aligned with college and work expectations;
- are clear, understandable, and consistent;
- include rigorous content and application of knowledge through high-order skills;
- build upon strengths and lessons of current state standards;
- are informed by other top performing countries so that all students are prepared to succeed in our global economy and society; and
- are evidence-based.

The Common Core Standards were announced in June 2009 and released the following year in June 2010. Full implementation will be achieved in 2015.[6]

Other Faculty

In the process of developing instructional objectives, many school districts ask teachers to get together on the basis of common grade levels or common subject-area interests. Typically, district administrators also provide teachers with objectives that have already been formulated either locally or by educators elsewhere. Sometimes it is appropriate to adopt some of those objectives as they are, but more often they must be modified to fit district expectations.

Textbooks

Assuming that the courses you are assigned to teach have been taught before, your first instinct is likely to be to look at the texts being used. Follow your instinct. To produce marketable texts, authors must focus on what practitioners in the field consider important. They must also include the most up-to-date knowledge in the field (look at the copyright date), must organize the information so it follows some logical order (look at the table of contents), and it must present that information in terms that students find interesting, relevant, and understandable (read sections of the text). With this much work already done, it makes good sense to examine the texts for ideas about objectives.

Concepts

While most texts do a good job of presenting important names, dates, events, skills, and techniques, few do as good a job identifying key concepts. As you look through texts for your course, isolate key concepts as you go. Operationally defined, a **concept** is a group of things, either concrete or abstract, that have enough elements in common to comprise a unique set. For example, the word "trees" represents a concept. When you think of trees, you may think of conifers such as pines, cedars, and firs, or deciduous trees such as oaks, maples, and birches, but you do not think of roses or lilac bushes. All are plants, but the trees have enough characteristics in common to be members of a unique set. The same idea holds for

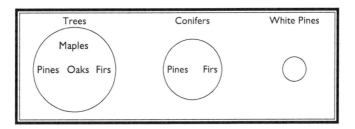

Figure 4.1 Organizing Concepts

abstractions. For example, when you think of governments, you may think of democracies, republics, dictatorships, or socialism, but you do not think of hermits or anarchy.

As you begin identifying key concepts in your subject area, focus on those most relevant to the course you are teaching and to units within that course. A diagram for organizing concepts is presented in Figure 4.1.

For example, if you were teaching general science, you might include a unit on trees. By analogy, "trees" is a beach-ball-size concept. It is large enough to contain many smaller elements.

If you were teaching a botany course, you might want to deal with trees in greater depth and devote an entire unit to coniferous trees. You would be substituting a baseball for the beach ball.

If you were teaching a course in advanced forestry, you might want an even narrower concept, such as white pines. In this case, the ball shrinks to the size of a golf ball.

If we are talking about instructional units two to four weeks in length, the broad unit on trees would have great breadth but relatively little depth, whereas the unit on white pines would have great depth but little breadth. The concepts you want to focus on should be appropriate to the course you are teaching.

The Learners Themselves

As the various national groups worked to develop standards for their respective subject areas, they worked from the perspective of subject area specialists. Tyler, and common sense, suggests that the needs and interests of students must also be considered, and this may pose a philosophic dilemma for some teachers. Some educators believe that there are certain things that students ought to learn whether they are interested in them at the moment or not. Others believe that unless the students are interested in the content, they will not cooperate in the teaching–learning process. The goal is to find a workable blend, but that is not easy.

One approach that may help is to examine the key concepts and skills identified for your subject area and to think of how to adapt them to the students you will teach. This does not mean adapting them to each student because then, instead of having objectives and standards for a course, you might end up with different objectives and standards for each student. Taking individualization to this extreme is tutoring and, while it might be best for individual students, it would destroy the whole idea of scope and sequence inherent in school curriculums. It is possible, however, to think in broad terms about your students. Is your course designed for beginning students or for seniors? Is it a general course or an advanced placement course? Is it elective or required? Are your students typically in the lower, middle, or upper socio-economic class; inner-city, urban, suburban, or rural? Using factors such as these, you can begin thinking about how to make the content relevant to your students by relating it to their lives. In doing this, it is important not to shortchange your students.

Teacher Expectations—The Pygmalion/Galatea Effects

There is a significant amount of research demonstrating that teacher expectations can have a measurable impact on student achievement and behavior. In 1968, **Robert Rosenthal** and **Lenore Jacobson** conducted a series of experiments in which teachers were told that certain students were "late bloomers" and could be expected to make rapid progress in their classes. In fact, the students were selected at random, but because the teachers expected them to do well and consciously or unconsciously treated them differently, they did make more rapid progress than their peers. The phenomenon, known as the **Pygmalion effect**, was also demonstrated when teachers were told that certain students were slow and could be expected to make only limited progress. Again, the students were selected at random and again, the expectation became a self-fulfilling prophecy.[7]

In 1982, Jere Brophy analyzed the research concerning the Pygmalion effect and concluded that the effect did exist but that the impact was minimal in most cases because teachers' initial expectations were fairly accurate and usually open to change based on actual work with the students.[8] The results of the Rosenthal-Jacobson studies were reviewed in 1983 by Harris Cooper and Thomas Good[9] and in 1984 by Stephen Raudenbush.[10] These reviews confirmed the initial findings. In 1991, Rosenthal reviewed 448 studies concerning the Pygmalion effect and found that these, too, confirmed his initial findings.[11] What you expect of students in terms of behavior and academic performance can affect the resulting behavior and performance. It is wise, therefore, to set high standards.

To the extent that high expectations are established and students are helped to achieve them, students begin to have increased confidence in their own abilities. This effect is known as the **Galatea effect**. With the Pygmalion effect, the expectations of others affect performance. With the Galatea effect, it is the person's own self-confidence that affects performance. It is a student saying to himself or herself, "I climbed that mountain, so maybe I can climb the next one." Clearly, having high expectations for students is better than having low expectations, but expectations alone will not get the job done. In order to get students to work willingly toward those high expectations, the expectations must be relevant to the students' lives.

Central to the task of making content relevant is identifying practical applications of the concepts and skills to be learned and then explaining those applications to students. In this effort, it is not very persuasive to explain that the content will be needed for a test or to pass the course. Students may not care, and they have certainly heard those arguments before. It is more persuasive to cite examples of how the concepts and skills will help students improve their performance in and out of school and/or how it can help them better understand and deal with the world around them.

For example, literature can be made more relevant to students if you seek out underlying themes rather than focusing mainly on technical aspects. Herman Melville's *Moby Dick* could be read with an emphasis on analyzing the plot structure, the setting, and the use of language. On the other hand, it could be read with an emphasis on its central themes of obsession and revenge. Since it is likely that students of all races and social strata know of instances where obsession or revenge motivated actions, they can relate the cause-effect relationships in the story to their own lives. It becomes relevant to them. Shakespeare can be read in the same way. History teachers can make it a point to demonstrate how events in the past frequently have the same basic cause-effect relationships as current events.

Typically, students are willing to put forth significant effort if they see some practical payoff. It is well worth the effort to view the content through the eyes of students, especially those who tend to regard all schoolwork as irrelevant. What would you say to those students to persuade them that the selected content can be of practical utility to them? Persuading them to participate in the teaching–learning process is more difficult than discussing content with peers, parents, or administrators because you are asking the students to invest their time and effort. Increase their incentive by explaining practical utility.

Studies of Contemporary Life Outside of School

A third area that Tyler suggested as a source of ideas for objectives is society as a whole. This source can be looked at from two perspectives. First, taxpayers pay for the educational enterprise and exercise legal control over the schools through state and local school boards. You should ask yourself if the objectives being considered are compatible with community goals. Some communities are composed primarily of factory workers, others of farmers, and still others of white-collar workers. Regardless of type, every community wants a good education for its children, but different communities prefer to emphasize different skills and areas of knowledge. To find out if ideas for objectives are compatible with community expectations, you should share their ideas with parents and other community members. In addition to whatever responses are elicited, such actions do much to forge good school–community relations. Such actions demonstrate recognition on the part of teachers that parents and other concerned citizens have parts to play in educating students and should have a voice in planning the educational program.

A word of caution. You may find out some things you do not like. For example, you may find that the community depends largely on one industry and, in order to keep that industry, it is "understood" that water and air pollution problems will be minimized or overlooked. Similarly, you might find that the community is predominately fundamentalist and wants students to be taught to accept a literal interpretation of the Bible.

While it is not likely that there will be serious conflicts between what you believe you should teach and what the local school board wants taught, if there is such a conflict, you have two choices. You can either adjust the objectives and content to the standards of the community, or you can seek employment in a district with objectives closer to your own. It is crucial to remember that once you sign a contract, you accept the obligation of following lawful administrative mandates. You are free to work within the system to change those mandates, but if you arbitrarily change or ignore them, you may be fired, regardless of your reasons.

The second perspective is to view the content with respect to its relevance to current society as a whole. Students are more likely to participate in the teaching-learning process if teachers can show that the topics being studied are of current interest in the world outside of school. One way to demonstrate this is to turn to recent editions of newspapers or popular magazines such as *Time*, *Newsweek*, *Reader's Digest*, *National Geographic*, and *Ebony* and look for articles that focus on some aspect of your instructional unit. The idea is to be able to point to an article in a recent issue of a widely read magazine or newspaper and show students that people nationwide are currently talking about, making use of, or researching essentially the same things that they will be studying. This approach helps students feel that what they are learning really is of some worth and relevance.

One more thought. We all know that empires rise and fall, and some people are already debating whether the American "empire" is beginning to fall. If the American "empire" rose in 1776, it turned 244 years old in 2020. By comparison, the Soviet "empire" rose in 1922 and fell in 1991, 69 years later; the British "empire" rose in 1600 and fell after 345 years, in 1945.[12] The relevant point here is that an increasing number of people think that our "empire" will surely fall if our educational goals continue to be the kinds of basic skills emphasized in the No Child Left Behind Act. While those goals are necessary, they are not sufficient to ensure our place as a world leader and keep our "empire" from falling. For that, new goals are needed.

Wallis and Steptoe, in "How to Bring Our Schools Out of the 20th Century" (*Time*, 2006), argue that our students must be highly competent in twenty-first-century skills, which include the following.

- Knowing more about the world: Students need to recognize that they are now "global" citizens. They need to know other languages and more about other cultures.
- Thinking outside the box: More emphasis is needed on creativity and innovation. Interdisciplinary combinations such as mathematics and art should become more common.
- Becoming smarter about new sources of information: Students "need to rapidly process what is coming at them and distinguish between what's reliable and what isn't. 'It's important that students know how to manage it, interpret it, validate it, and how to act on it.'"
- Developing good people skills: "We have to emphasize communication skills, the ability to work in teams and with people of different cultures." [13]

WHY PRECISE OBJECTIVES ARE USEFUL

In 1921, Boyd H. Bode spoke of the need for educators to give "consideration to what constitutes a good life in the social order."[14] He was concerned that rather than having broad educational goals that would result in good people living good lives in a good society, educators might focus on simplistic, perhaps even superfluous goals, because dealing with such goals is less difficult. He was concerned that we might narrow the goals so much that we would lose sight of the original intent. For example, in concerning ourselves with teaching students to spell and describe "democracy," we might forget about the larger goal of teaching them how to act as citizens in a democracy. He had good reason for concern, and you should have the same concern. No one wants to see students turned into stimulus-response subjects who learn things mechanistically. At the same time, it would be foolish to ignore the need for accountability.

While broad goals and state learning standards can point us in the right general direction, in order to implement them, we need to convert them into more precise instructional objectives. As teachers, we need to be able to tell students, parents, and anyone else who is concerned, in terms that are observable and measurable, exactly what students will be able to do when they complete a particular course that they were unable to do before taking the course.

Purpose and Parts of Precise Instructional Objectives

The purpose of precise instructional objectives is to explain to students, before instruction begins, exactly what will be expected of them after instruction. The objectives specify behaviors expected of students, not of you as the teacher.

Observable Terminal Behaviors

Observable terminal behaviors describe, in terms that can be seen and measured, exactly what students will be expected to do at the end of instruction. Objectives for the short term, say one class period, are called **enroute objectives**. Objectives for a semester or an instructional unit are called **terminal objectives**. In both cases, word choice is crucial. Experience has shown that words such as "know," "learn," and "understand" are less effective in describing expected behaviors than words such as "explain in writing," "underline," and "diagram." This is so because the words in the first group are not directly observable and can be interpreted in a number of ways. Most educators now know to avoid terms such as know, learn, and understand when writing objectives, but there can be other problems. Consider the science example:

Describe the effects of electromagnetic and nuclear forces, including atomic and molecular bonding, capacitance, and nuclear reactions.

Although there appears to be an observable behavior (describe), it is not clear if the description is to be oral or written. A bit of rewording clarifies the instructional intent: "Describe in writing …" or "Orally describe. …"

Some terms, such as "identify," "differentiate," and "solve," may appear less ambiguous than terms such as "know" and "learn," but they too describe purely mental activities. Objectives need to be worded so that the results of mental activity can be observed, for example, "identify by recording on a checklist," "differentiate in writing," or "write the step-by-step procedure." Specifying the expected overt activity sharpens the picture students have of what is expected, and this, in turn, tends to reduce anxiety. With the expected behavior clear, students do not have to try to guess your intent.

Often it makes sense to have students demonstrate competence orally. While this kind of competence demonstration has its place, particularly in sampling overall student competence on a day-to-day basis, it has a disadvantage. For example, if the objective is to orally state three measures of central tendency, the first student's correct response could simply be parroted by the other students. Therefore, if a terminal objective calls for an oral presentation, provisions must be made for each student to demonstrate it privately.

If it is likely that many terminal objectives will be demonstrated in writing, it is advantageous to state at the beginning of the list of objectives that each of the objectives will be demonstrated in writing unless otherwise specified. This eliminates the need to include the words "in writing" in every objective.

Sometimes, teachers have a particular behavior in mind but unintentionally specify a different behavior. Consider the following examples.

You will be able to

1. Demonstrate the ability to dissect a frog by orally describing at least three steps of the dissecting process.
2. Dissect a frog following standard dissection procedures and correctly label at least three organs.

Judging from the activities called for in the first objective, the teacher started with the intention of having students demonstrate the ability to dissect a frog. However, at some point, the teacher thought about having students describe the dissecting process, and both behaviors ended up in the objective. Now, it is not clear if the oral descriptions were to be in addition to, or in place of, the actual dissection. It is clear that the only way students can demonstrate the ability to dissect a frog is to actually dissect a frog. Having students orally describe three steps in the dissecting process might be a useful activity, but it is not equivalent to dissection.

The second objective communicates instructional intent more clearly, but it too has a problem. It calls for two behaviors, dissection and labeling. Assessment is complicated by the fact that a student might be able to demonstrate one behavior but not the other. A better solution would be to have two objectives:

3. Dissect a frog following standard dissection procedures.
4. Given a dissected frog, correctly label at least three internal organs.

The "terminal" part of "observable terminal" means at the end of the instructional unit. Teachers typically state about a dozen terminal objectives in the syllabus for a semester-long course. These objectives may be supplemented with narrower unit objectives, and these, in turn, are supplemented with daily "enroute" objectives. However, the dozen or so terminal course objectives in your syllabus will define the scope of your course and be of greatest initial interest to students, parents, and administrators.

Conditions

The function of conditions is to clarify the student's mental picture of any constraints that will affect the demonstration of the specified competence. Conditions frequently refer to time limits or to the use of aids or special equipment, but they can refer to whatever factors are considered important to the demonstration of the behavior. For example, a physical education teacher might consider it important to specify "using a regulation baseball" in an objective concerning the hitting of line drives. Doing so would answer the question of whether a baseball or a softball is to be used. Consider the following objectives.

You will be able to

5.   Describe in writing two possible advantages and two possible disadvantages associated with the use of precise instructional objectives.
6.   Without notes and in a paper of no more than one page, describe two possible advantages and two possible disadvantages associated with the use of precise instructional objectives.

Objective five includes an observable terminal behavior, "describe in writing," but students do not know if they will be allowed to use their notes. In objective six, doubts are removed. The condition that notes may not be used is stated clearly, and there is little room for misunderstanding.

While statements of conditions are usually helpful and are sometimes absolutely necessary to avoid misunderstandings, some care must be taken in their use. Conditions such as "after a lecture," "as was discussed in class," or "after reading Chapter 10" weaken an objective because they limit the sources from which a student may draw information. How students acquire knowledge or skills should *not* be specified in the objective. Certainly, it would not be your intention to penalize a student for acquiring information or skills outside the class, but conditions such as those just mentioned might allow such a penalty. If references to specific sources must be made, those sources should be nationally available (i.e., the American Medical Association). This helps avoid parochial views.

Another point to remember is that it makes little sense to try to state all conditions for all objectives. For example, the condition "with no aids" will probably be common to many objectives. To include those words in every objective would be repetitive and distracting. A more logical solution would be to state the conditions common to most objectives at the beginning of the list of objectives and to discuss the general nature of these conditions with students prior to instruction. It is common, for example, for a list of objectives to be preceded by a statement such as, "The following objectives must be demonstrated in writing and under test conditions unless otherwise specified." Such a statement leaves little room for misinterpretation but still enables the teacher to modify specific objectives.

As a general rule, specific conditions should be stated only when there is a possibility that doubts or misunderstandings may arise. If there is any doubt about whether conditions are needed in a particular objective, they should be included. If no conditions are initially specified in an objective, adding them at the time the competence is to be demonstrated is likely to result in strong and justified student resentment.

Minimum Acceptable Standards

The last element included in a precise instructional objective is a minimum acceptable standard of performance. The need for minimum acceptable standards is obvious. Unless you plan to assign a passing grade to every student who walks through your classroom door, you will need grading criteria. At the very least, you need to identify the minimal competencies that students must demonstrate to earn a grade of D, and factors such as perfect attendance and smiling a lot should not do the job. You need to decide how well each of the observable behaviors must be demonstrated in order to be deemed acceptable. In making this decision, you should keep the Pygmalion effect in mind. If you set low standards with the hope that virtually all students will be able to achieve them, students may, indeed, meet those low standards, but their potential for doing better or more significant work will not be tapped. If you set high standards and demonstrate, by word and deed, that you believe students *can* achieve them, there is a good chance student performance will rise to meet the standards. Go for the gold.

Minimum acceptable standards can be stated in quantitative and/or qualitative terms. As the name suggests, quantitative terms specify quantities such as six out of ten, or eighty percent. Qualitative terms specify particular qualities or points that are sought. The following are examples of objectives using quantitative and/or qualitative minimum acceptable standards.

7. Given four sets of symptoms, diagnose in writing the correct disease in *at least three* of the sets.
8. Write *at least six* precise instructional objectives, each of which includes an observable terminal behavior, conditions, and a minimum acceptable standard.
9. Explain, in writing, the proper use of the wood lathe, including (a) *the procedure for mounting material*, (b) *the proximity of the rest block to the material*, (c) *the speed of the chuck*, (d) *the proper use of the tool bit*, and (e) *at least two safety precautions*.

Objective seven utilizes only a quantitative standard (at least three). Objective eight combines a quantitative standard (at least six) with a qualitative standard (includes an observable terminal behavior, conditions, and a minimum acceptable standard). Objective nine includes a qualitative standard that describes the minimum elements necessary in a student explanation (points a–e).

Sometimes a quantitative standard can be confusing. For example, suppose that an objective called for students to solve a series of math problems with at least eighty percent accuracy. It is not clear whether students must correctly solve at least eight of ten problems or if the student could get each of the answers wrong but still end up with eighty percent of the points because of earning partial credit for each problem. Potentially confusing points such as this one need to be anticipated and clarified.

A common misconception concerning minimum acceptable standards is that the specification of lengths of answers is, by itself, sufficient to clarify what is expected.

Generally, this is not so. Just as you strive to be concise, you want to encourage your students to be concise. Specifying minimum lengths works against this by requiring students to fill up X amount of space, regardless of how much they know. Ideally, you want students to say what they have to say and stop. However, if you specify that a paper must be at least two pages in length, students will feel compelled to fill two pages even though they may only have a page and a half worth of information. They did not want to write that extra half-page, and you will not want to read it. Why require it?

You should always expect to be held to your word. With respect to objectives, this means that students may interpret your words literally and expect you to give them credit for doing exactly what you asked of them. In this sense, an objective is a contract. Consider the following objectives.

You will be able to

10. Describe, in no more than two pages, the results of World War II.
11. Type at least two letters in one class period.

In objective ten, a student could argue that he or she should receive full credit for achieving the objective for simply writing, "The Allies won." This answer would meet the requirement of "a paper of no more than two pages," but it confuses conditions with minimum standards. The main focus should be on content, not length. To give students some idea of expected length, specify a maximum length such as, "in no more than two pages." This gives students some idea of expected length but allows them to stop writing when they have said what they had to say. In addition, be sure to specify the content expected.

With objective eleven, a student could cause an embarrassing situation by typing just two letters such as an X and a Y. If one of your students did this, and you refused to give the student an A for the assignment, you could end up trying to explain to a parent or principal why you failed to say exactly what you meant. The argument would hinge not on the fact that the student outrageously and deliberately misinterpreted the instructional intent; it would hinge on the fact that you did not communicate clearly. The same could happen if the student turned in two messy, error-filled pages. In both cases, the quantitative limitations failed to convey the true minimum standards. You need to use language clearly, precisely, and concisely, especially when communicating instructional intent.

If time or length is a consideration for achievement it should be a minimum standard. For example, if an objective calls for students to run the 100-yard dash in no more than twenty seconds, the specification of time is crucial. Similarly, a teacher who is teaching how to summarize can include "in less than one page" as part of a minimum standard.

Qualitative standards often imply subjective judgments. This sometimes makes it difficult to describe the particular attributes or characteristics that must be included in the behavior to meet minimal standards. For example, the following objectives become increasingly clear as additional qualitative standards are added.

You will be able to describe the following in writing:

12. Results of World War II
13. Effects of World War II on France and Germany
14. Results of World War II in terms of two economic developments in France and two in Germany

Each succeeding objective communicates instructional intent more clearly and minimizes the chances for misunderstandings better than its predecessor. As more standards are added, the picture of the desired end product becomes clearer in the mind of the student. However, trying to include every possible point would make the objective so cumbersome that it would be virtually useless. For example, when evaluating papers, teachers typically consider factors such as logical organization, completeness, relevancy, neatness, and mechanics. Once it is explained to students (and specified in writing) that these factors are always considered, it is not necessary to include them in each objective. This will help keep objectives to a reasonable length.

Typically, sentences, including objectives, get longer as ideas are embellished with descriptions, examples, and sometimes other ideas. These embellishments are intended to clarify the main idea, but if they give the reader too many things to keep in mind, they have the opposite effect. Generally, sentences or objectives longer than about twenty-five words tend to be difficult to comprehend. Therefore, objectives should be written as single sentences no longer than twenty-five words whenever possible.

The fact that all possible qualitative standards are not included in each objective should not be taken as an abdication of your right, or professional obligation, to make judgments concerning overall quality, and this point should be made clear to students. You should simply acknowledge the fact that many instructional objectives deal with complex concepts or human behaviors. The objectives are attempts to convey, as clearly as possible, the true instructional intent by specifying as many relevant parameters as makes good sense. If students are expected to refer to particular ideas, points, or aspects when demonstrating a competence, those points should be identified in the objective, but terms such as "main ideas," "most important points," and "major aspects" should be used only with the understanding that you are willing to accept the student's opinion regarding these matters. Opinions cannot be graded. A teacher who is not precise in describing terminal behaviors or minimal acceptable standards should not hold students accountable for the consequences of misinterpretation.

SUMMARY

To be useful in the context of accountability for teachers and students, broad goals must be translated into behaviors that can be observed and measured. Precise instructional objectives identify expected learning outcomes in terms of observable terminal behaviors, conditions, and minimum acceptable standards.

Observable behaviors are overt and include behaviors such as "write," "orally state," and "physically demonstrate." Oral demonstrations of a competence pose a problem, because in order to be sure that each student has achieved the objective, each student must be assessed privately. You also need to be sure that each objective calls for only one behavior. Terminal behaviors are those that are demonstrated at the end of an instructional unit. Teachers generally specify terminal objectives in course syllabi and supplement those with narrower unit objectives and daily "enroute" objectives.

Conditions may be included in a precise instructional objective if they are needed to clarify the terminal behavior and avoid misunderstandings. Typical conditions include "under test conditions," "without aids," and "using calculators." It is common for teachers to include an observable terminal behavior and conditions in a single statement that precedes a list of objectives, for example, "The following objectives must be demonstrated in writing and under test conditions unless otherwise specified." If no conditions are built into the objectives, it is unfair to impose them at the time the behavior is to be demonstrated, since students would have had no way to prepare for them. There is no place in an objective for the specification of where or how students acquire knowledge of skills. Including such conditions might result in penalizing students for using knowledge or skills that are correct but are different from those covered in class.

Minimum acceptable standards may be stated quantitatively or qualitatively. Quantitative standards specify a quantity such as sixty percent or two out of three. Qualitative standards specify the qualities or points that must be included for the behavior to be deemed acceptable. When thinking about minimum standards, it is a good idea to remember the Pygmalion effect. Teacher expectations can affect student performance. Typically, the higher the standards (within reason), the higher the performance level. Further, remember the Galatea effect. As students' self-confidence increases, so does their willingness to take on ever more demanding tasks.

You should be more interested in the quality of student work than in the length of such work. It makes sense, therefore, to refer to maximum rather than minimum lengths. This gives students an idea of expected length while at the same time making it clear that students should stop writing when they have said what they want to say.

You should word objectives carefully to avoid having to admit that you said one thing but meant something else. Say exactly what you mean. Further, to make the objective as readable and clear as possible, state it as a single sentence of preferably no more than about twenty-five words. Once the components of objectives are understood, you can move on to the task of determining if they cover a range of thinking skills. That is the focus of the next chapter.

PRACTICE EXERCISES AND SELF-TEST
Practice Exercise 1: Identifying Weaknesses in Objectives

Some of the following objectives are stated in unacceptable form. Use the following rating scale to pinpoint the weakness(es) in each objective and check your responses with those furnished.

Rating Scale

A. Lacks an observable behavior
B. Lacks a minimum acceptable standard
C. Lacks both A and B
D. The behavior sought is not that which is to be demonstrated
E. The objective is acceptable as written

To meet the minimum acceptable standards for this course you must

1. Know the democratic principles upon which our country is founded.
2. Know the names of the US senators from your home state.
3. Be an alert and aware citizen.
4. Given a word processor, set the tab stops at designated points.
5. Take an active role in society.
6. Given two business letters, retype them in class without errors using block style.
7. Understand the plight of poor people in our country.
8. Orally list at least two organizations that are part of the United Nations.
9. Demonstrate proper CPR procedures by describing each step of the process in proper sequence.
10. Demonstrate the ability to write precise instructional objectives by achieving a score of at least seventy percent on a multiple-choice test dealing with the construction of such objectives.

Exercise 1—Answers: 1-C, 2-A, 3-C, 4-E, 5-C, 6-E, 7-C, 8-E, 9-D, 10-D

Practice Exercise 2: Rewriting Instructional Objectives

Rewrite each of the poorly written objectives to include an observable behavior, minimum standard, and conditions. Identify the observable behavior with a single underline and the minimum acceptable standard with a double underline. Examples of acceptable rewrites are shown below, but yours may vary considerably.

You will be able to

1. Explain, in writing, at least two democratic principles upon which our country is founded.
2. Write the names of the US senators from your home state.
3. Select a current legislative issue, write a one-page letter to your US senators expressing your views on that issue, and give at least two reasons for those views in the letter.
4. No changes are needed.
5. Write a letter to the editor of the local paper expressing your views on a current local problem and include at least two rationales for those views.
6. No changes are needed.
7. Orally state at least two factors inhibiting the elimination of poverty within our country.
8. No changes are needed.
9. Demonstrate proper CPR techniques using a mannequin under test conditions.
10. Recall and/or apply information concerning the structure of precise instructional objectives well enough to answer correctly at least eighty percent of a series of multiple-choice questions concerning such objectives.

Self-Test

Some of the following objectives are stated in unacceptable form. Use the following rating scale to pinpoint the weakness(es) in each objective and check your responses with those furnished.

Rating Scale

A. Lacks an observable behavior
B. Lacks a minimum acceptable standard
C. Lacks both A and B
D. The behavior sought is not that which is to be demonstrated
E. The objective is acceptable as written

You will be able to

1. Write a critical reaction to *Moby Dick*.
2. Orally state the names of two wartime presidents.
3. Recite the Pledge of Allegiance with no errors.
4. Demonstrate knowledge of proper tool handling by selecting a saw with which to cut plywood as opposed to hardwood.

5. Understand quadratic equations well enough to solve, on paper, any three that are given, without the use of aids and within thirty minutes.
6. Demonstrate easy mathematical skills with at least eighty percent accuracy.
7. Understand fully the terms volt, ohm, and alternating current.
8. Demonstrate good physical condition, in part, by running the mile in less than six minutes.
9. Understand written French
10. Be proud to be an American eighty-five percent of the time.

Self-test answers: 1-B, 2-E, 3-E, 4-D, 5-E, 6-C, 7-A, 8-E, 9-C, 10-A

KEY TERMS, PEOPLE, AND IDEAS

Precise instructional objective
Ralph Tyler, Robert Mager
Observable terminal behavior
Conditions

Minimum acceptable standard
Pygmalion effect
Galatea effect
Standards: Common Core State Standards

QUESTIONS FOR CONSIDERATION

1. Given that most objectives are subject-centered, to what extent should we be concerned about content integration (i.e., the idea of education as an enlightening and mind-broadening endeavor)?
2. Given that most curriculums and standardized tests focus on academic work, to what extent should educators be concerned about issues such as character development and citizenship?

ENDNOTES

1 Boyd H. Bode, "Education at the Crossroads" *Progressive Education* 8, (November 1931): 548.

2 Tyler, Ralph W., *Basic Principles of Curriculum and Instruction* (Chicago; University of Chicago Press, 1949).

3 Tyler, 1.

4 Tyler, 5–33. (In Tanner and Tanner, 2nd ed., 86)

5 *Geography for Life*, 9.

6 Common Core State Standards Initiative. Preparing America's students for success (2011), retrieved June 10, 2020, from http://www.corestandards.org/.

7 Robert Rosenthal and L. Jacobson, *Pygmalion in the Classroom* (New York: Holt, Rinehart, and Winston, 1968).

8   Jere Brophy, "Research on the Self-Fulfilling Prophecy and Teacher Expectations," *Teaching and Learning Program* (Washington, DC: National Institute of Education, 1982).

9   Harris M. Cooper and Thomas L. Good, *Pygmalion Grows Up: Studies in the Expectation Communication Process* (New York: Longman, 1983).

10 Stephen W. Raudenbush, "Magnitude of Teacher Expectancy Effects on Pupil IQ as a Function of the Credibility of Expectation: A Synthesis of Findings from 18 Experiments," *Journal of Educational Psychology* 76, no. 1 (Feb. 1984): 85–97.

11 Robert Rosenthal, "Teacher Expectancy Effects: A Brief Update 25 Years after the Pygmalion Experiment," *Journal of Research in Education* 1, no. 1 (Spring 1991): 3–12.

12 It Happened Timelines. History Timeline: World History Timeline from Ancient History to 21st Century. Retrieved June 8, 2020 from http://www.ithappened.info/ebook/world-history-timeline.pdf.

13 Claudia Wallis and Sonja Steptoe, "How to Bring Our Schools Out of the 20th Century," *Time* 168, no. 25 (Dec. 18, 2006): 51–56.

14 Boyd H. Bode, "Education at the Crossroads," *Progressive Education* 8 (November 1931): 548.

CHAPTER 5

Classifying and Using Precise Instructional Objectives

INTRODUCTION

Is someone who knows how a piece of equipment works more valuable to society than someone who simply knows how to operate it? Okay, the question is unfair because society needs people with both kinds of skills. However, the question points to a larger question: How much time do you want your students to spend learning how to do something (e.g., mastering a technique), as opposed to learning the theory underlying that technique? For example, in science we can teach students how to use a microscope and how to analyze blood and tissue. Knowing how to do those things is important, but they are purely technical skills. The people who use those skills most often are not the same people who decide what will be looked at and what will be analyzed. The people who make those decisions have to understand the technical skills, but they also have to think beyond them, and in today's worldwide economy, many of the technical skills are being carried out in other countries by people willing to work for far less than similarly skilled workers here. If we, as a society, want to maintain our edge in the worldwide economy, we need to prepare people to engage in higher-level thought. We need to prepare people who will know enough to decide what the technicians will do.

This chapter focuses on how to classify instructional objectives on the basis of the kinds of thinking they require of students. Being able to classify objectives will make it easier for you to help your students move from low-level, teacher-directed activities to higher-level, self-directed activities.

One of the best-known classification schemes was developed in 1956 and is described in a book edited by **Benjamin Bloom** entitled *Taxonomy of Educational*

Objectives, Handbook 1: Cognitive Domain.[1] Bloom's taxonomy (as it is popularly known) is divided into three domains, and each domain is divided into levels. The cognitive domain, delineated in Handbook 1, concerns the acquisition and manipulation of factual information.

The affective domain, delineated in Handbook II,[2] concerns the development of attitudes, values, and feelings. The psychomotor domain, delineated in a book entitled *A Taxonomy of the Psychomotor Domain,*[3] concerns the development of physical skills. The *Taxonomy of Educational Objectives, Handbook 1: Cognitive Domain* was revised in 2000. According to Krathwohl (2002), the six categories (Knowledge, Comprehension, Application, Analysis, Synthesis, and Evaluation) were retained but were renamed (Remember, Understand, Apply, Analyze, and Evaluate, Create) respectively. Synthesis was switched with Evaluation and renamed Create.[4] This chapter will familiarize you with all of them.

LEARNING OUTCOMES

You will be able, in writing, to:

1. List each major level of the cognitive, affective, and psychomotor domains.
2. Describe the distinguishing characteristics of each level of the cognitive domain.
3. Classify at least eighty percent of a given series of instructional objectives by correct domain and level, and explain the main factor justifying each classification.
4. Write one precise instructional objective at each level of each appropriate domain, given an instructional topic.

THE TAXONOMY AND ITS USES

The taxonomy of educational objectives was developed to help educators classify objectives according to the skills and abilities they elicit from students. When working with the taxonomic domains and levels, keep in mind that the taxonomy is a theoretical division of skills and abilities. Since we do not yet fully understand how the mind stores or manipulates information, we can only theorize that tasks such as memorizing basic number facts are less complex than tasks such as performing long division. The fact that it seems reasonable does not necessarily make it so. Further, the classification of any specific behavior must be made in relation to the task and the background of the individual performing that task.

Complicating the matter still further is that taxonomic divisions are more easily delineated on paper than they are in practice. Some objectives may not fit unequivocally into one specific level or even into one specific domain. The lines between domains and levels blend like lines between colors in a rainbow. This means that while most objectives can be clearly classified as to domain and level, the classification of others may be hazy. Fortunately, the possibility of haziness does not seriously lessen the usefulness of the taxonomy. Its power is not in its precision with respect to any one objective but in its ability to enable teachers to see, generally, whether they have included an appropriate range of skills and abilities.

The Cognitive Domain

The cognitive domain deals with the acquisition and manipulation of factual information. It is divided into six major levels, each divided into sublevels. When classifying objectives, it is usual to do so according to the major level. Examining some of the components is helpful to understanding the major levels. Table 5.1 represents the structure of the Cognitive Domain.

Remember

In the taxonomy, "Remember" is used as a label for the lowest level of cognitive activity. At this level, students are expected simply to have memorized information and be able to recall it. Over the years, memorization has often been criticized as a trivial or unnecessary learning step. The fact is, however, that unless we commit a great deal of information to memory, we would not have time to do much of anything. Consider how much you do each day by rote memorization. You do not have to think about every movement when you tie your shoes because you have memorized the process. You also memorized how to find your way to class, how to write your name, and how to write a check. These actions, which now require virtually no thought, took considerable concentration and time when you first learned to do them and, if you had not committed them to memory, they would still require a great deal of time and concentration. For verification, watch a three-year-old tying his or her shoelaces. The process of learning something to the point that you can use the information or skill with little or no conscious thought is called **automatization**.[5]

The range of things that can be committed to memory illustrates the complexity and richness of this level. Consider the following sublevels as listed and described in Krathwohl's 2002 article.

Remember, which is the first level in the cognitive domain, means the act of "retrieving relevant knowledge from long-term memory." It is divided into two main categories:

| 1.1 | Recognizing |
| 1.2 | Recalling[6] |

Table 5.1 Structure of the Cognitive Domain

1.0	**Remember**—Retrieving relevant knowledge from long-term memory
	1.1 Recognizing
	1.2 Recalling
2.0	**Understand**—Determining the meaning of instructional messages, including oral, written, and graphic communication
	2.1 Interpreting
	2.2 Exemplifying
	2.3 Classifying
	2.4 Summarizing
	2.5 Inferring
	2.6 Comparing
	2.7 Explaining
3.0	**Apply**—Carrying out or using a procedure in a given situation
	3.1 Executing
	3.2 Implementing
4.0	**Analyze**—Breaking material into its constituent parts and detecting how the parts relate to one another and an overall structure or purpose
	4.1 Differentiating
	4.2 Organizing
	4.3 Attributing
5.0	**Evaluate**—Making judgments based on criteria and standards
	5.1 Checking
	5.2 Critiquing
6.0	**Create**—Putting elements together to form a novel, coherent whole or make an original product
	6.1 Generating
	6.2 Planning
	6.3 Producing

Table adapted from D. R. Krathwohl, "A revision of Bloom's Taxonomy: An overview," Theory into Practice 41, no. 4 (Autumn, 2002): 215.

In thinking about Remember-level activities, it is sometimes useful to think of words that reflect those activities. Some of these words are define, identify, label, list, and state. These words reflect the fact that information has been recalled or recognized, but they give no indication of whether the student understands what has been recalled or recognized. This is characteristic of knowledge-level activity. The following are examples of objectives at the Remember-level:

1. Poor: Define the terms mean, median, and mode.
2. Better: Define terms such as mean, median, mode, and range as they pertain to measurement and evaluation. (Without the clarification, a student could define mean as being unkind, median as the area between opposite lanes of traffic, and mode as a form of transportation or communication.)

It is, of course, better to go beyond the call for definitions and to call instead for the recollection of appropriately complex information of lasting significance. For example:

3. Given a specific culture, such as Hindu or Muslim, orally list at least three characteristics unique to that culture.
4. Given a blank diagram of a plant or animal cell, correctly label all numbered parts.

Note: Keep in mind that while you will be giving students a specific culture or cell, you are preparing them to demonstrate the same behavior with any relevant culture or cell.

Understand

The second level of the cognitive domain is Understand. It means "determining the meaning of instructional messages, including oral, written, and graphic communication." The divisions within this level are as follows:

2.1	Interpreting
2.2	Exemplifying
2.3	Classifying
2.4	Summarizing
2.5	Inferring
2.6	Comparing
2.7	Explaining[7]

It is the view of many educators that this is the level most emphasized in today's schools. To the extent that this is so, it is disappointing because the understanding-level is low in the hierarchy of intellectual skills. This level indicates that the student can recall information and that the information has meaning to the student.

In thinking about Understand-level activities, it is sometimes useful to think of words that reflect those activities. Some of those words include convert, explain, describe, estimate, paraphrase, predict, and rewrite. If students must explain or describe something, be sure to include a minimum standard for the explanation or description. Ways to do this include calling for differentiating characteristics or for the use of cause-effect reasoning.

Examples of poorly written and well-written objectives at the Understand level are illustrated below.

1. Poor: Describe three elements of Baroque art. (A student could describe color, line, and perspective—elements that are central to other schools of art.)
2. Better: Describe at least three characteristics that differentiate Baroque art from Realistic art. (The call for characteristics that differentiate makes up the minimum standard for the description of the characteristics.)
3. Poor: Explain at least two causes of the fall of the Roman Empire.
4. Better: Using cause-effect reasoning, explain at least two causes that were the same for the fall of the Roman Empire and the Soviet Union. (The call for cause-effect reasoning makes up the minimum standard for the explanations of the two causes.)

Other examples of well written objectives include the following:
You will be able, in writing and under test conditions, to

1. Translate the formula for converting degrees Fahrenheit to degrees Celsius from sentence form to mathematical statement form.
2. Using cause-effect reasoning, explain at least two probable effects of either dramatically increasing or decreasing property taxes in a community.
3. Describe what is meant by the tone of a letter and cite examples of two tones.
4. Explain, in your own words, the formula for calculating the area of rectangles.

Note: Avoid "compare and contrast" because those terms, by themselves, do not provide sufficient guidance.

Apply

The third level of the cognitive domain is Apply. As used in the taxonomy, apply means the act of "carrying out or using a procedure in a given situation." This level is divided into two categories.

3.1	Executing
3.2	Implementing[8]

It is useful to think of the student understanding a principle or rule at the Understanding level and then using the principle or rule in a practical situation at the applying level. Some words that reflect such activities include change, calculate, convert, show, and solve. Examples of Apply-level objectives follow.

You will be able to, under test conditions,

1. Organize components into a news story using the inverted pyramid format given unorganized components.
2. Calculate the cost of carpeting the room to within five dollars given the dimensions of a room and the cost of carpeting.
3. Correctly convert to degrees Celsius, in writing, at least eighty percent of a series of temperatures given in degrees Fahrenheit.
4. Complete a balance sheet with no errors given journal entries for business transactions.

Analyze

The fourth level of the cognitive domain is Analyze. Breaking material into its constituent parts and detecting how the parts relate to one another and an overall structure or purpose.[9] The Analyze level can be classified into the following categories:

4.1	Differentiating
4.2	Organizing
4.3	Attributing[10]

Many educators consider analysis to be the first of the higher cognitive levels. The taxonomy includes three kinds of skills in the analysis level.[11]

The difference between application-level and analysis-level tasks is not clear sometimes. One of the key points of difference lies in the complexity of the task. At the application level, the task is so clear-cut that there is little question as to which rules, principles, and procedures need to be used. The focus is on using them correctly in a new situation and without prompting. At the analysis level, the task is more ambiguous. The elements, relationships, and organization principles sought are not so obvious and may not call clearly for the use of a particular rule or procedure.

It is important to remember that when you analyze something, you make objective observations. One test of the objectivity of the analysis is to ask whether three equally qualified experts would probably come to the same conclusion. For example, suppose that you gave three suits to three equally qualified tailors and asked them to determine which suit was best made. They would all look at things such as the quality of material, stitching, and cut, and assuming that one suit was in fact better made than the others, they would all identify that suit as being best made. Analysis is a matter of identifying the true state of affairs and being able to point to the factors that make it the true state of affairs.

Words that typically reflect analysis include diagram, differentiate, relate, and separate. Examples of Analysis-level objectives follow. Note that in each objective, the student is expected to determine the true state of affairs and to document that determination with specific facts—what and why.

1. Given a problem and two business letters written to resolve that problem, you will be able, in writing and under test conditions, to explain which letter is better written and identify at least three elements concerning its structure and/or tone to support that determination.

2. Given the relevant characteristics of a family, such as ages and number of children, and the costs and life expectancies of various kinds of carpeting, you will be able, in writing and under test conditions, to determine which carpeting would be most cost-effective.

3. You will be able, in writing and under test conditions, to explain what changes would have to be made in order for a cake to be properly prepared, given the elevation of a city in meters, metric measuring utensils, and a box of cake mix from a typical American store.

4. Given a standard 1040 tax form with its instructions and a description of a family's income and expenses, you will be able, in writing and under test conditions, to determine if it would be advantageous for the family to itemize deductions, and cite at least two factors from the form and description to justify that decision.

Writing Analysis-level objectives is more complex than writing objectives at other levels, so perhaps a step-by-description example might be useful.

First, state what previously unseen materials students will be given. These materials may include such things as pictures; excerpts of stories, editorials, or letters; short poems; descriptions; audio or video clips; and real things such as foods and artifacts. If you say something like "given a scenario" or "given a description of," be sure to include the critical components of that scenario or description so students have a clear idea of what they will be given to analyze. Many times, "such as" is useful.

1. Poor: Given a scenario describing a person taking a restricted drug, …
2. Better: Given a scenario describing factors such as the age, appearance, and actions of a person taking a restricted drug, …

Keep in mind that while you will be giving students specific materials to analyze, you are preparing them to make the same kind of analysis with any similar materials. Make your description of the materials broad enough so that it can apply to examples beyond those used for a given lesson and class. For example:

3. Given a course title, the grade and academic level of students in that course, and two lesson plans, ... (This description can apply to a variety of situations, not just the ones that you will provide in your lesson.)

4. Given a previously unseen poem, ... (Here, it is clear that students should be able to analyze any poem, not just the one that you are going to present to them.)

Second, call for the determination of subtle, unclear elements, relationships, or principles to arrive at a true state of affairs (the *what* part of the required *what* and *why*). If what is sought is relatively clear and easily discernible, it is likely that you are asking for only Knowledge-level thinking.

Third, call for the empirical basis (the observable facts and/or examples from the given material) that supports the analysis (the *why* part of the required *what* and *why*). For example:

5. Given a course title, the grade and academic level of students in that course, and two lesson plans, determine which plan is best (the *what* part), and cite at least three aspects of that plan that make it superior (the *why* part).

6. Given two previously unseen poems, determine which best exemplifies the Romantic period (the *what* part), and cite at least two aspects of that poem to support your analysis (the *why* part).

Evaluate

The fifth level of the cognitive domain is Evaluation. Evaluation is defined as the act of "Making judgments based on criteria and standards." While the act of making judgment and critiquing is valuable, the most important part of the activity is not the judgment itself; it is the justification of that judgment. This level is divided into the following categories:

5.1   Checking

5.2   Critiquing[12]

Students will be making judgments throughout their lives. The purpose of Evaluate-level objectives is to help students learn to justify their judgments. The justification can consist of logical reasoning (such as cause-effect), references to specific facts or examples, or the use of specific criteria, but it should not reflect a lack of thought (e.g., "My father believes this, so I believe it too"). It is wise to ask students to make value judgments about socially significant issues rather than simple short-term issues.

Do not confuse Analysis-level and Evaluation-level objectives. At the Analysis level, three equally qualified experts (i.e., the three tailors) would be likely to arrive at the same conclusion. At the Evaluation level, if each was asked which suit he or she thought was best, each of the three might reach a different conclusion, and that would be wholly acceptable, provided they could defend their conclusions with relevant, valid, and logical arguments. In a sense, you are asking for an opinion, and opinions, by themselves, cannot be judged acceptable or unacceptable. What can be judged is the quality of the defense, and that is what you are after at the Evaluation level.

Some of the linked phrases that reflect Evaluation-level thinking are "State your opinion about … and defend that position by citing at least three relevant facts;" "Take a position for or against … and defend that position by using cause-effect reasoning." Examples of Evaluation-level objectives follow. Note that in each case, the student is expected to make a value judgment. This is in contrast to the Analysis level, where the student was expected to determine the true state of affairs. At the Evaluation-level the focus is not on determining the true state of affairs; it is on having the student develop a rational justification for a value judgment.

You will be able, in writing and under test conditions, to

1. Explain in less than two pages which of two business letters you believe is more effective and support your decision by citing at least three specific facts or examples.
2. State your position with respect to whether students in the United States should learn the metric system and defend your position by citing at least three factual or cause-effect arguments.
3. Explain which economic system you believe has the greatest long-term growth potential and support your belief by citing at least three factual or logical arguments that are consistent with accepted knowledge.

Some additional pointers:

- Instructional objectives are neither test items nor activities; they are behaviors expected of individual students at the end of a three- to four-week instructional unit.
- Work done outside of class, such as homework, while usually valuable as a learning experience, is not acceptable as the demonstration of an objective unless you can verify that the student actually did the work (as opposed to a friend or parent).
- Each student's performance must be judged as fairly as possible. Therefore, be sure to ask only for things that are completely independent efforts as opposed to

asking for something that might require the participation of other students, such as a skit or a request to "persuade fellow students to. ..."

Create

The sixth level of the cognitive domain is Create. It means "putting elements together to form a novel, coherent whole or make an original product."[13] The taxonomy describes three forms at the creating level.

6.1	Generating
6.2	Planning
6.3	Producing[14]

In this context, "creating" means the assembling of parts into a new and unique whole. The production of unique communication consisting of words, sounds, shapes, colors, and actions that can be assembled to effectively convey ideas, feelings, or experiences to others is an example of processes at the creating level. The second kind of product, a plan or a proposed set of operations, would be any new plan or set of operations that would meet specified requirements. Those requirements could be given to, or developed by, the student along with the plan or set of operations. The last kind of product is the derivation of a set of abstract relations. A typical example would be the derivation of a hypothesis.

Although students will be using knowledge and skills already mastered as the basis of their creating activities, the teacher must not confuse the simple accumulation of related parts with creating. For example, the task of creating a nutritious menu might be accomplished simply by selecting X foods from Y food groups. Such an activity might be appropriate at the application level. If, on the other hand, the task was to create a one-day menu that would appeal to, and meet the nutritional needs of, a person with specified characteristics, such as a nine-year-old boy, or a high-school girl, the complexity of the task increases significantly and so does the creativity needed to accomplish it. Eliciting the higher-level thinking indicative of Create-level thinking requires more from a task than the mechanical application of rules and principles; the main focus must be on creativity and higher-level thinking. Some words that reflect create-level thinking include compose, construct, create, develop, devise, and design.

There are a few factors that complicate the writing of Create-level objectives. First, although the focus is on creativity, the product must still be evaluated. Pablo Picasso's works reflect a great deal of creativity, but suppose it was 1937 and Pablo was working on *Guernica* in your art class. (*Guernica* was Picasso's interpretation of the Spanish Civil

War as a surrealistic nightmare.) How would you have evaluated his work? It is likely that Pablo would have gotten an F and been sent to see the guidance counselor. If Picasso had to work within the accepted standards of his day, his creativity would have been stifled. The dilemma is that minimum acceptable standards are needed in classroom situations, but the more detailed those standards are, the more they limit the student's creativity.

Second, it is unwise to have students respond to hypothetical situations. Logically, if you ask students to enter the world of make-believe, you must be prepared to accept their ideas of what that world is like, regardless of how outlandish or bizarre. If you ask a student to describe what the United States would be like if we had a king with absolute power instead of an elected president, and the student said that all of our problems would be solved, give the student an A. In the land of make-believe, anything is possible. It is unwise to send students there and then try to grade what they say they see.

Finally, be careful not to ask students to do anything that you cannot do. For example, unless you could develop a politically and economically feasible plan to reduce the national debt, do not ask students to do so. Examples of create-level objectives follow.

You will be able, under test conditions, to

1. Poor: Write a poem in iambic pentameter. (Since the emphasis here is more on following a procedure than on creativity, this objective would be more properly classified at the application level.)
2. Better: Create a Mother's Day poem that uses iambic pentameter and reflects the Romantic period.
3. Compose for your local newspaper an original editorial of no more than one page, in which you describe a series of changes in the local governing structure that would make it more democratic.
4. Create a new ending to a given short story that is consistent with the original plot and characters but that differs from the original ending in at least two significant ways.

The Affective Domain

Since educators typically see their primary responsibility as helping students acquire and manipulate factual information, there was quick and widespread acceptance of the *Taxonomy of Educational Objectives, Handbook I* when it was published in 1956. However, when it came to *Handbook II*, which dealt with attitudes, feelings, and values, both the development and the acceptance of the handbook were slower. It was not until 1964 that *Handbook II: Affective Domain* was published. There was general agreement that **affects** such as emotions, attitudes, and values exist and profoundly affect human endeavors. There was also general agreement that a typical classroom, with its many human interactions, is one of the places where attitudes and values are shaped. The question was how much, if any, instructional time and effort should be focused on building or changing feelings, attitudes, and values.

Problems to Be Considered

Consider the following points. As a teacher, you will have a great deal to do with the feelings, attitudes, and values that are developed in your classroom regardless of whether you do or do not state affective objectives. Factors as varied as the way you dress and act and expect students to dress and act, and the way you interact with students and expect them to interact with each other, will work to shape students' feelings, attitudes, and values. For example, teachers who act dictatorially or use the language carelessly convey a different message to students than those who treat students as responsible people and take care to use the language properly. Your instructional objectives also help shape attitudes, feelings, and values. If the objectives focus primarily on low-level skills or seem irrelevant to students, attitudes in the class will be different than if the objectives focus on the attainment of high-level abilities that students perceive as relevant and important to their lives. Separate objectives that focus purely on attitudes, feelings, and values may not be needed.

Second, many people believe that it is the prerogative of parents or religious organizations to develop attitudes, feelings, and values, particularly as they reflect how we live our lives, and that schools should focus on cognitive and psychomotor development. Although teachers are tacitly expected to encourage values such as honesty and responsibility, they may inadvertently cause conflicts by espousing more complex or specific moral stances. Given the separation of church and state and the great diversity of moral thought in the United States, it is presumptuous for anyone to stand up and shine the light of Truth on everyone else.

Third, the only way to assess the attitudes or values people have is by observing what they do or say. Teachers who decide to write objectives in the affective domain must select observable behaviors that they believe will reflect particular attitudes or values. If they happen to select inappropriate behavioral indicators, their assessment of the affect will be distorted. For example, if an objective calls for students to be patriotic, how could that be assessed? Would it be sufficient to observe that the student stood and said the Pledge of Allegiance to the flag every day or knew all the words to the national anthem? If not, what behavior(s) would be adequate?

Fourth, assuming that teachers could gather incontrovertible information about whether each student did or did not achieve specific affective objectives, what could be done with that information? It would be difficult, for example, to defend raising or lowering a student's grade because he or she did or did not demonstrate a particular attitude.

In this age of accountability, teachers must be able to demonstrate that their grades were reported objectively and that they were not biased by questionable determinations of whether the student had or had not acquired certain attitudes, feelings, or values.

Finally, there is a conflict between the purpose of precise instructional objectives and the nature of objectives in the affective domain. The general purpose of precise instructional objectives is to clarify instructional intent so that teachers and students can work toward the same clear goals. Inherent in this idea is that students must know what the objectives are before instruction begins. However, knowing the affective objectives might prompt some students to demonstrate the expected behaviors only to please the teacher and to stop demonstrating them as soon as the course ended. The same *could* happen with objectives in the cognitive domain, but at least there, teachers are more certain of the validity of the behaviors being observed.

Given the problems described, many teachers choose not to write objectives in the affective domain. Regardless of whether teachers write such objectives, they should understand the affective domain because it describes the progression of commitment that we all go through as our attitudes, feelings, and values develop. Therefore, we will look briefly at each of the five levels of the affective domain and see what a typical objective might look like at each level.

Receiving (Attending)

1.1	Awareness
1.2	Willingness to Receive
1.3	Controlled or Selected Attention[15]

The lowest level of the affective domain is Receiving. At this level, the student is aware of the existence of a condition or problem and is willing at least to listen attentively to what others have to say about it. The element of commitment is not present, and the behavior is somewhat analogous to "sitting on the fence." The student is aware of an issue but has not yet made a decision about it. Words that reflect the Receiving level include asks, follows, names, replies, and uses. An objective, at this level, might be for the student to demonstrate a willingness to learn about drug abuse by contributing to an introductory discussion on the subject.

Responding

2.1	Acquiescence in Responding
2.2	Willingness to Respond
2.3	Satisfaction in Response[16]

The second level is Responding. At this level, the student is willing to go along with an idea or a value (such as being willing to follow school rules), actively volunteers to respond, and takes satisfaction in the response. The level of commitment is minimal, and the behavior is analogous to jumping off the fence but holding on to it and being ready to jump back at any moment. Words that reflect the Responding level include answers, assists, conforms, presents, and recites. An objective at this level might be for the student to display an interest in solving drug-related social problems by taking a stand in classroom discussions against drug abuse.

Valuing

3.1	Acceptance of a Value
3.2	Preference for a Value
3.3	Commitment[17]

The third level is Valuing. Here the student demonstrates that an attitude has been accepted and is consistently preferred over competing attitudes or values. The commitment is clear. The student has walked away from the fence and is willing to be identified as holding the attitude or value. Words that reflect the Valuing level include completes, initiates, invites, joins, justifies, and shares. An objective, at this level, might be for the student to indicate a commitment to social reform by becoming an active member of a community service organization such as Students Against Drunk Driving. Active membership constitutes a minimum standard because each organization operationally defines the term for its own purposes.

Organization

| 4.1 | Conceptualization of a Value |
| 4.2 | Organization of a Value System[18] |

The fourth level is Organization. As students become more aware of values, they eventually recognize that conflicts between values do arise and must be resolved by setting priorities on values. To do so, students should use higher-level cognitive thinking that will enable them to resolve value conflicts in a logical and defensible manner. They will then have greater confidence in their decisions. This level is a direct link between the cognitive and the affective domains. Words that reflect the Organization level include chooses, combines, compares, defends, organizes, and synthesizes. An objective at the Organization level might be for students to identify two conflicting values in their own lives and to describe how that conflict will be resolved.

Characterization

5.1	Generalized Set
5.2	Characterization[19]

The highest level of the affective domain is Characterization. At this level, a person has developed and internalized a value system to the extent that those values are clearly reflected in the person's behavior. When we think of a miser or a spend-thrift, we are thinking of someone who has reached the Characterization level. That person has reasons for holding those particular values and is satisfied with those values. Since students are in the process of developing their value structures, few will reach the characterization level while in high school. Words that reflect the Characterization level include acts, displays, performs, practices, and verifies. An objective at this level might be for the student to demonstrate a continuing commitment to the idea of social reform by studying to be a physician who specializes in drug abuse.

The Psychomotor Domain

The psychomotor domain is concerned with the development of motor skills and neuromuscular control. Objectives in the psychomotor domain often contain elements of the cognitive or affective domain (and vice versa), but the dominant characteristic and intent of the student's response is a physical movement. The curricular areas in which psychomotor skills receive major emphasis include typing, shorthand, home economics, industrial education, art, music, and of course, physical education. It is important to keep in mind, however, that virtually all other curricular areas depend, to one degree or another, on psychomotor skills. Speaking, gesturing, writing, and eye-hand coordination are all examples of psychomotor domain skills.

While the Psychomotor domain is of primary concern to physical education teachers, all teachers need to be aware of its elements. For example, in most school districts there is a concerted effort to include students with special needs in regular classrooms whenever possible. If such students are placed in your classroom, they may have physical disabilities and you will be expected to work with a special education teacher to develop Individualized Educational Plans (IEPs) for them. Knowledge of psychomotor development will be useful in that endeavor. Further, such knowledge is useful as you watch your own children develop.

There are a number of psychomotor domain taxonomies, but the one developed by Anita J. Harrow in 1972 is one of the clearest ways of classifying the neuromuscular development stages through which students pass. As with the cognitive and affective domain taxonomies, this psychomotor domain taxonomy depicts a continuum of simple to complex achievements, and its use can greatly facilitate the conceptualization and sequencing of appropriate objectives and experiences.

Reflex Movements

Reflex movements are involuntary actions that are typically elicited by some stimulus. Ordinarily, educators are not concerned with movements at this level because they are part of the repertoire of all normal children. More complex psychomotor skills can be developed from them with little or no difficulty. Educators typically concern themselves with these movements only when a student has some impairment that limits proper execution of the movements.

Basic Fundamental Movements

Basic fundamental movement patterns are developed in the first year of life. The movements build on the reflex movements and consist of such behaviors as grasping, reaching, manipulating objects, crawling, creeping, and walking. Ordinarily, basic-fundamental movement patterns are learned naturally, with little or no training. Educators typically do not formulate objectives for this level unless a student is observed having problems in this area. Special education teachers may provide appropriate activities for their students with regard to basic-fundamental movements, especially where muscular or visual impairment exists. An objective, at this level, might call for a student to skip for 20 feet.

Perceptual Abilities

Perceptual abilities focus on our awareness of the world around us and our abilities to use our bodies to interact with the world. The first of the five levels with this category is Kinesthetic discrimination—the ability to perceive one's body in relation to surrounding objects in space and to control the body and move its parts while maintaining balance.

Visual discrimination involves a number of components that are necessary for proper psychomotor execution. Visual acuity is the ability to distinguish form and fine details and to differentiate between various observed objects. Visual tracking is the ability to follow objects with coordinated eye movements. Following the movement of a ball would be an example. The third category of visual discrimination is visual memory. This is the skill to recall from memory past visual experiences or previously observed movement patterns such as dance routines or swinging a baseball bat. Figure-background differentiation is the fourth category of visual discrimination. Here the learner is able to select the dominant figure from the surrounding background. Evidence that individuals can differentiate figure and background occurs when they are able to identify the dominant object and respond to it. Ball catching and hitting thrown balls are evidence that the individual can differentiate figure and background. Consistency is the last category of visual discrimination. This is the ability to recognize shapes and forms consistently, even though they may have been modified in some way.

Auditory discrimination involves the ability of the learner to receive and differentiate among various sounds and their pitch and intensity, distinguish the direction of sound and follow its movement, and recognize and reproduce a post-auditory experience, such as the notes to play a song on the piano.

Tactile discrimination is the learner's ability to differentiate between different textures simply by touching. Being able to determine the slickness or smoothness of an object or surface may be essential to properly executing psychomotor movements where the body must come in contact with surfaces in the process.

Coordinated abilities incorporate behaviors that involve two or more of the perceptual abilities and movement patterns. At this level, the student is able to differentiate between the figure and the ground and to coordinate the visually perceived object with a manipulative movement. An example of an activity at this level would be to kick a moving soccer ball. Kicking the moving ball is the psychomotor evidence that there is coordinated discrimination ability. Clearly, perceptual abilities are not observable in isolation. Evidence that these abilities exist depends on the integration of various movements and cognitive skills. The following are examples of objectives written at the various levels in the perceptual abilities category:

You will be able to

1. Without any outside assistance, walk the full distance across a balance beam and back without falling on each of five tries (kinesthetic discrimination).
2. From an audio recording of a symphony orchestra, list the names of eighty percent of the instruments playing in any thirty-second segment of the recording (audio acuity).
3. Catch ninety-five percent of the baseballs batted from a distance of approximately fifty yards (coordinated activities).

Physical Abilities

The physical abilities of the learner are essential to efficient execution of psychomotor movements. Physical abilities constitute the foundation for the development of skilled movements because of the demands placed on the various systems of the body during the execution of these psychomotor skills. Physical abilities are the foundation for the development of highly skilled movements. Physical abilities include endurance, strength, flexibility, and agility.

Endurance is the ability of the body to supply and utilize oxygen and to dispose of increased concentrations of lactic acid in the muscles. The lack of endurance reduces the learner's ability to perform movements efficiently over long periods of time. Development of endurance requires strenuous activity on a sustained basis.

Strength is the relative ability to exert tension against resistance. The development of strength is accomplished ordinarily by gradually increasing the resistance through the use of weights and springs. The student's own body can also be used as resistance in exercises such as pull-ups and push-ups. Maintenance of strength requires the learner to utilize the muscles continually. Obviously, the strength required to perform various psychomotor movements depends on the nature of these movements as well as on the ability of the learner. For example, a greater amount of strength is required for wrestling than for fencing. Other activities that require a good deal of strength include football and gymnastics.

Flexibility refers to the ability to move bodily parts to the maximum limits imposed by the structure of the body's joints. Flexibility depends greatly upon the extent to which muscles can be stretched during movement without resulting in injury. Hurdlers, gymnasts, and dancers are among those who are most concerned about flexibility.

Agility is the ability to move with dexterity and quickness. Agility involves with deftness of manipulation, rapid changes of direction, and starting and stopping activities. Playing tennis, playing the piano or other musical instruments, and playing basketball are activities that require a good deal of agility. Examples of objectives at different levels of the physical abilities category include the following:

You will be able to

1. Following the Harvard-Step Test, have your recovery period pulse count decrease to a point at or above the next highest classification level when compared with the norms (endurance).
2. Correctly execute twenty-five push-ups and fifteen pull-ups with no more than a five-minute rest between the push-ups and pull-ups (strength).
3. While sitting on the ground in the hurdler's position, touch your extended foot with your fingers and hold this position for ten seconds (flexibility).
4. Complete the run-and-dodge course in less than twenty seconds (agility).

Skilled Movements

A skilled movement is the performance of a complex psychomotor task. Such movements are classified by the complexity of the skills themselves and by the proficiency with which they are demonstrated. The levels of complexity include simple adaptive, compound adaptive, and complex adaptive. Performance at each of these levels is classified as beginner, intermediate, advanced, or highly skilled.

Activities included in the skilled movement category are those that involve an adaptation of the inherent movement patterns listed in the Basic-Fundamental movements level. At the Basic-Fundamental movements level, the focus is on whether the learner can simply perform the movement. At the Skilled movements level, the focus is on the extent to which the learner has mastered the skill.

In differentiating among the three categories of skilled movements, the first involves a limited amount of sensory information and only a portion of the performer's body or body parts. The second involves the extension of the body parts through the use of an implement or tool. The third incorporates total body movement, in many instances without a base of support, and necessitates the making of postural adjustments due to unexpected cues.

Mastery levels within the skilled movements category go from beginner, to intermediate and advanced, to highly skilled. At the beginner level, the learner is able to perform the skill with some degree of confidence and similarity to the movement expected. This stage is somewhat beyond the trial-and-error learning of initial attempts at learning the task. When the learner can minimize the amount of extraneous motion and execute the skill with some proficiency, the person is categorized as being at the intermediate skill level. Once the individual can perform the skilled movement efficiently and confidently and achieve almost the same response each time, the skill level is judged to be advanced. At this level, the student's performance is usually superior in quality when compared with similar performances of peers. Highly skilled performances are usually limited to those individuals who use their skills professionally. These people are totally involved in the use of their skills. At the highly skilled level, factors such as body structure, body function, and acuity of sensory modalities and perceptual abilities become critical. Proper execution of the skills depends heavily on each of these components. The following are examples of objectives written at different levels of the skilled movements category.

You will be able to

1. In a five-minute test, type at a rate of forty words per minute and make no more than five errors (simple adaptive skill).
2. From a distance of twenty feet, putt a golf ball into the cup twenty-five percent of the time (compound adaptive skill).
3. Properly execute the following dives with a point rating of at least 4.5: forward one and one-half, one-half gainer, and one-and-one-half forward twist (complex adaptive skill).

Nondiscursive Communication

This category of behaviors consists of nonverbal communications used to convey a message to an observer. These involve such nonverbal movements as facial expressions, postures, and complex dance choreography. Two subcategories are included: expressive movement and interpretive movement.

Expressive movement is composed of many of the movements that are used in everyday life. The basic types of expressive movement include posture and carriage, gestures, and facial expressions. These means of expression are used to indicate the individual's emotional state. Expressive movements are not usually incorporated into typical secondary curricula. They are, however, used in modified form by learners in the area of fine arts and are included in the taxonomy for this reason.

Interpretive movements are art forms. They can either be aesthetic, where the movements are performed for the purpose of creating for the viewer an image of effortless, beautiful motion, or they can be creative movements that are designed to communicate some message to the viewer. In both cases, the performer must have a highly developed knowledge of body mechanics and well-developed physical and perceptual abilities. The following is an objective at the Interpretive Movements level: After selecting a piece of music, create your own movement sequence that contains recognizable rhythmic patterns, keeps time with the music, and communicates a message to the viewer on a contemporary social theme.

It should be noted that for many movements, there are several components. In such cases the learner may be instructed and evaluated on one or all of the components that make up a skill. Dividing the movements into component parts allows for more accurate evaluation and also provides the learner with more specific details that can be used to make movement corrections. Analysis of subcomponent skills is particularly useful for the highly skilled performer. However, a beginning learner may get confused if inefficient movements are analyzed in too much detail. The more advanced that learners become, the more likely they are to benefit from detailed analysis.

Testing Objectives for Clarity

Once you have ascertained that your objectives are technically correct and provide for student development at a variety of levels, check to see if they communicate instructional intent clearly. One way to do this is to ask other people to read each objective and explain what they think they would have to do to demonstrate competence. If their interpretation differs from yours, or if you find yourself saying, "What I really meant was … ," you should rewrite the misleading objective(s). This method is particularly useful if students are used as readers because they will be more representative of the potential "consumers" than anyone else. It may be, for example, that the reading level is inappropriate for the intended students. If a fellow teacher reads the objectives, this factor may pass unnoticed. If students read the objectives, they will be quick to point out that they cannot understand what is intended.

Using Precise Instructional Objectives

Once teachers have (1) gleaned ideas for instructional objectives, primarily by examining relevant learning standards established by the state, (2) converted those ideas into precise instructional objectives, and (3) classified the objectives into domains and levels to ensure that students will develop a range of skills and abilities, the next step is to get administrative approval to use them. School administrators are responsible for ensuring the implementation of an approved curriculum. For this to happen, the objectives of various courses must complement one another. Administrators can help see that they do, but only to the extent that they are aware of each teacher's objectives. It is prudent, therefore, to get administrative approval for course objectives and for any major changes in course objectives. This minimizes the chance of jeopardizing the success of the overall curriculum.

SUMMARY

The classification of objectives into domains and into levels within those domains enables educators to determine if those objectives include a desirable range of skills and abilities. The three domains include Cognitive, Affective, and Psychomotor, and the levels within them are considered to be cumulative. The domains and their levels are summarized below.

Cognitive Domain—Bloom, Benjamin S., 1956

1.00	Remember	Simple recall—no understanding necessary
2.00	Understand	Lowest level of understanding, demonstrated by translation, interpretation, and extrapolation
3.00	Apply	Utilization of rules, principles, and procedures in a mechanical way
4.00	Analyze	Identification of components within a whole, recognition of relationships among those components, and recognition of the organization of the whole
5.00	Evaluate	Making, defending, and supporting value judgments
6.00	Create	Combination of parts into a new and unique whole

(From Taxonomy of Educational Objectives: The Classification of Educational Goals: Handbook I: Cognitive Domain by B.S. Bloom et al. Copyright © 1956 by Longman Inc. Reprinted by permission of Longman, Inc., New York)

Affective Domain—Krathwohl, David R., 1964

| 1.00 | Receiving | Sensitization to the existence of certain phenomena and the willingness to direct attention to them. No commitment. |
| 2.00 | Responding | Sufficiently committed to seek out and discuss examples and to gain satisfaction from association with the value or attitude. Minimal commitment. |

3.00	Valuing	Behavior is motivated not by the desire to comply or obey, but by the individual's realization that some attitude or value has become important to him or her.
4.00	Organization	The resolution of value conflicts and the beginning of the organization of a value system hierarchy.
5.00	Characterization	Values are internalized and are reflected in the person's lifestyle.

(From Taxonomy of Educational Objectives: The Classification of Educational Goals: Handbook II: The Affective Domain by D.R. Krathwohl et al. Copyright © 1964 by Longman Inc. Reprinted by permission of Longman, Inc., New York)

Psychomotor Domain—Harrow, Anita J., 1972

1.00	Reflex Movement	Movements or actions elicited in response to some stimulus, but without conscious volition on the part of the learner
2.00	Basic Fundamental Movements	Actions such as reaching, crawling, and walking that are inherent movements, motor patterns based upon the reflex movements of the learner that emerge without training
3.00	Perceptual Abilities	Recognition of, and discrimination among, various perceptual modalities such as kinesthetic, visual, auditory, and tactile modes and coordinated abilities such as eye-hand coordination
4.00	Physical Abilities	Functional characteristics of organic vigor (endurance, strength, flexibility, and agility), which, when developed, provide the learner with a sound, efficiently functioning instrument (his or her body) to be used when making skilled movements
5.00	Skilled Movements	Development of increasing degrees of skill or mastery of movement patterns learned at earlier stages of development
6.00	Nondiscursive Communication	Use of movements such as facial expressions, postures, gestures, communication, and modern dance choreography to communicate

(From A Taxonomy of the Psychomotor Domain: A Guide for Developing Behavioral Objectives by Anita J. Harrow. Copyright © 1972 by Longman Inc. Reprinted by permission of Longman, Inc., New York)

Affective domain objectives are typically less precise and more time-consuming to write than objectives in the other domains. This is so, in part, because it is necessary to decide on an observable behavior that reflects the target affect. Determining which behavior is, in fact, an accurate reflection of an attitude, feeling, or value is difficult. Even if appropriate behaviors could be identified, dealing with Affective objectives in terms of grading poses other problems.

After instructional objectives are written, they should be classified and, if necessary, adjusted to ensure that a range of skills and abilities is developed. Ideally, the objectives will move students from teacher-directed, lower-level skills to student-directed, higher-level skills. The objectives should be checked for clarity by having others, particularly students, read and interpret them. Finally, the objectives should be approved by the administration to ensure that they fit into the overall curriculum. The following checklist might help in verifying the adequacy of objectives:

- Is the objective a single sentence, preferably of twenty-five words or fewer?
- What is the single observable behavior? Underline it.
- Is the behavior to be demonstrated under controlled conditions so there will be no question about who did the work? (No group work or homework assignments.)
- What is the minimum acceptable standard? Circle it.
- Is the standard reasonable in light of the ability level of the students?
- Could a parent or someone else who is not a specialist in the subject evaluate achievement of the objective as well as the teacher could?
- If there is a series of objectives, are they arranged from the lowest to the highest level?
- Describe two ways achievement of the objective will help students better understand or deal with the world outside of school.
- How does the objective help the student integrate knowledge or learn to learn?

PRACTICE EXERCISES
Practice Exercise 1: The Domains
Classify each objective as belonging to the Cognitive (C), Affective (A), or Psychomotor (P) domain.

1. Explain in writing which of two possible solutions to the problem of social unrest is more likely to eliminate the problem and cite two facts in support.
2. Recite the Emancipation Proclamation from memory with no more than two errors.
3. Install a PowerPoint presentation on a SMART Board so that it runs properly.
4. Show increased interest in band music by attending eight out of the ten concerts offered during the year.
5. Given ten quadratic equations, solve correctly on paper at least eight.
6. Demonstrate concern for the democratic principles of free enterprise by orally stating these concerns.
7. Show a growing interest in art by participating extensively in discussions about art forms.
8. Transfer bacteria from a culture to a Petri dish in a manner that produces properly spread colonies and no contamination.

9. Write an original short story that has appropriate sentence structure and organization and that meets the requirements of heightened action.
10. Given a series of paintings, explain, in writing, which one you believe is best and cite two elements of the painting in support.

Answers to Practice Exercise 1: 1-C, 2-C, 3-P, 4-A, 5-C, 6-A, 7-A, 8-P, 9-C, 10-C

Practice Exercise 2: Cognitive Domain

Classify each objective into its level in the cognitive domain. Check your responses against the answers provided. Resolve discrepancies, if any, by further study, analysis, or consultation with your instructor or peers. When in doubt, classify the objective at the highest level implied.

Levels of the Cognitive Domain

R. Remember	AP. Apply	E. Evaluate
U. Understand	A. Analyze	C. Create

1. Given three garments of varying prices, choose the garment you consider to be the best buy based on the garment's construction and cite at least two written reasons for the decision.
2. List, in writing, at least five factors that led up to the Spanish–American War.
3. Given a new list of possible reasons for World War I and World War II, classify them, in writing, under World War I or World War II with no errors.
4. State, in writing, four common ingredients in pastry.
5. Given the necessary material, compare, in writing, the state welfare program in Illinois to that in California on at least five points.
6. Explain, in writing, using at least five examples, why many Black people moved to the North at the end of the Civil War.
7. Given comprehensive material on the waste of natural resources, write an original legislative bill calling for conservation of a natural resource.
8. Write a unique legal, ethical, practical plan to increase student participation in school activities.
9. On a ten-minute written quiz on ceramics, explain three ways of hand-building a pot.
10. Given two sculptures, choose the one that you judge to be better and defend that choice by citing, in writing, at least three points of superiority in the selected piece.
11. Given the names of two Cubist painters, contrast and compare the styles of each painter in a one-page paper citing at least four similarities and three differences.

12. Solve ninety percent of the two-digit multiplication problems on a written math test.

13. Calculate and write down how much 1 gram of N HCI will have to be diluted to prepare 500 ml of 0.5 N solution.

14. Given a list of tasks that must be done during an eight-hour period, create a written work plan that organizes the tasks so that the time will be used efficiently to complete them.

15. Use Robert's Rules of Order to conduct a class election without any violations of procedure.

Answers to Practice Exercise 2: 1-E, 2-R, 3-A, 4-R, 5-A, 6-U, 7-C, 8-C, 9-U, 10-E, 11-A, 12-AP, 13-AP, 14-C, 15-AP

Practice Exercise 3: Psychomotor Domain

Classify each objective into its level in the psychomotor domain. Check your responses against the answers provided. Resolve any discrepancies by further study, analysis, or consultation with your instructor or peers.

Levels of the Psychomotor Domain

R. Reflex movements	PH. Physical abilities	B. Basic-fundamental movements
S. Skilled movements	P. Perceptual abilities	N. Nondiscursive communication

1. Given bacteria cultures, Petri plates, wire loop, and Bunsen burner, transfer bacteria from the culture tubes to the Petri dishes using proper streaking techniques and preventing contamination.

2. Type forty words per minute in a three-minute timed test with no errors.

3. Drive an automobile in heavy traffic, properly executing a right turn, a left turn, a lane change, a stop, and a parallel park.

4. Draw at least twenty-five Old-English letters demonstrating correct proportion and style.

5. Dance the waltz in proper time.

6. Given a series of ten pictures, point to the dominant figure (as opposed to background figures) in at least eight instances.

7. Without any outside assistance, demonstrate a unique dance routine that is coordinated with at least four minutes of music and that communicates the theme of "war."

8. Show an increase in grip strength of five pounds after two weeks of training.

9. Swim 1,000 yards in less than 19 minutes and have a heart rate of no more than 120 beats per minute after one minute of rest.

10. While battling against a complete defensive team, hit a pitched baseball safely three out of ten times.

Answers to Practice Exercise 3: 1-S, 2-S, 3-S, 4-S, 5-S, 6-P, 7-N, 8-PH, 9-PH, 10-S

KEY TERMS, PEOPLE, AND IDEAS

Taxonomy of Educational Objectives

Cognitive Domain, Benjamin Bloom, 1956—
   Acquisition and manipulation of information. The Cognitive Domain was revised by David R. Krathwohl in 2002.

Automatization—saves time by reducing the need for conscious thought about frequently done tasks

Affective Domain, David Krathwohl, 1964—
   Feelings, Attitudes, Values

Psychomotor Domain, Anita Harrow, 1972—
   Psychomotor development

QUESTIONS FOR CONSIDERATION

1. Since many state learning standards are conceptual in nature, and many items on state tests are application in nature, can taking the time to classify objectives help to bridge the gap?

2. To what extent should secondary teachers concentrate on objectives at the higher cognitive levels?

ENDNOTES

1   Benjamin S. Bloom, ed., *Taxonomy of Educational Objectives, Handbook I: Cognitive Domain* (New York: David McKay, 1956).

2   David R. Krathwohl, Benjamin S. Bloom, and Bertram B. Masia, *Taxonomy of Educational Objectives, Handbook II: Affective Domain* (New York: David McKay, 1964).

3   Anita Harrow, *A Taxonomy of the Psychomotor Domain* (New York: David McKay, 1972).

4   D. R. Krathwohl, (Autumn, 2002) *A revision of Bloom's Taxonomy: An Overview, Theory into Practice* 41, no. 4 (Autumn 2002): 212–18.

5   Shiffrin, Richard M., and Walter Schneider, "Controlled and Automatic Human Information Processing: Perceptual Learning, Automatic Attending, and a General Theory," *Psychological Review* 84 (March 1977): 127–90.

6   Krathwohl et al., *A Revision of Bloom's Taxonomy: An Overview*, 215.

7   Krathwohl et al., *A Revision of Bloom's Taxonomy: An Overview*, 215.

8   Krathwohl et al., *A Revision of Bloom's Taxonomy: An Overview*, 215.

9   Krathwohl et al., *A Revision of Bloom's Taxonomy: An Overview*, 215.

10 Krathwohl et al., *A Revision of Bloom's Taxonomy: An Overview*, 215.

11 Krathwohl et al., *A Revision of Bloom's Taxonomy: An Overview*, 215.

12 Krathwohl et al., *A Revision of Bloom's Taxonomy: An Overview*, 215.

13   Krathwohl et al., *A Revision of Bloom's Taxonomy: An Overview*, 215.

14   Krathwohl et al., *A Revision of Bloom's Taxonomy: An Overview*, 215.

15   Krathwohl, *Handbook II*, 98–115.

16   Krathwohl, *Handbook II*, 118–34.

17   Krathwohl, *Handbook II*, 139–51.

18   Krathwohl, *Handbook II*, 154–63.

19   Krathwohl, *Handbook II*, 165–74.

CHAPTER 6

Whole-Class Instructional Activities

INTRODUCTION

If you are doing a complex job, is it better to have more or fewer tools available to you? Most of us would agree that it is better to have more tools because then you are more likely to have the right tool for a specific task. Most of us would also agree that teaching is, indeed, a complex task. Therefore, it is the purpose of this chapter to help you acquire some instructional tools. The chapter will focus first on some generic teaching skills—skills that are useful across subject-area and grade-level lines. Attention will then shift to an examination of whole-class instructional activities and how they can be used to capture and maintain student interest, enliven your classes, and help students achieve the stated objectives. With the right activities, students will look forward to your class and are more likely to be successful.

LEARNING OUTCOMES

You will be able, in writing, to:

1. Define terms such as set induction, higher-order questioning, practice, and closure, and cite an example of each that is relevant to your subject area.
2. Explain at least two procedures likely to increase the effectiveness of three given whole-class instructional activities such as informal lectures or general discussions.
3. Given a precise instructional objective, select a sequence of three relevant, whole-class activities and cite at least two factors likely to make those activities, in that sequence, at least as good as sequences of other activities.

4. Watch videotapes of parts of two lessons in which the teachers are using the same instructional technique (lecture, discussion, etc.), and determine which teacher is using the technique more properly and cite specific examples from the tape to support your analysis.

GENERIC SKILLS

In education, generic skills are skills that are useful in a variety of instructional settings. It is important to keep in mind that the following list of skills is *not* all-inclusive, nor does use of the skills guarantee student learning. Consistent use of these skills is, however, likely to enhance student learning, so it is wise to include these components in every lesson plan.

Set Induction

Set induction refers to establishing a particular mindset, an anticipation of what is to come, at the beginning of a lesson. It gets students ready to learn. Ideally, what you do during the first minute or two of the lesson will actively involve the students and lead logically into the rest of the lesson. For example, if you were a history teacher and the class was about to begin a unit on transportation, you could begin by telling students to open their textbooks to page 101 and read the first few paragraphs. Ho-hum. On the other hand, you could hold up a gold-painted railroad spike and ask how that might be relevant to the unit. It is likely that some, if not all, students will remember hearing about how a gold spike was used to complete the transcontinental railroad, and they will be eager to demonstrate their knowledge. It is, of course, possible that some students may have never seen a railroad spike and will wonder why you are holding up a big gold-colored nail. Some explanation may be needed, but a favorable set will have been induced and all it required was a little forethought and planning.

Communicating the Objective

Once student interest in the lesson has been stimulated, the next step is to communicate the lesson's objective. While it is true that most lessons build on one another, and that some carry over from day to day, it will facilitate your planning and students' learning if the instructional objective for each lesson is made clear. This enroute objective can be communicated by writing it on the board, projecting it, or by orally explaining it; in any case, a moment or two should be taken to discuss the objective. This will help to ensure that students understand what they are supposed to be able to do at the end of the lesson. It is essential that students see the objective as being relevant to their lives. Some teachers advocate writing the objective on the chalkboard and leaving it there for the entire period to help students focus their attention. That is a good idea.

Stimulus Variation

Most people learn about the world around them via their senses of sight, sound, taste, touch, and smell. However, if you think of your own classroom experiences, you will probably agree that most of them focused on just sight and sound. It is recommended that you make use of the other senses as well. For example, instead of having students learn about Hawaiian luaus by reading, hearing, and/or seeing pictures of them, why not have them plan and conduct one? Actual participation would involve all the senses and would likely result in a long-remembered experience. Variety is "the spice of life," and instruction should be "spiced up" with a variety of activities. However, you must be certain to select activities that directly contribute to the achievement of specific instructional objectives. The objectives should drive the activities.

Review/Repetition

The purpose of review is literally to give students another view of the material. The most effective method is to have the students themselves provide the main points. This is so because if some students failed to understand a point when you first presented it, they might very well fail to understand it again if you present it in the same way during a review. If students present main points, they are likely to do so somewhat differently than you originally did, and their phrasing or examples might help other students better understand.

There are at least three ways of handling review or repetition. **Simple repetition** takes place when you ask a student to paraphrase a main point after it has been discussed but before you move on to the next point. **Spaced repetition** takes place periodically throughout a lesson, typically at the end of important blocks of information. **Massed repetition** takes place at the end of the lesson and is typically thought of as review. It is here that student involvement is most useful.

Practice

Once skills or techniques are introduced, the best way to develop proficiency with them is through practice: if you want to swim well, get in the water and practice. **Analogous practice** is similar, but not identical, to the terminal behavior. For example, students in a beginning swimming class would be engaging in analogous practice if they practiced correct breathing techniques standing by the pool and making appropriate arm and head movements. They would be engaging in **equivalent practice** if they were in the water and actually practicing their breathing technique while swimming. **Guided practice** is typically used in initial practice sessions so that you can give students frequent corrective feedback concerning their efforts and help them avoid making mistakes. **Independent**

practice is useful once students have somewhat mastered basic skills and are unlikely to make serious mistakes.

Closure

Just as every lesson has a beginning, every lesson has an end. There is a big difference however, between a planned ending and having the bell ring mid-sentence. There are two major purposes of closure. The first is to give students a sense of accomplishment—a feeling that they took a step in the right direction, that they accomplished something more than just attending one more class. The second purpose is to relate the information just learned to previous experiences, previously learned information, and/or information yet to be learned or events likely to happen. This bridge building helps students make a meaningful whole out of what might otherwise be isolated pieces of information.

WHOLE-GROUP INSTRUCTION

Whole-group instruction takes place when all students engage in a teacher-directed, academically oriented activity such as an informal lecture or a guided discussion. The fact that the teacher typically uses such activities to provide students with planned and organized information leads to the identification of many such activities as direct instruction activities. Research by **Rosenshine**,[1] **Evertson** et. al.,[2] **Jones and Jones**,[3] **Ornstein and Levine**,[4] and others indicates that students taught via direct instruction tend to score higher on standardized achievement tests than students taught by other methods. This is particularly true with low-achieving students and with low-level objectives. Many teachers also like whole-group direct instruction because it allows them to control the selection and pace of instructional activities, thus simplifying classroom management.

The Madeline Hunter Method

In 1984, **Madeline Hunter** described a lesson-planning structure called Instructional Theory in Practice (ITIP). Among other things, this structure identified a set of generic skills that provided a paradigm for planning systematic and effective, direct-instruction lessons. This set of skills came to be called the Hunter Method and includes the following skills:

1. Anticipatory Set—Stimulate interest and focus attention.
2. Objective and Purpose—Explain to students what they should be able to do by the end of the lesson and why it is important to them.
3. Instructional Input—Select instructional activities that will help students achieve the stated objective.

4. Modeling—Show students how the information is used, or skills are performed. Use many examples.
5. Checking for Understanding—Sample student understanding before they practice.
6. Guided Practice—Monitor initial practice carefully to help students avoid or overcome errors.
7. Independent Practice—Practice with minimal teacher supervision.[5]

In 1987, Barak Rosenshine also identified generic skills that characterized direct or explicit instruction. Those steps were as follows:

1. Begin each lesson with a short statement of goals.
2. Briefly review previous material.
3. Present new material in small steps that require students to practice after each step.
4. Give clear and detailed instructions and explanations.
5. Provide a high level of active practice for all students.
6. Guide students during initial practice.
7. Ask many questions, check for student understanding, and get answers from all students.
8. Provide systematic feedback and correction.
9. Obtain a student success rate of eighty percent or higher during initial practice.
10. Provide explicit instructions for exercises, and where possible, monitor and help students.
11. Provide for spaced review.[6]

Both sets of skills call for the teacher to focus clearly on an academic objective, communicate the objective to students, provide extensive content coverage, and actively engage students. Both sets of skills are useful in planning and teaching direct-instruction lessons. Effective teaching, however, is a complex whole and it is not likely that any single set of skills or steps will be best for all teachers in all circumstances. Teachers need to make informed choices about objectives, content, and methods, and the more information they have, the more informed those choices can be.

What follows are descriptions of various instructional techniques that typically fall under the whole-class, direct-instruction heading. These techniques are most appropriate when objectives call for students to acquire information or understand concepts.

Instructional Activities

Formal and Informal Lectures

Lecturing has fallen into some disrepute, partly because too many lectures were poorly done by too many teachers. A good lecture, one that is well planned and delivered smoothly and with conviction, can be an exciting learning experience and will be perceived as such by students. However, a good lecture is more than the recitation of fact after fact. It requires the careful linking of facts into meaningful blocks of information, and the linking of those blocks. The time spent planning a truly good lecture precludes all but an occasional use of this method by most teachers.

Rather than striving for the perfect "formal" lecture, that is, a lecture in which students do little except listen to a virtuoso performance, most teachers do better to concentrate on identifying those points, skills, and procedures that will enable them to deliver "informal" lectures, providing for student participation rather than passive student reception. This approach has the advantages of being well within the capabilities of most teachers, involving students, and, therefore, being more effective. From this point on, the term lecture refers to the informal lecture.

Purposes of Lectures

Lectures are used appropriately to (1) quickly and concisely present a great deal of new and integrated information, (2) clarify relationships among general points or between specific causes and effects, (3) explain procedures, and (4) point out inferences, inductions, deductions, and assumptions. Some of this information could be provided on handouts or even better, by putting notes online. Lectures, however, allow you to add emphasis by voice inflection, to make instant modifications on the basis of student reactions, and allow for spontaneous student responses and questions, thus making it possible to clarify points as they are raised by the students.

Planning Lectures

There are a number of appropriate lecture-planning procedures, but perhaps the most common is to construct a word or phrase outline. As the first step in this process, write down the specific instructional objective students will be able to achieve after listening to and participating in the lecture. The kinds of objectives for which lectures are most appropriate are generally those at the low cognitive levels. For example:

1. Explain in writing at least two economic causes of World War I.
2. In no more than one page, define ethnocentrism and illustrate it with at least two examples.

Objectives such as these are appropriate to lectures because their terminal behaviors are not time-consuming (and thus do not detract too much time from the lecture), and they do not require much, if any, student practice. Students can be expected to achieve such objectives simply by virtue of having been exposed to the information.

The lesson's objective should serve as the standard against which all prospective elements of the lecture are measured. Elements that clearly contribute to student achievement of the objective should find their way into the word or phrase outline, whereas those that contribute little or nothing should be discarded. This procedure assures cohesiveness and facilitates evaluation of the lecture's effectiveness.

Word or Phrase Outlines

The outline may consist of short sentences, phrases, or even single words. In fact, many teachers find that they can lecture most effectively if they reduce their notes to a minimum using single words or short phrases. Voluminous notes, either in the form of lengthy outlines on sheets of paper or many brief items on index cards, tend to inhibit rather than help. Faced with detailed notes, many beginning teachers tend to refer to the notes more often than necessary, simply because they are there. In some cases, the referrals become so frequent that the lecturer is, in effect, reading the notes. Further, voluminous notes tend to tie the lecturer to the podium, increase the probability of losing one's place, and decrease opportunities to make eye contact with students. Still further, if you make frequent referrals to notes, you create the impression of not knowing your content. Extensive notes, in most cases, simply do not add to the smoothness and polish of a final delivery. Outlines can frequently be shortened by simply eliminating the word 'the' and by using phrases rather than sentences.

The lecture outline should serve to spark memory, not be a source of new information. It should contain the key phrases, facts, figures, names, and dates that are at the heart of the material. The outline should organize the material into logical blocks and subdivide these blocks into manageable sizes to facilitate student learning. When first beginning to plan lectures, it is a good idea to write down the approximate time each part of the lecture should take.

Another part of planning concerns checking the content for its suitability for the students' level. It is easy to make notes without realizing that students may not be familiar with certain terms, especially those that are technical or complex. If such terms are used, they should be starred or underlined to remind you to define and explain them.

Instructional Aids

Plan on using appropriate instructional aids. Almost any lecture will hold students' attention longer if pictures, maps, graphs, cartoons, or similar support materials are used. The time to consider such aids is when the lecture is being planned.

Teaching Students How to Take Notes

There are two parties in an informal lecture, the lecturer and the students. You can increase your effectiveness by helping students learn how to take notes. For example, you can hand out a list of instructions such as the following:

1. Notes for each day should start on a separate page, carry the date and title of the lecture and, if the lecturer is a guest, his or her name.
2. A consistent outline format should be used, such as the following:
   I. Major topic (Outline Format)
      A. Subheading (Logical Organization of Content)
         1. Explanations (sequential steps, causes and effects, etc.)
            a. Further explanations
               i. Proper indentation—easy reference. Sentences of more than one line should begin under first word of first line (as shown here).
               ii. Notes tend to be more useful if students write down only major points rather than trying to copy the lecture virtually word for word.
3. Students should look for techniques such as restating, rephrasing, and listing points on the board or overhead projector as clues that these are major points.
4. Contextual clues such as "There are *three* main facts here …" are often used at the beginning of a series of points and can facilitate the outlining of information.
5. The development of a personal shorthand system for abbreviating frequently used words and phrases can save considerable time.
6. There are advantages to writing neatly enough so that rewriting the notes is not necessary. Students can read and study neatly written notes in less time than it takes to recopy them. Some students, however, find that the act of recopying or rephrasing notes assists in learning. Tell students about both approaches and let them decide which is best for them.
7. As the notes are being taken, space may be left to add personal thoughts, comments, questions, and reactions.
8. Some students, particularly visually handicapped students, may benefit from taping lectures.

Some educators advocate teaching students the double-column, Cornell System, of taking notes. Using this system, students leave a 2 1/2-inch margin on the left of their note paper. This space is used to write in key words or to formulate questions answered in the notes. Both procedures are likely to help students learn and remember key ideas.[7]

Still other educators advocate constructing a website and putting class notes on the website so that when students are in class, they can concentrate on what is being said and have time to think about and comment on what they hear.

Delivering the Lecture

Capture Interest

Even after considerable effort has been made to prepare a lecture well, it may still be ineffective because of weak delivery or style. As with any other instructional procedure, lectures are enhanced by the stimulation of student interest *at the very beginning.* This initial interest arousal is enhanced by involving students as directly as possible and should "tune them in" to what the lecture is about. You need to induce a favorable anticipatory set. There is some evidence that teachers who can initiate lessons well can elicit more learning than teachers who do not concentrate on the initial stages of a presentation.[8] The use of humor, a relevant joke or cartoon, is often an excellent way to begin a lecture.

Language usage can also contribute to or detract from the effectiveness of a lecture. Using language of appropriate complexity and formality is an art worth practicing. If new words are to be introduced, clearly identify and define them so students will understand their meanings in the context in which they are used. Using complex language early in the lecture may cause students to "tune out" because they feel the lecture is going to be "over their heads." If this happens, it is difficult to recapture their interest.

Explain Organization of Material

Good lecturers explain to students how the lecture is organized. Common organizations include cause-effect relationships, chronological order, easy-to-difficult, concrete-to-abstract, or rule-example-rule. Explaining to students how the information is organized will help them orient their thinking and organize their notes.

Use Instructional Aids

The effectiveness of a lecture is increased by visually reinforcing verbal information. If students *see* important facts, figures, names, and dates as well as *hear* them, the probability of their being remembered increases. Further, varying the stimulus can, in itself, be a device helpful in refocusing the attention of students whose interest may be wandering. Among the most common visual aids are posters, maps, charts, chalkboards, overhead projectors, and document cameras. These devices are easy to use and provide sufficient latitude for creative utilization.

Gestures

Just as the use of formal visual aids adds to the interest of a lecture, so do physical movements. Appropriate gestures can help punctuate sentences and emphasize important points. When you walk about, you provide visual stimulation, but be sure that your movements and gestures stop short of being distracting.

Voice—Modulation and Rate

The way you use your voice also influences your effectiveness. Voice inflections, for example, can place emphasis on particular points and can dramatize quotations and asides. By varying the pitch and volume of your voice, you can add the variety necessary to capture the interest of the students. Rate, too, is important. In everyday conversations, we can comprehend spoken information at the rate of about 250–300 words per minute,[9] but lectures are not everyday conversations. If you want students to be able to take notes and to listen to what you are saying, as opposed to simply hearing it, slow down to about 120 words per minute.

All teachers *can* improve their lecture delivery techniques. For example, audio and videotape recorders can be used to help detect problem speech patterns and distracting physical movements. By taping segments of a lesson and dividing the number of words spoken by the number of minutes elapsed, you can calculate the words per minute. Listening to an audio tape or watching a videotape of yourself will also reveal tendencies to speak in a monotone, mispronounce particular words, use personal pronouns, or insert words such as "you know" "um," or "uh." We tend not to realize our own idiosyncrasies until we listen to ourselves and analyze what we hear.

Use Lots of Examples

The use of numerous and relevant examples has been shown to facilitate student understanding of content. Generous use of examples, analogies, and illustrations will help to keep student interest high and produce more learning. It is also a good idea to ask students for examples. When citing examples, it is particularly important to keep in mind what was said about cognitive field theory. Students will come to your class with their own backgrounds, i.e., cognitive fields. If your examples are not consistent with what the students have experienced, i.e., with their cognitive fields, the examples will be useless.

Involve Students

When students are actively involved, their interest is higher, and you can assess their responses to determine the extent to which they understand. Student participation is best encouraged by careful planning. Sets of key questions can be prepared and asked at appropriate places in the lecture. The experienced teacher is constantly aware of nonverbal cues and student behaviors such as blank stares, the slow shaking of a head to indicate disagreement, or a raised hand. Prompt attention to these cues can help students stay on track. Having students reiterate points by answering questions will often clarify important points for students who are still struggling with a new idea.

Summarize

A good lecture concludes with a summary and review of the main points. While this activity can be done orally, it may be helpful to students if visual aids are used for reinforcement. Visual reinforcement helps to emphasize important points and it gives students a chance to double-check notes, fill in points they may have missed, and correct errors.

Summary

In summary, the lecture is one of the most often used instructional procedures. Lectures have the advantage of enabling you to present a large body of information in a relatively short period of time, and they are relatively easy to direct and control. Possible disadvantages are that lectures can (1) encourage passive, rather than active, student participation; (2) inhibit much of the student-teacher interaction needed for proper evaluation of the instructional process; (3) foster unquestioning acceptance of presented material; (4) fail to capitalize on student curiosity or creativity and (5) tend to center more on the content than on what students are to do with the content. Each of these problems is avoidable.

Questioning

The main purposes of questioning are to (1) find out how well students understand a particular block of information, (2) shift student attention from one point to another, (3) increase retention of important points by isolating and emphasizing them, (4) point students in the right direction before starting assignments, and (5) elicit higher-order thinking on the part of students. Questions can be asked that call for analysis, synthesis, and evaluation. All higher-order questions provide practice for students in formulating and orally communicating specific answers to specific questions.

The "Overhead" Questioning Technique

Using the following steps of the "overhead" questioning technique may prove helpful in increasing the effectiveness of questioning:

1. *State the question clearly and precisely.* A question such as, "What about microcomputers?" for example, gives the student little direction for an answer. It is necessary to ask a follow-up question to clarify the first question. It would be better to ask, "How does a microcomputer differ from a large computer?" or "How could a microcomputer be used in this class?"

2. *Pause after asking the question and allow it to "hang overhead."* When you ask questions in a classroom, you generally want all students to think about the answer. To encourage this, ask the question clearly and then pause before calling on someone. Let the question "hang" over everyone's head. The pause gives students a chance to think about the question and encourages all students to do so, since they do not know who is to answer.

One researcher found that teachers typically allow only one second after asking a question before expecting a response. The researcher also found that when the **"wait-time"** was increased to three or four seconds, more students tend to provide more appropriate responses.[10] Even three or four seconds may be too short a time. Many students have learned that if they just sit quietly, many teachers will get so uncomfortable with the silence that they will answer their own questions. If a student does not volunteer an answer, call on someone.

3. *Call on students at random.* Since it is desirable for all students to think about the questions, do not follow any pattern when calling on students. Any pattern, be it a seating arrangement, an alphabetical arrangement, or any other kind of sequence, has the effect of reducing attention on the part of those students who feel they will not be called on.

4. *Provide immediate feedback to students.* Indicate the appropriateness of students' answers. If an answer is not wholly correct, try to use the part that is correct or state the question to which the given answer would have been appropriate. Cues or hints can be used to help students answer appropriately, but care must be taken. If the hints are too obvious, students may feel embarrassed and be reluctant to answer in the future. Do nothing that might embarrass a student and do all that you can to help each student succeed.

Categorizing Questions

The nature of questions should be varied to ensure differing types of responses. One way to check on variety is to compare the kinds of responses expected with the levels of the cognitive domain.[11] The following examples may be helpful in placing questions into appropriate categories.

1. *Remember (simple recall).* "What are the three basic parts of a precise instructional objective?"
2. *Understand (basic understanding).* "What is meant by the term *in loco parentis*?"
3. *Apply (basic use).* "Traveling at sixty miles per hour and with no stops, how long would it take to travel the approximately three hundred miles from Chicago to St. Louis?"

4. *Analyze (pulling an idea apart).* "Which words or phrases in this article, if any, make it biased?"
5. *Evaluate (making and defending a judgment).* "Which of these three lesson plans would you most prefer to follow and why?"
6. *Create (putting together something new).* "Assuming that the basic objectives of this course stay the same, suggest one or two alternative ways students might be helped to achieve those objectives."

Another way to categorize questions is according to their essential function.

1. *Lower-order questions.* A lower-order question may be defined as any question that has served its purpose as soon as an acceptable answer is given. Typically, such questions come from the first three levels of the cognitive domain, although virtually any question that can be answered with one or two words can be considered a lower-order question.
2. *Higher-order questions.* A higher-order question requires students to analyze, synthesize, or evaluate. Answers to higher-order questions usually include cause-effect reasoning and/or the citation of relevant facts in support of an initial response.
3. *Probing questions.* A probing question is asked to encourage students to go beyond initial responses and to explain themselves further. An example of a probing question might be, "Good, you are right so far, now can you give us an illustration?" By asking students to provide examples, illustrations, and rationales, you can frequently determine the depth of their understanding more accurately than by using lower-order questions alone. Probing questions often begin with "why."
4. *Cueing questions.* As the name suggests, cueing questions are used to provide cues or hints to help students arrive at the correct answer. Avoid making the cues too obvious. You do not want to embarrass students; you want to help them be successful.
5. *Open-ended questions.* An open-ended question has no definite right or wrong answer. For example, if your purpose is to encourage students to go beyond the recollection or explanation of previously acquired information and to hypothesize, project, and infer, it might be appropriate to ask what they think about the probability of extraterrestrial life forms. Such questions are particularly useful at the beginning of a discussion.
6. *Convergent questions.* Convergent questions are arranged in a series and are designed to "converge" on a particular point or idea. For example, questions such as "Are there fewer or more farmers now than twenty years ago?" and "How do farm subsidies affect consumer prices?" could be used to help students

focus attention on the issue of government farm subsidies. Convergent questions may be used to induce a principle or deduce an answer.

7. *Divergent questions.* Divergent questions are asked to draw students' attention away from one point and to stimulate thinking about different, but related points. Divergent questions are particularly useful in inspiring student discovery of analogous situations. "What present-day parallels do we have, if any, to the Athenian agora?" is an example of an analysis-level question being used to stimulate divergent thinking.

Encouraging Participation

Encouraging students to ask questions is a skill that can be developed. Aside from asking reasonable questions, as opposed to questions about trivial points, perhaps the most important things you can do with respect to questioning is to make it clear that asking thoughtful questions does not indicate ignorance, it indicates a willingness to learn. In all cases, you should respond to students' questions thoroughly, courteously, and in a friendly manner. You should also indicate the importance of students' questions by comments such as "That was a good question because ..." Finally, *never* humiliate or embarrass a student who gives a wrong answer. To encourage student participation, treat students as you want to be treated.

Demonstrations

Demonstrations have the unique advantage of enabling students to observe the demonstrator doing something instead of simply talking about it. It is a form of modeling. A correctly conducted demonstration, whether of some laboratory procedure, physical skill, or other action, is usually a stimulating instructional experience simply because it is being done "live." A typical objective calling for a demonstration would be: "Following Red Cross guidelines, apply an arm splint to a subject within three minutes."

Planning Demonstrations

To make demonstrations effective, you must sometimes break down complex procedures into separate components and decide what components can be adequately demonstrated in the time available. For example, it is not likely that a home economics teacher would have time to demonstrate how to assemble ingredients for a cake, use alternative ingredients when one or more of those called for is not available, blend the ingredients, bake the cake, frost it, and discuss pitfalls, all within a typical classroom period. The task would need to be divided.

Having decided what can adequately be demonstrated in the time allowed, the next step is to plan each component. Depending on the nature of the demonstration, initial steps may include an overview description of the skill, process, or procedure. If machinery or equipment of any kind is to be used, safety aspects *must* be stressed. In fact, if your course exposes students to particular hazards, school rules typically require that safety precautions be prominently posted in the room at all times and followed meticulously.

An outline of main points may be written on the chalkboard for quick reference, or students may be given handouts containing this information. Detailed descriptions should not be unnecessary. New terms, labels, and relationships should be dealt with before the demonstration begins and should be clearly pointed out and explained as they are encountered during the demonstration. It is also wise to test all the equipment prior to the demonstration to be used to be sure it functions properly.

Conducting the Demonstration
Before the demonstration is begun, be sure that all students can see and hear clearly. This is important, so do not make assumptions; check. If small instruments or fine manipulations are called for, schools so equipped often use a closed-circuit TV camera or videotape equipment. Many classrooms in which large numbers of demonstrations take place are equipped with mirrors above demonstration tables.

Effective demonstrations blend verbal skills and psychomotor skills. Gifted demonstrators are able to use the full range of questioning skills, drawing students' attention to crucial steps and to the way each step is carried out. Exaggerated movements should be avoided because they might confuse or mislead students when they practice the movements themselves.

If students are watching a demonstration in order to learn how to do something themselves, they should be allowed to practice as soon after the demonstration as possible. Student questions should be answered, but the sooner students practice the skills or procedures they just saw, the fewer mistakes they are likely to make.

If the practice session is to result in some product (as opposed to resulting in the improvement of some process), examples of satisfactory and unsatisfactory products should be made available so students can compare and contrast their own products with the models. The use of models is a good idea for all assignments because it helps students be successful. Opportunities for creative responses in the development of a product should be encouraged as long as established standards are maintained.

As students practice the skill or procedure, you should provide individual corrective feedback and encourage students to assess their own performances. This is particularly important when dealing with students with special needs. Allowances should be made for individual differences. For example, if the instructions begin, "Using your right hand," left-handed students are likely to find the movement awkward. Student's idiosyncrasies should cause concern only if they are likely to inhibit future performance.

If a demonstration involves valuable or potentially dangerous material or equipment, you must carefully compare the cost and/or dangers involved with the expected benefits. If material or equipment is too valuable or too dangerous, it would be wise to choose a different procedure.

Guest Speakers

The chief purpose of inviting guest speakers into a classroom is to help students achieve specific objectives by giving them access to people with expertise in a particular area or who have views different from those already explored in class. The presence of a guest speaker also establishes direct contact between the classroom and the "real" world.

Planning for Speakers

The value of a guest speaker is maximized when students are involved in selecting the speaker. When the class identifies a particular area in which a speaker can provide a unique contribution, a list of potential speakers should be compiled. The names of prospective speakers should then be cleared with the principal or other appropriate administrator and permission obtained to invite them to speak to the class. Administrators may be able to suggest individuals who are willing to speak to classes and who have been well received in the past. They can also help you avoid trouble.

When talking with prospective speakers, it is a good idea to let them know the age and grade level of the students, the topic being studied, how much the students already know about the topic, and what type of unique contribution he or she might make. Assuming that the speaker can come when needed, it is a good idea to discuss the general format of the presentation, suggest that time be allowed for questions and answers, and ask if a tape recording may be made. It is also useful to provide the speaker with a list of questions to which students had been unable to find satisfactory answers.

Conducting the Activity

On the appointed day, have a student meet the speaker at the entrance to the school and act as an escort to the classroom. You should formally introduce the speaker to the class. After the presentation is complete, it is your responsibility to tie loose strands together and bring about closure. Points may have been made that will require further study, and aspects of the content presented may need to be related to previously learned material and to the instructional objective underlying the presentation. If students do not suggest writing a thank-you note, you should remind them of the need to do so and make sure that one is written, carefully checked, and sent.

Field Trips

The logical extension of bringing part of the world into the classroom is taking the class into the "real" world. Field trips are useful because they give students firsthand experience available in no other way. It is not likely, for example, that many students would get to see the printing of a newspaper unless they saw it on a school field trip. Similarly, many students are first introduced to art museums, concerts, and professional plays via field trips.

Planning Field Trips

Field trips should be related directly to specific instructional objectives, and these objectives should be used as a springboard to produce specific questions to be answered by students while they are on the field trip or on their return. During a trip, many activities and new experiences will be competing for the students' attention, and the questions will help focus their attention on the most important activities and experiences.

Student involvement during each step of planning a field trip helps generate interest and make the trip more worthwhile. For example, while some students are building questions that focus attention on important points, others may gather information about the facilities at the site of the field trip. This latter group may wish to write for information on the availability of guided tours, admission costs, dates and times the facility is open, specific clothing requirements, and the availability of food. Still another group may obtain information about transportation. Even though you could probably make all the arrangements, students should help. Doing so will help them learn such things as whether school district regulations allow classes to use school buses for field trips, whether this use is dependent upon the buses being returned in time to transport students home after school, whether the distance is such that students will have to leave particularly early or return after school hours, how to charter a bus if necessary, and the importance of school insurance policies that cover field trips and the ramifications for private automobile use.

Permission Slips

Most schools require that the parents or guardians of students going on a field trip sign permission slips. These slips are not legal documents meant to protect schools and teachers from a lawsuit; they are simply devices to assure school administrators that parents know where the students will be going that day and approve of the trip. You can extend the utility of permission slips by including details parents would wish to know, such as departure and arrival times, whether students are to bring food with them or purchase it, and special clothing requirements.

Other Considerations

All these considerations may be influenced by board and administrative policies concerning absences from other classes, providing for students who are unwilling or unable to go, securing enough qualified chaperones, and dealing with special cases such as financially or physically handicapped students or students with particular religious or dietary restrictions. There may also be regulations concerning taking along a first-aid kit or extra cash. Students should be asked to demonstrate that they know where the bus will be waiting for the group should they get separated, and what time it is scheduled to leave the field trip site. It should be made clear to students that their behavior will reflect on the school as a whole. They can either tarnish or polish the school's reputation and its relationships with the community. Be sure that all students are together before leaving the field trip site. It is considered good practice to return with as many students as you had when you left and, preferably, the same ones.

Follow-Up Procedures

Proper follow-up activities are particularly important with respect to field trips. Unlike other instructional activities, field trips involve other faculty by keeping students from attending their classes. If the field trip does not yield worthwhile results, the sponsoring teacher may find it difficult to secure permission for other trips. This possibility, coupled with financial problems, has caused some boards of education to require very strong rationales for field trips. When the field trip has focused on specific objectives and students are given adequate preparation, follow-up discussions and evaluations are easy. General and ambiguous reactions to the trip, while perhaps of passing interest, are not the main concern. The experience should be evaluated on the extent to which it helped students achieve the stated objective(s).

Potential Problems

If chartered transportation is needed, it must be paid for, and this may be an inhibiting factor. Depending on the student population, it may be unfair to expect parents to contribute enough money to cover both the incidental expenses of their children and the transportation costs. This poses a dilemma. If students are asked to raise the needed funds, regardless of what they might learn about business operations during the fundraising, time for that activity will come at the expense of study time. To the extent that we want students to do well academically, we should do all in our power to free them to study. If the needed funds can be provided by parents or the PTA, there is no problem. If funds become a problem, a different activity should be considered. If money is collected, it is important to give each student a receipt and to keep a copy, and to keep accurate and public records. Some schools have adopted specific procedures concerning the handling of money and if such procedures exist at your school, follow them explicitly.

School-community relations tend to improve as interaction between the two increases. Guest speakers and field trips provide interaction and thus help to improve school-community relations.

General Discussions

The purpose of general discussion is to give students practice in on-the-spot thinking, clear oral expression, and asking and responding to questions. Such discussions are also useful for assessing the diversification of views and exploring ideas.

Preparation

Your initial step should be to gather, and make available to students, appropriate background information, materials, and sources. The success of a discussion depends on the degree to which students are informed and prepared. This preparation can be done as homework and will be facilitated if students are given a series of key points to look for or think about. It is a good idea to prepare a list of key questions for use in stimulating or changing the direction of the discussion. These questions can guide discussions along those lines most likely to contribute to student achievement of the instructional objectives.

Since one of the aims in discussions is to encourage student-to-student communication, it can be helpful to arrange desks or chairs in such a way that students can comfortably see each other. Circular, semicircular, or horseshoe arrangements are useful.

Procedures

First, explain the ground rules. For example, all comments and questions will be impersonal; ideas, not the people who suggest them, will be the focus of the discussion. Common courtesies will be followed such as raising a hand to be recognized, not interrupting, and not monopolizing the time. If there are consistent violations of the rules, students may wish to establish a process for helping their peers who are lax in proper participation procedures.

Potential Problems

Sometimes teachers unconsciously allow one or two students to monopolize the discussions. This can be avoided by asking for the comments and opinions of those students who do not volunteer, but care should be taken not to force such participation. If students feel threatened, their participation will decrease rather than increase. Asking for opinions rather than for specific facts is a good way to encourage participation without posing a threat.

Digressions can be a problem in any discussion. Some digressions may have meaning and relevance for students, but you must decide if the digression is important enough in its own right to allow it to continue. The point of the discussion is to help students achieve a particular objective. Digressions that are frequent or long may jeopardize the achievement of the particular objective and by extension, the timely completion of the unit as a whole.

Exploratory Discussions

A central purpose of exploratory discussions is to stimulate student thinking and inter-action. General discussions have a similar purpose, but there is a difference between the two. General discussions typically focus on academic or emotionally neutral topics. Exploratory discussions can focus on controversial issues (such as premarital sex, use of illegal drugs, and abortion) and thus provide opportunities for students to discuss such issues without fear of censure. Such discussions help make students aware of the other students' views and can thus help them become more tolerant of differing viewpoints.

Procedures

In conducting an exploratory discussion, you must define the topic clearly and make sure that students understand that there will be no negative criticism of other stu-dents' views during the discussion. This does not preclude disagreement and alternative views, but if a tone of ridicule emerges, students will become reluctant to voice further opinions, thus defeating the purpose of the discussion. While the later scrutinizing of a general class feeling is not threatening to individuals and can cause little harm, the scrutinizing of a particular student's opinion or comment may cause negative atten-tion to be focused on that student. This may result in an unintended and undesirable reaction. Typically, divergent and probing questioning will predominate throughout the discussion.

Potential Problems

One of the problems of exploratory discussions is that they are often explorations into the affective domain, and it is sometimes not clear just what was gained by students. Students themselves may feel that little was accomplished. To minimize these difficul-ties, you can synthesize the various contributions and use them as a basis for further instructional experiences that are more precisely defined. There may be few concrete accomplishments directly attributable to an exploratory discussion, but it is likely that some students will be enlightened by the variety of opinions held by their peers and will gain new insights.

Exploratory discussions may also be used in conjunction with a resource person knowledgeable in the area to be studied. The function of such a person would be to present new ideas and opinions to which students could respond.

Brainstorming

The purpose of brainstorming is to generate a wide variety of creative ideas concerning a problem in a short period of time. To conduct a brainstorming session, you act as a facilitator whose primary responsibility is to see that proper procedures are followed.

Procedures

After the problem is identified, explain that the point of the brainstorming session is to acquire as many creative ideas as possible as quickly as possible. Everyone is encouraged to contribute any idea, regardless of how strange it may seem. Make it clear that no idea or contribution is to be discussed, evaluated, or criticized during the brainstorming session and that each idea suggested will be added to a written list of ideas.

The effectiveness of brainstorming sessions depends on rapid pace, short duration, and close adherence to the rule that no idea or contribution during the brainstorming is to be discussed. At the end of the session, the students will have a number of suggestions written down relating to the central topic. You then help the students divide the ideas into general categories and move into an exploratory discussion in which the various ideas are discussed.

Potential Problem

If discussions are allowed to interrupt the brainstorming session itself, the necessary free-wheeling atmosphere is inhibited.

Guided or Directed Discussions

A directed discussion is appropriate if students are to be guided through a series of questions to the discovery of some principle, formula, relationship, or other specific preselected result. In guided discussions, students are given practice in inductive or deductive, step-by-step thinking. **Inductive reasoning** goes from the specific to the general. Students are led to conclusions about a set of things by the examination of only a few members of that set. People in China typically have two arms and two legs, as do people in France, the United States, and South Africa. It is reasonable to assume, therefore, that all people typically have two arms and two legs. **Deductive reasoning** goes from the general to the specific. A common form of deductive reasoning is **syllogistic reasoning**. A syllogism consists of a major premise assumed to be true of a whole class of things, a minor premise that identifies an entity as a member of that class, and a conclusion that is inescapable if the major and minor premises are true. For example:

Major Premise—All men are mortal.

Minor Premise—Socrates is a man.

Conclusion—Socrates is mortal.

There is some danger in using directed discussions, because you may have already determined what the students are to discover. If students become too frustrated in the chain of logic leading to the discovery, they may react with the attitude, "Why didn't you just say so in the first place?" and the value of the experience will be lost. Many teachers who use this technique feel that using it for only ten- or fifteen-minute blocks of time works best. Once the conclusion is reached or the principle is discovered, it makes sense to switch to another instructional experience to make use of that conclusion or principle. It has also been found helpful to begin guided discussions with a statement such as, "There is an underlying point here" or "Let's see if we can reach a conclusion concerning. …" Statements such as these help set the stage for the guided discussion and minimize the possibility of students' seeing the experience as guesswork.

An analogy might be made between a guided discussion and a computer-assisted instruction program. In both, the most likely student responses to questions must be anticipated and appropriate questions (or instructions) planned. Both are designed to provide reinforcement for correct answers and both are built around a series of sequential steps. The important difference is that, in a guided discussion, you can monitor the interaction very closely and modify the remaining questions to capitalize on some unexpected student response.

If used cogently, guided discussions can provide a rich instructional experience. Students enjoy discovering and solving, and once they have "discovered" a principle, they remember it longer than if it is simply explained to them.

Reflective Discussions

Reflective discussions are used to assist students in developing analytical skills, arriving at alternative explanations, finding solutions to selected problems, and classifying ideas into major categories. These skills relate directly to objectives at the higher cognitive levels (i.e., analysis, synthesis, and evaluation). A typical objective for a reflective discussion might be, "You will explain orally how some aspect of daily life would differ if we lived under a socialistic government."

Preparation

A good way to begin a reflective discussion is to define a particular problem relative to the instructional objective and then devise a series of open-ended questions to encourage a variety of responses. Additional specific questions will be generated and asked spontaneously during the discussion.

To help maximize the benefit of reflective discussions, one student can be delegated to list the identified main points of each response on the chalkboard. To supplement this listing, you can elicit from the class appropriate headings for clusters of responses that have points in common. In this way, as students are given practice in classifying ideas and in analysis skills, a basis is provided for predicting and hypothesizing solutions to the original problem.

Potential Problems

Unlike guided discussions, which can often be conducted at a rapid rate since you have prior knowledge of the result, reflective discussions should be conducted at a relatively slow pace and include periods of silence. Time must be allowed for students to consider alternate possibilities and to think about the ramifications of those possibilities. Many teachers feel that the slowness of reflective discussions is a serious drawback and that the time they require can be used in more valuable ways. Other teachers feel the "thinking" time required is one of the strongest attributes of reflective discussions and use the discussions frequently. In deciding how often to use reflective discussions weigh these factors and balance the time used against the opportunities for divergent responses, large-scale student participation, practice in classification, and reflection. At their roots, these are all matters that reflect your philosophy of education.

Evaluation of Discussions

Discussions are time-consuming instructional procedures in relation to content gained by students, especially in comparison with experiences such as reading assignments or lectures. The advantage most forms of discussion have over these other activities, however, is that they capitalize on student curiosity and creativity, encourage participation, and allow for development of higher-level thought processes.

Discussions, like all instructional procedures, must be evaluated to determine effectiveness. The best way to judge a discussion is to determine if students can achieve the instructional objective for which the discussion was chosen as the learning activity.

Teachers sometimes find it useful to note which students do or do not contribute to discussions and what types of contributions are made by individuals. It is sometimes found, for instance, that even though students did not participate vocally in a discussion, they were involved mentally and developed analytical skills. Nonparticipation may indicate that the student needs special, individualized help, but it may also mean that these students are simply thinking about what is being said. By comparing evaluation results with patterns of participation, it may be possible to determine which students need the maximum amount of encouragement to participate, since participation, in their cases, might aid learning.

The quality of students' responses is a valid indicator of the effectiveness of discussions. When students make comments indicative of muddled thinking or misconceptions, you have at least two choices. You could ask the student to explain the factual basis for the response. The risk here is that there may be no factual basis and the student will be embarrassed and get very defensive. Another approach is to point out that while some people share that particular view, there is considerable evidence that supports a different view. Sometimes, students make extreme points purely for effect, to impress their peers or to elicit special attention from the teacher. If it becomes clear that a student is engaging in "artificial" participation, attempting to take care of the problem during the ongoing discussion is likely to produce denials or challenges by the concerned student and should be avoided. A private conference is usually more fruitful.

Effective evaluation of discussions takes thought, but the potential for improvement makes the effort worthwhile. The more discussions are used and evaluated, the more polished you will become in their use.

Contests

Competitiveness is at the heart of our democratic way of life and it is reflected in school in activities as varied as sports, elections for school councils, and competition for college admission. You can bring some of the excitement of competition into your classroom by having occasional contests.

The simplest way to do this is to assign all students a block of content to study and to prepare a list of questions going from simple to complex. The following day divide the class into teams either randomly or by some variable such as gender or height. Then, have each "team" sit together and follow a quiz show format. Ask a question of the first member of Team One. If that person answers correctly, the team earns two points. If the person cannot answer or answers incorrectly, but someone else on the team can answer correctly, the team earns one point. If no one on Team One can answer the question, but someone on Team Two can answer correctly, Team Two earns two points. The first person on Team Two is then asked a question and the process is repeated. This procedure is repeated until all students on each team have had a chance at a question.

To stimulate a sense of teamwork, a different format, one that links whole-group with small-group activities, can be used. For example, students could be divided into groups of four to six students each. Fewer students in a group tend to make the competition unwieldy because of the number of groups that result. Larger groups tend to reduce the amount of teamwork that takes place among members. With the teams known before-hand, all students are given a block of content to study. If this format is followed, the questions you prepare can be more complex than with the first format. This is so because it is likely that members of each team will work together to some extent and will come to class well prepared. The following day, the quiz show format can be used, but each team is allowed to earn points only on the questions answered correctly by the team. Play-offs between the teams having the greatest number of points are also possible.

In using contests, it is crucial that the questions asked be seen as fair. This means that a good deal of thought needs to go into their development. The earliest questions should be at the Knowledge or Comprehension level and should be designed not only to sample student knowledge, but also to enable students to earn points quickly. Once each team has amassed some points, its members will have a stake in the activity and this will increase interest and participation. This interest and participation is then likely to continue even when the questions become more challenging. Variations of these formats include (1) specifying a maximum amount of time to be allowed for each question, (2) having teams construct and pose questions to each other, and (3) having students submit questions to you, and you select questions from among those submitted. With option three, it is a good idea to have an understanding with the students that if there are not enough suitable questions submitted, you may use other questions that you have developed.

SUMMARY

There are a number of generic skills that are useful in many instructional settings. Among those skills are set induction, communicating the objective, stimulus variation, review/repetition, practice, and closure. As useful as these skills are, it is crucial to remember that good teaching is more complex than simply sequencing a set of skills and using them mindlessly.

You will be responsible for the progress of your class as a whole and a good deal of your time is likely to be used in whole-group, direct, instruction. Research indicates that if instruction is predominately teacher-directed and academically oriented, students are likely to achieve higher scores on achievement tests than if instruction is predominately student-directed. Madeline Hunter and Barak Rosenshine identified sequences of skills typical of direct instruction. Those sequences begin with inducing a favorable mindset and communicating the objective, include the use of a variety of instructional activities, and conclude with a review, practice, and closure.

Lectures are used mostly as a way to convey information quickly and concisely. Formal and informal lectures differ in that informal lectures provide for student involvement. In planning a lecture, you should prepare a word or phrase outline and appropriate visual aids. Students should be taught to take notes in an outline or double-column format. While delivering the lecture, speak at about 120 words per minute, maintain eye contact with the students, use a great many examples, and make use of visual aids. Conclude by asking students for main points.

Another commonly used whole-group technique is questioning. When using the "overhead" questioning technique, ask a question of the whole group, allow it to "hang over everyone's head" for at least four or five seconds, and then ask for an answer. Call on students randomly to increase attentiveness and participation. Questions can be categorized according the levels in the cognitive domain, or according to function. Some of the function types include probing, cueing, open-ended, convergent, and divergent.

Demonstrations have the advantage of enabling students to see something being done as opposed to being able to only hear about it being done. You should practice the demonstration beforehand, arrange students so they can see clearly, explain all safety precautions, explain each step as it is being done, and have students practice the skill or procedure as soon after the demonstration as possible.

Guest speakers and field trips have the advantage of exposing students to the "real world." Both activities should be cleared with the principal. Field trips have two drawbacks that need careful consideration. First, taking students out of school interferes with the instructional plans of other teachers who have those students in class. Enough such disruptions can threaten the integrity of the entire curriculum. Second, if funding for a trip is required, expecting students to raise that money detracts from the time they should spend studying. Fund raising activities for any purpose are, therefore, highly questionable.

Discussions can help students acquire new information, but they are particularly useful in giving students practice in voicing ideas and defending points of view. Regardless of the type of discussion, it is a good idea to ensure that students are prepared by making specific assignments prior to the discussion. Friendly competition can be utilized in the classroom by pitting teams of students against one another in contests that follow quiz show formats.

KEY TERMS, PEOPLE, AND IDEAS

Generic skills—useful in many instructional
  settings
Set Induction
Communication of the Objective
Stimulus Variation
Review/Repetition

Simple, Spaced, Massed Repetition
Practice
  Analogous, Equivalent
  Guided, Independent
Closure

Direct Instruction—(Madeline Hunter, Barak
  Rosenshine, Alan Ornstein)
  Formal and Informal Lectures
  Word or Phrase Outline
  Cornell System
  Overhead Questioning Technique
  Wait-time
  Probing, Cueing, Convergent and Divergent
  Questions
  Demonstrations
  Guest Speakers

Field Trips, Permission Slips
Discussions
  General
  Exploratory
  Brainstorming
  Guided/Directed
  Reflective
  Inductive Reasoning
  Deductive Reasoning
  Syllogistic Reasoning
Contests

QUESTIONS FOR CONSIDERATION

1. Using cause-effect reasoning, orally explain why you do or do not believe that whole class activities should be your primary instructional mode.
2. In your particular content area, use cause-effect reasoning to orally explain why you think that having students "learn by doing" is or is not an effective way to use instructional time?

ENDNOTES

1   Barak V. Rosenshine, "Content, Time and Direct Instruction," in *Research on Teaching: Concepts, Findings, and Implications*, eds. Penelope L. Peterson and Herbert J. Walberg (Berkeley: McCutchen, 1979), 28–56; Barak V.Rosenshine, "Explicit Teaching," in *Talks to Teachers: A Festschrift for Nate Gage*, eds. David Berliner and B. V. Rosenshine (New York: Random House, 1987), 75–92.

2   Carolyn Evertson, C. Anderson, L. Anderson, and J. Brophy, "Relationship Between Classroom Behaviors and Student Outcomes in Junior High Mathematics and English Classes," *American Educational Research Journal* 17 (Spring 1980): 43–60.

3   Vernon F. Jones and Louise S. Jones, *Comprehensive Classroom Management: Motivating and Managing Students*, 3rd ed. (Boston: Allyn and Bacon, 1990).

4   Allan C. Ornstein and Daniel U. Levine, "School Effectiveness and Reform," *Clearing House* (November-December 1990), 115–18.

5   Madeline Hunter, "Knowing, Teaching, and Supervising," in Using What We Know About Teaching, ed. Philip L. Hosford (Alexandria: Association for Supervision and Curriculum Development, 1984), 175–76.

6   Rosenshine, "Explicit Teaching and Teacher Training," 34.

7   Walter Pauk, *A User's Guide to College: Making Notes and Taking Tests* (Providence: Jamestown Pub., 1988), 7.

8   Robert F. Schuck, "The Effect of Set Induction upon Pupil Achievement, Retention and Assessment of Effective Teaching in a Unit on Respiration in the BSCS Curricula," *Educational Leadership Research Supplement* 2, no. 5 (May 1969): 785–93.

9   Robert Heinich, Michael Molenda, and James D. Russell, *Instructional Media and the New Technologies of Instruction*, 4th. ed. (New York: Macmillan 1993), 181.

10   Mary B. Rowe, "Wait-Time and Reward as Instructional Variables," *Journal of Research in Science Teaching* (February 1974): 81–97.

11   D. R. Krathwohl, *A Revision of Bloom's Taxonomy: An Overview*, 2002, accessed August 4, 2020 from https://www.depauw.edu/files/resources/krathwohl.pdf.

CHAPTER 7

Small-Group and Individualized Instructional Activities

INTRODUCTION

People continually compete for things as varied as money, power, and a "better" life for themselves and/or for their children. Our schools, with their emphasis on whole-group instruction, do much to further the spirit of competition, because each student is typically competing with all others for recognition and grades. However, if we are to produce citizens who are able not only to compete, but to also work together in joint ventures, perhaps we ought to do more to further the spirit of cooperation. At the same time, students also need to develop the skills needed to work independently. Therefore, this chapter will focus on small-group and individualized activities. The more you know about different instructional procedures, large-group, small-group, and individualized, the more you will be able to vary instructional procedures and thus help students develop a wide range of skills and understandings.

LEARNING OUTCOMES

You will be able, in writing, to:

1. Explain what concepts are central to cooperative learning strategies such as STAD and TGT, and how the steps of those strategies attend to those concepts.
2. Describe each of the five steps of the "scientific method."
3. Identify an "ill-structured" problem suitable for a problem-based learning project in your subject area and explain at least three kinds of information students would need, outside of your subject area, in order to complete the project.

4. Construct a self-instructional package that could be used for enrichment by students in your subject area.

SMALL-GROUP ACTIVITIES

Small-group and individualized activities usually follow whole-class activities. Whole-group activities are most often used early in each instructional unit, because they effectively help students acquire the facts, figures, names, dates, sequences, and other components that make up a well-developed knowledgebase. However, the acquisition of such a knowledgebase does not automatically lead to the development of higher-level skills. Students need to be given opportunities to combine pieces of information into meaningful wholes, voice and defend positions, and critically analyze what they see, hear, and do. It is here that small-group and individualized activities are most useful.

Small-group activities, because of the more direct and continuous involvement of individuals and because of the increased opportunities to check ideas against those of others, facilitate achievement of complex tasks. This is particularly so when those tasks require the use of skills and knowledge that cut across subject-area lines because students can divide the workload and capitalize on each other's strengths. Further, you can use small-group activities to make students more responsible for their own learning. This happens when students identify problems of particular interest to them and plan how to work to solve those problems with little or no teacher direction. The opportunity to maximize the relevance of instruction to the needs and interests of students reaches its epitome in individualized activities.

Proportions of Whole-Group versus Small-Group Activities

A point of continuing discussion is the proportion of time that should be devoted to whole-group versus small-group instruction. Some teachers argue that most instructional time should be devoted to whole-group, direct instruction because: (1) students must have a common and strong knowledgebase on which to build and large-group direct instruction is the most efficient way to build that knowledgebase, and (2) large-group, direct instruction tends to minimize classroom management problems. Other teachers argue that most of the time should be devoted to small-group or individualized activities because: (1) students learn best by doing, (2) students who cover less content, but who spend more time considering and working with it, will acquire longer lasting knowledge ("less is more"); and (3) learning to work in groups is essential for success in the twenty-first century. Given the fact that teachers typically work with 120–180 students every day, it is likely that large-group instruction will continue to predominate, but it should not exclude small-group and individualized activities. We want to produce citizens who can cooperate as well as compete with each other.

Determining Group Make-Up

Putting students in groups of three or four seems to result in the greatest productivity. Larger groups tend to be unwieldy and to subdivide on their own, and pairing students typically results in too many groups. Some teachers favor **heterogeneous** grouping, the assigning of one or more high, middle, and low achievers to each group. Variations of heterogeneous grouping include grouping students randomly or in alphabetical order. The advantage of heterogeneous grouping is that it tends to maximize social development because students learn to work with people with widely varying abilities. The disadvantage is that the brighter students may simply do most of the work, rather than helping the slower students.

Other teachers favor **homogeneous** grouping, the assigning of students to groups on the basis of common ability levels, interests, or friendships. The advantage of homogeneous grouping is that people tend to congregate and work best with others who have abilities and interests similar to their own. The commonalties provide a motivating force and also enable students to get to work more quickly. The disadvantages are that such grouping amounts to segregation and because of their commonalties, students in such groups tend to digress more than students in heterogeneous groups. Further, if slower students are grouped together, their joint efforts are not likely to match those of high-ability students who were grouped together.

Clarifying Overall Purpose

Regardless of how groups are formed, it is your responsibility to ensure that all students understand how their work will benefit them individually and contribute to their achievement of course objectives. Before groups are formed, you should explain the need for each person to do his or her part if the group, and the class as a whole, is to accomplish its task. It is a good idea to discuss the potential problem of having one or two group members do less than their share of the work. Students can be asked to suggest procedures for minimizing the problem and with dealing with it if it occurs. A written operating plan clarifying who is to do what by when helps to minimize the problem. Ultimately, it is your responsibility to monitor and grade each individual's work.

Concluding

When small-group activities are completed, results should be shared with the entire class. This enables all students to benefit from the work of each small group and it also provides you with an opportunity to publicly commend the members of the groups for their efforts. Panel discussions and debates are among the activities that provide opportunities for the dissemination of group results. Descriptions of small-group strategies follow.

Panel Discussions

The purpose of a panel discussion is to enable a small group of students to delve deeply into an area of interest and then to act as a source of information for the rest of the class. To arrange a panel discussion, appoint panels of three to five students. Each group takes responsibility for selecting a chairperson, dividing research responsibilities, and setting up a time schedule. You intervene only if the responsibilities assigned to, or assumed by, some students are inappropriate for their ability levels. For some students, it may be necessary for you to provide specific advice, references, and sources. There will be little benefit to those students however, if you or other panel members do most of the work.

When the panel is ready to act as an authority, the chairperson or other moderator may follow several courses of action. One approach is for the moderator or chairperson to explain briefly what the panel is prepared to discuss with the class, introduce the panel members, identify their individual areas of special interest, and begin accepting questions from the class.

In another approach, the moderator or chairperson briefly introduces the topic to be discussed and then introduces each of the panel members, allowing each about five minutes to discuss or explain his or her particular area of interest. The moderator or chairperson then summarizes the findings and opens the panel to questions and comments from the class. This procedure has the benefit of providing the rest of the students with information on which to base questions.

In both approaches, the moderator or chairperson ensures that all panel members participate on an equal basis and that sufficient time is left for a final summation. Time is also allowed for the teacher to bring the panel discussion to a close near the end of the class period, to establish the relationship of the discussion to the instructional objective, and to bring about closure.

Debates

Debates are similar to panel discussions because small groups of students work together gathering information. The difference between the two is that with debates, the purpose of each group is to present facts, ideas, and values relevant to a particular view of a controversial issue. In conducting debates, each panel is given a certain amount of time to present its case and to answer questions about it. When all panels have made their presentations and answered questions, the class, as a whole, can discuss the issue and try to reach consensus.

Role Playing/Skits

Role playing is useful for dramatizing particular social problems and for increasing student empathy for the feelings, viewpoints, and problems of other members of society (affective domain objectives). Students might be asked, for example, to play the role of a pro-choice or pro-life activist and to cite at least three arguments they might use to persuade others to join their cause.

To use role playing successfully, you must make certain that all students understand that they will be playing specific roles, acting the way they believe their assigned characters would behave. A ground rule should be that the role playing will be stopped if students step out of their roles or begin to get too emotionally involved.

Once the ground rule is understood, identify the specific roles and "positions" of the participants and a situation in which two or more people interact. After this is done, students should be asked to volunteer to play the roles. No one should be forced to participate.

Participants should then be allowed to confer briefly about how they intend to act out the situation (not to rehearse) and should then act it out. Usually, two or three minutes are sufficient for students to decide how they intend to present the situation and another ten minutes for the actual presentation.

Before any discussion of the presentation takes place, it is sometimes worthwhile to have a second set of students confer and act out the same situation. After the second presentation, students can compare and contrast pertinent points. No effort should be made to evaluate the students' performances. The focus of the discussion should be on the differing perceptions of the roles by the participants and nonparticipants, on an attempt to understand the probable feelings and beliefs of the person(s) in the real situation, and on an examination of personal rationales for values held.

It should be noted that there is some risk associated with the use of role playing. If students play their roles too convincingly, other students may suspect that they are not acting at all and that they are saying and doing what they personally believe. If this happens, the seeds of dissension may be sown and tentative relationships that might have flowered between or among students may be stunted. These subtle, but significant, risks may well outweigh any potential gains.

Cooperative Learning

All small-group activities foster cooperative learning, but some strategies are more likely to be effective than others. **Robert Slavin** at Johns Hopkins University has done extensive research on what he refers to as Student Team Learning strategies, or cooperative strategies. He maintains that three concepts are central to effective Student Team Learning: (1) team rewards, (2) individual accountability, and (3) equal opportunities for success. He was also instrumental in developing four main cooperative learning strategies: (1) Student Teams—Achievement Divisions, STAD; (2) Teams-Games-Tournament, TGT; (3) Team-Assisted Individualization, TAI; and (4) Cooperative Integrated Reading and

Composition, CIRC. The STAD and TGT strategies are adaptable to most subjects and grade levels, while the TAI and CIRC strategies work best, respectively, in grades 3–6 and in reading and writing.[1] All of the strategies are intended for use after whole-group instruction, to extend knowledge and provide opportunities for teamwork.

Student Teams—Achievement Divisions (STADs)

When using the STAD strategy, Slavin recommends putting students in teams of four and mixing membership on each team with respect to ability levels, sex, and ethnicity.

> Students then work together within their teams to make sure that all team members have mastered the lesson. Finally, all students take individual quizzes on the material, at which time, they may not help one another.
>
> Students' quiz scores are compared with their own past averages, and points are awarded based on the degree to which students meet or exceed their earlier performance. These points are then summed to form team scores, and teams that meet their criteria may earn certificates or other rewards. The whole cycle of activities, from teacher presentation to team practice and quiz, usually takes three to five class periods.[2]

The STAD strategy incorporates Slavin's three main concepts. Students are accountable for their own learning because they take quizzes individually. In order for the team to earn rewards they must help each other succeed and, since "team scores are based on students' improvement over their own past record, there is equal opportunity for all groups to be successful."[3]

Teams-Games-Tournament (TGT)

> The TGT strategy uses the same teacher presentations and teamwork that STAD does, but replaces the weekly quizzes with weekly tournaments in which students compete with members of other teams to contribute points to their team scores. Students compete at three-person "tournament tables" against others with similar past records in mathematics [or other subject areas]. A "bumping" procedure, which consists of changing students' table assignments weekly based on their performance in each tournament, keeps the competition fair. The winner at each tournament table brings six points to his or her team, regardless of which table it is; this means that low achievers (competing with other low achievers) and high achievers (competing with other high achievers) have equal opportunity for success. As in STAD, high-performing teams earn certificates or other forms of rewards.[4]

Problem-Based Learning

Problem-based learning is, perhaps, the single best way to introduce students to the complexities of "real-life" problems. Central to using problem-based learning is student familiarity with the "scientific method."

The Scientific Method

Although **Sir Francis Bacon** (1561–1626) did not invent the steps that came to be called the **"scientific method,"** he was one of the earliest thinkers to recommend induction and experimentation as the basis of the scientific method. He made his recommendation in 1620 in a book titled *Novum Organum* (New Organon, referring to Aristotle's book on logic, the *Organon*).[5] The procedure he recommended has been reduced to the following steps:

1. Identify the problem.
2. Formulate a hypothesis (a probable solution or explanation).
3. Gather, evaluate, and categorize available data.
4. Reach some conclusion (either reject or support the hypothesis on the basis of the evidence acquired).
5. Take some action appropriate to the results.

Using Problem-Based Learning—Constructivism

Rather than simply describing the procedural steps of problem-based learning, we illustrate those steps via a problem-based learning exercise that was completed by students at the **Illinois Math and Science Academy (IMSA)**. The IMSA is a state-funded, residential, magnet school that selects top students from the state of Illinois and provides them with a three-year high school experience focusing on math and science and delivered via an innovative curriculum. The project was entitled *Jane's Baby* and it was the privilege of this author to be present when W. J. Stepien demonstrated the steps involved, in brief form, at a workshop.

Preparation

Before starting his demonstration, Stepien explained how he and his colleagues prepared for the project. The first step was to decide on an ill-structured problem. They wanted students, on first seeing the problem, to be able to apply the general knowledge and reasoning skills they had accumulated to date. However, they also wanted students to see that "real-life" problems are typically far less well-defined than classroom assignments and that they typically cannot be solved by turning to large amounts of well-organized information. One of the problems they selected involved an anencephalic fetus.

After selecting the problem, the IMSA faculty thought it through and identified some of the issues that students would be likely to encounter. They then identified the kinds of resources students were likely to need in their investigations and verified that those resources were available. Some materials could be made available in the classroom, but part of the power of problem-based learning is that students find out that they need to look for answers outside the classroom. If resources are scarce, teachers should consider putting some of them on reserve in the school library or in other central locations. If students are going to use resource people, the teacher needs to talk with them to make sure that they are willing to work with the students. If so, the teacher must then explain that they are not to simply tell students the answers; they are to help students understand what questions need to be answered and to guide them toward the appropriate information. Only then can the students be referred to these human resources. In this case, since students might well seek advice from a doctor, a teacher talked with a doctor who agreed to work with students if they asked. It should be noted that teachers typically spend more time preparing a good problem-solving project than preparing any other kind of instructional activity.

Procedure

Students were given the following scenario:

> You are the head of pediatrics at a large city hospital. Jane Barton is one of your patients. Doctor, what will you do in the case of Jane's baby?
>
> Jane Barton is pregnant. She first came to see you about two weeks ago after she and her husband received the results of tests ordered by her family doctor. The tests indicate that Jane and Ralph's baby is anencephalic. The couple is concerned about the fetus and wonders what to do if Jane cannot deliver a normal, healthy infant.[6]

A medical report of the situation was attached to the scenario.

Identifying the Problem

After reading the scenario and the medical report, students were asked if a problem exists and if so, what it was. Students agreed that two problems existed: (1) what to tell the Bartons and how to assist them, and (2) there were many things they needed to learn about.

Stating a Hypothesis

A hypothesis is "a tentative assumption made in order to draw out and test its logical or empirical consequences."[7] As the first step in stating hypotheses, students were asked to list, in three columns on the chalkboard, what they knew about the problem, what they needed to know, and what they should do. Part of their work is shown in table 7.1.

Table 7.1 Jane's Baby

What do we know?	What do we need to know?	What should we do?
Jane Barton is pregnant.	What is the medical description of anencephaly?	Order another test to confirm the diagnosis.
Jane is married.	What is Jane's general health?	Discuss the condition of the fetus with the Bartons before too long.
Medical tests indicate that her baby is anencephalic.	Does she have children?	Have technology ready to help the baby at birth.
Jane and Ralph feel that their baby might not be norm.	What test did she have? How accurate is it?	Use the tissue/organs of the fetus in some way.
Jane has been referred by another doctor.	Is abortion possible in this case?	
Anencephalic babies do not live very long.	What is the law on abortion in our state?	
It has something to do with the brain.	How do Jane and Ralph feel about abortion?	
	Are there alternatives to abortion in this case?	
	How long do anencephalic babies live?	
	What is their "quality of life"?	

Stepien, William J., Shelagh A. Gallagher, and David Workman, "Problem-Based Learning for Traditional and Interdisciplinary Classroom," *Journal for the Education of the Gifted* vol. 16, no. 4, Summer 1993, 338–357.

Students concluded that, in this situation, they could not state the hypotheses until they had more information. This, in itself, was a major step because it brought home the ill-structured nature of many "real-world," problems.

Gathering, Evaluating, and Categorizing Data
Since a major purpose of problem-based learning is getting students to gather, interpret, and evaluate information on their own, it would be self-defeating for the teacher to act as a major source of information. A better role is that of resource person, one who helps point students to the sources of information, rather than as a supplier of data. This is in contrast, for example, to guided discussions in which the teacher not only provides information, but also directs students to predetermined outcomes. In this case, students found it necessary to get and consider information about how long anencephalic infants typically lived; what kinds of procedures would be covered by insurance; what state and/

or federal laws said about abortion, organ transplants, and the use of fetal tissue for research; religion; and ethical and moral issues.

As they gathered data, the students established, modified, strengthened, and discarded hypotheses. It frequently happened that new information generated the need for still more information, so students had to continually engage in analysis and synthesis. To aid them in their work, they were given problem logs. Part of one such log is shown in Table 7.2.[8]

Table 7.2 Problem Log for Jane's Baby

Log Exercise

1. Based on your current understanding of Jane's situation, write a statement of the problem you face.
2. Provide a medical description of anencephaly. (Provide your own drawing to clarify your verbal description,) Specifically,
   a. What causes anencephaly?
   b. What is the prognosis for an infant born with anencephaly?
   c. Describe the nature of cranial abnormalities in an anencephalic infant.
   d. What brain functions are missing in an anencephalic infant? What functions are present?
3. Describe the ethical dilemma(s) you and the Bartons face in this situation.
4. Now that you have investigated this problem, what is your advice to the Bartons?

Stepien, William J., Shelagh A. Gallagher, and David Workman, "Problem-Based Learning for Traditional and Interdisciplinary Classroom," *Journal for the Education of the Gifted* vol. 16, no. 4, Summer 1993, 338–357.

Reaching a Conclusion
In a typical classroom assignment, once the data are gathered and analyzed, students are ready to conclude either that the evidence warrants the support or rejection of the hypothesis. In the minds of many, any conclusion reached by the students is less important than the practice they got in applying the scientific method to a problem. In the case of Jane's Baby, a number of possible conclusions were considered.

Take Some Action
As the final step, students take some action. In a typical classroom assignment, students might demonstrate the objective by writing a letter to someone arguing for a change in

policies or practices. In the case of Jane's Baby, students, in their roles as doctors, had fifteen-minute "consultations" with Mr. and Mrs. Barton (played by volunteers from the community and faculty). In these "consultations," students became aware of two other aspects of the problem: (1) who actually had to make decisions, and (2) the communication skills needed to help the patients understand the problem and the risks involved in each possible solution.

Advantages/Disadvantages

The chief advantages of problem-based learning are that it helps students: (1) learn how to deal, systematically, with ill-structured problems—problems that involve a number of interrelated factors; and (2) recognize that some problems, and perhaps most "real-life" problems, have multiple answers, none of which may be clearly right or wrong. Few other instructional procedures call for students to deal, simultaneously, with factual data and with ethical and moral values.

The chief disadvantage is the amount of preparation time required. When teachers spend hours preparing materials for lectures, discussions, or contests, they can often use those materials the following year with relatively few changes. However, in problem-based learning, each class of students should be given a new problem. If this is not done, students in a current class might very easily get needed information from students who dealt with the problem earlier and thus short-circuit the learning process. Developing new projects, however, is a time-consuming task. In the long-term, teachers can capitalize on the power of problem-based learning and minimize preparation time by developing a sequence of problems. This enables the teacher to use a different problem each year for four or five years. Another option is to try to arrange for resources as they are needed, but if the project stalls because of a lack of appropriate resources, the teacher will have wasted a lot of student time and enthusiasm. Stepiens has written an informative article concerning ways to engage students by having them take on the roles of scientists, doctors, artists, and historians. It is titled "Problem-Based Learning: As Authentic as It Gets,"[9] and anyone interested in using problem-based learning, as opposed to simply talking about it, is likely to find the article highly useful.

Out-of-Class Assignments/Homework

There are at least four purposes served by out-of-class assignments, or homework:

1. *Helping students acquire new information.* When you assign a section of a book to be read as a basis for a future discussion or ask students to view a particular TV program or videotape, you are asking students to acquire new information. This information can be dealt with during class time, but it is acquired outside of class.

2. *Providing practice in particular skills.* Some skills, such as word processing, solving mathematical problems, and golf swings, can be polished by repeated practice (well, maybe all but the golf swings). It would be a poor use of class time to provide extended periods for such practice, but students can practice out of class.

3. *Giving students practice in long-term planning.* Some assignments, such as term papers and projects requiring correspondence, require a good deal of student planning. The fact that students must plan ahead to achieve the objective is, in itself, a valuable experience. Some teachers see such value in it that they consider it, alone, to be sufficient justification for such assignments.

4. *Providing for student creativity and particular student needs.* In-class activities generally force students to be one of a group and leave little opportunity for them to demonstrate skills unique to them as individuals or to engage in instructional activities they feel are of particular interest to them personally. By working with individuals in planning out-of-class assignments, teachers can do much to make school relevant and interesting.

Despite the strengths of these advantages, there is considerable controversy about out-of-class assignments. Proponents point out that the chief responsibility of students should be to study, and that many valuable educational activities cannot be completed solely within the four walls of a classroom or within usual class meeting times. Opponents argue that many students have neither the time nor the environment in which to do the work. They also point out that once students leave the classroom there is no assurance that they will be the ones actually doing the assignment. Friends, relatives, or parents may do the actual work.

Some research concerning homework was surveyed in "Developing Homework Policies. ERIC Digest."[10] It shows that

> "Increased homework time resulted in higher grades for high school seniors of all ability levels. Moreover, through increased study, lower ability students achieved grades commensurate with those of brighter peers."[11]

> "One to two hours of homework a day were associated with the highest levels of reading performance for 13-year-olds. For 17-year-olds, reading performance increased as the amount of time spent on homework increased. Students spending more than two hours a night on homework showed the highest performance levels."[12]

> "Schools that assigned homework frequently showed higher student achievement levels than did schools that made little use of homework."[13]

Few people argue for the abolition of all homework, but some, such as Cooper, report that studies show that "Elementary school students get no academic benefit from home-work—except reading and some basic skills practice—and yet schools require more than ever. High school students studying until dawn probably are wasting their time because there is no academic benefit after two hours a night; for middle-schoolers, 1 1/2 hours."[14]

Clearly, the research concerning homework is inconclusive, but the arguments for reasonable out-of-class assignments are both logical and reasonable. Students who complete meaningful out-of-class assignments benefit from them. The following steps will help make such assignments effective.

For frequently assigned work such as reading assignments or answering specific questions, assignments can be written on the chalkboard, preferably in an area of the board reserved for this purpose. Students quickly learn to check the board for new assignments, and they can copy them down at any time during the period. If the assignment is unique or not clear-cut, it is better to provide each student with a handout that details the assignment and the grading criteria. Students should know what qualities are associated with each grade, *D* through *A*. Soliciting and answering questions about the assignment should provide further clarification.

If the assignment is long-term in nature, a due date should be established, with point penalties detailed for work turned in after that date. Students should be encouraged to bring in drafts of partially completed work for periodic appraisal. If the assignment is individualized, the teacher should make sure there is agreement on exactly what is to be done, by when, and what the final product is to be. The teacher can facilitate student accomplishment of out-of-class assignments by making sure that required instructional materials are available. Needed books, magazines, videotapes, and other materials should be placed on reserve in the library.

Make sure that students understand exactly what they are to do and how the assignment will be graded. Some schools have set up telephone accessible databases that enable students or parents to call a number and find out what homework has been assigned. Other schools require that such information be available on-line and have links on their websites for it.

All assignments should be carefully evaluated and promptly returned to students with notations concerning strengths and weaknesses. All teachers, regardless of subject area, are responsible for helping students improve their writing. Therefore, all teachers should point out errors in spelling, punctuation, and grammar in all student work. The careful grading and prompt return of assignments will assure students that their work is important and is being used to help them succeed. Further, the prompt grading of assignments helps the teacher detect students' problems and evaluate the effectiveness of instruction. While it may not be practical to return students' work the day after it is received, it should be returned before students are again asked to make use of the skills and knowledge they practiced. They need the benefit of your feedback to avoid making mistakes a second time. To make it more likely that assignments of three or more pages can be returned promptly, it is useful to schedule due dates at the end of the week. This gives the teacher the weekend to grade the papers.

Some teachers, fearing that students will not complete homework assignments at home, allocate class time to work on assignments. While it might be reasonable to have students start assignments during class time, particularly if the assignment involves procedures or concepts that might be difficult for students to understand, it also has a major drawback. If teachers complain, on one hand, that there is never enough instructional time to accomplish what needs to be accomplished, it is difficult to justify using very much, if any, of that time having students do things that they should be doing at home. For example, if something is to be read. If you use class time for that reading, there will be that much less class time available to discuss and analyze what was read. One way to induce students to do homework is to have a short, five- or ten-point quiz over it the next day. Tell students that they can use the total of their quiz scores to replace a low grade on a test or paper (more about this when we get to the assessment chapters). A reasonable rule of thumb is that if some work can be done at home, it should be—just do not overdo it.

Individualization

It is likely that even Og, the caveman, realized that individual differences exist, and Plato described how societies could become virtually utopian if they recognized and accommodated individual differences. Schools, however, have always had difficulty implementing the idea. The **Winnetka Plan** was put into practice in 1919 by Carleton Washburne (1890–1968), Superintendent of Schools in Winnetka, Illinois. In the Winnetka Plan, teachers agreed on a set of objectives and then developed self-instructional materials that enabled each student to progress at his or her own rate. Students self-tested themselves prior to being tested by the teacher and moving on to new objectives.[15] In the same year, a similar plan, the **Dalton Plan**, was put into practice by Helen Parkhurst (1887–1973), at an ungraded school for crippled children in Dalton, Massachusetts. It was adopted by a high school in Dalton in 1920.[16]

Neither the Winnetka nor the Dalton plan gained wide acceptance, largely because students were willing to accept the freedom made possible by the individualization and self-pacing, but they were unwilling to accept the responsibility that had to go along with it. Unwilling may be a bit too harsh. It must be remembered that schools have been, and continue to be, highly structured places. Students are not typically given a great many choices and virtually none with respect to when to do certain tasks. Having become accustomed to supervision and guidance by teachers, and the need to meet deadlines, it is not surprising that students put off and/or failed to complete work when freed of the supervision, guidance, and deadlines.

In 1971, educators at Illinois State University experimented with a large-scale, self-paced, competency-based teacher education program called the **Professional Sequence**. As did the Winnetka and Dalton plans, the Professional Sequence seemed like a good idea. Students would complete a series of required and optional self-instructional packages and would demonstrate competencies via written tests, lesson plans, and actual teaching in microteaching and high school classroom settings. Although the ISU educators were familiar with the self-discipline problem inherent in the Winnetka and Dalton plans, they believed that it would not be a problem at the university level. The juniors and seniors in their program would be motivated not only by the prospect of graduation but also by the prospect of teacher certification. They were wrong. Aside from older and married students, an unacceptably large percentage of the students failed to complete the program in a timely manner. It was stopped in the early 1980s and the program returned to the more traditional format of scheduled classes.

Individualization, like peace on earth and good will toward men (and women), is an excellent idea, but it seems impractical in the context of mass education and limited time. Also, there is a difference between a self-paced competency-based program in which the responsibility for progress is on the shoulders of the student, and an individualized approach in which the student's progress is monitored by a teacher, but there are ways to combine both ideas in a limited way.

Self-Instructional Packages

Self-instructional packages are a form of out-of-class assignments that enable teachers to maximize the individualization of instruction. Self-instructional packages are built around specific instructional objectives and include a carefully sequenced set of learning activities that students can complete at their own rates. Such packages are ideal for enrichment activities and for Individualized Education Plans. They typically include the following parts:

1. A brief rationale that explains how the information and/or skills to be learned can be used by the student;
2. One or more precise instructional objectives;
3. A preassessment instrument to help the student identify areas of strength and weakness;
4. Either all the information the student needs to achieve the objective, or references to specific sources of information;

5. Practice exercises; and
6. Specific grading criteria if the objective calls for a paper or similar product, or directions of when and where to take a test if the objective is to be evaluated in that way.

Assuming that effective self-instructional packages are constructed, you need to use them with care. In particular, you need to talk with the prospective user and get his or her agreement to do the work by a certain time. This face-to-face discussion, and the student's willing commitment to do the work, should set the stage for a successful learning experience and for helping the student move toward independence.

Contracts/Portfolios

Another way to individualize instruction to the maximum extent is to use contracts. To do this, you and the student agree on a particular task to be done, a specific timetable, and specific D through A grading criteria. To help ensure that the student makes timely progress, the timetable should include periodic progress checks.

One major advantage to contracts is that students can play the major role in selecting the project, establishing the timetable, and developing the grading scale. They can take a major role in planning their own learning and in making it relevant to their own lives. The major disadvantage is that students, typically, have had very little practice in planning their own learning. Teachers have always selected the topics to be studied and spelled out learning activities. When they are given the opportunity to do these things with little teacher direction, students are lost. They often do not know how or where to begin, and some will be forthright enough to say, "Please, just tell me what to do and I'll do it." Helping students learn to assume increasing control over their own learning and lives should be one of the overall objectives of all teachers, but it does take time and patience.

One increasingly common use for contracts is in the development of student portfolios—compilations of products that show either growth over time, or the student's best efforts academically and creatively. Since students play a major role in establishing the terms of learning contracts, they frequently have a greater commitment to perfecting the product.

One downside of contracts and portfolios is that, because they are highly individualized, the more they are used, the more difficult it becomes to maintain a coherent curriculum with recognizable breadth and depth. Another downside is that as students demonstrate competencies in different ways, it becomes increasingly difficult to assess each student's progress in way that is seen as fair by all students. Everything has a cost.

SUMMARY

Small-group activities usually increase student involvement and interaction. Since the results of small-group work are shared with the entire class, all students benefit from the in-depth work of separate groups. Students can be assigned to small groups heterogeneously, to maximize the interaction among students with differing abilities or interests, or homogeneously, to capitalize on common ability levels or interests. In either case, groups of about four students tend to maximize productivity.

Panel discussions and debates are particularly useful for enabling the class as a whole to benefit from the in-depth work of groups of students. Regardless of how students are assigned to panels or teams, procedures for dealing with students who may not do their share of the work should be discussed. Ultimately, it is your responsibility to evaluate and grade each student.

Role playing can be an effective technique in helping students to increase their awareness of the attitudes and feelings of others. A potential problem in role playing is that students may act out their own feelings or attitudes, or that other students may believe that this is happening. If this happens, long-lasting ill feelings may be generated.

Four cooperative learning strategies were investigated and developed by Robert Slavin. Common to all four are the concepts of team rewards, individual accountability, and equal opportunities for success. Two of the strategies, Student Teams—Achievement Divisions (STAD), and Teams-Games-Tournament (TGT), are particularly useful in grades 6–12.

Problem-based learning is an excellent way to introduce students to the complexities of "real-life" problems. Teachers prepare extensively by identifying an ill-structured problem, exploring the kinds of issues that students are likely to encounter, making sure that appropriate human and other resources are available, and developing enroute tasks to be accomplished by certain times. Students then follow the scientific method in attempting to solve the problem. Problem-solving learning almost always cuts across subject-area lines and, if done properly, requires students to balance factual information with ethical and moral values.

Out-of-class assignments can help students learn. Assignments should be written on the board or given in the form of a handout. It is crucial that students understand exactly what they are to do and exactly how the assignment will be graded. Homework should be returned to students before they are called on to use the skills or knowledge a second time, and feedback concerning content and mechanics should be provided for all assignments.

Self-instructional packages and contracts enable teachers to maximize the individualization of instruction. Self-instructional packages are typically prepared by the teacher and given to students for purposes of enrichment or as part of Individualized Education Plans. Experiences, such as those with the Winnetka and Dalton plans, demonstrate that students often lack the self-discipline to use self-instructional material without close supervision.

Contracts are agreements between a teacher and students concerning exactly what is to be done, by when, and exactly how the product will be evaluated. Since the student plays the major role in planning and carrying out a contract, the result often reflects that student's best efforts. For this reason, the products of contracts are often included in portfolios of the students work.

KEY TERMS, PEOPLE, AND IDEAS

Small-Group Activities
  Heterogeneous
  Homogeneous
Cooperative Learning, Robert Slavin
  Student Teams—Achievement Divisions
  (STAD)
  Teams-Games-Tournaments (TGT)
  Problem-Based Learning

Structured Problems
  Scientific Method, Sir Francis Bacon
  Panel Discussions/Debates
  Role-Playing
Out-of-Class Assignments/Homework
  Winnetka Plan, Dalton Plan
Self-Instructional Packages
  Contracts/Portfolios

QUESTIONS FOR CONSIDERATION

1. How do you plan to deal with the problem of helping students learn to work cooperatively while also helping them prepare for standardized tests that focus exclusively on individual efforts?

2. Assuming that you may want to use some small group activities, what steps do you plan to take to ensure that you are able to assess each student's independent efforts?

ENDNOTES

1   Robert E. Slavin, *Cooperative Learning: Theory, Research, and Practice* (Englewood Cliffs: Prentice-Hall, 1990), 3.

2   Slavin, *Cooperative Learning*, 3–4.

3   Slavin, *Cooperative Learning*, 4.

4   Slavin, *Cooperative Learning*, 4.

5   Alexander Hellemans and Bryan Bunch, *The Timetables of Science* (New York: Simon and Schuster, 1988), 130.

6   William J. Stepien, Shelagh A. Gallagher, and David Workman, "Problem-Based Learning for Traditional and Interdisciplinary Classroom," *Journal for the Education of the Gifted* 16, no. 4 (Summer, 1993): 338–357.

7   Merriam-Webster Online Dictionary, "hypothesis," accessed August 4, 2020, https://www.merriam-webster.com/dictionary/hypothesis.

8   Stepien, Gallagher, and Workman, "Problem-Based Learning for Traditional and Interdisciplinary Classroom."

9   William Stepien, and Shelagh Gallagher, "Problem-Based Learning: As Authentic as It Gets," *Educational Leadership* 50, no. 7 (April 1993): 25–28.

10   Yvonne Eddy, *Developing Homework Policies*, ERIC Digests, 1984, accessed August 5, 2020, https://www.ericdigests.org/pre-921/homework.htm.

11   Timothy Keith, "Time Spent on Homework and High School Grades: A Large-Sample Path Analysis," *Journal of Educational Psychology* 74 (1982): 248–53.

12   Barbara Ward et al., *The Relationship of Students' Academic Achievement to Television Watching, Leisure Time Reading and Homework* (Denver: Education Commission of the States, 1983), 41.

13   Michael Rutter et al., *Fifteen Thousand Hours: Secondary Schools and Their Effects on Children* (Cambridge: Harvard University Press, 1979).

14   Valerie Strauss, As Homework Grows, So Do Arguments Against It, accessed August 10, 2020, http://www.washingtonpost.com/wp-dyn/content/article/2006/09/11/AR2006091100908.html.

15   Carleton W. Washburne and Sidney P. Marland, *Winnetka: The History and Significance of an Educational Experiment* (Englewood Cliffs: Prentice-Hall, 1963). In Saettler, 65.

16   Helen Parkhurst, *Education on the Dalton Plan* (London: G. Bell and Sons, 1922).

CHAPTER 8

Planning Daily Lessons

INTRODUCTION

Few professionals, whether in entertainment, business, politics, sports, or any other field, would willingly go before a group of people without adequate preparation. You, as a professional educator, should not do so either. In teaching, preparation goes from a syllabus, to unit plans, to daily lesson plans. It is the daily plans that enable you to take the overall instructional strategy exemplified in a unit plan and divide it into segments that can be completed in single class periods. Further, lesson plans help ensure that you include all that you intended to include, and that students leave the room with a sense of accomplishment. This chapter will help you learn about some of the basic components of lesson plans, and the steps for writing lesson plans. Such plans will go a long way toward helping you and your students, be successful.

LEARNING OUTCOMES

You will be able, in writing, to:

1. List at least three components of a lesson plan.
2. Given a precise instructional objective, describe at least two instructional activities that are logically associated with the objective and explain how these activities will help students achieve the stated objective.
3. Take a position for or against requiring student teachers to construct daily lesson plans, and in no more than two pages, defend that position by citing relevant facts and using cause-effect reasoning.

4. Construct, for each of three, sequential, lessons of a given time length, a plan no longer than two pages that includes
    (a) a precise instructional objective at the comprehension level or higher;
    (b) the content necessary for students to achieve the objective;
    (c) a variety of instructional activities that explain the steps to be followed in teaching the lesson and which, across the lessons, incorporate both large- and small-group activities as well as a range of mediated instruction; and
    (d) the materials needed other than those normally found in a classroom.

LESSON PLAN COMPONENTS

What goes into a lesson plan is determined, in part, by how experienced the teacher is. For example, beginning teachers are wise to construct a detailed plan. Such plans enable them to list the main points they intend to cover, plan for a variety of activities, and have those activities conclude in time for an appropriate closure and evaluation. More experienced teachers may find that simply listing the objectives and the activities is sufficient. It should be noted that some administrators may require all their teachers to follow a particular lesson plan format. Regardless of its format, if you are a beginning teacher, and if your plan for each lesson includes the components described in this chapter, your instruction is likely to be more effective than if it does not.

State and National Standards

Your lesson plans should be based on state and national learning standards (e.g., Common Core Standards), so it is wise to include the main standard that is the focus of that lesson in the plan. This may be expected by your principal, but even if it is not, including the standard will make it clear that you are basing your instruction on the state standards.

Objectives

The main source of objectives for daily lesson plans should be the list of objectives generated for the course or unit. Since these terminal objectives typically represent fairly complex behaviors, it is likely that each will need to be divided into a series of less complex, enroute, objectives. These will be the day-to-day objectives that help students develop, step-by-step, the needed skills and knowledge.

To be most effective, enroute objectives should be written so that students can clearly see some out-of-class applicability. One way to do this is to focus on concepts and skills rather than on isolated facts, incidents, or literary works. For example, rather than focusing on Herman Melville's *Moby Dick* as a novel in and of itself, focus on Moby Dick as an example of stories that deal with obsession and revenge. Not many students are likely to encounter a white whale in or out of class, but most will encounter feelings of obsession or revenge. A sea-going story written in 1851 can, with the right emphasis, be highly relevant to students today.

When developing enroute objectives it is important to think in terms of the time available for each class period. When people complete a task, whether it is shoveling a driveway, mowing a lawn, dusting a house, or baking a cake, they derive a sense of accomplishment from completing the task. Students are people. If you write enroute objectives so that they can be completed in a single class period, students will be able to walk out of the room feeling that they accomplished something—that they took a small but definite step toward reaching the final goal. That is a good feeling for students to have, and it is within your power to provide it. Students come to your class day by day, so it is wise to plan lessons that can be accomplished day by day.

Sometimes lessons do carry over to a second day. While this is usually less desirable than completing each lesson in a single class period, it is not a fatal flaw. Plans can be made to work in a two-, three-, or even a four-day time frame. However, it should be noted that stopping properly in mid-lesson is easier said than done. Under ideal circumstances, lessons include closure, a summary, review, and at least a sampling of student competence. This kind of lesson provides students with a feeling of accomplishment and serves as an impetus to further learning. Some elements of the ideal lesson will have to be omitted or at least modified if the lesson is carried over to a second day. However, if possible breaking points are built into the plan, and if close track of the time is kept, it is possible to summarize, review, and lay the groundwork for the next day's work at any of the planned stopping points.

Keeping track of time is important in all lessons. If you go off on a tangent, at the end of the period you are likely to find that there are still a few points that need to be covered. Trying to make those last points after the class should be over and half the students are out the door is not recommended. Conversely, teachers who end up with extra time at the end of a lesson are likely to have to deal with the classroom management problems that typically occur when students are not actively engaged in meaningful activities.

When writing objectives, keep in mind that in most lessons it is not practical to each student demonstrate the objective(s). To do so in most cases, each student would have to write something, and this would consume too much time if done daily. An alternative is to call for an oral demonstration. This enables you to randomly call on students to explain a major point or to demonstrate all or part of a skill. While you cannot be sure that the performance of the randomly chosen students accurately reflects the abilities of all other students, it is a reasonable and practical way to sample competence at the end of most lessons.

Content

The content section of a lesson plan should include all the information students need to achieve the objective. This means that all of the needed names, dates, facts, figures, definitions, explanations, cause-effect relationships, and even examples, should be there. There are at least three reasons for making the content section so complete.

First, people often temporarily forget information, even if they know it well. For example, you may have had the experience of being asked for a name or a phone number, not being able to recall it at the time, but then having it spring to mind hours later. It is almost as though your mind continued searching for the name or phone number past the time you needed it and called you back when it was found. When that happens socially it is simply a bit embarrassing and frustrating. If it happens to you in your classroom, it is not only embarrassing; it could lead students to doubt your knowledge. If you have the needed information in the lesson plan, a quick glance at the plan solves the problem.

Second, you are likely to have more than one section of a class. What may happen is that in your first section you will cover all the information you intended to cover. However, in later sections, since you will remember having covered certain points, you may not cover them "again." The problem would become apparent when students in the earlier sections were able to use certain information or skills and students in later sections were unable to do so. Having the content in the plan and following the plan with each section will help avoid this problem.

A third problem concerns substitute teachers. If all goes well, you and your family will remain healthy. Even so, it may become necessary for you to miss a day or two of school and a substitute teacher will be called in. Typically, the substitute teacher will be competent and willing and able to follow well-made lesson plans. Therefore, well-made lesson plans can help minimize the loss of instructional time.

What has just been said concerning completeness should not be misinterpreted. You should not try to write into a lesson plan every single thing that will be covered. You are not writing a script; you are listing highlights to help ensure that crucial points are not forgotten or unintentionally omitted.

To make the content most useful it should be arranged in a word or phrase outline and organized with appropriate headings. The idea is to construct the plan so that you can conduct the lesson smoothly. A word or phrase outline makes it easy to glance down to check a fact or to see that nothing is being omitted. If the plan is too detailed you will end up looking at it so much that students will begin to wonder if you know what you are talking about or if you are just reading material from the plan.

The actual form of the plan will depend on the teaching-learning activities selected. A lecture, for example, is facilitated best by a word or phrase outline of factual information. A discussion moves most smoothly if the plan consists of key statements, examples, and pivotal questions with possible answers. Activities such as demonstrations or experiments can progress smoothly if the content consists of procedural steps and descriptions, whereas art lessons might require limited verbal but extensive visual content, such as slides or pictures. Regardless of the form of the content, it should still contain the minimum data students need to achieve the objective.

Some instructional objectives require that students demonstrate a skill that is not dependent on specific content. For example, suppose the objective calls for students to write a precise instructional objective at each level of the cognitive domain so that each objective builds logically on its predecessor. Aside from the technical information about the structure of precise instructional objectives, the content of the objectives could concern any subject area. Trying to concoct hypothetical content, other than for use as examples, would be pointless. In lessons of this kind, providing the basic factual information and guidelines for practice may be all that is needed.

Instructional Activities

In a lesson, the first thing most teachers must do is to check attendance and report absences. In most states, you are legally responsible for students assigned to your class unless you report that they are absent. This should take no more than a minute. A seating chart may be helpful, and some teachers go so far as to take pictures of their students and put the pictures on the seating chart. Some teachers then allow another minute or two for announcements and/or the collection of homework.

The lesson actually begins with a set induction that lasts a minute or two. A good set induction does more than get the students' attention; a shout or slamming a book on a desktop can do that. A good set induction stimulates interest, actively involves the students, leads logically into the lesson, and again, lasts only a minute or two.

The next step is to communicate the objective. Some teachers simply explain what students will be able to do at the end of the lesson. A better idea is to write the objective on the board and leave it there throughout the period. This makes it easier to refer to the objective throughout the lesson. In either case, the objective should be stated in terms of what students will be able to do, as opposed to what you want. Therefore, rather than say, "At the end of the period I want you to be able to. ..." it would be better to say, "At the end of the period you will be able to. ..." The communication of the objective, and the provision of any needed feedback, should take only a minute or two.

From this point on, the range of activities is limited only by your own creativity. Here is where you choose to lecture or to use small-group activities, to have a discussion or to use videotape, or perhaps, CAI. The activities should facilitate student achievement of the lesson's objective and should include a closure to build bridges to previously learned content and to content yet to come. The evaluation should at least sample the extent to which students have achieved the objective(s).

Use a variety of instructional techniques and activities in each lesson. One way to do this is to divide the class time into three different parts and have a different activity for each part. For example, a math teacher may begin by going over homework problems for the first activity during which students will have an opportunity to correct work and ask and answer questions. The next activity might pertain to introducing new material, and the third activity would provide students the opportunity to practice working with the new material in small groups. With such a variety, students are not likely to get bored.

As each activity is listed, record the estimated time for it in the time column. Since these are estimates, try to avoid blocks of less than three or four minutes (except for the taking of attendance, set induction, and communication of the objective). Be sure to add up the minutes to see that all the available time is accounted for and, conversely, that you have not listed seventy minutes of activities for a fifty-minute period. Beginning teachers tend to overestimate the time needed for various activities and thus end up trying to improvise in order to use up excess time. A safer course of action is to include, on a separate sheet, additional content and activities relevant to the objective. These can be used to fill unexpected free time. It is better to have too much material than not enough.

Evaluation

In the description of instructional activities, one activity should be student demonstration of the stated competence. Because of limited time, oral explanations are often more practical than having each student write or do something. Ultimately each student will need to apply the skills and knowledge to achieve the terminal objectives. The evaluation component should contain space for you to write comments concerning student achievement of the objective, the reaction of the class to particular activities, and possible ways to improve the lesson.

Closure

A lesson should not end because the end-of-period bell rings. It should end because the teacher and students have completed the planned activities. The last of these activities should include linking the information and/or skills just learned to previously learned information and/or experiences and to information and experiences yet to come. This is consistent with the thinking of the field theorists and of educators such as Dewey and Herbart. By linking information to known information, students can make better sense of the whole, and by linking information to information yet to come, you help prepare students to learn more.

Plan B

Since teachers are not superhuman, we cannot control absolutely everything that happens in and out of the classroom. Therefore, it is possible that your lesson plan will have to be altered while you are teaching. For example, a fire drill has been called, a discussion went longer than planned, students did not understand a concept you were teaching, or you were called away from your room for an emergency (another teacher tended to your classroom while you were away, of course). Perhaps part of your lesson just did not work the way you had planned. With any of these, it is a good idea for you to be prepared with alternate ideas for the lesson.

If a lesson has gone too long, you should have some idea of what items can be taken out and covered another day. You may not necessarily want to cut out the last item listed in your lesson. If a lesson ended sooner than you anticipated, you will need to have something for your students to do that is not busy work. Planning for this will help minimize classroom management problems.

This section of your lesson plan should be short, with just one or two sentences of ideas on what to do if a lesson runs too long or too short. Keep it simple and be prepared to use it with whatever worksheets or videos you might need.

Accommodations for Inclusion

Remember that for each lesson you teach, accommodations for inclusion must take place according to IEP standards. As the teacher, you should have copies of your students' IEPs, and if accommodations are called for, you will have to ensure that they are met in your classroom. You could include the accommodations in the activities section of your plan, but it is better to have a separate section with a list of all accommodations needed for your students with IEPs. Listing needed items such as extra time on written work, basic outlines of lectures, or worksheets printed in Braille will help you in the long run as you can verify quickly whether you are prepared.

Materials

It is a good idea to use instructional aids. They help stimulate interest and provide a change of pace. In this section of the lesson plan, list only those materials that will be needed but are not usually in the classroom. For example, do not use time or space to list things such as a whiteboard or an overhead projector if these materials are standard equipment in the room. However, if you need a second overhead projector, a specific DVD, a VCR player, or a large-screen monitor, listing them will remind you to make sure they will be available when needed. Since not all lessons require special materials or equipment, it is not necessary to include this component in every lesson. It is also a good idea to list the overheads and handouts you will need for this particular lesson. You may choose to keep a copy of each with the lesson plan. Also, remember that students can do more than use their eyes and ears. Utilizing the other senses makes lessons all the more interesting. Food is usually welcomed as an instructional aid, but if you use it, be alert to the fact that some students may be diabetic or allergic to some foods.

Sources

Hopefully, you will be teaching for a long time and, logically, you may well want to use a unit or lesson more than once. You will find it easier to modify, extend, or update material if you cite, in standard footnote or endnote format, the sources of your information as you build them into the original plans. Think about the times you wrote term papers, included a particular fact or quote, and then wasted hours trying to find its source because you forgot to document it as you used it. Avoid the problem. Document as you go. Using at least two current sources helps ensure that the information is accurate.

It should be noted that despite the best-made plans, a lesson may still not be successful. You can do your part and even more, but you cannot do the students' part. If they choose not to cooperate, even the best plans will be ineffective. However, students are not fools. They want to be successful, so the surest way to encourage their participation is to show them how the skills and knowledge to be learned will be of practical utility to them, helping them deal with life and problems outside of school. Relevance, relevance, relevance = success, success, success.

Miscellaneous Components

Since lesson plans reflect the needs of the teachers who write them, not all plans have the same components. Virtually all plans include the components described previously, but other components can be added. For example, the date, title of course and/or subject, grade level, and title of the unit can be added, and sections for homework assignments and special announcements can also be added.

Length

Writing lesson plans almost always poses a problem. On one hand, you want plans that are complete enough to function as useful guides. On the other hand, logic and experience will tell you that you that: (1) you will not have time to generate two or three-page plans for each lesson, and (2) long plans are more cumbersome to use than shorter plans. A good rule of thumb is to keep the entire plan to no more than two pages. As you gain more experience, you may find that you can be successful with a plan that consists of the objective and a list of timed activities.

SAMPLE LESSON PLANS

Having examined typical lesson plan components, we will look next at how they might be combined into a lesson plan. The sample plans cover a variety of subject areas and include a variety of formats. All are workable and useful, but they are only samples. Other structural formats are possible for the plans and other learning activities might be equally effective in helping students achieve the same objectives. The comments in parentheses are included to help explain the various components. They would not be included in an actual lesson plan.

Sample: Concept Lesson

Dept.: English

Course: World Literature

Previous Unit: Conflict and Resolution in Greek Drama

This Unit: Character Motivation in Elizabethan Drama

Next Unit: Social Issues in Contemporary Drama

Grade Level: 10

Illinois Learning Standard: Analyze how complex characters (e.g., those with multiple or conflicting motivations) develop over the course of a text, interact with other characters, and advance the plot or develop the theme. (Illinois Learning Standards: English Language Arts (ELA), 2020, https://www.isbe.net/Pages/English-Language-Arts.aspx or https://www.isbe.net/Documents/ela-standards.pdf.)

Objectives

You will be able to orally define terms such as tragedy, tragic flaw, and hubris as they relate to literature and list at least two attributes of a tragic hero.

Content

A. Attributes of a hero

 1. Mythological heroes–Hercules, King Arthur, Joan of Arc; divine origins, great strength, great leaders
 2. Historical heroes–George Washington, Abraham Lincoln, Martin Luther King, Jr.; wisdom, intelligence, dedicated to helping others
 3. Literary heroes–Pony Boy, Harry Potter, Queen Amadala; brave, strong, fearless, fight for the rights of the underdog

B. Define tragedy

 1. Tragedy–a serious drama typically describing a conflict between the protagonist and a superior force (as destiny) and having a sorrowful or disastrous conclusion that excites pity or terror

2. Aristotelian–of or relating to the Greek philosopher Aristotle (384–322 BC) or his philosophy

C. Attributes of a tragic hero–see Tr. 2

1. Hamartia–tragic flaw, sometimes called the character flaw; a flaw in the character of the hero of a tragedy that brings about his downfall; a Greek word

2. Hubris–exaggerated pride or self-confidence often resulting in retribution; a Greek word

Instructional Activities

Minutes

(2)	1.	Take attendance and make any necessary announcements.
(2)	2.	Go over homework, if any, from previous day.
(2)	3.	Begin by showing students a Frodo action figure. Ask for volunteers to tell what they know about Frodo. Ask if Frodo is a hero and ask for specific examples to support their choice.
(2)	4.	Display objectives on Tr. 1 on the overhead projector and discuss.
(2)	5.	Brainstorm attributes of heroes. Write terms and concepts from students on board.
(5)	6.	Distribute Ho. 1 and divide class into four groups. Tell groups that they are to determine if the literary, mythological and historical characters listed on the Ho. classify as heroes and give specific examples to support their choice.
(5)	7.	Ask volunteers to share who they picked as a hero and what attributes heroes should have.
(5)	8.	Ask volunteers to define "tragedy." Discuss "tragedy" as it relates to literature.
(2)	9.	Display Tr. 2 and discuss attributes of tragic hero.
(10)	10.	Distribute Ho. 2 and have previous groups decide if the heroes on Ho. 1 are tragic heroes.
(5)	11.	Ask volunteers to share who they picked as a tragic hero and to give specific examples.
(2)	12.	Close by telling students that the concept of a tragic hero began with Greek drama but that the concept had to be altered for contemporary drama because of our democratic society.
(2)	13.	Evaluate by having students (1) orally define terms such as tragedy, tragic flaw, and hubris as they relate to literature, and (2) orally list at least two attributes of a tragic hero.

Total Minutes (46)

Materials

Frodo action figure, two transparencies, and two handouts

Students with Special Needs: None

Sources

Applebee, Arthur N., et al. *The Language of Literature.* Evanston, IL: McDougal Littell. 2000. pp. 682–793.

Meyer, Michael. *The Bedford Introduction to Literature.* Boston: Bedford/St. Martin's. 2005. pp. 115–120.

If there is additional time …

Content

- Attributes of a villain

1. Antagonist—one that opposes another esp. in combat
2. Foil—one that serves as a contrast to another
3. Villain—a scoundrel in a story or play

Instructional Activities

Minutes

(5)	1.	Write the word "antagonist" and tell students that the character who tries to stop the hero is called the antagonist, or sometimes the "villain" or "foil."
(10)	2.	Have students return to their groups or divide them into new groups. Ask groups to determine the antagonist of each of the heroes on Ho. 1.

Total Minutes (15)

Note: Used with the permission of John B. Thompson

Appropriate Preparation

Appropriate preparation is one of the most important components of effective teaching. Lesson plans demonstrate that planning. The following checklist includes the components that will help make a lesson plan a useful document.

I. Objective
   a. Clearly specifies an observable terminal behavior and a minimum acceptable standard
   b. Is relevant to students and has some practical or long-term usefulness

II. Content
   a. Contains accurate information and, where appropriate, examples and anecdotes
   b. Goes beyond what is in the students' text and beyond the superficial
   c. Is complete enough to enable students to achieve the objective and for a reasonably competent substitute teacher to teach the lesson
   d. Arranged in a word or phrase outline format
   e. Enough content for the length of the lesson (and a bit more)
III. Learning activities provide for
   a. An appropriate set induction and the communication of the objective
   b. Stimulus variation with respect to modes of presentation (lecture, discussion, etc.) and the appropriate use of media
   c. Practice—analogous and/or equivalent
   d. Review—main points provided by students, not the teacher
   e. Closure—builds bridges to content learned earlier and to content or experiences yet to come
   f. Evaluation—Should parallel objective(s)
IV. Materials: Includes all materials needed for the lesson except those normally in the classroom

SUMMARY

No single thing can guarantee your success in the classroom, but planning and implementing relevant and interesting lessons is, without a doubt, a critical factor in your success and in the success of your students. Good plans benefit you because knowing what you are trying to accomplish and how you intend to accomplish it gives you a sense of confidence. It also demonstrates to your students that you are serious about teaching and are willing to work hard to help them succeed.

The basic elements of a lesson plan include: (1) a state standard, (2) one or more precise instructional objectives that are relevant to students' lives and to the state standard, (3) content needed by students to achieve the objective(s), (4) three or more instructional activities, (5) evaluation, (6) provision for closure, (7) materials, (8) accommodations for students with special needs, and (9) sources.

Good plans benefit students because in most cases you will be able to follow your plans as written and students will engage in a sequence of activities that are logically linked and they will leave the room with a feeling of accomplishment. As long as students feel they are making progress toward a goal that is relevant to them (you will want to revisit the relevance issue with them repeatedly), they will cooperate in the teaching-learning process. If they do that, both you and they will be successful.

A short-term advantage to lesson plans for a student teacher or a beginning teacher is that you can demonstrate your intention to act professionally by bringing well-constructed plans to your cooperating teacher or principal. Since these are the people who will be evaluating you, getting their input and acting on it can help improve your teaching and your ratings.

QUESTIONS FOR CONSIDERATION

1. Why do you think that assigning approximate times to activities in a lesson plan is or is not worth the time that it takes?
2. How can lesson plans play an important role in self-improvement?

CHAPTER 9

Principles of Preparing and Administering Tests

INTRODUCTION

The main reason teachers evaluate students is to determine the extent to which those students have achieved specific instructional objectives. This information helps students identify areas of strength and weakness and gives them a basis for comparing their abilities to those of other students. The information also provides a basis on which teachers can assess the effectiveness of particular instructional procedures and materials. Further, the data are used by students, parents, other teachers, admissions officers, and employers to make decisions about educational and vocational options. For all of these reasons, evaluation that is as accurate and unbiased as possible is needed.

This chapter begins with a review of the purposes of assessment and examines some of the basic principles and terminology related to measurement and evaluation. Its main focus is on ways to prepare objective and subjective tests, administer such tests, and use alternate forms of evaluation. Since the grades students get are the most frequent cause for student and parent concern and since grades are determined based on students' performance on tests, this chapter and the following chapter that focuses on calculating and interpreting grades, should be of particular interest to you.

LEARNING OUTCOMES

You will be able, in writing, to:

1. Define terms such as measurement, evaluation, reliability, validity, objective, and subjective as they apply to measurement and evaluation.

2. Explain how criterion-referenced and norm-referenced evaluation differ and cite at least one example of how each could be used in your subject area.
3. Construct a multiple-choice test that (1) samples the content included in an instructional unit; (2) consists of six questions, each with four choices; (3) includes two analysis-level questions; and (4) meets the criteria for questions as described in typical texts that deal with measurement and evaluation.
4. Construct a one-item essay test that (1) samples the content included in an instructional unit; (2) asks a question at the analysis or synthesis level; (3) includes content-based, *D–A* grading criteria; and (4) includes a model answer.
5. Develop an evaluation procedure that assesses student achievement with a method other than an objective or essay test, and includes the specific criteria by which grades of *A–F* could be objectively determined.

BASIC TERMINOLOGY
Test

In this discussion, the word test means to sample student abilities. It is essential to recognize that even under ideal circumstances, tests are not perfect instruments and that at any given time, students may have health or emotional problems that will keep them from doing as well as they might otherwise. Although we might be able to carry out grade calculations to twenty decimal places, we are still dealing with samples of abilities, not absolute measures. With different questions, or even the same questions but a different day, the sample results might be very different.

Measurement

There is a difference between measurement and evaluation. Measurement has to do with quantifying something by assigning numbers to it. We measure height and weight, but even here, the measures are not exact. Given the fact that educators are trying to assess a complex mix of skills and knowledge, it should not be surprising that the tests, papers, and projects that make up our measurement tools are relatively imprecise. This means that we must engage in evaluation as well as measurement.

Evaluation

Evaluation means making a value judgment. To be as accurate as possible, a value judgment should be based in part on whatever measurement data are available, but it should go beyond that data to include assessments about such factors as the student's ability to write and speak effectively, to organize ideas clearly, and similar qualities that defy simple quantification. Evaluations are more holistic assessments than are measurements.

Validity

Neither measurement nor evaluation makes much sense unless we measure and evaluate the right thing. Validity refers to how accurately an instrument measures whatever it is supposed to measure. There are at least three kinds of validity to consider.

Content or face validity reflects the extent to which a test covers what was taught—not what the syllabus or objectives called for, but what was actually taught (hopefully, there will be a perfect match). Teachers sometimes construct tests that seem to cover the content taught but, in fact, do not. For example, if the instruction focused on developing understandings of trends and issues, the test should give students the opportunity to demonstrate their understanding of those trends and issues. If the test focused on specific names and dates, or the grammatical correctness of responses, its content validity would be low.

Predictive validity measures how well performance on one test or task reflects probable performance on other tests or task. For example, the ACT and SAT college entrance exams are given because they provide some insight into the probable success of students in college. Performance on the test is used to predict performance in college. Preassessment tests sometimes have high predictive validity.

Construct validity has to do with the ability of a test to assess psychological constructs such as honesty or tolerance. Teachers do not usually deal with construct validity, but it is useful to know the term because some standardized tests, such as those used by many government agencies and large companies, assess psychological constructs.

Reliability

Reliability refers to how consistently an instrument measures whatever it measures. It refers to the test results, not to the instrument itself. To the extent that the results are reliable, the relative positions of scores will remain the same on repeated administrations of the test or on the administration of an equivalent form of the test. Students who score high on one form will score high on an equivalent form. If the results are not reliable, students who score high on one form may score low on an equivalent form. If you administered a senior-level trigonometry test to a group of freshmen in an English class, the scores would probably be low. They would be just as low if you then administered an equivalent form of the test. The content validity of these tests would be zero, because they did not test what was taught. The reliability, however, would be high because the relative positions of the grades on each form of the test would likely stay the same.

The degree to which a test is reliable is expressed as a decimal known as a **reliability coefficient**. These coefficients range from the highest degree of reliability (1.00) to the lowest (.00). It is also possible for a test to have a negative reliability coefficient, possibly as low as minus 1.00. This would indicate that those students who scored highest on one measure scored lowest on the other. Reliability coefficients of .65 and higher are desirable.

Generally, longer tests are more reliable than shorter tests. For example, commercially available tests, such as college entrance exams and standardized achievement tests, frequently have hundreds of items and require hours to complete. Their length contributes to their reliability: many questions mean it is unlikely the test will miss large areas of the student's relevant skills or knowledge. If the student took an equivalent form of the test, the same skills and abilities would be assessed, and the score would be close to the previous score unless new skills or abilities were acquired between tests.

Because long tests are time-consuming, teacher-made tests usually do not consist of hundreds of items. A test of about fifty items is long enough to yield reliable results and is not too long for students to complete within a class period. When planning a multiple-choice test, teachers should allow about thirty seconds for each four-choice item. A fifty-item test should take about twenty-five minutes to complete. Since time is needed to take attendance, make announcements, and distribute and collect the test, more time is needed. In order to allow students as much time as possible to recall and apply their skills and knowledge, a full class period should be used for a major test.

The same factors that make longer tests more reliable than shorter ones apply to semester grades. Teachers who use a variety of performance samples including tests, papers, and projects to assess students' abilities can justifiably have more confidence in the reliability of their grades than can teachers who rely on a mid-term and final exam plus a paper or two.

A word needs to be said here concerning grading on the basis of improvement. Some teachers believe that it is appropriate to grade students on the amount of progress they personally made, regardless of whether stated objectives were actually achieved. An example might be for a physical education teacher to ask students to run the fifty-yard dash or do push-ups at the beginning of the semester and tell them that their final grade will depend on the extent of their improvement. Most students will quickly see that it is to their advantage to do poorly at the outset so that at the end of the semester, it will seem as though they made large gains. The reliability of this measurement technique is not high.

Criterion-Referenced Evaluation

Criterion-referencing means that the grade reflects performance relative to some preset standard. A passing grade means that the standard has been met; a failing grade means that the standard has not been met. For example, the minimum acceptable standard of a precise instructional objective spells out what constitutes a D-level demonstration of a particular ability, assuming that D represents the lowest passing grade. A driving test is an example of a criterion-referenced test. As long as you pass, it does not matter if you get the lowest passing grade or 100 percent.

Since the scores on a criterion-referenced test are either pass or fail, all the items should be about equally difficult. Differences in difficulty levels would be necessary if a spread among scores were needed, but none is. Students either pass or fail the test and, if the instruction was successful, many more students will pass than will fail. Beyond knowing if a score was above or below the minimum passing grade, the exact score does not matter.

The most common applications of criterion-referencing are those in which cut-off scores are established for such things as competence tests and entrance tests. A certain score must be obtained in order to move on or to be considered for admission. Most other forms of evaluation are norm-referenced.

Mastery Learning

Mastery learning is a way of using a criterion-reference point. That point is a specified level of mastery. In its "pure" form, mastery learning requires that, instead of holding time stable and allowing achievement to vary within the fixed time span, achievement is held stable, and time is extended until the student reaches the desired level of mastery. There are, obviously, practical difficulties in implementing mastery learning in its "pure" form. However, teachers can use the idea of mastery in the traditional time-stable, achievement-varies framework.

In the normal course of affairs, students do an assignment, it is graded, returned, and everyone moves on to the next topic. To the extent that time allows, you can help students improve their levels of mastery and, at the same time, you can make it possible for them to improve their grades. You can do this by letting them redo the assignment and averaging the original grade with the grade on the redone work. While this process does not guarantee mastery, it has a number of advantages.

The most obvious advantage is that if students redo the work, taking advantage of the feedback you provided on the original work, their degree of mastery will increase. Secondly, the averaged grade will be higher than the original grade (if, for some reason it is not, let the student keep the original grade), so the student's semester average will be higher than it might otherwise have been. Finally, and most important, you are giving the students the opportunity to put forth additional effort to help themselves. If, at the end of the semester, some students are not doing well, and if those students did not take advantage of opportunities to redo work, they will find it difficult to blame anyone but themselves for their grades. The opportunity to redo work helps make students more accountable for their own actions. It is a good idea, even if your workload does not permit its use for all assignments.

Norm-Referenced Evaluation

Norm-referencing means that the grade reflects performance relative to the performance of some norming group. A norming group is a group of people who have some relevant characteristic in common, such as grade level or age. The students in a class constitute a small norming group, whereas all high school seniors who take a college entrance examination constitute a large norming group.

Since our society is basically competitive, teachers need data that allows them to rank-order students according to abilities. It is not enough to separate students according to those who can and cannot do something. Finer distinctions are needed, and norm-referenced evaluation provides them. To rank-order students in terms of demonstrated abilities, the teacher must create test items of varying difficulty levels so that differing ability levels can be assessed.

Although norm-referenced tests require items of varying levels of difficulty, they do not require trick questions or questions that deal with trivial points. Most students prefer to do well, rather than poorly, on tests and are willing to study to do so. Their desire to do well will be lessened if the instruction focuses on important skills and ideas but the test includes questions that focus on relatively unimportant points. Students can make a serious attempt to learn important skills and information, but they cannot learn every possible bit of information. What follows are some principles that can help teachers develop effective tests.

BASIC PRINCIPLES OF ASSESSMENT AND EVALUATION
Obtain Enough Samples

Students need feedback in order to identify strengths and weaknesses and the more feedback you provide, the more students are able to correct mistakes and achieve the objectives. On the other hand, it is not practical to test every day and, even if it were, too much testing sends the wrong message to students. It tells them that grades, per se, are all-important. A balance is needed.

Students should not have to go more than a week without feedback concerning their progress. This feedback may take the form of grades on a formal test or paper, comments written on homework assignments, or comments made to individuals during class discussions. The behaviors called for in the objectives dictate the kinds of activities in which students will need to engage and the most appropriate forms of feedback about progress. Since the purpose of the feedback is to help students form or shape their abilities in order to demonstrate specific objectives, evaluations carried out during instruction are known as **formative assessment**. Evaluation carried out at the end of the instructional unit is called **summative assessment**—it sums up the skills and knowledge included in the unit.

Obtain Different Kinds of Samples

At the end of each grading period and at the end of each semester or year teachers are required to give each student a grade—a single letter to represent the achievements of weeks and weeks of work. That grade should reflect the student's achievements as accurately as possible. Some of the achievements might be assessed via objective tests such as multiple-choice or matching tests. Other objectives will require students to use skills and knowledge in more creative and holistic ways. To assess achievement of these objectives, teachers use essay tests, papers, and projects of one kind or another. The point is that the accurate assessment of students' achievements requires the use of a variety of assessment techniques.

Another reason to vary assessment techniques is that students respond to assessment instruments in different ways. For example, some students take objective tests well while others "freeze up" on such tests. Some students write well, while others are more adept at demonstrating their knowledge orally. Still others are better at completing projects that require the utilization of knowledge, such as constructing a tape-slide sequence or manipulating a hypothetical stock portfolio. If only one or two assessment techniques are used, the real extent to which students have mastered skills and knowledge may be masked by their reaction to the assessment mode itself. A variety of assessment techniques is needed.

Drop the Lowest Grade

There is another advantage to frequent assessments. They make it possible to drop a low grade. Tests only sample skills or knowledge and these samples can be flawed by factors such as less-than-perfect test items or a student's health when the test was taken. If you have ten or more samples of each student's skills and knowledge, you can afford to drop the lowest grade. Dropping the lowest grade will not seriously distort a student's achievement pattern, but it will help minimize the effects of a low score, regardless of the reason for that score. Knowing that the lowest grade will be dropped acts as an incentive for students to continue working, despite the low grade. They know that their averages can always be improved and, just as important, they know that even though you did not have to do it, you did something extra to help them succeed. An alternative to dropping a grade outright is to allow students to replace a low grade on a test or paper with the grade on some optional activity such as their grade on a self-instructional package.

Assess Student Effort

The issue of student effort is one that troubles many teachers. On one hand, it is necessary to have students' grades reflect their actual achievements. On the other hand, it does not make good sense for teachers to ignore honest effort of the part of students even if it does not translate into adequate achievement levels. One way to reflect effort and attitude is to report them in supplementary comments. This may help students' morale, but it will not help their grade.

Another approach is to provide a way for students to earn points by demonstrating effort. For this technique to work, students must be able to demonstrate extra effort as opposed to additional content-area work or greater ability. The difference is significant. Students who are not doing well in your class are not likely to be able to do additional content-area work or demonstrate greater ability. The reason they are not doing well in the first place is because they are having difficulty with the content and tasks already required. Make it possible for them to earn extra credit by doing things they can do.

One way to do this is to award extra points, perhaps five, for every paper that is turned in with no spelling, punctuation, or grammatical errors. These errors most often reflect carelessness rather than lack of ability, so students could earn the extra points by simply taking the time to carefully proofread their work. Whatever extra credit work is available must, in fairness, be available to all students. Do not inadvertently structure it so that only the better students can take advantage of it.

In order to keep achievement and effort points separate, the points for effort should *not* be added to the grade for the paper. They should be reflected by a separate notation on the paper. If a student got 75 points out of 100 for achievement and the full 5 points for effort, the grade on the paper should appear as 75/100 +5. Use a separate column in the grade book to keep track of the extra points each student accumulates. Since all students have the same opportunity to acquire the extra credit points and the awarding of those points is objective, the total number of points each one earns is a fair measure of effort demonstrated.

Use Quizzes

For purposes of this discussion, quizzes are short tests, usually consisting of one to ten questions, which students complete in less than ten minutes. In an ideal world, all of your students would come to class every day prepared for the work at hand. Since we do not live in an ideal world, it is possible that some of your students will choose to attend to other matters rather than preparing for your class. You do not have to like this situation, but you do have to recognize it and deal with it.

One way to encourage students to prepare for your class is to build into your syllabus, and announce on the first day of class, that a short quiz will be administered at the beginning of each class period. The point value of each quiz will be small, perhaps just five or ten points, but the fact that students know they will be taking the quiz may act as an incentive for them to prepare.

Some teachers prefer to use surprise quizzes. The possible use of such quizzes should be included in the syllabus. During the discussion of the syllabus, students can be told that the surprise quizzes are a kind of Damoclean sword. Since the possibility of a surprise quiz is always there, it is wisest for them to come to class prepared every day.

Whether announced or surprise quizzes are used, you can increase their incentive value by dropping the lowest quiz grade and/or by allowing the sum of the quiz points to substitute for a low grade on a test or paper. Your interest is not so much in the quiz grades themselves as it is in encouraging students to come to class prepared.

Paper and Pencil Tests

Paper and pencil tests are not the only kind of assessment instruments that teachers should use, but they will probably be the most common. There are three basic reasons for this. First, paper and pencil tests present the same task to all students under the same test conditions. This means that the test results provide a reasonable basis for sampling and comparing student progress and/or ability with respect to the relevant skills and knowledge. Second, paper and pencil tests generate products (students' responses) that are easily stored. This means that the tests and the results can be kept readily accessible for analysis or review either to improve the test or to explain to students or parents how a grade was determined. Third, paper and pencil tests can be used equally well to broadly sample students' knowledge or to probe deeply into particular areas.

Objective Tests

Questions that require true-false, multiple-choice, matching, or completion answers are called forced-choice or "objective" tests. They are forced choice because students are forced to select or construct responses from a given or very limited range of options. They are "objective" only in the sense that there is no need to make value judgments about the answers. They are clearly either right or wrong. There are, however, many value judgments made during the construction of objective tests. For example, it is the teacher who decides which questions to ask, how many questions to ask, and what vocabulary to use. These judgments are largely value or subjective judgments.

Objective tests are popular for a number of reasons. First, such tests are intended to sample broadly, but not deeply. Rather than asking one or two questions, which might be the "wrong" questions for some students, objective tests ask many questions about different aspects of the topic, thus sampling students' knowledge more broadly. The typical analogy is to compare objective tests with digging post holes in a field. You dig a lot of holes, but none are very deep. By contrast, essay tests are analogous to digging wells; they are few, but they are deep. Further, objective tests are easy to score and they lend themselves well to item analyses, so teachers can continually improve items and develop a test bank of valid and reliable questions.

Objectives tests encourage students to focus on and organize pieces of information rather than focusing on the whole. This could result in students knowing isolated facts but having little idea of the relationship of those facts to each other or to the whole. This problem can be minimized or avoided by writing questions that require students to use information rather than simply recall it. For example, rather than asking a series of questions that require the recollection of the amount of cholesterol in various foods, ask a question in which students look at two recipes and determine which one contains the least cholesterol. Here they use information in a practical way, rather than simply recalling it.

General Rules

What follow are some general rules that can guide the construction of good objective test items.

I.   *Keep the objective clearly in mind.* For example, a terminal objective might call for students to recall and apply information concerning educational philosophies, the goals of education, learning theories, instructional models, and the structure and classification of objectives well enough to answer correctly at least sixty percent of a series of multiple-choice questions concerning these topics. If so, be sure all questions relate directly to one or other parts of the objective.

II. *Keep the language simple.* Unless the purpose of the test is to survey the extent of students' vocabularies, there is no point in using unfamiliar words or phrasing questions in a way that is difficult to understand. Students will be justifiably angry and frustrated if they get answers wrong because they did not understand what was being asked rather than because they did not know the right answer. Compare the following two examples:

1a. The physical relationship between most petroleum products and most purely aqueous solutions is generally such that physical interaction and diffusion of the two is severely limited. (A) True (B) False

1b. As a general rule, oil and water do not mix. (A) True (B) False

It should be noted that it *is* appropriate to expect students to become familiar with the jargon associated with particular subject areas. It would be unfortunate, for example, if a chemistry student kept visualizing little furry creatures every time the instructor mentioned the word mole (a unit of measurement in chemistry). However, there is a difference between using appropriate jargon and using overly complex or unfamiliar words and phrases. Ask questions as simply and concisely as possible to help ensure valid and reliable test results.

III. *Ask students to apply, rather than to simply recall, information.* If students can apply the information they learned, it is likely that they have committed it to memory. It does not follow, however, that because students have memorized information, they can also apply it. This being the case, it is better to write questions at the application level than at the knowledge level. Consider the following examples:

2a. The area of a rectangle is found by multiplying the length by the width.
(A) True, (B) False.

2b. A room 10 feet wide and 12 feet long has an area of 22 square feet.
(A) True, (B) False.

The computation involved in example 2b is not difficult, yet it enables students to apply what they learned and thus emphasizes learning for the sake of practical application rather than learning for the sake of passing tests.

IV. *Make sure that each item is independent.* Check questions to be sure that one question does not provide a clue to some other question or that the answer to one question is not crucial to the answer of another. Both situations decrease the reliability of the test results. For example,

3. The number of square feet in a room 12 feet long and 12 feet wide is
   A. 24.
   B. 48.
   C. 98.
   D. 144.
   E. 240.

4. At $10.00 per square yard, what would it cost to carpet the room described in question three?
   A. $160
   B. $240
   C. $480
   D. $980
   E. $1,440

Given these two questions, any student who answered question three incorrectly would almost certainly answer question four incorrectly. Other than having the student get two items wrong instead of just one, nothing was gained by linking the questions. It would have been more advantageous if questions three and four had been combined, for example, "How much would it cost to carpet a room 14' × 12' *if carpeting costs $10 a square yard?" The extra space could be used for a separate and distinct item.*

V. *Do not establish or follow a pattern for correct responses.* Regardless of how clever an answer pattern is, some student will eventually discover it and compromise the test results. The problems involved with detecting compromised tests and doing something about them are far greater than any possible advantage to patterning responses.

VI. *Do not include trick or trivial questions.* Sometimes teachers are tempted to ask questions that require extended effort for correct interpretation or that deal with unimportant points. This temptation may stem from being unable to build items as quickly as one would like, or from a desire to ensure a widespread among test scores. When used, trick or trivial questions not only reduce the validity and reliability of tests, but they may have a powerful negative effect if they antagonize students.

VII. *Be sure that there is only one correct or clearly best answer.* When you go over the test with students, they are likely to have questions. You will be able to satisfy most students if you are able to go through items and explain why each wrong answer is, in fact, wrong. However, whether an answer is right or wrong should never come down to your saying, "Because I said so," or "Because that is what it says in the text." You should be able to cite more than one source for specific facts and you should give students the option of bringing in other sources if they believe those sources justify their answer.

VIII. *Avoid trivia.* A test uses valuable instructional time, so use that time to emphasize crucial points. Consider the following.

5a. The first microcomputer was the
   A. Altair 8800.
   B. Apple.
   C. Radio Shack Model I.
   D. Commodore PET.
   E. IBM PC.

5b. The "computer revolution" began when the first fully assembled microcomputers became commercially available in the
   A. early 1960s.
   B. late 1960s.
   C. early 1970s.
   D. late 1970s.
   E. early 1980s.

For most students, knowing that the Altair 8800 was an assemble-it-yourself microcomputer available in 1975 is of less long-term value than knowing that the "computer revolution" began in the late 1970s, when microcomputers first became commercially available. Ask questions that have long-term value.

Multiple-Choice Items

Multiple-choice items are particularly useful because they can sample cognitive skills ranging from simple recall through analysis. The following examples illustrate several levels of cognition that are based on Bloom's *Taxonomy of Educational Objectives, Handbook 1: Cognitive Domain*, which was revised in 2000.

Remember

The purpose of knowledge-level questions is to have students recall information; however, be sure that the information to be recalled is worth remembering. If students are asked to recall information that they perceive as relevant and useful, they are more likely to take the teacher and the course seriously. Consider the following.

A. Knowledge of Specific Facts
    6a. A sodium ion differs from a sodium atom in that it
        A. is an isotope of sodium.
        B. is more reactive.
        C. has a positive charge on its nucleus.
        D. exists only in solution.
        E. has fewer electrons.
    6b. To be at the proper rate of development, a child between the ages of __ should be in the __ stage.
        A. 4 and 9 / realism
        B. 3 and 7 / pre-schematic
        C. 5 and 10 / transitional
        D. 6 and 11 / schematic
        E. 5 and 8 / post-transitional
B. Knowledge of Principles and Generalizations
    6c. If the volume of a given gas is kept constant, the pressure may be diminished by
        A. reducing the temperature.
        B. raising the temperature.
        C. adding heat.
        D. decreasing the density.
        E. increasing the density.

Note: Do not confuse "would" with "should." "Would" implies an opinion and opinions cannot be graded. "Should" implies a correct course of action, and that can be graded.

Understand

The purpose of comprehension-level questions is to have students translate from one symbol system to another, to interpret (put into their own words), or to extrapolate (go beyond the data given). Consider the following.

7. "Milton! Thou shouldst be living at this hour; England hath need of thee; she is a fen of stagnant waters." –Wordsworth. The metaphor, "She is a fen of stagnant waters," indicates that Wordsworth felt England was
    A. largely swampy land.
    B. in a state of turmoil and unrest.
    C. making no progress.
    D. in a generally corrupt condition.

Apply

The purpose of application-level questions is to have students apply skills and knowledge to problems and situations that are new to them. Consider the following.

8a. When a geyser first begins to erupt, hot water overflows the orifice and is followed by a rush of steam mingled with hot water.

The first overflow of hot water aids in the production of steam because
    A. less water needs to be heated.
    B. more water can seep into the fissure from the surrounding rocks.
    C. the higher the pressure, the greater the steam produced.
    D. the lower the pressure, the lower the temperature at which steam is produced.
    E. the water that overflows is necessarily below 212 degrees F in temperature.

See *Taxonomy of Educational Objectives, Handbook I: Cognitive Domain*, pp. 131–143.

8b. The scores on a test were 95, 90, 90, 85, 70, 60, and 0. What is the mode?
    A. 47.5
    B. 70
    C. 81.66
    D. 85
    E. 90

Whenever possible, anticipate the mistakes the student might make. In example 8b, 47.5 is the mean of the highest and lowest scores, 70 is the mean, 81.66 is the mean of the middle three scores, and 85 is the median. The advantage of creating options in this way is that you can use the students' wrong answers to diagnose the source of their difficulty.

Analyze

The purpose of analysis-level questions is to have the student engage in higher-order thinking. This can be done by having the student examine a whole, looking for its constituent elements, for relationships between and among elements, or for organizational patterns. Depending on the objective, the "whole" could be a poem, a musical excerpt, an editorial, a hypothetical situation, a picture, or even a rock sample, but it is necessary that students be given something to examine that requires careful analysis. Further, to help ensure that analysis-level thinking is taking place, it is useful to have the student identify the true state of affairs and why it is the true state of affairs. Consider the following.

9a. Three weeks ago, John came down with the flu from an outbreak at school. He got over it about a week ago, but now his brother Tim has come down with the same viral infection. John would like to visit Tim but is not sure if he should. John should be told

A. not to spend too much time with Tim because his own immune system could be exhausted from fighting the virus the first time.

B. not to visit Tim because his own cells will have stopped producing interferon by now.

C. to visit Tim because his own helper T-cells will remember how to fight the virus properly.

D. to visit Tim because his own red blood cells will remember how to produce a specific kind of interferon that combats the virus.

9b. The Education for All Handicapped Children Act of 1975 (Public Law 94142) requires that all children with disabilities be educated and that they be educated in the least restrictive environment. Which of the following was the most critical assumption made by the drafters of the legislation?

A. That all students would be willing to be in the "least restrictive environment" in order to be in compliance with the law

B. That regular classroom teachers could provide for the needs of disabled students about as well as could the special education teachers

C. That sufficient funds would be available since special education students frequently need special materials

D. That special education teachers were not doing a very good job with their students so the students should be placed in regular classrooms whenever possible

Principles for Writing Multiple-Choice Items

A. *Put as much of the item as possible into the stem.* The stem of a multiple-choice question is the part that asks the question or states the problem. Typically, students read the stem once or twice, but they read the options many more times. You can reduce their reading time, thus allowing more thinking time, if you put most of the reading material in the stem. Further, if the stem does its job properly, it gives the student an idea of what is sought before reading the options. Consider the following.

10a. The term "junk" food
    A. refers to a food that has few essential nutrients but high caloric value.
    B. refers to a food that has neither essential nutrients nor caloric value.
    C. refers to a food that has both high nutritive value and high caloric value.
    D. refers to a food that has both high nutritive value and low caloric value.

10b. The term "junk" food refers to foods that are _____ in nutrients _____ in calories.
    A. *low / but high*
    B. low / and low
    C. high / and high
    D. high / but low

In example 10a, the options contain repetitive words, which not only take students time to read, but might also confuse students. Rather than writing options that contain repetitive words, build those words into the stem where they will only have to be read once.

In example 10b, the options are shorter than the stem (which is, itself, a good guide), and the stem clearly and concisely asks the question while providing sufficient data to help the student start thinking about the correct answer.

B. *Make options plausible.* When testing, you are not trying to trick students, you are trying to differentiate between those who know and those who are pretending to know. You want all options to look reasonable to someone who is unsure of the information. In example eight, you saw how to anticipate the kinds of mistakes students might make and build options on that basis. This can help create plausible options.

You must also take care that students cannot safely ignore options because they are so clearly wrong. Going back to example 10b, you can see that option

D is clearly a wrong choice and will be ignored by students. Something that is high in nutrients and low in calories is not likely to be considered "junk" food. Writing options such as this wastes your time and the students' time.

C. *Beware of Grammatical Clues.* Sometimes teachers point to right answers with inadvertent grammatical clues. For example, the word "an" is almost always followed by a word beginning with a vowel. The word "a" is almost always followed by a word beginning with a consonant. A student who knows this basic rule may be able to use it to identify correct choices or to eliminate incorrect choices. You can avoid the problem by using "a(n)" rather than "a" or "an." Another grammatical clue is the inappropriate use of singular and plural forms of words.

D. *Length may be a clue.* In trying to add enough information to make the right answer right, teachers tend to make that option longer than the others. This, itself, may be a clue to students who are just guessing. Check to be sure that all options are about the same length.

E. *Avoid "always" and "never."* It is safest to operate on the premise that there is likely to be an exception to every rule. This being the case, there is little reason to use "always" or "never." Students are generally safe ignoring options that specify "always" or "never," and they know it. Those word constitute an unintentional clue.

F. *Use "all of the above," and "none of the above" with care.* The use of "all of the above," is weak because as soon as students see any two correct answers, they know that "all of the above" must be the correct choice. The use of "none of the above" is sometimes useful to see if students have confidence in their knowledge. For instance, in example eight the correct answer (E), could have been replaced with "none of the above." Students who knew what the mode was, would recognize that it was not listed. Students who were unsure would likely go back and select one of the wrong choices.

G. *Focus on the rule rather than the exception to the rule.* When students study for a test they try to learn the true state of affairs: what is, rather than what is not. When writing questions, write them so they call for the true state of affairs rather than for the exception. Consider the following.

11a. Which of the following are NOT parts of a central processing unit?

    A. RAM units

    B. Resistors

    C. And/or gates

    D. Transistors

11b. Which of the following is part of a central processing unit?

    A. RAM

    B. A monitor

    C. And/or gates

    D. A keyboard or other input device

If it is necessary to use a negative, be sure to call attention to it by capitalizing it. Students will be looking for what is rather than the exception. Help them notice the change in focus or, better yet, reword the question so the negative is eliminated.

H. *Check for correct spelling and punctuation.* Proofread each question and its choices to make them as easy to read as possible and to eliminate errors. Any time that you make a spelling or grammatical error students are likely to notice, and during a test that distraction wastes time for the students.

If the stem is part of a statement that will be completed by one of the choices, it should end with a colon. A colon must follow an independent clause. In this case, each choice should begin with a lower-case letter and end with a period because the stem, plus the choice, will form a complete sentence.

If the stem is a complete question, it should end with a question mark (for example, "Which of the following best describes a CPU?"). In this case, the choices would begin with capital letters but would not end with periods unless they were complete sentences.

I. *Make "visual packages."* Your intent should be to help students do as well as possible on the test. You can make things a bit easier for students if each question and its options make up an easy-to-read "visual package." After writing the stem, skip a line between it and the choices. This makes it easier for students to separate those components. List choices one under the other on separate lines. This takes more space than listing them on one or two lines, separated by commas, but it makes it easier for students to consider them. Then, be sure to keep entire questions (stem and choices) together on a single page. If there is not room on a page for the stem and all the choices, move the entire question to the following page. This will eliminate the need for students to flip back and forth and will reduce the chance of students missing an option altogether.

True/False Questions

True/false questions are often singled out as prime examples of the superficiality of objective testing, and they often stand justly accused. Superficiality, however, is not an inherent weakness. True/false questions can be written at the comprehension, application, and even analysis levels. Consider the following.

Remember

12. Most high school teachers who use computers for their own preparation work use the computer for word processing. (A) True (B) False

Understand

13. The statement X + Y – Z is the equivalent of Z – Y + X. (A) True (B) False

Apply

14. A man earning $250 a week would earn $13,000 a year if he worked every week. (A) True (B) False

Analyze

15. If every teacher were given his or her own computer, the most difficult problems currently limiting wider use of computer-assisted instruction would be solved. (A) True, (B) False.

   Any superficiality in true/false questions is there because the teacher failed to use the tool properly. However, it is true that students who have no idea of the correct answer still have a one-in-two chance of guessing correctly. Their chance of guessing correctly drops to one-in-four on multiple-choice questions with four questions, and to one-in-five when the questions have five options. Given the 50:50 chance of guessing correctly on true/false test questions, many teachers prefer to use multiple-choice questions. If you do choose to write true/false questions, the following points may help.

   15a. *Be sure that every item is wholly true or wholly false.* Consider the following example.

16. Most high school teachers who use computers for their own preparation work, use the computer for word processing and database management. (A) True, (B) False

   While it is true that most high school teachers who use computers for their own preparation work use them as word processors, it is not true that they also commonly use them for database management. The fact that the statement is partly true and partly false could result in unnecessary arguments.

   16a. *Whenever possible, avoid such terms as "generally" and "usually."* These terms, while not as obvious giveaways as "always" and "never," are still open to varying interpretations.

Matching Items

Matching items are used most easily to measure low-level cognitive skills such as recall and comprehension. A typical matching test might ask students to link people with events or dates. Variations include asking students to match terms with numbers on a diagram or to match labels for a chart, graph, or map in which such labels have been replaced by letters or numbers. Guidelines for the construction of matching items follow.

A. *Keep the number of items to be matched short.* If students are required to search through more than ten or so items as they respond to each question, they will spend valuable time just searching. Their time would be better spent responding to another series of items in another question.

B. *Make sure that all items concern one topic.* Unless all items are concerned with one topic, students can simply eliminate some options as being irrelevant to some questions. This reduces the reliability of the test.

C. *Include more possible answers than questions or stipulate that some answers may be used more than once or not at all.* These steps will minimize the possibility of students arriving at the right answer via the process of elimination.

D. *Arrange the options in some logical order such as chronological or alphabetical.* This will make it easier for students to search through the options and will help avoid providing unintentional clues.

Completion Items

Completion items depend almost entirely on the student's ability to recall a key word or phrase. This poses two problems. First, most secondary school teachers are after more than rote memorization. Second, teachers recognize that many people, particularly while in stressful situations such as a test, have difficulty recalling specific words, names, or dates. For these reasons, completion items are not used as frequently as other kinds of test items. Here are some points to keep in mind if completion items are written.

A. *Write items that can be completed with a single word or a short phrase.* There is a difference between a completion item and an essay exam. When students are required to fill in more than a word or two, the grading of the item is complicated, and it ceases to be a completion item.

B. *Be sure that only one word or phrase can correctly complete the sentence.* In a phrase such as, "The first World War began in _____." either a date or the name of a country could be correct. Guard against this by trying different words or phrases to see if there are correct alternatives. Revise each item until only the word or phrase sought can be used correctly.

C. *Put the blanks near the ends of the sentences so the student is guided toward the correct response.*

D. *Make all the blanks the same length.* Sometimes unintentional clues are provided when teachers try to make the size of the blanks correspond to the size of the word or phrase to be inserted. The items should be clear enough to make this kind of clue unnecessary. Make all blanks the same size—usually five or six spaces.

E.   *Do not put more than two blanks in any item.* The more blanks in the item, the greater the chance the student will be unable to determine just what is sought.

Preparing Tests and Students

Regardless of the type of objective test used, there are some things that teachers can do to help students succeed. First, divide the test into discreet sections and order the sections, and the questions in them, so they reflect the order in which the information was originally presented or learned. This makes it easier to verify that the test reflects the major topics covered and that the number of questions per section is proportional to the amount of time spent on that topic in class. People tend to remember sequences better than isolated facts, so if the test questions follow the same sequence as the original instruction, students will find it easier to remember specifics than if questions about those specifics appear randomly throughout the test.

Second, schedule major tests for a Monday and conduct a formal review session, with the test in hand, on the preceding Friday. The review session helps the students focus on the ideas and information that will be tested. They should be told how many sections and questions are on the test, what each section will cover, how many questions will be in each section, and the type of questions that will be included (multiple-choice, true-false, etc.). They should also be told how many points the test will be worth, how much time they will have for the test, and that they should bring sharpened pencils with erasers, and work to do if they complete the test early. Giving students this information will help reduce their anxiety. There are fewer unknowns.

In going over the information included in each section, teachers should proofread the test again and to be certain that there are no questions on the test that have not been covered in class or in assigned readings. Students may also raise questions that did not occur to them during the course of instruction so these, too, can be answered.

Scheduling tests for the beginning of a week, and reviewing at the end of the previous week, works to the advantage of students because it gives them the weekend to study. All of these steps will help students succeed.

Subjective (Essay) Tests

Essay tests are useful in assessing students' abilities to synthesize and evaluate because they call on students to gather, organize, interpret, and evaluate data, draw conclusions, make inferences, and express their thoughts coherently. However, essay tests are inherently biased in favor of those students who can write quickly, neatly, and effectively. They also take considerably longer to grade than objective tests. Since teachers often deal with about 100 students per day, it should not surprising if more objective, than essay, tests are given. Nonetheless, you are likely to use essay tests at some point and the following principles will help make those tests effective instruments.

Principles for Constructing Essay Tests and Reviewing

A. *Be definite about what is expected from students.* As questions are formulated, keep in mind the types of thought processes in which students are to engage, and the types of points that should be included in their responses. Consider the following.
    17. Discuss the effects of World War ll.
    18. In your opinion, what was reflected by the Republican wins in the House and Senate in 1994?

    Example 17 provides so little direction that students would not be able to formulate precise answers. Some students might concentrate on military effects, others on social effects, others on technological effects. The structure of the question is too broad. Depending upon the teacher's intent, some students would find they had included some of the appropriate information while others would find they had not, even though all might have been able to formulate acceptable answers had they known more precisely what the teacher expected.

    Example 18 presents an even worse problem; it asks for an opinion. Opinions may differ from one another, but that does not make some right and others wrong, regardless of what may have been covered in class or in outside readings. Teachers who ask for opinions should be prepared to award every answer full credit. For example, a perfectly acceptable answer to question 17 might be, "Not much."

B. *Describe the task clearly.* Provide sufficient direction so that if students have the necessary information, they will be able to formulate acceptable answers. Compare the preceding two examples with the following example.
    19. Outbreaks of the flu are an all too common occurrence in schools, offices, and other places where large numbers of people come into daily contact in close quarters. Assuming the environment is reasonably sanitary, explain what factors, other than those listed above, are necessary for a virus to infect a sizable portion of the population. Also explain how a virus of this sort infects individuals, being sure to describe, in order (if there is any), which defenses the host organism will use against the virus and why those defenses will be used.

    Here, the teacher is quite clear about what is expected and has described the task clearly. A student who possesses the requisite information should have little difficulty. A student who does not have that information will find it difficult to write anything that makes much sense.

C. *Specify grading criteria.* Specifying grading criteria is critical because each student's responses must be evaluated with the same yardstick and the stated criteria constitute that yardstick. To construct grading criteria, make a list of the important, points that would have to be included in an answer to earn a grade of D. These are the points that you expect all students to know, so there should be more criteria here than in other grade categories. As the criteria go from D, to C, to B and on to A, they should reflect increasingly complex qualitative, not quantitative differences.

A quantitative difference refers only to differences in number. For example, asking for two of something in the D category, three of those things in the C category, and four in the B category reflects only that the student can recall two, three, or four elements. That, alone, tells you nothing about how well the student understands those elements. For that, qualitative differences are needed.

A qualitative difference refers to the quality of something. It focuses on substantive differences in understanding and/or skill ability. To reflect this, the elements of each grading category should include two three examples of the kind of detail that a student earning that grade would be likely to include. Remember to include the actual details, not allusions to them. In the next category, include examples of the somewhat more complex details that a student earning the next higher grade would be likely to include, etc.

A. Grading criteria should consist of the actual names, dates, facts, definitions, and cause-effect relationships that you would have to see in a student's answer to justify a grade of D, *rather than an allusion to actual content.*

Example of an allusion: Name the three branches of our Federal government.

Example of a good criterion: Name the three branches of our federal government as the legislative, executive, and judicial branches.

B. The *D*-level criteria should include elements reflecting all aspects of the question even though *D*-level students might provide relatively superficial information to some parts or omit some parts altogether.

C. Unless you are teaching a composition course, do *not* include factors such as spelling, punctuation, grammar and organization. It is the responsibility of all teachers to grade all written work on the basis of both content and mechanics, but such factors should be assessed separately. To do otherwise would decrease the validity of the test.

A partial set of grading criteria for question 19 might include the following.

1. To qualify for a grade of *D*, student must explain that
    A. Full-scale outbreaks are possible only if a large portion of the population has never been exposed to the virus.
    B. An individual's first line of defense is the skin and mucous membranes.
    C. At least one secondary line of defense such as phagocytes, helper T-cells, and interferon an individual will use against the virus. Use terminology correctly.
2. To qualify for a grade of *C*, the student must explain the above information and include the following:
    A. The virus must be displaying a lytic life cycle to be contagious.
    B. A correct description of two defenses, after that of the skin and mucous membranes, an individual could use to fight a virus, but not necessarily getting them in the right order.
3. To qualify for a grade of *B*, the student must explain the above information and include the following:
    A. The reason a large part of the population has or has not been exposed to, or has or has not been vaccinated against, the virus.
    B. A detailed description of the phagocyte and antibody defense mechanisms in correct order of activation with an explanation of why each defense is used.
4. To qualify for a grade of *A*, the student must explain the above information and include the following:
    A. A detailed description of the interferon defense mechanism in correct order of activation and a correct explanation of why the defense is used.
    B. Correct identity of the part of the virus's life cycle that the defenses attack.

What follows in example 20 is another essay question that

- requires an answer that goes well beyond the definition of terms and the recollection of sequences of events and instead, requires the assimilation of facts and the demonstration of cause-effect reasoning;
- is a single question rather than a collection of questions;
- is free of superfluous information;
- provides sufficient structure and guidance; and
- should take about twenty minutes for a reasonably able student to answer.

It is followed by good *D–A* criteria.

20. Enzyme activity depends on the integrity of its structure. Explain why factors affect protein structure should affect enzyme activity and how inhibitors act to inhibit enzymatic activity. Draw figure(s) to illustrate if necessary.

Grading Criteria

1. To qualify for a grade of *D*, the essay must:
    A. Define enzyme as protein catalyst that can speed up a reaction but cannot make a reaction happen if it is thermodynamically unfavorable.
    B. Point out that in addition to amino acid sequence that usually defines a peptide, all enzymes have 3-D structure and any change in this structure may result in loss of activity.
    C. Identify at least two factors that can change the 3-D structure such as temperature, pH, or ionic strength.
    D. Define the process of loss of spatial structure as denaturation, the reverse process as renaturation.
    E. Define inhibitors as substances that can specifically inhibit a given enzyme's activity.
2. To qualify for a grade of *C*, the above criteria must be met, and in addition, the student must:
    A. Define activation energy as the energy barrier that a reaction must overcome.
    B. Describe enzyme spatial (3-D) structure correctly as the following: The primary structure as sequence; Secondary structure as a-helix and b-sheets; Tertiary structure as further folding of the first two structures; Quarterly structure as subunits, usually held together with disulfide bonds.
    C. Identify forces that sustain the spatial structure of enzymes as hydrogen bond, disulfide bond and hydrophobic interaction. Forces that interrupt these bonds such as increased temperature are the cause of denaturation.
    D. Define activity center as part of the enzyme's spatial structure where substrate binds specifically.
3. To qualify for a grade of *B*, the above criteria must be met, and in addition, the student must:
    A. Point out coenzyme (vitamins) and cofactors (minerals) as needed for activity too.
    B. Discuss lock-and-key and induced-to-fit models of enzymatic action.
    C. Define competitive and allosteric inhibitors: Inhibitors disrupt access of substrate by direct competition or by changing shape of enzyme so that substrate will not fit.

4. To qualify for a grade of A, the above criteria must be met, and in addition, the student must:
   A. Discuss the formation of enzyme's spatial structure, including post translational modification before leaving cell and role of chaperons.
   B. Discuss thermodynamic aspect of enzyme's high affinity and specificity. Pointing out that when substrates bind or induced to bind, it greatly increased local concentration and reducing energy barrier.
5. Write out a sample A quality answer. This step is helpful in two ways. First, by writing out the response yourself, you get some idea of how long it takes to do the job. You can then use that information, together with your knowledge of the writing abilities of your students (gathered, perhaps, during a preassessment test) to estimate how much time it will take students to answer the question. Second, your answer can serve as a model answer against which each student response can be compared. This will help increase the reliability of your grading. Do this for five or six questions, each similar in complexity to example 20.
6. Review. Reviewing for objective tests makes good sense and so does reviewing for essay tests, but the techniques differ. When reviewing for objective tests, you go over the general content in each section of the test. When reviewing for essay tests, give the students copies of the five or six questions you developed and explain that on the day of the test, you will select two or three questions to be answered. You will have a good idea of how many questions you can expect students to answer because you took the time to write out A-level responses yourself. Consider the advantages of handing out the questions.

First, since students do not know which questions they will be called on to answer, those who intend to be successful will study all the questions. This, in itself, is beneficial since it increases the likelihood of students understanding not only isolated facts, but how those facts relate to one another with respect to five or six central issues or points.

Second, although students do not get copies of the grading criteria, you have the grading criteria in hand so you can go over the main idea in each question. This enables students to identify areas where their knowledge is weak, so they have a better idea of where to focus additional study time.

Third, during the test, students will be expected to first mentally gather and organize data and to then express the relationships among the data clearly, concisely, and in writing, in order to demonstrate their in-depth understanding of some complex whole. This is not an easy task nor is it one for which students have had much practice. Giving them the questions ahead of time allows them, if they wish to do so, to work together and practice the skill. Even though these cooperative efforts are beneficial, they do not happen all that often. You can increase the likelihood of their taking place if you give students the test questions. Keep in mind that the test grades are less important than the learning that should take place as students prepare for the test.

7. Make sure that students have sufficient time and materials to do the job. One of the unique strengths of essay tests is the opportunity they provide for students to analyze relationships among points within a topic or problem and to formulate responses by synthesizing the information they possess. Even if students have the questions beforehand, they need to recall information when they take the test, organize their thoughts, perhaps outline their answer, and then write it legibly. If students are unduly pressed for time, their responses may not reflect their abilities as accurately as they might have otherwise. Writing out model answers and then adding to the time it took you to write out those answers provides a way of estimating how many questions you can reasonably expect students to answer in a given period.

Many teachers find it easier to read responses that are written in ink on lined paper. Responses written in ink is easier to read than those written in pencil because the graphite in the pencil "lead" creates more of a glare, especially under electric light. The lined paper helps ensure that lines of text are reasonably straight. The fact that students cannot erase is offset by the fact that they can cross out. Further, it is a good idea to insist that students identify the number of the question they are answering. This helps avoid misunderstandings later.

8. Compare each response with a model answer. There is a tendency, after grading a few responses, to begin comparing those read later with those read previously. This tendency can be offset by making frequent reference to the model answer(s) that you prepared to estimate the time students would need to write their answers.

9. Grade all responses to each question, then go back and grade all responses to the next question. This procedure solves two problems.

First, it reduces the halo effect: the probability that if a student did an outstanding job on the first question, the grader will evaluate that student's next answer more favorably than if the first answer was wrong or mediocre. The reverse can also happen where a poor first answer causes the grader to be more critical of the student's second answer. Grading all responses to each question avoids the problem.

Second, grading all responses to each question before moving on to the next question enables the grader to see if a significant number of students (perhaps more than one third) missed the same point(s) or misinterpreted something in the same way. The omission or difference will conflict obviously with the grading criteria. If this happens, the most likely explanation is that something was said in class, or appeared in what students read, that was misleading. In this case you would want to adjust the grading since it would not be fair to deduct points for something that might be, at least partially, your fault.

10. Avoid mixing essay items and objective test items on the same test. The intellectual operations required to synthesize a response to an essay item are significantly different from those required to select a response to an objective test item. This mental "shifting of gears" takes time. Of greater importance is the fact that students have no way to adequately judge how much time to spend on each part of such tests. If you want to help students do as well as possible, administer objective and essay tests on different days.

ADMINISTERING TESTS

A. *Help keep the honest students honest.* Tests are stressful situations and, while most people are honest, given enough stress, some may be tempted to cheat in order to pass. If cheating occurs it poses major problems. How can you be sure that student A was, in fact, cheating from student B? Did student B deliberately allow student A to see the answers? If cheating did occur, what should be done? It is a mess, and it makes sense to do what you can to avoid the problem.

When possible, arrange chairs in rows so that there is an empty row of chairs between the rows of students. When students are sitting directly behind one another is it more difficult for them to see another person's answers than if they are sitting side by side.

Actively proctor the test. Rather than grading papers from a previous class or doing other work, keep an eye on the students. Whenever a student looks up, he or she should see your smiling face. Knowing that you are watching will, by itself, help deter cheating.

B. *Number each test and have students record the number on their answer sheet.* This procedure helps ensure that all copies of the tests are returned in their entirety. This, in turn, makes it possible for the teacher to administer the same test to other students and still be reasonably sure that the test is not "out." Further, it is easier to store answer sheets than entire tests. Some teachers go so far as to tell students that points will be deducted if they make any marks on the test, thus further ensuring that the tests can be used with other students.

C. *Do not answer questions after the test has started.* If you recall, when you took your SAT or ACT exam certain procedures were followed to help ensure that all students took the test under as nearly alike conditions as possible. It is a good idea to follow the same procedures when you administer your own tests.

Before the test starts, ask if students have any last-minute questions that arose while they were studying. If they do, answer them even in the unlikely case where one or two might be virtually the same as questions on the test. However, announce that once the test starts, no questions concerning the test will be answered. Students are to interpret and answer each question as best they can.

There are sound reasons for following this procedure. If individual students have questions and you go to them and privately provide additional information, you will be acting unfairly to all the other students. They, too, might benefit from the additional information. However, trying to avoid this unfairness by interrupting the test and calling everyone's attention to the points in question poses its own problems.

Interrupting students during a test destroys their train of thought. This, itself, might cause students to forget an important point and/or put down a wrong answer. Further, enough interruptions could seriously detract from the time students have to think about each question.

A wiser course of action is to take time to go over the test carefully before using it during the review and to go over it again, in your mind, as you review. If any questions need to be revised or any points clarified, you can attend to them prior to duplicating the test. If the test has already been duplicated, any needed corrections or information could be written on the chalkboard and gone over prior to the test. Once the test starts, allow students to work on it without distractions or interruptions.

PERFORMANCE-BASED ASSESSMENT

Properly constructed performance-based assessment (PBA) projects can assess a student's understanding of the topic, their ability to use their knowledge and skills to construct a product, and their ability to make a clear and concise presentation that reflects their knowledge and skill. Not many forms of assessment can do all of those things.

You will be able to

A. Write a mailable one-page letter to a company or politician in which some problem is delineated, a desired course of action is outlined, and supporting rationales for that action are given. ("Mailable" is a business term used to denote a letter that is free from errors in spelling, grammar, punctuation, usage, etc., and ready for signature and mailing.)

B. Given a spreadsheet program, use its various operations and functions to build a grading program that will calculate the mean and median of sets of scores as they are input and continually update the total points earned by each student. Write a brief explanation of the sequence of the steps and of what takes place at each step.

C. Construct a poster approximately 2' x 3' designed to sway people's opinion for or against some controversial issue and describe in less than three pages how each element (such as color, message, design, and figure placement) helps make the poster a powerful communicator.

The elements included as part of the minimum acceptable standards for these objectives spell out the criteria to be used in assessing achievement. To achieve each objective, students must use higher-order thinking skills and, unless students demonstrate these skills, they cannot meet all the criteria. For example, suppose a student wrote the following letter in response to the first objective.

Dear Sir:

I recently purchased a new Doohicky, and it does not work right. Neither the store I purchased it from nor your factory representative accepted responsibility for the Doohicky's malfunction, and now I'm tired of fooling with it and want a refund. Unless I get the refund within two weeks, I will turn the issue over to my attorney.

Sincerely yours,

This letter contains all the elements suggested in the objective, but its lack of specifics and its tone leave much to be desired. What can be done?

The following steps may be useful as you think about constructing a performance-based assessment project.

1. Identify a relevant state standard and then state a precise objective for a component of the project. The following is an example of objectives for a performance-based assessment instrument. After choosing one of the seven biomes,
    a. compare the physical, ecological, and behavioral factors that influence interactions and interdependence of organisms in a three- to six-page reflection paper;
    b. create a PowerPoint presentation consisting of a minimum of eight, but no more than fifteen slides that demonstrate appropriate technical skills such as the dimming of points and the use of graphics; and
    c. present the research to your fellow classmates in an oral presentation that demonstrates appropriate skills such as maintaining eye contact and proper speech.
2. Construct a three-part description of the project. The use of the following headings is recommended.

a. Understanding the Topic. Under this heading provide an overview of the kinds of knowledge and skills that should be demonstrated and the salient points that should be included. Cite some sources to which students can turn for relevant information. Specific criteria concerning this skill area should be included in the Understanding the Topic section of the rubric.

b. Product. Under this heading provide an overview of the technical qualities expected of the product. For example, if PowerPoint slides are expected, and some slides have multiple points, one criterion might be whether one point was dimmed before the next point was revealed. If the product is a poster, one criterion might focus on the extent to which the lettering is appropriate. Specific criteria concerning this skill area should be included in the Product section of the rubric.

c. Presentation. Under this heading provide an overview of the presentation skills expected. These might include, but are not limited to, such things as maintaining eye contact, not reading from or talking to a screen or board, and not using slang or street language. Specific criteria concerning this skill area should be included in the Presentation section of the rubric.

3. Specify additional requirements. For example, you might want to require that as the students work, they present their work to you periodically, typically once a week, so that you can assess their progress. This also helps ensure that students are doing their own work. If the project requires the use of materials that students must acquire on their own, you might want to set limits on the amount of money that can be spent so that students with more money do not have an unfair advantage over students with less.

4. When possible, provide a model. Models are helpful from a number of standpoints. Regardless of how explicitly written the criteria are, seeing an actual product will help students more clearly understand what is expected. This understanding is further clarified if both good and bad models are provided, and explanations of why they are good and bad are included. By using written models, audio tapes, DVDs, and/or three-dimensional products, you can provide models for virtually every kind of behavior or product students are expected to produce.

5. Create a rubric. A rubric is, typically, a tabular grading scale with cells that reflect level of performance. Each cell of the rubric must contain factors that qualitatively (as opposed to quantitatively) differentiate one level of performance from another.

As was the case with the grading criteria for essay tests, the rubric for a performance-based assessment project should focus on qualitative rather than quantitative differences in answer quality. Qualitative differences focus on substantive differences in understanding and/or skill ability. To reflect this in the rubric, in the first cell in a given row, include two three examples of the kind of detail that an *A* student would be likely to include. Remember to include the actual details, not allusions to them. In the next cell, include examples of the somewhat less complex details that a *B* student would be likely to include, etc. Qualitative standards are more appropriate than quantitative standards for performance-based rubrics.

It is recommended that you divide your rubric into sections labeled Understanding the Topic, Quality of the Product, and Quality of the Presentation. In the Understanding the Topic section, include criteria that focus on the extent to which the student has demonstrated an understanding of relevant principles, practices, and concepts. Examples of factors that might reflect differences in grades include, but are not limited to, such things as accuracy, the ability to select relevant points, the ability to apply the information in a unique way, completeness, and the quality of the sources of information.

In the Quality of the Product section, describe what is to be produced. In many cases, performance-based projects result in a product such as a poster, PowerPoint presentation, model, diorama, or series of overhead projections. In each case, there is a range of expertise used to construct the product. It is this range that will be the basis for the criteria for this section. For example, in the case of posters, factors that might reflect differences in ability levels include, but are not limited to, such things as the extent to which lettering is properly sized and legible, the use of colors that are appropriate to the topic, and the extent to which elements on the poster are balanced and contribute the unity of the whole. In the case of projected presentations, examples of factors that might reflect differences in ability levels include, but are not limited to, such things as whether the student, when presenting a series of points on one slide, dims (or covers) one point before revealing the following point; and the extent to which the student avoids the unnecessary use of animation and sound. In the case of an artifact, such as a model or diorama, examples of factors that might reflect differences in ability levels include, but are not limited to, the extent to which diorama depictions are accurate and utilize real things such a cloth as opposed to paper depictions. If a model, such as a bridge is expected, weight-bearing ability might be a relevant element to assess.

In the Quality of the Presentation section, remember that students will spend considerable time and effort on the performance-based project, so having them make a presentation about their project serves two purposes. First, it gives the student an opportunity to show and tell. Each person gets their ten minutes on stage. Second, it gives the students an opportunity to develop their presentation skills and you an opportunity to assess them. Examples of factors that might reflect differences in presentation skill abilities include, but are not limited to, such things as the volume and speed of speech, the speaker's ability to maintain eye contact with the audience and his or her avoidance of street language and terms such as "uh," and "you guys."

An Example of a Performance-Based Assessment

What follows is an example of a performance-based assessment instrument. It is intended for use with high school students in biology and was submitted by Peter J. Miller.

State Goal: Compare physical, ecological, and behavioral factors that influence interactions and interdependence of organisms.

Instructional Objectives: After choosing one of the seven biomes,

1. compare the physical, ecological, and behavioral factors that influence interactions and interdependence of organisms in a three- to six-page reflection paper;
2. create a PowerPoint presentation consisting of a minimum of eight, but no more than fifteen slides that demonstrate appropriate technical skills such as the dimming of points and the use of graphics; and
3. present the research to your fellow classmates in an oral presentation that demonstrates appropriate skills such as maintaining eye contact and proper speech.

Description of the Project

Overview: In this activity you will research a biome of your choice, with teacher's approval. Selecting thirteen organisms (five plants and eight animals) and two cycles of nature, demonstrate an understanding of the intertwining relationships between them that make the biome what it is. The computer lab will be used on Tuesday and Thursday for four weeks for research, and Monday, Wednesday, and Friday of the fifth and sixth weeks for typing and PowerPoint creations. Any additional time needed will have to be conducted outside of the normal class period. When researching, be sure to copy URLs or write down the other sources of information to use as references for the reflection paper and presentation. Progress will be checked bi-weekly and six weeks will be allotted for the completion of this assignment. On Monday of the seventh week, you will be expected to give your presentation. The following guidelines should be used for this assignment:

1. Begin by selecting a topic and creating a topic and tentative calendar showing what will be done by when and have both approved by the instructor.
2. Create an outline of the content that will be needed to complete the project.
3. List the most likely sources to turn to for the information, keeping in mind that the use of sources is required.
4. Check your progress bi-weekly with your calendar and instructor.

5. Create the written part of the project. The focus here is to demonstrate the extent to which you understand the topic. The expected qualities will be expected in the form of a reflection paper, and are included in the rubric and are as follows:

Understanding of the topic / reflection paper: The reflection paper should include, but not be limited to the following:

A. The paper should be between three and six pages in length, single spaced with double spacing between paragraphs, Times New Roman, 12 font, and references.

B. A minimum of, but not limited to, thirteen organisms (five plants and eight animals) along with two natural cycles.

C. Two symbiotic relationships must exist.

D. Explanations of the nature cycles and their impact such as being a limiting factor on the biome.

E. A food-web or chain.

F. Impact of the weather and climate as abiotic factors.

G. Predator-prey relationships.

H. Intertwinements within niches.

I. Population densities in relationship to carrying capacity.

J. Density dependent limiting factors.

K. Impacts that human species have had on this biome.

L. Environmental characteristics of the biome.

M. Locations in the world.

N. Challenges faced by the biome.

O. Check the rubric for expected grouping patterns and ways of presenting the information.

PowerPoint presentation: The PowerPoint must include, but not be limited to, the following:

A. Organization. Presents findings and conclusions in an organized manner.

B. Content. Uses at least 12 examples (A through N) containing physical, ecological, and behavioral factors that influence interactions and interdependence of organisms from each of the components.

C. Presentation/Text Elements. Presentation included at least four slides with graphics and sounds. Backgrounds look good with chosen font styles and color for easy readability. Use of italics, bold, and indentations enhances readability. Text is appropriate in length for the target audience and to the point. The background and colors enhance the readability of text. The fonts are easy to read (e.g., Arial) and point size varies appropriately for headings and text.

D. Check the rubric for any other expectancies for this part of the project.

Oral presentation: The oral presentation should include the following:

A. Correct volume.
B. Good posture.
C. Eye contact.
D. Enthusiasm.
E. Introduction and conclusion.
F. Question and answer time at the end of presentation.
G. Consult the rubric for all expectancies for this part of the project.

The rubric: A rubric can be used for grade determination with points possible totaling 100 points for the reflection paper, 50 points for the PowerPoint, and 50 points for the oral presentation for a total of 200 possible points for an overall project grade.

RECORDING AND POSTING GRADES

The easiest way for students and parents to interpret the grade on a given test or paper is to see the number of points earned, in relation to the number of points possible. For example, 85/100. Letter grades such as B, B+, A, and A+, cannot provide the useful X out of Y information. Further, at some point, letter grades need to be converted into numbers in order to calculate statistics such as the mean and the median. Reserve letter grades for use on report cards, where they are typically required. Further, if extra credit is earned on a particular assignment, keep those points apart from the points for achievement, both on the papers returned to students and in your grade book. You need to be able to differentiate between the two sets of points.

It is a good idea to date and initial each paper as you grade it. This eliminates any question of who graded it or when. These may sound like bothersome steps, but they tend to eliminate problems and they take little time or effort.

Confidentiality is important. When graded work is returned to students, the teacher should hand each student's paper or test directly to the student. The quality of each student's work is a confidential matter between each student and the teacher. For this reason, it is *not* a good idea to have students grade each other's work. If you make an assignment, you should grade it. Doing so protects the confidentiality of grades, lets you provide appropriate encouragement and reinforcement, and enables you to more quickly identify, and help students deal with, problems.

Students and parents get upset, and justly so, when they see a grade on a report card that is unexpectedly low. (They rarely get upset if the grade is unexpectedly high.) Students should know at all times where they stand with respect to grades. If you recall, it was suggested that on the last page of the course syllabus, space be provided for students to keep a running record of the points possible for each assignment and the points they actually earned. You can, however, do more.

Teachers who take time to learn how to use a grading or spreadsheet program will save themselves hours of work and be able to easily post grades. Posting grades makes good sense pedagogically, but the confidentially of student grades must be protected. Your school may have a policy of whether grades may be posted and, if so, how. Generally, confidentiality can be protected by using either a school assigned identification number or the last four digits of the student's Social Security number to identify the grades.

After the first assignment is graded, grades should be posted and left up until the next assignment is graded. At that time the printout should be replaced with one showing the grades for all past assignments and those for the latest assignment. If such a cumulative printout is continually posted, all students will have access to all relevant grading information. Everything will be public.

Whether grades are kept in a grade book or in a computer program, most teachers list their students in alphabetical order according to last names and record grades for each student as they are earned. A computer can easily generate a printout of names and the associated grades. Such a printout or listing however, could not be posted without compromising grade confidentiality.

One way around this problem is to assign each student an identification number, such as the last four digits of their Social Security number or their school ID number. When the printout is generated, leave off the column with the students' names and arrange the ID numbers from high to low or low to high. Unless a student deliberately gives his or her identifying number to others, confidentiality is assured when grades are publicly posted.

Assigning Grades

The Traditional A–F Scale

Grades in schools are typically assigned on an A–F scale. This scale is based on the idea that a grade of A represents outstanding work, B represents above-average work, C represents average work, D represents below-average work, and F represents failing work. Unfortunately, there is a phenomenon known as **grade inflation**. Essentially this means that many people now expect, and receive, grades of A or B for average work, and C for below-average work. Virtually no one receives a grade of F.

Grade inflation causes a number of problems. First, it makes it impossible to recognize truly outstanding students, because so many less able students also receive grades of A. Second, if students start off believing that a grade of C is "no good," they are likely to become discouraged and stop trying, when their performance is, in fact, average. Third, inflated grades mislead students into believing they are more competent than they really are. Fourth, inflating grades makes liars out of teachers. Think about the stories of high school graduates who cannot read or do simple arithmetic. Assuming that such stories are true, the only way those students could have passed the courses necessary to graduate, is if their grades were falsified—if teachers gave them passing grades when they earned failing grades. Grade inflation is still very much with us and you can be part of the problem or part of the solution. That choice is yours.

One way to begin dealing with grade inflation is to point out to students that the objectives in the course syllabus represent *D*-level work, the minimal acceptable standard. Explain also that students who keep up in class will have little difficulty meeting those standards and that most students will likely end up with grades of *C* or higher. Students who want to earn the higher grades must meet higher standards. That choice is theirs.

The most common way to use the traditional A–F scale is to have the lowest *A* equal ninety percent of the available points, the lowest *B* equal eighty percent, the lowest *C* equal seventy percent, and the lowest *D* equal sixty percent. Some teachers raise or lower the cut-off points for various grade categories, but the basic approach remains the same.

The greatest advantage of this approach is that virtually everyone understands it. It is the traditional approach to grading. Another advantage is that it is administratively convenient; a whole semester's work is summed up and recorded with a single letter.

A significant disadvantage is that the letter grades have no relationship to the complexity of the work required. For example, there is a significant difference between the level of work required for an *A* in a regular history class and that required for an A in an advanced placement class, yet the best students in both classes will get As.

Grading Subjectivity

All grading methods have one point in common: they all depend on some subjective decision about what percent to use as the lowest *A*, *B*, *C*, or *D* or what SD cut-off points to use. Some educators argue that since all grading methods ultimately depend on subjective decisions, none is any better or worse than any other. The advantages and disadvantages balance out. However, unless your school has a policy concerning grading, you will have to make some choices, and there are some crucial points you should consider.

Perhaps the most important factor is fairness. Students should be confident that everyone in the class will have their achievement reported on the same basis. Explaining how the grades will be determined, and keeping a cumulative grade list posted, do much to generate that feeling of confidence.

Closely associated with fairness is consistency. Once you decide on a grading system you need to use it consistently so that students know that the established procedures are followed for everyone, all the time. Changing grading procedures capriciously would have the same effect as changing course objectives capriciously. No one would know what to expect or how to prepare and they would soon stop caring; the rules might change again next week.

The grades should be relatively easy to calculate, explain, and understand. As a conscientious teacher, you will have more to do than you will have time in which to do it. There is, therefore, no point in developing a complex grading scheme that requires a great deal of calculation time on your part, or that will take you a relatively long time to explain to students or their parents. The less complex it is, the less time you will need to devote to it and the easier it will be for everyone to understand it.

Students need to understand one other point. The point total they accumulate represents their lowest possible grade but not necessarily the grade they will receive. For example, if the cut-off for a B was 900 points, and a student ended up with just 900, that student would get the B even though he or she might have been obnoxious throughout the semester. However, if a student ended up just a few points short of the cut-off, say with 895 points, and had earned all or virtually all of the extra credit points available, you might exercise your professional judgment and also award that student a B.

The question of just where to draw the line between one grade and the next may not be clear-cut. Once the student has clearly achieved all the objectives necessary for a D, if you believe that the number of points keeping the student from the next higher grade is relatively inconsequential given the total number of points involved, give the student the benefit of the doubt. You and the student will sleep better.

After the Test

After test has been administered, the grades calculated, and the graded tests handed back to students individually, the next step is to go over the test with the students. This is a good idea for a number of reasons. First, it provides an opportunity to call to students' attention any questions the item analysis identified as causing problems to many students. A good approach here is to explain what the right answer is and why it is right, and then explain why each of the wrong answers is wrong. If students have further questions about these items, answer them.

Then, encourage students to ask questions about any other questions, but establish a ground rule. Explain that you are quite willing to consider answers other than the ones keyed as correct. However, you want to ensure that only those students who have particularly strong and relevant explanations to support alternative answers, get credit for those alternative answers. Therefore, if a student believes he or she has a strong and relevant explanation for an alternative answer, he or she should see you after class or after school to discuss the matter. This policy provides for needed flexibility, yet it prevents all students who chose a particular wrong answer from getting credit for it if only one student is able to build an adequate case for that option. After going over the test, it and the answer sheets should be collected. This will help ensure test security, thus enabling the teacher to use some or all of the items in the future.

Reporting Grades

There are three basic ways of reporting students' achievement. The most effective method is in a parent-teacher conference. Such a conference allows two-way communication, lets you show examples of the student's work, and allows discussion of other relevant issues with parents. Most schools have time set aside for parent-teacher conferences, but relatively few parents attend. One way to encourage attendance is to involve parents early, and a good way to do this is to mail home a copy of the course syllabus. Parents may not take the time to carefully read either the syllabus or the cover letter that you send home with it, but the fact that you took the time to send it, and to solicit their involvement, will tell parents that you care and want to see their son or daughter do as well as possible. This realization may prompt some parents who might otherwise have stayed home to come to a parent-teacher conference.

A somewhat less effective method is a phone call. Phone calls still allow for two-way communication and they do not take very long. In fact, some teachers make it a point to call each student's parents once or twice a semester to report on something good that the student did. Such a phone call can pay big dividends. Imagine yourself as a high school student who comes home to have Mom say, "I got a call from your teacher today." Your first question, probably with some dread, is likely to be, "What did he (or she) want?" If Mom says that the call was to let her know that you had done something particularly well, think of your reaction. You will be pleased, and you are likely to think well of the teacher. Students who think well of their teachers rarely cause classroom management problems.

A still less effective reporting method is a letter or an email. By using a word processor, you can write a general letter or an email describing what objectives students were working toward during the marking period. Then, as you prepare the letters or emails, and with little effort, you can personalize each one by adding information concerning the achievements and efforts of that student. This method allows for only one-way communication, but it enables you to better explain what the student has been doing better than the use of a report card.

Report cards are the most common, and least informative, way to report student achievement. All that parents see is a list of courses and a corresponding list of letter grades. By themselves, report cards provide no insight as to what is being learned in each course and, consequently, no insights as to what parents might do to help their children be more successful. The best one can hope for is that, if a parent sees a grade lower than they would like, they will call the teacher for more information. It does not happen often.

SUMMARY

Teachers use measurement and evaluation techniques in order to determine the extent to which students have achieved specific objectives. The information acquired also enables teachers to assess the effectiveness of instructional activities and materials, and it enables students to compare their abilities against specific criteria and against the abilities of peers.

Since tests only sample skills or knowledge, teachers can have greater confidence in the semester grades they record if those grades are based on a fair sampling of student achievement. The more grades that are averaged, the more likely the average will reflect the students' abilities. Further, with ten or more grades on tests and papers, the lowest grade can be dropped without seriously affecting reliability, thus giving students an incentive to continue working even though they may have done poorly on one test or paper.

Variety is also important in measurement and evaluation because students have different abilities. Some may take objective tests well, others may do better on essay tests, and still others may demonstrate their abilities best by completing projects. Varying assessment methods increases opportunities for students to demonstrate their skills and knowledge, thus increasing their opportunities to be successful.

Teachers should check the validity of their tests. Face or content validity reflects the extent to which the test assesses what was taught. Predictive validity reflects the extent to which performance on one test can be used to accurately predict performance on some other test or task. Construct validity concerns the extent to which a test measures psychological constructs such as honesty or tolerance.

Dealing with student effort is often difficult. One effective technique is to find ways in which students can demonstrate effort as opposed to ability in the subject area. One way is to award extra points to papers that have no spelling, punctuation, or grammatical mistakes and to accumulate those extra credit points in a separate column in the grade book. At the end of the marking period, an examination of the extra credit column will help show how much effort the student demonstrated during that period.

Test reliability refers to the consistency with which the test measures whatever it measures. Reliability tends to increase with the number of items because as the number of items increases so does the extent of knowledge being sampled. The more adequate the sampling, the more likely it is that students will do equally as well if tested with an equivalent form of the test. Reliability coefficients extend from 1.00 for perfect correlation, to .00 for no correlation, and to minus 1.00 for perfect negative correlation.

Criterion-referenced tests are those in which students either meet or fail to meet certain criteria. If the criteria are met, the student passes; if not, the student fails. Criterion referencing can be used to establish cut-off points for admission to programs or schools and for similar purposes, but most often teachers need norm-referenced tests.

Norm referencing means that a student's performance is assessed in relation to the performance of students in some norming group. A norming group consists of members that have some relevant characteristic in common, such as age or grade level.

The most common type of evaluation instrument is the paper and pencil test. These tests present the same task, under the same conditions, to all students and result in a product that can be easily examined and analyzed. Objective tests are used to sample abilities through analysis-level thinking, with respect to a fairly large topic. About thirty seconds should be allowed for each four-choice multiple-choice item, so about fifty items can be used per test.

Essay tests are used to sample higher-level abilities, such as the abilities to analyze, synthesize, and evaluate. Since different thought processes are involved with each kind of test, students will do best if objective and essay questions do not appear on the same test. When reviewing for essay tests, the teacher should give the students the actual questions to be asked and should go over, but not hand out to students, the associated criteria. Students should be told that they will be asked to answer two or three specific questions.

Performance-based assessments that require the integration of many skills and pieces of information are most useful because they emphasize the application of what is learned. Because students have weeks to work on a performance-based assessment project, and have a large say in what it will concern, they are typically see the project as more relevant than a test and are willing to work hard to ensure a quality job. These factors prompt more and more teachers to use performance-based assessments in lieu of midterm and final exams (with the approval of their principal).

Assessments that require the integration of many skills and pieces of information are most useful because they emphasize the application of what is learned. Before any test is administered, the teacher should conduct a formal review with the test in hand. The teacher should go over each part of the test explaining what topics are covered, what content is sampled, and how many items are in each part of the test. When reviewing for essay tests, the teacher should give the students the actual questions to be asked and should go over, but not hand out to students, the associated criteria. Students should be told that they will be asked to answer two or three specific questions.

Objective Tests

I. Advantages

    A. Provide a broad sampling of students' knowledge

    B. Present the same problems and the same alternatives to each student

    C. Minimize the chance of student bluffing

    D. Permit rapid scoring with little or no need for subjective decisions

    E. Permit items to be improved on the basis of item analysis

    F. Permit increased reliability through item improvement.

II. Disadvantages

    A. Cannot be used to assess abilities to synthesize or create

    B. Increase the probability of guessing

    C. Require a relatively long time to construct items

III. Utilization Factors

    A. Construction and administration

        1. Keep the language simple.

        2. Ask students to apply rather than simply recall information.

        3. Make sure that each item is independent.

        4. Do not establish or follow a pattern for correct responses.

        5. Do not include trick or trivial questions.

        6. Do not answer questions after the test has started.

    B. Multiple-choice items

        1. Put as much of the item as possible into the stem.

        2. Make all options reasonable.

        3. Make all options about the same length.

        4. Do not provide unintentional clues.

        5. Avoid the use of all-inclusive or all-exclusive terms (always/never).

    C. True/false items

        1. Avoid when possible since chance of guessing correctly is one in two.

        2. Be sure that each item is wholly true or wholly false.

        3. Be sure that items are not dependent on insignificant facts.

        4. Avoid the use of negatives and, if used, call attention to them by underlining and/or capitalizing the negative word.

    D. Matching items

        1. Limit the number of items to be matched to ten or less.

        2. Make sure that all items concern a single topic.

        3. Have more answers than questions or stipulate that some answers may be used more than once or not at all.

        4. Arrange options in some logical order.

    E. Completion items

        1. Write items that can be completed with a single word or a short phrase.

        2. Be sure that only one word or phrase can correctly complete the sentence.

        3. Put the blanks near the ends of the sentences.

4. Make all blanks the same length.
5. Do not put more than two blanks in any one item.

Essay Tests

I.   Advantages
   A. Allow sampling of students' abilities to create, analysis, synthesize, and evaluate
   B. Provide an in-depth sampling of students' knowledge of a specific topic
   C. Enable students to develop the skills of organizing pieces of information and demonstrating their understanding of how those pieces interrelate to form a complex whole
   D. Help students learn to express themselves coherently and concisely in writing
II. Disadvantages
   A. Reduced reliability and validity compared with objective tests
   B. Inherently biased in favor of students who write well
   C. Time-consuming to grade
   D. Increased chance for students to bluff
III. Utilization Factors
   A. Be definitive about what kinds of things students are to include in their answers.
   B. Make sure that students have sufficient time and materials to do the job.
   C. Compare each response with a model response and with a list of grading criteria.
   D. Essay tests and objective tests take about the same amount of time in total. With objective tests more time is spent constructing the items than in grading the answers. With essay tests just the opposite is true.

Performance-Based Assessment

I.   Advantages
   A. Permits the assessment of a students' knowledge of a topic, ability to construct a project, and ability to make a clear and concise presentation about that product.
   B. Performance-based assessments require students to synthesize broad areas of knowledge and skills in a way that cannot be duplicated in typical paper and pencil tests.

C. Students typically have a large say in what the project will concern and so they see it as being more relevant to their lives outside of class than other forms of assessment.

II. Disadvantages

A. The construction of the rubric is time-consuming since each cell must contain factors that qualitatively differentiate one level of performance from another.

B. If choices are allowed with respect to the product, e.g., a PowerPoint presentation or a poster; grading is complicated.

SO HOW DOES THIS AFFECT MY TEACHING?

The single greatest measure of the effectiveness of a teacher is the extent to which his or her students can use what they learned. This was true in 450 BC, when the Elder Sophists made their living selling their abilities to help students learn to speak in public, and it remains true today. If the students of the Elder Sophists had been unable to successfully speak in public, the teachers would have soon gone out of business. One does not get much more accountable than that.

Teachers today must also be accountable. Helping students learn is just part of the job. To demonstrate that they have learned, you must develop measurement and evaluation techniques that enable them to clearly and adequately demonstrate their abilities. They have to be able to use what they have learned. Their demonstration of their abilities is the way you demonstrate your accountability.

Further, think about the things that you consider when you assess your own instructors. The chances are good that an important point is the ability of the instructor to fairly assess what was taught. Your students will look at this same point when they assess you. Do what you want your instructors to do. Specify, in the objectives, what students are supposed to be able to do after instruction, provide appropriate instruction, and then assess the extent to which students have achieved the objectives. This is the honest and fair way to do business and it provides the greatest opportunity for you and your students to be successful.

KEY TERMS, PEOPLE, AND IDEAS

Tests = Samples of students' abilities

Measurement = Assigning numbers

Evaluation = Value Judgments

Validity = Measures what was taught—Content or Face, Predictive, Construct

Reliability = Consistency of test results, 1.00 to .00, and −1.00 to .00

Criterion-referenced—Pass or Fail

Mastery Learning—Allowing students to redo work—average the original and redo grades

Norm-referenced—Performance relative to performance of a norming group

Objective Tests—No value judgments required with respect to answers

Stem—The part of the question that poses the problem

Visual Package—Listing all choices for multiple-choice questions under one another and keeping the stem and all choices on a single page

Subjective Tests—Value judgments required with respect to the answers

Formative Assessments—Assessment carried out during instruction to provide ongoing feedback regarding students learning

Summative Assessments—Assessments carried out at the end of the instruction to provide a summative assessment of students' skills and abilities

Performance-Based Assessments (PBA)—Assess a student's understanding of the topic, their ability to use their knowledge and skills to construct a product, and their ability to make a clear and concise presentation that reflects their knowledge and skill

QUESTIONS FOR CONSIDERATION

1. Are midterm and final exams the most effective way of assessing what a student knows and is able to do at the end of a semester or year, or are there better alternatives?

2. To what extent do you believe that criterion-referenced measures are more productive than norm-referenced measures in helping students work together cooperatively?

3. Are essay tests suitable for all content areas?

4. Why will you or will you not use performance-based assessment projects?

5. What are the advantages and disadvantages of essays tests and performance-based assessments?

SUGGESTED READINGS

Additional information concerning the construction of objective and subjective tests, can be found in the following sources:

1. Thorndike, Robert L., and Elizabeth Hagen, *Measurement and Evaluation in Psychology and Education*, 5th ed. (New York: Macmillan, 1991).

2. Linn, Robert L., and Norman E. Gronlund, *Measurement and Assessment in Teaching*, 7th ed. (Englewood Cliffs, N.J.: Prentice-Hall, 1995).

CHAPTER 10

Student Assessment and Teacher Evaluation

INTRODUCTION

While classroom instruction looks vastly different than it did several decades ago, assessments in schools still look relatively similar. Many schools continue to rely on traditional multiple-choice tests as a means to assess student growth and achievement, despite the ways in which instruction has changed. Educators today are expected to differentiate and tailor their instruction to meet specific student needs, yet standardized assessments are rarely differentiated for students. Classroom work today may reflect a more *hands-on* approach, through experiments, papers, projects, and other assessment activities. Classrooms look very different now due to the use of the ever-evolving technology, and instruction structures. This chapter examines contemporary assessment and evaluations practices that are based on students' growth models and attempts to determine the extent to which current assessment models and theories are aligned with modern knowledge about learning and teaching. Furthermore, this chapter also includes a section dealing with teacher evaluation. The information in this section can help you to improve your own teaching effectiveness, attaining high teaching ratings, and eventually achieving tenure.

LEARNING OUTCOMES

You will be able, in writing, to:

1. Define terms such as formative and summative assessment.
2. Describe at least three advantages of formative and portfolio assessments.

3. Discuss at least two types of portfolio assessments.
4. Explain at least three procedures teachers can use to assess their own effectiveness including both process and product assessments.

ORIGINS OF STANDARDIZED TESTING

Standardized testing got its start in the early 1900s when Horace Mann introduced the concept of using achievement exams to gain "objective information about the quality of teaching and learning, monitor the quality of instruction, and compare schools and teachers within each school."[1] The tests revealed differences in student knowledge and achievement, which were used by the school to make sound academic decisions and determine a more rigorous academic plan. Mann's achievement exams were so successful that they quickly rose to the top as the most widely spread method across the country for assessing learning.

This testing method held true, until the time of WWI, when the United States Army required a method for quickly identifying potential officers among a large batch of recruits; thus, a new type of assessment was developed that could efficiently and effectively gauge a soldier's academic abilities through the use of a new scoring method. It was so successful that it quickly became the new model for many achievement tests.[2] Standardized testing now had a new face, and student tracking became widely used in order to sort students into different categories of varying abilities.

In 1965, standardized testing once again shifted, when the first federal laws were passed requiring the use of standardized assessments. This act, known as Title 1, was the first time in the nation's history that education acknowledged the role of the federal government in educational decisions and opportunities. Title 1 channeled money into under-funded schools, but in return, school districts were required to prove that funds were being used to increase student achievement and success through standardized test scores.[3]

The federal government now had a viable role in education, and during the 1970s, the term "educational accountability" was coined. Demands on the field of education increased, and school districts, administrators, and teachers were being held accountable for student test scores. In order to increase student test scores, it was suggested that schools and teachers make changes to their curricula to ensure that what students were learning matched what was being assessed on standardized tests. In 1974, Congress issued an increased use of standardized testing to "improve school programs and curricula" and by 1980, thirty-three states mandated "competency testing" with over two hundred million tests administered annually to determine "academic readiness."[4] The United States' use of standardized testing was on the rise, and the turn of the century brought forth a second wave of standardized testing reform, designed to correct the declining student achievement levels indicated by the use of such tests.

No Child Left Behind (NCLB) and Standards-Based Reform

In 2001, the **No Child Left Behind Act** was passed, and though it continued to use testing as a measurable way to evaluate student success, it placed a greater emphasis on accountability and government involvement. Prior to NCLB, education was left mainly to the state legislation and local districts. For the first time, the states were united under the umbrella of control by the federal government, who deemed what students will be taught, how federally funded resources will be used, and that schools will be held accountable by the success measured on standardized tests. Because such important decisions are based on these test results, they are considered high-stakes tests.[5]

Previously, students may have been tested one to three times over the course of their K–12 schooling, while under the NCLB Act, students are now tested annually from grades three to eight in a variety of subjects such as reading, mathematics, and science. With no national test, each state was allowed to make their own test, but the policy stated that schools and students must show improvement, known as Adequately Yearly Progress (AYP), and be on course to reach 100% efficiency for all groups of students on their state test by 2013. Each state was to decide what was proficient and an adequate rate of progress for each group. School districts passing AYP were given a monetary reward for exceeding expectations. Schools that fell behind faced the loss of federal funding and autonomy, unable to make educational decisions regarding teaching materials, methods, and practices. They were subjected to various school improvement, corrective action, or restructuring plans imposed by the state. Additionally, test scores were now made public, per public reporting, in order to determine the success of each individual district and school. Parents and the public were given information regarding the educational progress of each school and district in each state.

As a result of NCLB, states and the federal government were able to scour over annual test results, as well as the various progress tests administered three times a year in order to show academic readiness and success. The data indicated a gain in low-level skills, but a severe decrease in problem-solving and real-world application skills. To reverse this downward spiral, politicians and government officials called for a more challenging set of curriculum standards. Many felt that students would learn more and show their knowledge if they were actively trying to problem solve. It was decided that meaningful development of knowledge should occur through context of application; therefore, it was determined that making the curriculum more demanding would enable student learning. As a result, the Common Core Standards were developed and launched in 2009.

Testing in the Era of Common Core and PARCC

During his first term in office, President Obama signed into law the American Recovery and Reinvestment Act of 2009 (ARRA). Part of the ARRA legislation is a grant fund that was intended to provide the states with a $4.35 billion grant fund entitled Race to the Top (RTTTP).

> [This legislation] is a competitive grant program designed to encourage and reward States that are creating the conditions for education innovation and reform; achieving significant improvement in student outcomes, including making substantial gains in student achievement, closing achievement gaps, improving high school graduation rates, and ensuring student preparation for success in college and careers; and implementing ambitious plans in four core education reform areas. Race to the Top will reward States that have demonstrated success in raising student achievement and have the best plans to accelerate their reforms in the future. These States will offer models for others to follow and will spread the best reform ideas across their States, and across the country.[6]

One of the four main goals of the Race to the Top funding was "adopting standards and assessments that prepare students to succeed in college and the workplace and to compete in the global economy."[7] Consequently, the Common Core State Standards (CCSS) were developed and launched in 2009. The CCSS movement has been adopted by a majority of the states in the US. The Common Core State Standards are a set of standards intended for K–12 schools in three content areas including English language arts, mathematics, and science. In addition, those standards were intended to prepare students for college and careers. The Common Core State Standards became an opportunity for schools to reform their curriculum and ways of instruction in order to ensure that students are engaged in challenging tasks and higher order thinking skills in hopes that students will be more college and career ready. Along with the development of new standards, new assessment programs were created.

The Partnership for the Assessment of Readiness for College and Careers (PARCC) was developed in order to measure student achievement with respect to the Common Core State Standards. The federal Race to the Top legislation set high expectations for PARCC assessment. It is important to note that these standards and the assessments associated with it were met considerable opposition.

With the Common Core State Standards, came a more serious call for accountability. While accountability was a common thread through the previous decade's educational reform, it took on a different look this time. Standardized testing quickly became *high stakes* in that the consequences of scores directly impacts a person's life and opportunities.

Citing evidence that "high-stakes testing can be a driving force behind fundamental change within schools,"[8] the federal government could now use test scores to determine "how students were doing according to subgroups, like race and income level, and hold schools accountable for their performance."[9]

For students, test results can include placement on certain academic tracks, grade retention, high school graduation eligibility, and college readiness. For teachers, it could potentially determine continued employment.

A federal requirement was issued that every state receiving a waiver from NCLB must make student scores a significant part of teacher evaluations. The idea behind test-based accountability is that it will provide students, teachers and administrators an incentive to work harder as well as help identify struggling students and schools. Supporters of test-based accountability claim it will raise student achievement by increasing student motivation, promote parent involvement, improve curriculum and instruction, and "promote quality teaching" through "threat of sanctions,"[10] while others note that the biggest concern with this type of high-stakes testing is that it "may be fundamentally flawed, and may narrow the intended curriculum."[11] As a result of NCLB and the Common Core Standards, educators have developed varying attitudes and perceptions regarding high-stakes testing.

With the adoption of the new Illinois Learning Standards which incorporated the Common Core State Standards, the state has retired many of its old tests and replaced them with new, innovative assessments that will provide educators with reliable data to help guide instruction. Often aided by technological advances, these assessments will allow for students to better showcase their skills.[12]

The National Center for Fair and Open Testing supports these new assessment reforms as it is expressed in their position statement, which states that, "what is distinctive about assessment for learning is not the form of the information or the circumstances in which it is generated, but the positive effect it has for the learner."[13] Here, formative assessment is labeled as assessment for learning and is completely differentiated from summative assessment. The main goal of assessment to improve learning is emphasized, not as a concern for a score on a summative test. Formative assessments are about improving learning because they focus on process and ongoing progress.

DEFINITION AND TYPES OF ASSESSMENTS

Assessments are considered an important part of teaching and learning. Without sound assessment practices, educators will not be able to determine the extent of students learning and academic progress. Assessment determines students' abilities in comparison to specified levels of knowledge and skill. Ultimately, educators use assessments to make educational decisions for and about students' learning and teachers' performance.

Assessments include a variety of different methods that allow students to demonstrate evidence of learning that can range from observations, student portfolios, and running records to large-scale standardized tests.

In his book *Classroom Assessment: What Teachers Need to Know*, W. James Popham, defines educational assessment as "a formal attempt to determine students' status with respect to educational variables of interest."[14] Educators use two standard types of assessments to measure student knowledge and abilities. Popham, like many other educators, breaks those assessment into two main categories: **formative assessment** and **summative assessment**.[15] He defines formative assessment as, "the use of assessment-elicited evidence intended to improve unsuccessful yet still modifiable instruction."[16] He defines summative assessment as, "the use of tests whose purpose is to make a final success/failure decision about a relatively unmodifiable set of instructional activities."[17]

Formative Assessment

Formative assessment informs both teachers and students about student understanding at a point when timely adjustments can be made. These adjustments help to ensure students achieve, targeted standards-based learning goals within a set time frame.[18] If students are not involved in the assessment process, formative assessment is not practiced or implemented to its full effectiveness. Students need to be involved both as assessors of their own learning and as resources to other students.

To aid in the formative process, technology such as Google Docs allows for collaborative, in-process feedback, which can encourage students to consider feedback and apply new knowledge and skills immediately. Ultimately, this is a more effective means when expecting to see improvement in student writing (among other fields of study). Taking technology-based feedback a step further in the article "Integrating Technology and Literacy," Frank Ward suggests the Google extension *Kaizena Shortcut* as a more effective and efficient means than Google Docs as it allows educators to include voice recording among other forms of feedback (https://www.edutopia.org/blog/integrating-technology-and-literacy-frank-ward).[19]

It would be valuable for students to see every assessment as an opportunity for future growth; however, the current understanding of assessment practices is contrary to this belief. Therefore, assessments are broken into two main categories: *formative assessments* and *summative assessments*. These categories are not based on the type of assessment; instead, an assessment is determined to be either formative or summative based on its purpose and position in the learning process. Gorlewski reiterates this point well by stating, "If an assessment is designed to provide feedback to improve teaching and learning (some quizzes or "tickets out the door," for example), it is formative.[20] Even though such a quiz may be scored and recorded, its primary intent and use label it as formative."[21]

It is the purpose not the mode of the assessment that determines the categorization of the assessment.

There are many forms of formative assessments; however, the three that are commonly used among educators include observation checklists, peer/self-evaluation, and running records. These assessments are noted to improve student learning and teaching. They allow teachers to understand misconceptions about students and the concepts with which they are struggling. They also help students be more successful because they help students address their own misconceptions and better understand the concept before they are tested again on the summative assessments.[22]

Observation Checklists

An observation checklist can identify learning objectives and behaviors that are used to determine whether a student shows the behaviors or skills listed. The observations associated with the items on the checklist allow the teacher to have a clear sense of what the student is able to do at a specific moment of time.[23] This evidence can be recorded and used as feedback for students about their learning or as anecdotal data shared with them during conferences. In the classroom, teachers should identify specific outcomes that are aligned to the common core standards to assess. Then, they need to decide the criteria that indicates if the student is showing that outcome. Developing a data gathering system and documenting all observations is critical to help identify patterns of performance. Finally, use the information gathered to share with students and modify instruction.

There are both advantages and disadvantages to using observations and checklists. This type of formative assessment helps teachers to easily check off what students know and are able to do. They are easy to update for each standard being assessed, and they can be used with a variety of assessment strategies. Potential disadvantages of using them are that there is subjectivity involves in the observation process. Different teachers could rate a student differently and overlook certain details about the specific learning target. If there are too many checklists, the teacher could become overwhelmed with all of the record keeping. Checklists may not indicate how well a student performance in all situations and settings.

Peer/Self-Evaluations

Self and peer evaluations are defined as "students reflecting on and judging the quality of their work or learning experience, based on evidence and explicit criteria, for the purpose of improving their work in the future."[24] Having students evaluate themselves and each other is a beneficial technique that has an impact on student performance through increased self-efficacy and increased intrinsic motivation. This is of course is contrary to traditional teaching methodology. Self-evaluations can take place in student-led conferences through rubrics, goal setting activities, and by keeping a portfolio of their own work samples.

The advantages of self-evaluation include the opportunity for students to reflect on their own work and evaluate their strengths and weaknesses. It can also provide the teacher with information about the student's attitude towards education. Self-evaluations can sometimes be difficult to interpret objectively because students may overestimate their own abilities.

Running Records

Running records are another data collection tool that can help drive reading instruction in the classroom. According to TeacherVision, "Running records help teachers' measure students' progress, plan for future instruction, and provides a way for students to understand their progress."[25] This adds more information on the student in order to place the student in the proper interventions and give them the instruction that they need. Running records are meant to be ongoing assessments and should be administered early in the year and repeated often throughout the year to monitor reading progress.

There are more advantages to running records than challenges. Running records give a more authentic view of a student's oral reading ability because they are done frequently throughout the entire year. It can show many different areas of reading difficulty through one setting. It can help ensure that students are reading at the appropriate guided reading level and it allows for students to be grouped together by their needs. Disadvantages could be that students may feel uncomfortable while reading, which would result in a change of reading behavior, and teachers may feel that intensively listening to one student disrupts the behavior management of the rest of the class.

While formative assessment is crucial to students learning, summative assessments are demonstrably vital as well. After a teacher establishes a learning target, facilitates instruction and opportunities for practice, and provides feedback, students require an opportunity to demonstrate their abilities in relation to the learning target. The key factor here is alignment. In other words, the target, instruction, practice, feedback, and assessments should all connect because they are all based on a particular skill or concept.

Summative Assessment

Summative assessments provide information at the student, classroom, and school levels. If they are aligned with curriculum and instruction, as well as common core standards, they can provide information about students' learning at the end of an interval of instruction and about student's achievement of specific learning outcomes. According to W. James Popham, summative assessment "takes place when educators collect test-based evidence to inform decisions about already completed instructional activities such as when statewide accountability tests are administered each spring to determine the instructional effectiveness of a state's schools during the soon-to-be completed year."[26] Examples of the three types of summative assessments include Discovery Assessment, DIBELS, and PARCC assessment.

Discovery Assessment

Discovery Assessment, a computer-based assessment that tests language arts and math, is used to give another data point to use for responsive to intervention. Discovery Assessment presents scores within a range, that makes it possible for us to compare student progress from one test to the next test. This test is taken quarterly. Test results from the Discovery Benchmark series are compared each year to specific state criterion referenced test results and demonstrate over 80% predictive validity in grades two through high school. According to Discovery Education

> Teachers see how their classes are responding to various instructional approaches and progressing toward meeting state specific NCLB proficiency standards and levels. Parents and students see individual student strengths and opportunities and set targets for achievement. Problem solving teams have a solid set of data from which to recommend additional assessments, interventions, or tiers.[27]

The advantages of Discovery testing are that it can be scored analytically, results can be obtained quickly, and specific criteria for performance can be established to the curriculum. Some disadvantages to this assessment are that they are time consuming to give to the students which creates stress on the teacher and the student. It is also computer based which allows for students to simply click an answer and move on without giving the question any thought. Students that also do not have practice with computer-based assessment are at a disadvantage from students who grew up around a computer. Another disadvantage is that it evaluates a student's performance on one particular day as opposed to formative assessments that give you data throughout the year.

Dynamic Indicators of Basic Early Literacy Skills (DIBELS)
According to Wikipedia

> [DIBELS] is a set of procedures and measures for assessing the acquisition of a set of K-8 literacy skills, such as phonemic awareness, alphabetic principle, accuracy, fluency, and comprehension. The theory behind DIBELS is that giving students a number of quick tests, educators will have the data to identify students who need additional assistance and to monitor the effectiveness of intervention strategies.[28]

Students in Kindergarten through second grade are assessed on their phonemic aware-ness and phonics skills. DIBELS benchmarking is done by either a team of teachers or individual classroom teachers four times a year. Scores earned at different times during the year are used to determine whether a student's performance and progress is increas-ing, decreasing, or staying the same. Each student is individually pulled to read passages and answer comprehension type questions on the reading passage. Students in first grade through fifth grade are tested on their reading fluency; students in third through fifth grades are tested on their comprehension. Oral reading fluency (ORF) is the score used more often at my school. This test measures how accurately and quickly the student can read in one minute. It is a significant measure for first through third graders. The ORF does include a retell portion as well as the DAZE assessment of comprehension. The DAZE assessment requires the students to circle the best word from a list to complete the sentence.[29]

There are many advantages to DIBELS testing. First of all, results can be obtained quickly. The assessment is free and quick. Teachers can sign up for a free account and download the materials for no cost. Because the DIBELS assessment tests areas separately, teachers can quickly see if students are struggling in a certain area of reading. The test could point out that a student is having trouble with comprehension or he needs more instruction in phonics. The test is given individually to each student; so, if a teacher has a large classroom, this could be inappropriate. Giving the test may take up a large amount of classroom time. Anytime assessments have to be given, that's less instruction time that students are receiving.

Partnership for Assessment of Readiness for College and Careers (PARCC)

The Partnership for Assessment of Readiness for College and Careers (PARCC) is the state assessment and accountability measure for Illinois students enrolled in a public school district. PARCC assesses the New Illinois Learning Standards Incorporating the Common Core and will administer to students in English language arts and mathemat-ics (Illinois State Board of Education). The PARCC assessment includes two summative portions—a performance-based assessment (PBA) and an end-of-year assessment (EOY). There are two formative components that can be used at the beginning and mid-points of the year.[30] These exams are intended to be used as indicators of student needs and progress for teachers to identify and address.

PARCC assessment advantages including building problem solving skills because the test will require skills that colleges demand. Also, since it was created by over 800 colleges, it will help ensure that students will graduate high school and be ready for college.[31] It is also supposed to help make teachers accountable by providing a direct way to gauge learning and improve classroom performance. One of the major disadvantages has to do with the technology associated with it. Many schools are struggling to get computers together with the appropriate Wi-Fi infrastructure needed to handle the volume of testing. Since the test requires students to use technology, many students from low-income areas do not have as much experience using the computer and software, which could put them at a disadvantage. Finally, as with all high-stakes tests, there is a lot of teacher anxiety because teachers feel they need to teach normal curriculum while also preparing students for such an important test.

In conclusion, experienced and effective teachers use assessments to inform what they teach (curriculum) and how they teach it (instruction). Summative assessments enable teachers to pull data to see whether or not students have mastered certain skills while formative assessments help evaluate whether a student is understanding the material while the unit is being taught and address misconceptions students might have before the districtwide common summative assessment takes place. While there are positive and negatives to all types of assessments, I do believe that a balance between both formative and summative assessments needs to take place for exceptional teaching and learning to occur.

Portfolio Assessment
Definition of Portfolio Assessment

While we are still mainly using summative assessment, there is a better way to show the processes of the students' knowledge and abilities through the use of portfolio assessment. A portfolio assessment involves the collection of work samples from a student over time as opposed to a paper pencil test. Portfolio-based assessments come in many ways and truly show the students understanding of skills and or concepts that were being taught that are not a multiple choice or short answer questions in a test. Portfolio-based assessments can show the students' growth and understanding of a concept by allowing the students to select what they want to learn and a chance to reflect on the concept. Portfolio-based assessment is not an assessment that can be thrown together; there are challenges with developing and implementing this assessment as well as benefits. The students' ownership of what they are learning and motivation to do well in school is a key part of portfolio assessment. With the correct information and knowledge of portfolio-based assessments, an educator can develop and implement a sound assessment that shows the students' growth and progress.

Popham defines portfolio-based assessment as "a systematic collection of one's work."[32] This work can be either an assignment or a project that allows an educator to see the student's thought processes and reflection. Portfolio-based assessment can document both individual students' accomplishments and specific course goals across a curriculum.[33] As it documents both accomplishments and course goals, portfolio-based assessment cannot be thrown together overnight.

Challenges of Portfolio Assessment

There are many challenges that educators face while developing and implementing portfolio-based assessments. Challenges include but are not limited to interfering with teaching, identifying what should be included in the portfolio, and the perceptions of individual school districts regarding the use of portfolio-based assessments. Portfolios can interfere with teaching because it does take time to manage and document what goes into the students' portfolios.[34] Educators have to manage the time in the class, prepare to hold conferences with the students to help select what needs to go into their portfolios, and provide time for the students to reflect on the process.[35] Since portfolio-based assessment will be different for each student, more time will be needed to make sure the students fully understand what is being asked of them. Popham stated, "It would be educationally unwise to select portfolio assessment as a one-time measurement approach to deal with a short-term instructional objective."[36] This is true because a portfolio assessment shows growth over time and gives students a chance to self-reflect on the process they use when completing a project.

Selecting what type of portfolio to use is challenging because there are many types of portfolios and each has their own content. Educators must understand the difference between the types of portfolios: working portfolio, display portfolio, or assessment portfolio.[37] Since portfolios are a record of the student's work over time in a variety of modes to show the depth and development of the students' abilities, it is the educator's responsibility to make sure that the student is showing their growing skills in the class for which they are developing the portfolio-based assessment.[38]

The last challenge for implementing portfolio-based assessment is the individual school district. School districts have different beliefs and understanding of portfolio assessment. School districts that are implementing portfolio-based assessment may only want it a certain way, which can be a challenge. If it is not fully explained or there is a lack of professional development to implement and develop it, there will be a lack of buy-in from the faculty. The faculty needs to be able to have time to accept and understand why the district is using portfolio assessment.[39] When an educator wants to use a portfolio for their own class, it is suggested that they receive backing from their administration, so time is not wasted on development and implementation of a procedure that has not been accepted.

Benefits of Portfolio Assessment

Even with these challenges there are many benefits of using portfolio-based assessments. Portfolios encourage students to take ownership of their work, and they create a connection between process and product. The assessment develops collaboration, reflection, and discussion. When students have ownership of their "own" portfolios, they become more motivated because it provides the students with meaningful learning. [40] students who feel that they have ownership in what they are learning are more invested and to produce a product that they are proud of. [41]

While the students are producing a product, they are also developing their own process. [42] Portfolios give students a chance to understand how the product relates to the process by facilitating self-reflection about each assignment and or project that is added to their portfolio. This self-reflection encourages students to explain their process and feelings during the developing of their product. [43]

Students not only develop ownership of their learning along with the comprehension process, but they are also experiencing and developing collaboration, reflection, and discussion skills. [44] An integral component of portfolio-based assessment is teacher–student conferences. The students and teachers collaborate to select the best product to include in the student's portfolio. [45] This collaboration helps students develop skills that they will need later in life outside of high school. Students develop ownership of their portfolio by discussing why they do or do not want to add a certain product into their portfolio. During these conferences between the teacher and student, students are able to reflect on the process and discuss it with the teacher. These conferences also help the student and teacher decide what would be the best assignment or project to add in the portfolio by reflecting on the process. During the conference, the student and teacher will be able to also discuss and provide feedback on the student evaluation and teacher evaluation, which leads to open communication and collaboration.

Portfolio Assessment in Secondary Education

There are lot of challenges and benefits with using portfolio-based assessments in secondary education. With the educational focus being to make students college and career ready, students need to learn and understand the skills and concepts for life after high school. For students to fully understand the process, educators need to understand how to develop and implement a sound assessment that shows the student's growth and process. Portfolios should focus on valued outcome, processes, and strategies; they should also mirror real world work and use multiple forms of evaluating students' work. [46]

To develop and implement portfolio assessments, educators must first understand why the portfolio is being created, who the portfolio is for, what processes we are trying to show, how time and materials will be managed, and how the portfolio will be shared and evaluated. [47] Once the teacher understands and answers these questions above, educators are ready to implement portfolio-based assessment. While answering those questions, educators must also keep these seven key ingredients in their mind: educators must make sure students "own" their portfolio; educators must decide on what work samples to collect, where they will store work samples, and the criteria to evaluate portfolio work;

students must evaluate their own portfolio products; conferences to be held; and parent involvement.[48] These seven ingredients will help educators develop a meaningful portfolio assessment that is age appropriate for their students.

Steps for Implementing Portfolio Assessment

To implement portfolio assessment, follow these simple steps:[49]

1. Determine the purpose of the portfolio. What do you want the students to be able to show and gain from the portfolio? What are the learning targets you want your students to meet to show growth and understanding?
2. Identify what type of portfolio you are going to have the students use. Is the portfolio going to be a binder, or is it going to be electronic? Will the portfolio be a working portfolio, display portfolio, or assessment portfolio?[50]
3. Determine the source content. What are you going to have the student put in their portfolio?
4. determine the scoring criteria of the portfolio. How are you going to evaluate the portfolio?
5. determine the criteria for the student's self-reflection. What do you want your students to gain from the self-reflection?
6. Review the student's portfolio with them. Collaborate, reflect, and discuss the content of the portfolio.
7. Plan for time for students to self-evaluate the content of their portfolios. Allow students to be able to grade and take ownership in their own evaluation.
8. Plan times to conference with the students about their portfolio. Once an educator has taken the time to develop the portfolio-based assessment, implementing it becomes easy. Educators just need to remember the "seven key ingredients" and provide enough structure and modeling so the students understand what to do when working on their portfolios.[51] Remember, time and planning can make the process of portfolio assessment run smoothly and proficiently. It is unwise to select portfolio assessment as a one-time measurement approach to deal with a short-term instructional objective.[52]

Overall, portfolio-based assessments are beneficial to secondary education. Portfolios can show the thought process of a student's product and help connect the process and product to the concept or skill. With the use of portfolio assessment, students will be able to use the portfolio for college interviews and job interviews to show their abilities. With the push to show student's growth and process of learning, portfolios give educators a chance to see the growth through sample work and self-reflections. For students to be college and career ready when they finish the graduation requirements of their school, portfolio-based assessment will show students sample work and self-reflection while developing the skills to communicate and collaborate.

TRADITIONAL TEACHER EVALUATION METHODS

This section of chapter ten discusses several methods for evaluating teachers' performance. It is divided into two areas. The first area describes traditional teacher evaluation methods. The second area describes contemporary teacher evaluation methods that were instituted after 2010. Contemporary teacher evaluation methods are strongly connected to student growth models.

Process

There are two major ways by which teachers are evaluated: process and product. Process evaluation is the more common because it focuses on what is going on in the classroom. Evaluators can make judgments about what they see then and there. While some evaluators look to see if the blinds on the windows are evenly raised or if the chalkboard is clean, most use evaluation forms containing questions most of us consider reasonable. A small sampling of such questions follows.

1. Are the course and lesson objectives clearly understood by the students?
2. Does the lesson focus on a planned and identifiable objective?
3. Are students asking, or responding to, thought-provoking questions?
4. Are students actively, as opposed to passively, involved in the lesson?
5. Does the teacher encourage students to think for themselves?
6. Does the teacher provide helpful comments on returned papers and tests?
7. Does the teacher seem well prepared?
8. Are appropriate instructional aids used?
9. Is there sufficient stimulus variation to stimulate and maintain interest?
10. Does the teacher seem genuinely interested in each student's progress?
11. Are the skills and knowledge to be learned relevant to out-of-school life?
12. Is the room appropriately decorated with relevant bulletin boards, appropriate resources, etc.?

Product

One of the reasons process evaluation is so common is that its counterpart, product evaluation, must wait until learning has taken place. Product evaluation focuses on how well students are able to achieve the stated objectives. To determine this, evaluators can look at such things as student products and demonstrations, and at test scores, but they cannot look at these things as often as they can observe the instructional process. It is wise to remember that regardless of how well you do on process evaluations, if your students do not achieve the approved objectives or produce the expected results, you are not likely to be rehired.

Administrative Evaluations

When administrators (or anyone else) evaluate, they tend to do so from a particular perspective. As a consequence of their educational philosophy and their experiences, they have a mental picture of how the ideal teacher should look and operate. A good part of your rating will depend on the extent to which that picture is matched by you and your performance.

It is common for the evaluator, often the principal, to meet with the teacher before the evaluation. One of the things discussed during this preconference is the evaluation form. If you have the opportunity, be sure to go over the form carefully so you have a clear idea of what is expected. If the kinds of things on the evaluation form do not lend themselves well to your style of teaching, ask if you can share your lesson plans with the evaluator and if those plans can be the basis of the evaluation. If the course objectives have already been approved and the plans look reasonable, the evaluator may be quite willing to base the evaluation on them. This will enable you to be evaluated on how well you do what you say you intend to do rather than on a generic evaluation form alone.

You may also be given the choice of having the evaluation on a predetermined day or having the evaluator come in unannounced. If given this choice, it is wise to choose the unannounced visits. If the visit is announced, the evaluator will expect to see you at your very best. Maybe you have heard of "Murphy's Laws,"; one of them says that if anything can go wrong, it will, and at the worst possible time. It is wiser to tell the evaluator to come in unannounced and to see you as you are. If you do the kinds of things recommended so far, the evaluator will find few faults.

Peers

As a beginning teacher it will not take long for you to identify at least one other teacher in the building who you believe is doing an exceptional job. When that happens, it is appropriate to ask that teacher to sit in during some of your classes and suggest ways in which you might improve. You are likely to have more confidence in the suggestions of a person of your own choosing than in suggestions provided by an administrator who may or may not be familiar with your subject area.

Students

No one sees your day-to-day performance more frequently than your students, so it makes good sense to ask them to evaluate you. Forms for evaluations by students typically include questions similar to those listed previously in the Process Evaluation section, but teachers are free to develop their own forms. Students can also be asked to bring in written or typed evaluations that focus on what they like most and least about the teacher and the course.

It is common for student evaluations to vary widely, and you need not be devastated if a student says things that are unkind or even untrue. The power of student evaluation is in their sheer numbers. If one or two students mention a particular problem, you may choose to ignore it. It is more difficult to ignore that problem if it is cited by many students, particularly if the same problem is cited over the course of two or three semesters. However, unless you ask for student input, you might never know what problems are interfering with student learning. Getting student input gives you one more basis for analyzing, and improving, your own teaching, and thus being better able to help your students succeed.

There is a difference of opinion about whether students should be asked to sign their evaluations. Some educators believe that if students are asked to sign their ratings, they will not rate a teacher poorly or cite problems, even if such a rating is deserved, for fear of having their grade lowered. Other educators argue that students are likely to take the evaluation more seriously if they have to sign their name. If students' grades are kept public (using ID numbers to protect confidentiality), students should have little to fear by being honest. Nonetheless, they may be fearful. A compromise is to encourage students to sign their evaluations but make it optional.

Teacher Performance Tests

A teacher performance test (TPT) is a test that you, as the teacher, give to yourself. One way to use a TPT is to specify one or two precise instructional objectives that students can achieve within a single class period and which you have reason to believe concern information or skills that are new to the students.

Next, establish a minimum acceptable level of class performance. This standard is different from the minimum acceptable standard specified in the objective(s). Here, you use your own judgment to decide on a minimum percentage of students who must be able to demonstrate the objective(s) before you will consider the lesson a success. There is no one "right" percentage.

The final step is to go ahead and teach the lesson. If the minimum number of students established as a cut-off point are able to demonstrate the objective, you have reason to believe that, for those students, under the conditions that existed, you did an effective job. Reach over and pat yourself on the back. Of course, success with one lesson might have been a matter of luck, but you can verify the findings by using the same process frequently. If the expected number of students are unable to demonstrate the objective(s), you will know to look more closely at what actually took place during the lesson and to try some other procedures.

Audio and Video Recordings

So much takes place during a typical lesson that it is difficult to recall, afterwards, all that went on. Let machines help. Most schools have audio tape recorders, and many have video tape recorders as well. Taping the TPT (or any other lesson) can provide highly useful information. You may find, for example, that you talk too fast, tend to cut off students' responses, or neglect to reinforce students for their contributions. Because of the wealth of information that can be gleaned, many educators believe that the most effective form of self-evaluation is to view a video tape of a lesson while checking what you see against the plan for that lesson. This enables you to see how well you were able to do what you planned to do, and how much students were actively and appropriately involved.

Interaction Analysis Techniques

In addition to simply listening to or watching a playback of a lesson, you could utilize an interaction analysis technique. One of the most common of these was developed by Edmond J. Amidon and Ned A. Flanders (1967) and is known as *Flanders's Interaction Analysis*. This technique is based on the delineation of nine categories of student and teacher verbal behaviors. The analyst uses the numbers assigned to each category of verbal behavior to encode, every three seconds, the kind of interaction (if any) that is taking place at that moment. The list of numbers can then be analyzed to determine if particular interaction patterns are used to the exclusion of other patterns and whether the interaction pattern recorded was what the teacher intended. The technique is useful for quantifying verbal interaction patterns and it is not intended as a technique for determining whether those patterns are good or bad. Judgments of that sort should depend more on the kind of interaction intended and the extent to which the interaction pattern facilitates students' achievement of the specified objectives. Another interaction analysis system was developed by Morine, Spaulding, and Greenberg.[53] Either system can help ascertain what actually transpired during the lesson and help to quantify that information.

CONTEMPORARY TEACHER EVALUATION METHODS

Teachers in Illinois have been assessing students using various methods for years to check for understanding and assign appropriate grades. In 2010, the Illinois General Assembly passed a bill that changed the way teachers look at assessments. The Performance Evaluation Reform Act (PERA) (Senate Bill 315; Public Act 96-0861) was passed by the Illinois General Assembly and signed by the Governor in January 2010.

In summary, "PERA" requires, among other things, that "Upon the implementation date applicable to a school district or other covered entity, performance evaluations of the principals/assistant principals and teachers of that school district or other covered entity must include data and indicators of student growth as a 'significant factor.'"[54] By September 1, 2012, principals, assistant principals, teachers in contractual continued service (i.e., tenured teachers) and probationary teachers (i.e., non-tenured teachers) were to be evaluated using a four-rating category system (Excellent, Proficient, Needs Improvement, and Unsatisfactory). Anyone evaluated after September 1, 2012 must first complete a pre-qualification program provided or approved by the Illinois State Board of Education (ISBE).

Because the student growth portion of teacher evaluations is new to school districts in Illinois, many administrators and teachers are currently looking at assessments given in classrooms to determine if existing testing is reliable or if assessments need to be altered or created in order to be effective in showing student growth.

Teachers around the country use a variety of assessments to measure growth. With multiple assessments used, teachers can gather more data and more effectively determine student understanding and growth.

There are several types of research that are focused on student growth. Many studies have been researching the types of assessments being used to measure students learning, others are looking at the data collection systems, and others still look into how student growth is being tied into teacher evaluations. The following are examples of some of the research that is been conducted on measuring students' growth.

Current Student Growth Models

Currently there are several data collection systems for tracking student growth out there which are being used as part of teacher evaluations. These assessments are known as performance-based assessment methods or PBAMs. Some examples of PBAMs are student learning objectives (SLOs) and value-added models (VAMs). Research has also been done to determine which growth method is best suited to show growth for different types of learners, including gifted learners.

Performance-Based Assessment Methods (PBAM)

In 2014 a study was done on performance-based assessment methods (PBAMs) to find which of the PBAMs are used frequently or not used, as well as opinions about their applicability and the reasons for preferences reasons of these methods and opinions about the applicability of them. Six information technologies teachers working in Ankara, Turkey were part of the study. According to Daghan and Akkoyunlu, "Two of the teachers are male (33.3%) and four of them are female (66.7%). The lowest vocational seniority of the teachers is three years and the highest one is ten years of teaching experience. The teachers were interviewed, observations took place, and document analysis methods are used. All the data was then reviewed, and a result was found."[55] Two main questions were asked to each of the six teachers. The questions are as follows, "What have you experienced in terms of the phenomenon?" and "What contexts of situations have typically influenced or affected your experience of the phenomenon?"[56] The study found that teachers are not using the PBAMs enough. Portfolios, projects and performance tasks are used, but the other methods almost never are. I have an idea about these PBAMs. In my opinion, it is impossible to have students acquire the attainments and to support them with these methods at the same time during a lesson hour. Some participants said, "PBAMs enable me to see student progress from beginning to end," which is a statement in favor of using PBAMs.[57] These statements are few and far between when it comes to using PBAMs. From this study it seems teachers are unwilling to use new assessment methods, or any new concept, because of unfamiliarity with it and a lack of proper training. To help teachers use PBAMs at a satisfactory level, they should be supported through in-service trainings, in-school briefings, and professional development programs. Two factors, namely "the social system" and "time" should be taken into consideration while attempts are made to make PBAMs, a relatively recent development at schools, popular and adoptable. This is a similar case with VAMs and SLOs. These methods of showing student growth are becoming part of the teacher evaluation with little regards to the proper training or checking for understanding on the teachers' behalf.

Student Learning Objectives (SLO)

With the need for methods of assessment which show student growth, teachers have been creating their own and school districts have been piloting different methods to show student growth for teacher evaluations. From this came student learning objectives (SLOs). The SLO process is similar in each district. "During the first months of school, each teacher identifies strengths and weaknesses of students. Teachers set learning goals aligned with standards; two sample districts require teachers to identify the instructional strategies to be used. Each teacher submits assessment goals to the principal, who has responsibility for reviewing and approving the SLOs. To promote consistency, three of the sample districts also require that SLOs be approved by the district office. Spring assessments-selected at the beginning of the year by the teacher-are used to measure growth. Teachers in the SLO sample districts receive feedback at the end of the school year or the following summer."[58] Research was done in 2015 by Angus, English, Gill, and McCullough to compare and look into the usefulness of both SLOs and VAMs (value-added models). This study was designed as a qualitative study on alternative student growth measures. Research questions consisted of "How are alternative student growth measures incorporated alongside state assessment-based value-added models, measures of professional practice, and other elements of evaluation systems? For what purposes other than teacher evaluation are alternative student growth measures used? How do alternative student growth measures compare with ratings based on classroom observation and ratings based on state assessment–based value-added models in differentiating teachers?"[59] The questions were answered by interviewing teachers, school administration, and union representatives in eight districts. "In total, the study team interviewed 18 district administrators, 11 principals, 14 teachers, and 6 teachers' union representatives across the eight districts."[60] Four of the districts were using added-value models and the other four districts were using student learning objectives. Both of these districts adapted student growth models early on in the required process. The study found that alternative growth measures have been used for many purposes other than teacher evaluation, but SLOs are unique in their use to adapt and improve instruction. The majority of teachers using SLOs met their student growth goal in all four districts using this method. "All the respondents from districts that used student learning objectives noted that the proportion of teachers meeting student learning objective goals (a binary measure) was lower than the proportion rated as satisfactory under comparable binary (satisfactory or unsatisfactory) measures based on classroom observation that were used in previous years."[61] There were mixed feelings and results for districts using added-value models. The evidence of validity and reliability were unclear as well. Teachers in these districts also showed a wide range of teacher effectiveness. It was also noted, SLOs have more added value. They are used in making decisions about data driven instruction, professional development, and help to increase collaboration. The researchers found a few limitations to their study. One limitation was the small number of districts participating in the study. Also, VAMs showed to not be useful for informing instruction without additional information, and SLOs create a conflict of interest. More research is needed on the statistical properties of the alternative measures, the approaches districts are taking to offset implementation costs, and innovative solutions to overcome implementation challenges.

Value-Added Models (VAM)

Other studies have been done on solely value-added models and how they work with different types of assessment. In 2014, Austin, Berends, Gerdeman, and Stuit did a study "to compare estimates of teacher value-added based on two different assessments, the study selected districts whose students took the criterion-referenced Indiana Statewide Testing for Educational Progress Plus (ISTEP+) and the norm-referenced Measures of Academic Progress (MAP) in the same school year. The analysis examines reading and math achievement data for grades 4 and 5 in 46 schools in 10 Indiana districts for 2005/06–2010/11."[62] This study was designed as a quantitative study on the variability of added-value models. "The value-added estimates were calculated using a covariate-adjustment model that predicts the students' posttest scores based on their pretest scores and student and classroom characteristics. The average difference between students predicted and actual posttest scores provides the basis for estimating teacher value-added."[63] Three strategies were used to compare the estimates. One strategy looked at the correlations of the estimates. "A second strategy constructed transition matrixes to document how the quintile rankings of estimates of teacher value-added differed between the two assessments."[64] The final strategy classified value-added estimates. According to Austin et. al., "The findings indicate yearly variability between the two tests in estimates of teacher value-added. [...] The comparison of quintile rankings found that an average of 33.3 percent of estimates of teacher value- added ranked in the same quintile on both tests in the same school year. However, across all comparisons, 28.1 percent of estimates had at least a two-quintile difference between ISTEP+ and MAP scores."[65] The researchers found a few limitations to the study. One limitation was the possibility for missing data. Other limitations were the study's inability to be generalized to other districts or states, only a single year was used, and the source of the variability could not be determined. In another study done on VAMs each district works with an outside provider to develop and implement its VAM, and all four districts apply the same VAM approach to alternative assessments that they are using for state assessments. Teachers in the four districts using alternative assessment-based VAMs receive written performance feedback about prior-year performance each fall, along with training to interpret the feedback. When selecting and designing alternative growth measures, districts using SLOs chose them as a teacher-guided method of assessing student growth, while those using alternative assessment-based VAMs were motivated to use VAMs partly to take advantage of existing assessments. Both VAMs and SLOs have pros and cons and depending on how they are going to be used may determine which method is best suited for each district. Also, assessment and growth models are not created equal.

Growth Model Pilot Program (GMPP)

Not all students may thrive using certain growth models. In 2014, Rambo-Hernandez and Ryser did research to determine which growth model shows the best data for educators and to conclude how gifted learners are impacted when using assessment data to determine student growth in education through the use of Growth Model Pilot Program (GMPP). Student data was collected in both elementary and middle-level grades. In 2005, nine states were used to pilot some of the first growth models, which consisted of three different categories: transition matrix models, trajectory models, and projection models. One of the goals of the Growth Model Pilot Program (GMPP) was to predict whether non-proficient students would successfully attain proficiency over a given period of time. The second goal was to identify which levels of performance students must achieve at each grade level in order to be considered proficient. The transition matrix model compared academic growth to performance categories (basic, proficient, advanced). The trajectory model highlighted the difference between the performance target and the baseline test score. Lastly, the projection model estimated future scores based on current performances. The growth model used by pilot states included five different categories to monitor student growth. Those five categories were categorical, gain score, regression, value-added, and normative. These categories correspond with the three categories implemented with the GMPP and require the use of a vertical scale (performance scores). "As a result of the study, it was found that the average AYP increase using the original growth models was 2% in eight of the pilot states and 34% in the ninth state."[66] While the study did show growth towards proficiency, one of the main concerns with the data collected was that the researchers only focused on proficiency. Unfortunately, the growth model didn't focus on tracking growth in gifted students who already score at or above proficient. It was also found that the results of different types of growth models varied based on grade level and state. They also found that all tests, regardless of what type, will show error at some point. While researchers did see increases in all growth models implemented in education, it was concluded that growth models need three components to truly track growth of all students. The growth models should include at least three observations or test scores, the test scores should be comparable across time, and a measure of time must be collected for each test. The three test scores allow educators to estimate a growth path or plan for each individual student.

In conclusion, student growth is not new, but it is becoming more widely talked about and reviewed. It has more of an impact now than ever before on both students and teachers. Now we must look into and decide what way is best to monitor and report on student growth as it applies to teacher evaluations, professional development, and student learning. There are several different models to show growth, VAMs and SLOs being two of the most popular. Some apply to teacher evaluation and some do not yet. Some states have started using student growth as a part of the teacher evaluation while other states have yet to make the move. Some teachers are willing to jump right into the new systems, while others find all the new and added workload to be overwhelming. There are many pros and cons the idea of student growth and the new models, but what needs to happen now is decisions on what is going to show the best results for the students.

SUMMARY

Teacher evaluation is just as important as student evaluation. A particularly useful approach is to videotape a lesson and then assess the extent to which it followed the lesson plan and the extent to which students could achieve the lesson's objective. Other techniques, such as student, peer, and administrative evaluations, may provide useful information, but no single piece of information should be considered conclusive. A good teacher is continually trying to improve and is continually seeking feedback. The single best feedback is the success of the students. A teacher's success is dependent on the success of his or her students.

KEY TERMS, PEOPLE, AND IDEAS

Standardized Testing

No Child Left Behind (NCLB)

Standard-based Reform

Common Core State Standards

PARCC Testing

Formative and Summative Assessments

observation checklists, peer/self-evaluation, and running records

Discovery Assessment, DIBELS, and PARCC assessment

Portfolio Assessment

Teacher Evaluation Methods

Teacher Performance Test

Student Growth Models

Performance Based Assessment Methods (PBAM)

Student Learning Objectives (SLO)

Value Added Models (VAM)

Growth Model Pilot Program (GMPP)

QUESTIONS FOR CONSIDERATION

1. To what extent do you agree or disagree with the idea of designing teacher-made tests so that they prepare students for standardized tests?
2. What politically and economically feasible way is there to deal with students who, for whatever reason, fail to pass mandated state tests?

ENDNOTES

1 C. J. Gallagher, "Reconciling a tradition of testing with a new learning paradigm," *Educational Psychology Review* 15, no. 1 (2003): 83–99, https://doi.org/10.1023/A:1021323509290.

2 N. T. Edwards, "The historical and social foundations of standardized testing: In search of a balance between learning and evaluation." *Testing and Evaluation* 10, no. 1 (2006): 8–16, retrieved from http://jalt.org/test/edw_1.htm.

3 N. T. Edwards, "The historical and social foundations of standardized testing," 8–16.

4 C. J. Gallagher, "Reconciling a tradition of testing," 92.

5 D. Johnson and B. Johnson, "*High stakes testing,*" December 23, 2009, retrieved from http://www.education.com/reference/article/high-stakes-testing1/.

6 US Department of Education, Race to the Top Program Executive Summary, 2009, 2. Retrieved June 1, 2020 from https://www2.ed.gov/programs/racetothetop/executive-summary.pdf.

7 US Department of Education, Race to the Top, 2.

8   L. M. Abrams, J. J. Pedulla, and G. F. Madaus, "Views from the classroom: Teachers' opinions of statewide testing programs," *Theory Into Practice* 42, no. 1 (2003): 18, DOI: 10.1207/s15430421tip4201_4.

9   H. Sweetland Edwards, "Leaving Tests Behind," *Time* 185, *no.* 5 (Feb. 16, 2015): 30.

10   Abrams, Pedulla, and Madaus, "Views from the classroom," 18.

11   L. M. McNeil, *Contradictions of school reform: Educational costs of standardized testing.* (New York: Routledge, 2000).

12   A. Foxal and D. L. Brown, Assessment, March 17, 2017. Retrieved from Illinois State Board of Education: https://www.isbe.net/Pages/Assessment.aspx.

13   The National Center for Fair and Open Testing, FairTest, 2009, https://www.fairtest.org/search/node/position%20statement.

14   W. J. Popham, *Classroom Assessment: What Teachers Need to Know* (7th ed.). (New Jersey: Pearson, 2014), 8.

15   Popham, *Classroom Assessment.*

16   Popham, *Classroom Assessment*, 12.

17   Popham, *Classroom Assessment*, 12.

18   C. Garrison and M. Ehringhaurs, *Formative and Summative Assessments in the Classroom, 2015.* Retrieved November 23, 2020, from Association of Middle Level Education: https://www.amle.org/wp-content/uploads/2020/05/Formative_Assessment_Article_Aug2013.pdf.

19   F. Ward, "Integrating Technology and Literacy," edutopia.org, March 25, 2016. https://www.edutopia.org/blog/integrating-technology-and-literacy-frank-ward.

20   J. Gorlewski, "Research for the Classroom: Formative Assessment: Can You Handle the Truth?" *The English Journal* 98, no. 2 (2008): 94–97. Retrieved November 23, 2020, from http://www.jstor.org/stable/40503394.

21   J. Gorlewski, "Research for the Classroom," 95.

22   N. Bakula, "The Benefits of Formative Assessments for Teaching and Learning," *Science Scope* 34, no. 1 (2010): 37–43. Retrieved November 23, 2020, from http://www.jstor.org/stable/43184055.

23   C. J. Marsh, "A critical analysis of the use of formative assessment in schools," *Educational Research for Policy and Practice* 6 (2007): 25–29. https://doi.org/10.1007/s10671-007-9024-z.

24   P. Black and D. William, "Assessment and Classroom Learning," *Assessment in Education* 5, no. 1 (1998): 26. https://www.gla.ac.uk/t4/learningandteaching/files/PGCTHE/BlackandWiliam1998.pdf.

25   TeacherVision, "Running Records," February 8, 2007, 1. https://www.teachervision.com/reading-aloud/running-records.

26   Popham, *Classroom Assessment.*

27   Discovery Education Response to Intervention (RTI) Management Tool Guide, n.d. Retrieved March 20, 2021, from http://docplayer.net/30342907-Discovery-education-assessment-response-to-intervention.html.

28   "DIBELS," Wikipedia, last modified May 27, 2020, https://en.wikipedia.org/wiki/DIBELS.

29   College of Teaching and Learning, University of Oregon. Dynamic Indicators of Basic Early Literacy Skills (DIBELS). Retrieved from https://dibels.uoregon.edu/assessment/dibels#measures.

30   Illinois State Board of Education, *PARCC - Partnership for Assessment of Readiness for College and Careers*, 2015. Retrieved November 23, 2020, fromhttps://www.isbe.net/parcc.

31   Illinois State Board of Education, *PARCC*.

32   Popham, *Classroom Assessment*.

33   D. Kelly-Riley, N. Elliot, and A. Rudniy, "An Empirical Framework with ePortfolio Assessment," *International Journal of ePortfolio* 6, no. 2 (2016): 95–116.

34   C. Gillespie, K. Ford, R. Gillespie, and A. Leavell, "Portfolio Assessment: Some Questions, Some Answers, Some Recommendations," *Journal of Adolescent & Adult Literacy 39, no. 6* (1996): 480–91. Retrieved November 23, 2020, from http://www.jstor.org/stable/40014037.

35   G. Hewitt, "The Writing Portfolio: Assessment Starts with A," *The Clearing House 74*, no. 4 (2001): 187–90. Retrieved November 23, 2020, from http://www.jstor.org/stable/30189658.

36   Popham, *Classroom Assessment, 243.*

37   C. Danielson and L. Abrutyn, *An Introduction to Using Portfolios in the Classroom* (Alexandria, VA: Association for Supervision and Curriculum Development, 1997).

38   K. Cole et al., "Portfolio Assessment: Challenges in Secondary Education," *The High School Journal 80*, no. 4 (1997): 261–72. Retrieved November 23, 2020, from http://www.jstor.org/stable/40364458.

39   G. Ring and B. Ramirez, "Implementing ePortfolios for the Assessment of General Education Competencies," *International Journal of ePortfolio* 2, no. 1 (2012): 87–97. Retrieved March 2017, from http://www.theijep.com/pdf/ijep62.pdf.

40   Popham, *Classroom Assessment*.

41   D. Schunk, *Learning Theories: An Educational Perspective* (7th ed.), (Boston: Pearson, 2016).

42   J. Lombardi, "To Portfolio or Not to Portfolio: Helpful or Hyped?" *College Teaching* 56, no. 1 (2008): 7–10. Retrieved November 23, 2020, from http://www.jstor.org/stable/27559345.

43   W. Kicken et al., "The Effects of Portfolio-Based Advice on the Development of Self-Directed Learning Skills in Secondary Vocational Education," *Educational Technology Research and Development* 57, no. 4 (2009): 439–60. Retrieved November 23, 2020, from http://www.jstor.org/stable/40388642.

44   H. Noden and B. Moss, "Professional Development: A Guide to Books on Portfolios: Rafting the Rivers of Assessment," *The Reading Teacher* 48, no.2 (1994): 180–83. Retrieved November 23, 2020, from http://www.jstor.org/stable/20201398.

45   T. Goolsby, "Portfolio Assessment for Better Evaluation," *Music Educators Journal* 82, no. 3 (1995): 39–44. Retrieved November 23, 2020, from http://www.jstor.org/stable/3398900.

46   Cole et al., "Portfolio Assessment."

47   W. Rickards et al., "Learning, Reflection, and Electronic Portfolios: Stepping Toward an Assessment Practice," *The Journal of General Education* 57, no. 1 (2008): 31–50. Retrieved November 23, 2020, from http://www.jstor.org/stable/27798089.

48   Popham, *Classroom Assessment.*

49   D. Sweet, *Student Portfolios: Classroom Uses, November 1993.* (J. Zimmermann, Editor, Office of Educational Research and Improvement (OERI) of the U.S. Department of Education) Retrieved November 23, 2020, from Office of Research Education Consumer Guide. https://www2.ed.gov/pubs/OR/ConsumerGuides/classuse.html.

50   Danielson and Abrutyn, *An introduction to using portfolios in the classroom.*

51   Popham, *Classroom Assessment.*

52   Popham, *Classroom Assessment.*

53   G. Morine, R. Spaulding, and S. Greenberg, *Discovering New Dimensions in the Teaching Process* (Scranton, PA: International Textbook, 1971), vi.

54   Illinois State Board of Education. Performance evaluation reform act (PERA) and Senate Bill 7. Retrieved from https://www.isbe.net/Pages/Educator-Evaluations.aspx.

55   G. Daghan and B. Akkoyunlu, "A Qualitative Study about Performance Based Assessment Methods Used in Information Technologies Lesson, *Educational Sciences: Theory and Practice* 14, no. 1 (2014): 333–38.

56   Daghan and Akkoyunlu, "A Qualitative Study," 335.

57   Daghan and Akkoyunlu, "A Qualitative Study," 336.

58   English et al., Alternative student growth Measures for teacher evaluation: Profiles of early-adopting districts. *National Center for Education Evaluation and Regional Assistance, 2014, 1.* Retrieved from http://ies.ed.gov/ncee/edlabs/regions/midatlantic/pdf/REL_2014016.pdf.

59   M. H. Angus et al., "Alternative student growth measures for teacher evaluation: implementation experiences of early-adopting districts. Regional Educational Laboratory Mid-Atlantic, 2015, 3. Retrieved from http://files.eric.ed.gov/fulltext/ED558160.pdf.

60   Angus et al., "Alternative student growth measures for teacher evaluation: implementation experiences of early-adopting districts," 3.

61   Angus et al., "Alternative student growth measures for teacher evaluation: implementation experiences of early-adopting districts," 4.

62   M. J. Austin et al., "Comparing estimates of teacher value-added based on criterion- and norm-referenced tests," Regional Educational Laboratory Midwest, 2014, 1. Retrieved from http://files.eric.ed.gov/fulltext/ED544674.pdf.

63   Austin et al., "Comparing estimates of teacher value-added based on criterion- and norm-referenced tests," 4.

64   Austin et al., "Comparing estimates of teacher value-added based on criterion- and norm-referenced tests," 4.

65   Austin et al., "Comparing estimates of teacher value-added based on criterion- and norm-referenced tests," 5.

66   Gail R. Ryser and Karen Rambo-Hernandez, "Using Growth Models to Measure School Performance: Implications for Gifted Learners," *Gifted Child Today* 37, no. 1 (December 2013): 19. https://doi.org/10.1177/1076217513509617.

CHAPTER 11

Classroom Management

INTRODUCTION

One of the greatest concerns felt by most beginning teachers is whether they will be able to establish and maintain a classroom atmosphere conducive to effective teaching and learning, or in short, whether they will be able to control their classes. More than maintaining a good classroom atmosphere, classroom control involves helping students learn to be responsible for their own actions.

This chapter examines principles of classroom management, how helping students meet some basic human needs can help minimize or eliminate problems, some approaches to dealing with problems if they arise, and some of the legal terms and factors that may help guide your actions in the classroom. The intent is to provide you with information and techniques that you can use to prevent most common classroom management problems and to deal humanely and effectively with any that do arise.

LEARNING OUTCOMES

You will be able, in writing, to:

1. Explain at least two basic management principles and their supporting rationales.
2. Select any two levels of needs described by A. H. Maslow and explain at least two things that can be done to help students satisfy those needs in a classroom.
3. Given a videotape or written description of a classroom management problem, determine whether an operant conditioning, reality therapy, or limiting

involvement approach is most appropriate and cite specific factors from the tape or description to support your decision.

4.   Define terms such as *in loco parentis*, case law, slander, libel, extortion, assault, and battery.

BASIC MANAGEMENT PRINCIPLES

There are many classroom management rules and principles, but the following are likely to prove particularly useful to you.

The Goal Is Self-Control

One of the primary missions of all teachers is to help students learn to control their own actions and take responsibility for those actions. Young children lack the foresight to anticipate the consequences of many of their acts, so parents and primary-grade teachers assume much of that responsibility. This helps protect youngsters from impetuous actions that might be harmful. As children get older and more experienced, they mature; they become more able to anticipate consequences and, thus, more aware of the need for self-control. Parents and teachers, who, for various reasons, are slow to give up the control they have, hinder the maturation process. The situation is analogous to learning to ride a bicycle. It is helpful to have someone hold the bicycle when you are first learning to balance, but if the helper does not let go, you will never master the skill or be able to use the bicycle to its fullest advantage. Teachers need to let go of some control in order to provide opportunities for students to practice the skill of self-control. If students do not practice the skill, it will be difficult for them to master it.

One way to "let go" is to minimize the number of rules imposed. Teachers are required to enforce all rules set forth by the school board and the school administration. These are usually written in a handbook that is given to each student at the beginning of the school year. All teachers, and particularly beginning teachers, should read the school rules carefully because they are contractually obligated to enforce them, and they should make that point clear to students. Beyond those rules, however, teachers have a great deal of latitude. Some teachers, for example, find that they need just one rule: *You may do whatever you like as long as you do not disturb anyone else.*

Such a rule may sound like an invitation to chaos, but it is not. One reason for this is that the rule is so reasonable that students are reluctant to violate it. Teachers who take such an approach might find the following steps useful:

1.   Before the semester begins, construct a syllabus and supporting unit plans that focus on the acquisition of useful information. Be sure that you can show students the personal and social significance of the material to be learned. Build a rationale that answers the question "Why should I learn this stuff?"

2. On the very first day of class, distribute, and then discuss, the course syllabus. The discussion of the objectives and week-by-week schedule will communicate to students that you have done your homework, that you have thought seriously about the course and its relevance to the students, that you have confidence in them, and that the plan is a workable one that will enable them to achieve worthwhile goals.

3. Explain that you will help students learn the skills and information described in the syllabus, but that you cannot control their actions, only your own. Therefore, although you intend to do your best to conduct interesting and informative lessons and to help each student achieve useful objectives, students must decide whether they want to learn. In order to get anything out of the class, they have to put something in: effort.

While the choice to learn or not learn, to put forth effort or to coast, is up to each student, the choice to disturb others is not. Students who do not want to learn can do other work, doodle, or daydream, as long as neither you nor students who wish to learn are disturbed or distracted. This is not really much of a concession, because if students choose not to learn they will do these other things anyway. You are simply recognizing a fact and trying to impose a condition on it. However, because you give students the option of simply sitting quietly and doing nothing, if they choose to cause a problem, their choice makes them seem unreasonable. Since few students want to appear unreasonable to their peers, the rule acts as a deterrent against disruptions.

Rely on Natural Consequences

A natural consequence is one that follows an action without the necessity of human intervention. For example, if you continually consume more calories than you expend, you will put on weight. If you fall asleep while driving on the highway, you are likely to have an accident. If you daydream during class, you may miss some information and may not be able to perform tasks requiring that information.

Schools do not deal with life and death issues, and failing a course does not condemn a person to a life of abject slavery. Nonetheless, many students and parents expect that if a student is not doing well, the teacher will come up with some way to save the day. Do not do it. At the beginning of the semester, explain that you have no intention of trying to live students' lives for them, and in part, this means that you will not shield them from the consequences of their own actions. If they do not pay attention, do not complete assignments, or they miss class because they are discussing their unacceptable behavior with an administrator, their grades are likely to suffer, and they may end up failing the course. You will not fail them; they will fail themselves.

This approach to classroom management shifts responsibility for proper student behavior from the teacher to each student, where it belongs, and it gives students the opportunity to develop self-control. Students are denied that opportunity if you closely supervise and control their every move.

Helping Students Succeed

People would rather be successful than unsuccessful, and to the extent that you can help students succeed, they will tend to be cooperative. Success means the achievement of some goal or the satisfaction of some need or desire, so the first thing teachers must do in order to help students be successful is to identify some of the basic needs and desires that motivate their behavior. As it happens, the groundwork has already been done.

MASLOW'S HIERARCHY OF NEEDS

In 1943, Abraham H. Maslow described a hierarchy of human needs beginning with basic physiological needs and extending through needs for safety, love, esteem, and self-actualization. He theorized that people would devote their attention to at least partially satisfying their most basic needs before they diverted their efforts to satisfying less basic needs.[1] For example, you might, at one time or another, have had to miss part of a play or movie in order to use a restroom. The physiological need was more powerful than the desire to watch the entertainment. Teachers can make use of Maslow's work because the needs he described are the motivating forces behind many student actions. Understanding the hierarchy of human needs may help teachers understand how they can help students meet those needs in the classroom. This will help minimize or eliminate many classroom management problems.

One word of caution. In thinking about why particular students may be causing problems, you need to keep your own qualifications in mind. Unless you are a certified psychologist or a licensed physician, you should not try to diagnose or treat any suspected psychological or physical problem. Teachers are employed to teach the content they are certified to teach, not to play amateur psychologist, physician, or minister. Any attempts to do so may do more harm than good (regardless of good intentions), and they may delay or prevent the proper thing from being done.

Physiological Needs

Maslow identified physiological needs as the most basic and powerful of all human needs. For example, the first concern of a person who is drowning, starving, or dying of thirst is to satisfy that crucial need for air, food, or water. Teachers do not often encounter situations involving actual survival; nevertheless, physiological needs can prompt behavior problems.

Air

People work best when they are reasonably comfortable. If a room is too cold or too warm, smells bad, or simply lacks adequate air circulation, students will soon begin paying more attention to the discomfort than to the lesson. Teachers who ignore such problems will appear to be unreasonable or unaware of the world around them. Neither image is helpful. A better course of action is to acknowledge the problem and to try to solve it. Sometimes it helps to simply open a window, but in some cases it may be necessary to move to a different place. In any case, the acknowledgment of the problem and the effort to solve it are important. These steps show students that the teacher cares about them and this alone will help minimize potential behavior problems.

Food

One could argue that it is the responsibility of parents to feed their children, but since the passage of the National School Lunch Act in 1946, schools have taken on part of that responsibility. Most students come to school adequately fed, but they are in a period of rapid growth and are frequently hungry. Do not be surprised, therefore, if students are somewhat less attentive toward the end of the period immediately preceding lunch. Hunger is a powerful force, and hungry students would rather contemplate a hamburger than an algebraic equation. This does not mean that teachers should allow students to snack during class (since that would be likely to disturb the teacher and the rest of the class), nor does it mean that a teacher should end instruction early. What it does mean is that if you are aware of basic human needs, you are more likely to understand students' actions—in this case, why they may be less than fully attentive.

If you suspect that a student is getting too little to eat or is suffering from malnutrition (perhaps from dieting too rigidly on their own, or perhaps the family is financially unable to provide appropriate meals at home), the proper course of action is first to discuss the issue privately with the student and then, if necessary, to alert the appropriate school administrator. Your primary function is to provide food for thought. Others are employed to deal with the question of food for the body.

Water

The need for water is not usually a great problem, but callous teachers can make it into one. If a student asks for permission to get a drink of water and is refused for no good reason, you will appear to be unreasonable. If students believe that you are unreasonable, you will find it difficult to elicit student cooperation and can expect continual challenges to your authority.

On the other hand, some students use requests for drinks as a way of avoiding work or disrupting the class. One effective way to handle this problem is to meet with such students privately and express concern for their health. Tell students that you will keep track of their requests and, if there seems to be a problem, that they will be referred to the school nurse. If the requests were just excuses, the idea of having to talk with the school nurse will quickly end the problem—people like to keep their personal habits personal. If the requests continue, there might, in fact, be a problem and a visit to the nurse would be appropriate.

Using the Bathroom

The need to eliminate bodily wastes is a very real and basic need and requests to go to the bathroom should be granted immediately. If you suspect that students are making the request in order to avoid work or to disrupt class, the same strategy as used with the excessive water-drinkers should be used. You should meet with such students privately and express concern for their health, and explain that if they cannot attend to their needs before or after class, an appointment will be made for them to see the school nurse. Students are even less likely to want to discuss their toilet habits with a nurse than to discuss their requests for drinks, so the problem will quickly end. If the need is real, a referral might result in finding and treating a disease or malfunction at an early stage.

Sleep

Today's teenagers have full schedules. In addition to attending school and doing homework, many students engage in extracurricular activities and some hold part-time jobs. As a result of trying to attend to so many things, some students do not get the sleep they require and may therefore doze during class. Certainly, such students are less likely to sleep if a class is interesting and informative, but even then some students may still get drowsy. One way to help students fight drowsiness is to announce to the class that anyone who feels sleepy should feel free to get up and stand in the back of the room for a while.

Unfortunately, some students may fall asleep in your class and even though they may not be snoring, the very fact that they are sleeping will distract you, and it will distract other students. You will need to take some action.

The first time a student falls asleep, it would be appropriate to indicate via nonverbal cues that someone nearby should awaken the student. It is important to avoid embarrassing the sleeper. Once awake, the student can be brought into the class activities by being asked a not-too-specific question or by being asked for an opinion. If the problem persists, you should meet with the student privately, express concern, and use the referral strategy. In some cases, students may not be able to control their amount of sleep: they may work late to help support their family, or they may not go to sleep at a reasonable hour due to noise. These problems should be referred to an appropriate administrator. Your primary responsibility is to teach. Others are employed to deal with out-of-school problems.

Interest in the Opposite Sex

Interest in the opposite sex is normal, and it begins to manifest itself during the early teen years. Educators are well aware of the hormonal changes affecting students, and they try to help students adjust to their new needs by providing instruction about reproductive systems, social expectations, and how to avoid sexually transmitted diseases. This instruction provides students with useful information, but in some cases the hormones appear to override the thinking process.

You need to be aware that teenagers are sometimes preoccupied with sex. They have just undergone pubescence, and they are naturally curious about their bodies and their attractiveness to the opposite sex. Some concern about physical development and some flirting is to be expected. If the interest interferes with academic performance, then the teacher needs to intervene. The intervention should take the form of a private conference to discuss with the student the need to separate physical concerns from academic concerns. Since the issue is a sensitive one for most students, one conference is usually enough. If the preoccupation continues or if the student brings out a concern that may reflect a physical problem, referrals to appropriate school staff may be in order.

Safety Needs

Once physiological needs are at least partially met, Maslow contends that people will turn their attention to the next most powerful need, physical safety. As was the case with physiological needs, safety needs concern survival, such as not being killed by wild animals or by other people. In today's schools there are three main sources of physical harm: other students, the curriculum itself, and physical punishment.

The US Department of Education estimates that each day about one hundred thousand students carry guns to school and that each hour more than two thousand students are physically attacked on school grounds.[2] Further, more than four hundred thousand crimes are reported in and around our schools, and many more go unreported.[3]

There is little that teachers can do to protect students against violence by other students, because most of that violence takes place when teachers are not present, as in restrooms, before or after school, or in congested, hectic situations, such as crowded hallways or lunchrooms. If such violence is a serious problem in your school, the school administration may decide to have police patrol the school grounds and hallways and/or to install metal detectors. Having to take these steps is unfortunate; first because it is an admission that education alone is not sufficient to induce social order and second, because it is expensive. It reduces the number of dollars available to meet other educational needs. In some cases, however, there is no choice. Without that protection, education in some schools is not practical.

While you may not be able to do much about violence outside your classroom, you can take steps to prevent it in your classroom. One step is to establish and follow a routine. If you begin each class on time, greet students, take attendance, make announcements, and then move directly into the lesson, students will understand what to expect in that class and what is expected of them. This understanding will help generate among students a sense that the classroom is a special place, a place to learn, not a place to continue out-of-class discussions or fights. The classroom becomes more of a safe and secure haven.

The Curriculum Itself

A second source of safety concerns for students is the curriculum itself. Handling a welding torch in a shop class, putting a cake into a hot oven in a home economics class, or jumping off a diving board in a physical education class, are activities that may, depending upon the previous experiences of individual students, cause them great concern. It does not matter that the activity is one that can easily be performed safely; what matters is the student's perception of danger. It is the perception that must be dealt with because that is what the student sees as real.

It is best to avoid problems, so it is wise to examine planned activities and to identify any that have caused concern for students in the past or that might cause concern for students. If any such activities are identified, it makes sense to make a special effort to show students how those activities should be done and how to avoid common mistakes. While you do not want to generate fears where none exist, students need to know that having concerns about some things is not wrong or "dumb," and that if they have such concerns you are willing to work with them, individually, to help them get the job done.

It may happen that a student does not ask for extra help but shows great reluctance to engage in an activity during class. The student should not be pressured, either physically or by fear of ridicule, to engage in the activity. You should move on to another student and discreetly arrange to talk with the fearful student after class or after school. Great care should be taken to avoid embarrassing the student. Most of us are fearful of one thing or another, but none of us would want that fear to be the source of public ridicule or embarrassment. If you handle the problem with sensitivity and tact, you will do much to strengthen your rapport with the class.

When meeting with the student privately, discuss the problem and offer additional time and help. It should be made clear, however, that credit for achieving the objective can only be given if the objective is, in fact, achieved. The student's fear may be so great that he or she chooses to lose credit for the objective rather than attempt the activity. Make it clear that this is an acceptable choice. There is no point in telling the student that unless that particular objective is achieved, his or her academic career is ruined. First, such a statement is not true. There are other objectives that can be achieved and other things the student can learn. Second, an understanding attitude may, over a little time, help the student overcome the fear and achieve the objective. Your job is to help students succeed. Helping them overcome fears helps them succeed.

Corporal Punishment

A third source of student concern for safety is physical punishment. Although hundreds of years ago teachers, such as Hillel and Comenius, argued that physical punishment has no place in the instructional process, the practice is still with us. In fact, as recently as 1988, 50 percent of 2,118 adults surveyed approved of the use of physical punishment.[4]

The legality of corporal punishment is in the hands of each state, because there is nothing in the U.S. Constitution about education. In April of 1977, the U.S. Supreme Court, in *Ingraham vs. Wright*, ruled that the provision against cruel and unusual punishment does not apply to school children.[5] Nonetheless, many state boards of education have banned the use of corporal punishment, some for pedagogical reasons, and others out of fear of lawsuits. Within those states that have not formally banned corporal punishment, many local school boards have done so. Even in districts that have not banned it, many principals have done so. It is important to keep in mind that once a rule or law is passed at one level, no one at a lower level has the right to unilaterally change or ignore that rule.

It is reasonable to ask why so many teachers favor corporal punishment, and the answer is not hard to find. Imagine yourself as a primary grade teacher who has just told a student, for the third or fourth time, to stop poking other students. The student looks up at you and says, "No." After your attempts, and perhaps the attempts by the principal or school counselor to reason with the student have failed, what would you do? You are charged with the education of 20–30 small children. Students such as your poker have apparently not learned appropriate social skills at home, and they see no reason to listen to you or to anyone else. The problem is that there is no natural consequence for their continued misbehavior. Lacking other workable alternatives, many teachers see corporal punishment as the most appropriate substitute for a natural consequence.

You, however, will not be teaching primary grade students and, at the high school level, the arguments against physical punishment are strong. First and most important, using force rather than reason contradicts the intent of the educational process. Educators are trying to help students learn to solve problems by using brains rather than brawn. If educators themselves use force, the brains versus brawn argument is seriously weakened. This, of course, is equally true at the primary grade level, but there the students may be too young to understand the concepts involved.

Second, although physical punishment may be expedient and may provide some immediate satisfaction to the punisher, it teaches the student very little other than not to get caught. If a teacher is unable to explain the rationale for or against a particular act with sufficient clarity to convince a student, it is unlikely that a session with the paddle will do the job.

Still further, while educators might be able to use physical punishment in the lower grades, because they are so much bigger than the students, older students are unlikely to submit meekly to such treatment. In the interest of self-preservation, teachers should abstain from physical punishment.

If a student is subjected to physical punishment, you should not administer it. Your role as a concerned helper is too important to jeopardize by assuming the role of bully. Further, if physical punishment is administered, it should be done in the presence of at least two adults. Lawsuits are likely to arise out of charges of physical abuse, so a witness may be needed in court. Avoid the problems. With the exception of occasional congratulatory pats on the back, teachers should keep their hands off students.

Love Needs

Maslow's description of love needs centers on the love that usually exists between husband and wife, between parents and children, and among siblings. The need for this kind of nurturing love and sense of belonging is only indirectly related to classroom management, because a teacher's sincerest concern for a student cannot replace the love and concern of a mother, father, brother, or sister. Further, you are not employed to act as a substitute mother, father, brother, or sister; you are employed to teach.

Nonetheless, you should recognize that students who are deprived of love at home suffer a deficiency as debilitating as that resulting from the deprivation of food or sleep. Students who suffer from a lack of parental concern, nurturing, and love are likely to be less stable emotionally and more easily depressed than their more typical peers. A teacher who learns of such a problem can make special efforts not to amplify the problem at school.

While it is not true that all students who come from single-parent homes suffer from a lack of love, the following statistics are not encouraging.

> About 24 percent of single women age 18 to 44 had borne a child (as of June 1992), compared with 15 percent a decade earlier. The proportion of single mothers more than doubled among women with one or more years of college (4.4 percent in 1982; 11.3 percent in 1992) and nearly doubled among women with a high school diploma, 17.2 percent in 1982; 32.5 percent in 1992.
>
> Out-of-wedlock childbearing increased among all racial and ethnic groups between 1982 and 1992. About two-thirds (67 percent) of births to black women in 1992 were out of wedlock, compared to 27 percent for Hispanic

women and 17 percent for white women. Comparable figures in 1982 were 49percent, 16 percent, and 10 percent, respectively.

In 1992, about 65 percent of teenage (15–19 years old) births were out of wedlock. Ninety-four percent of black American teenage births were out of wedlock, compared to 60 percent of Hispanic and 56 percent of white teenage births.[6]

Nearly 30% of all family groups with children were maintained by single parents in 1993, a significant increase from 12% in 1970. A child in a one-parent situation was just slightly more likely to be living with a divorced parent (37%) in 1993 than with a never-married parent (35%).

Although two-thirds of all single parents were white, one-parent situations are much more common among black Americans than white. About 65% of all black family groups with children were maintained by single parents versus 25% of comparable white family groups. Among Hispanics, single parents represented 35% of family groups with children.[7]

The statistics just cited make it clear that many students have less than an ideal family life and are, in many cases, parents themselves. One thing you *can* do with respect to love needs is to maintain your classroom as a place where students are safe from physical abuse and from psychological abuse such as ridicule and embarrassment. This can be done, in many cases, by generating among students a sense of unity and security. This, in turn, can be facilitated by having a set of common goals, treating students with respect and insisting that they treat you, and each other, with respect. If these things are done, your room is likely to become an island of calm and sanctuary. Students will know that when they are in your room, they are safe and that you care about them as individuals. In an otherwise threatening and turbulent world, students would value such a place.

Self-Esteem Needs

The need for self-esteem is the need for a sense of worthiness in one's own eyes and in the eyes of others. Although this need is less basic than the preceding needs, it is more directly related to classroom management and more amenable to teacher manipulation.

One aspect of self-esteem is a one's sense of oneself as a person—the need to be accepted as one is. You should make it clear by words and actions that your first, and greatest, concern is for each student as a person. People are not perfect, and it is reassuring for students to know that when they make a mistake, they will not be regarded as inherently bad. It is the act, not the person, that rates the disapproval. This stance enables you to continue working with students who sometimes cause problems. It becomes a matter of "John, I do not like what you did, but I believe that you have done better and will do better," rather than, "John, I do not like what you did and therefore I want as little to do with you as possible." The first stance allows for cooperation in the future, whereas the second tends to end the relationship.

The same is true if students do poorly in your class. It is important to remember that despite your best efforts to demonstrate the usefulness and relevance of what you are teaching, not all students will recognize that usefulness and relevance. Consequently, those students may not put forth the effort required to learn, although they may go through the expected motions of working on projects, doing library work, or even sitting with the book in their laps for hours. Their poor performance means only that they are not doing well in your class. It is likely that those students have a host of talents that you, yourself, lack. For example, they may be better than you at playing basketball or football, cooking or taking care of a house, or stealing cars. Low grades do not necessarily reflect stupidity.

Internal Recognition

Self-esteem has two parts. The first and most important part is the recognition, by individuals, that they are being successful—that they are developing new abilities, new knowledge, or new control over their lives, or are acquiring some other desired thing or state. Think back to the time you learned to ride your bicycle or to swim. The chances are good that one of the first things you did after learning the new skill was to show off your new ability to Mom or Dad. You were proud, and you felt good about yourself. That is what self-esteem is all about—earning a sense of accomplishment.

Earning the sense of accomplishment is crucial. Students are unlikely to feel good about themselves if they get high grades for relatively simple work. The symbol (whether it is a gold star, a high grade, money, or some other reinforcer) is not sufficient, by itself, to produce the feeling of pride and accomplishment that builds self-esteem. To exist at all, the feeling must be earned: it must be based on having made a real gain.

One way teachers can help students achieve is by helping them help themselves. For example, if a student is having difficulty learning a skill, it might be useful for the teacher to break the skill into separate components and encourage the student to work on each component independently, with minimal teacher assistance. This "systems analysis" approach should help the student eventually overcome the larger problem. The procedure requires careful monitoring of each student's progress, but it helps students more accurately perceive their abilities, and it builds their self-esteem as they see their abilities increase through personal effort.

Allowing students to redo all or some assignments is another way to help them develop self-esteem. No one feels good about doing poorly, but if you provide a second chance and additional guidance, it is likely that the students' competence will increase, and it will take their self-esteem with it.

Sometimes students are so caught up with their failures, that they lose sight of the fact that they are making some progress. When students are not doing well, examine their overall performance and isolate the things that they do well. If you then take those students aside and point out the progress they have made and the likelihood that more can be made, they are more likely to develop a feeling of accomplishment. Such students may not feel great about their work, but they will not feel hopeless either. You cannot give students a sense of accomplishment as you might give a five-dollar bill, but you can help students realize their actual achievements, and that is important.

External Recognition

A second part of self-esteem is having other people recognize your accomplishments. Remember running to show Mom or Dad that new ability? You did not do that until you were confident that you had acquired the skill; that had to come first. Immediately thereafter, however, you wanted everyone to know. Much the same is true of your students. Having worked and practiced developing new skills that they perceive to be important, they will want others to know of their accomplishments. Acknowledging students' achievements boosts their self-esteem. Posting good work on bulletin boards is a common way elementary school teachers share students' achievements, and grades on report cards are common at all levels. However, if you are serious about helping students feel good about themselves, a phone call to their parents once in a while to tell them about a piece of good work or some good class participation will go a long way. The parent will certainly tell the student about the call, and the student will feel good. Most people feel awkward about blowing their own horns, but few object if someone else does it for them. Take the time to point out the accomplishments of students to parents, other teachers, and administrators, making sure that the accomplishments represent real gains in skills and abilities. The better students feel about themselves, the better work they are likely to do. The more successful they are, the more successful you will be.

The need for peer acceptance is great among teenagers. If they cannot satisfy that need by doing well in some socially accepted arena (such as school, music, or sports), they may try to satisfy the need by demonstrating to peers that they can challenge an authority figure and win. From the students' standpoint, winning may be measured by the degree to which they can get away with some rule infraction, by publicly proving that some rule is outdated or logically inconsistent, by causing a teacher to lose patience, or by using up class time. Regardless of the outcome, such students accomplish part of their goal simply by focusing attention on themselves.

Challenges and confrontations can be minimized if teachers follow a routine of beginning class promptly, explaining the objective, and moving directly into the lesson. This routine focuses the attention of the class on a specific objective. Once the lesson is underway, any issue raised that is not relevant to the work at hand should be deferred. Students raising such issues should be told that the work at hand must continue, but that the issue can be discussed immediately after class. By refusing to argue during class, the teacher minimizes the peer reinforcement that the student might get. Further, and equally important, deferment provides a cooling-off period. This increases the likelihood that the issue can be discussed objectively.

Teachers need to be careful not to use sarcasm, ridicule, or humiliation for any reason. It is particularly important to guard against sarcasm. Teachers have many opportunities to make remarks that seem clever, and perhaps even funny, but that may offend some students. Think twice before speaking. A sharp tongue can inflict deep and lasting wounds, and it can surely destroy any rapport that might be developing.

Keeping grades confidential helps minimize student embarrassment and humiliation, and it protects your own integrity. It is generally no secret who is doing well in a class and who is not, but if you become the source of information about who is and is not doing well, you are betraying a trust. Further, many schools have strict rules prohibiting the sharing of confidential information such as grades.

Perhaps the best advice is the oldest. "Do not do unto others what you would not have them do unto you."

Self-Actualization Needs

The last need described by Maslow is the need for self-actualization, or the need to develop as fully as possible.[8] This need is directly related to classroom management. Students who believe that their time and efforts will help them make useful and relevant gains in abilities or will open up new areas of personal development, are likely to be more willing learners.

One of the most crucial steps you can take to help students meet their need for self-actualization is to ensure that the course objectives focus on the higher levels of the cognitive or psychomotor domains. Such objectives require the integration of skills and knowledge and usually reflect abilities relevant to life outside of school. Discuss these abilities with students and, further, show how the content clearly relates to current events in business, industry, research, the arts, or some other human endeavor. These steps will help students see that they will be learning interesting and valuable information and that they are, in fact, enhancing their own abilities.

It is also important for students to use their newly acquired abilities. Individual or group projects can provide opportunities for students to utilize new skills and to see how their study has paid off. Further, to the extent that the projects involve people other than the teacher, students will be demonstrating their abilities to different adults, thus helping build their self-esteem.

In review, many classroom management problems can be avoided if teachers recognize that, in most cases, students' actions are motivated by basic human needs. By consciously helping students satisfy those needs, teachers will eliminate many of the causes of classroom management problems.

GUIDELINES FOR MINIMIZING DISCIPLINE PROBLEMS

Using the background information on human needs, along with other psychological principles and common sense, the following set of ten guidelines can be helpful in organizing to preclude discipline problems.

1. *Minimize Physical Distractions.*

   Students who are concerned about their physical well-being are likely to pay less attention to the classwork at hand. Simple steps, such as assuring a continual flow of fresh air through the room, maintaining a comfortable temperature, eliminating glare on the chalkboard, and establishing a reasonable policy concerning leaving the room for drinks or trips to the restroom can help eliminate the causes of many "discipline problems."

2. *Treat Students with Respect.*

   Remember that students are fellow human beings and deserve to be treated with the same degree of respect and courtesy that adults extend to any of their peers. Students are likely to treat you the same way you treat them.

3. *Explain the Big Picture.*

   Taking the time to explain to students what the course is about, what skills and abilities students will gain, and how those skills and abilities can be of practical utility to them, helps give students the big picture. Letting students know what will be happening and when, treats them like adults. They have a sense of direction and a timeline to use in assessing progress.

4. *Maintain Reasonable Expectations.*

   Your expectations of students, and your confidence in your own ability to help them succeed, will have an effect on their performance. Many teachers, hoping to ensure student success, have expectations that are far too low. They have the effect of cheating students by depriving of the opportunity to truly excel. At the same time, teachers should not set unreasonably high expectations. The solution is not complex. Set expectations that you believe are reasonable even if they are higher than most students originally think they can achieve. Present them with a mountain, not a mole hill. Further, do not feel guilty if it is necessary to expect more work from students than they think should be required. Make it clear that it requires hard work to achieve most worthwhile goals.

   At first, this step will not make you popular, but you are not in a popularity contest. You are in business to help as many students as possible become as competent as possible. If you are willing to work with students individually, you will find their frustration at having to work hard seems to speed learning. The mildly uncomfortable feeling that students get when their initial efforts do not always lead to immediate success continues until they achieve the objective. The sooner the task is completed, the sooner the frustration ends. If you expect too little from students, this sense of frustration will be lacking, the work may be viewed as busy work, and the final sense of achievement students could otherwise have experienced will be minimized. At the same time, unattainable goals or artificial barriers to goal achievement must be eliminated or students will become overly frustrated, and this frustration may be manifested in the form of discipline problems.

When students successfully complete your course, it seems more desirable for them to say, "I worked like a dog, but I really learned useful stuff," as opposed to "We had a lot of fun, but we didn't learn much." Your students may be young, but they are not stupid. They do not want to waste their time and effort. They may not love you for making them work hard, but they will take pride in their accomplishments, and they will respect you for doing what you were supposed to do.

5. *Use a Variety of Instructional Experiences.*
   A frequently cited cause of discipline problems is student boredom. You can combat this by building into your lessons a variety of learning experiences. Not every student will be equally interested in each experience, but by having a number of different experiences, you increase the probability of gaining and holding the interest of students more of the time. Interested students are less likely to cause discipline problems.

6. *Provide Prompt Feedback.*
   Students are generally very interested in finding out how they did on any given task, and they are young and do not have a lot of patience. If feedback is not forthcoming fairly soon after the task is completed, students are apt to think that the teacher did not regard the task as very important. This feeling will continue to grow as such instances multiply, with the eventual result that students will feel that whatever they do in that particular class is of little value. Such an environment is open to the generation of discipline problems. As a general rule, a second assignment should not be given until the first is corrected and handed back. That is one reason why it is a good idea to have written assignments turned in on Fridays. You then have the weekend to correct the work.

7. *Provide Positive Reinforcement.*
   When evaluating students' work, many teachers concentrate upon the identification and correction of errors. This is useful in that if you do not point out mistakes, students will not know about, or be able to correct, them. However,

if you do not also recognize those things students have done well, they may become discouraged and resentful. Their needs for esteem and self-actualization will go unsatisfied and they may seek other, undesirable sources of satisfaction. It is a good idea, therefore, to point out sections of students' work that are well done and to encourage students to use those sections as models for the less well-done portions. Sincere, positive reinforcement can go a long way toward making corrections more palatable and toward satisfying student needs.

8. *Be Consistent.*

   If students perceive inconsistencies in a teacher's reactions to problems, or if they believe a teacher is being unfair, their respect for that teacher will decrease. Once a teacher loses the respect of his or her students, discipline problems will begin to increase.

9. *Foster Peer Approval.*

   As was pointed out earlier, peer approval or disapproval is an important element in the life of most adolescents. At times this force may motivate students more than any other single element. If you are able to gain the respect and approval of the majority of your students, potential troublemakers will recognize that they risk peer disapproval if they cause problems.

   It must be pointed out that, although teachers can accept most forms of student support and can allow most forms of peer pressure to bear on students causing discipline problems, the tool cannot be used indiscriminately. Peer pressures such as physical reprisals, ridicule, sarcasm, and humiliation cannot be tolerated. If teachers condone the use of such measures, the very student respect that generated the support in the first place will be lost.

10. *Avoid Punitive Action.*

    This principle is one of the most difficult for beginning teachers to follow. Many people have become accustomed to an eye-for-an-eye philosophy. When a student causes a problem for a teacher, that teacher's first inclination may be to cause at least as great a problem for the student. There is, however, little evidence to support the idea that punitive action will have any lasting effect on deviant student behavior. Nonetheless, what follows is an examination of common punitive actions.

A. *Detention.* This option punishes teachers as much as students, since someone must supervise the detention. Often the student is bused to and from school or has an after-school job, and the hardship caused makes the punishment excessive. In other cases, students may be involved in sports or some after-school club and the detention may therefore deprive them of one of the few school experiences that is keeping them from dropping out.

B. *Extra schoolwork.* There seems to be no evidence to support the idea that assigning extra schoolwork is helpful in eliminating discipline problems. In fact, it is likely that the assignment of such work will cause students to associate all schoolwork with unpleasant experiences and thus cause more harm than good.

C. *Repetitive sentences and the like.* The use of repetitive sentences and similar busywork assignments has been widespread among teachers for years. There must be teachers somewhere who have found this device effective in maintaining good discipline, but locating such a teacher proves to be difficult. Such tasks are likely to cause students to equate schoolwork with busywork and to dislike both.

D. *Special seating assignments.* Special seating assignments usually take one of two forms. In the first form, a seat is isolated from the rest of the class and students are assigned to it essentially as objects of ridicule. Ridicule is not acceptable as a discipline device.

Another form of special seating is to attempt to separate friends or arrange seats in a way that will minimize student interaction. This procedure is less satisfactory than using friendships in a positive way to foster intrinsic motivation. Further, if they want to, separated students will still find ways to communicate despite the teacher's efforts.

E. *Physical labor or exercise.* The use of physical work or exercise is fraught with danger. A student who is asked by a teacher to do as little as move a desk, and who is hurt in the process, is in a position to sue the teacher. In some schools, asking or telling students to engage in physical labor is specifically forbidden. Exercises, such as running the track, doing push-ups, and so on, are sometimes used in physical education classes as punishment. The same reservations apply here that applied in the assignment of schoolwork as punishment. How are students going to build an intrinsic desire for exercise if the teacher considers it distasteful enough to use as punishment?

F. *Lowering of grades.* In some school districts there are policies that condone the lowering of an academic grade for disciplinary reasons. This practice is analogous to withholding a diploma as punitive action, when all necessary requirements have been met. In this case the courts have ruled that the diploma must be awarded.[9] In the case of grades, unless the grading criteria are clear and public, a teacher may be accused of lowering a grade because a student caused discipline problems. Lowering grades is difficult to defend logically because once a student has achieved an objective and demonstrated a competence; it is senseless to deny the accomplishment. Teachers who engage in this practice will be deemed unfair by their students and will quickly lose a large measure of student respect.

G. *Banishment from the classroom.* Sending a disruptive student from the room may solve a problem for the moment, but it definitely causes another problem, and may cause still more. The immediate problem caused by sending a student from the room is that it denies the student access to ongoing instruction. Forget, for the moment, that the student obviously did not want the ongoing instruction. If that student's academic achievement is considered important, the teacher will eventually need to spend extra time helping that student learn the missed material. Further, you are legally responsible for your students while class is in session. By sending a student from the room, you remove that student from your direct supervision and may, therefore, be held liable if the student is injured or gets into additional trouble.

BEHAVIOR MODIFICATION: OPERANT CONDITIONING

All learning is intended to modify behavior, but the term **behavior modification** is most commonly used in reference to classroom management. A more exact term would be **operant conditioning**, a term made popular by B. F. Skinner. Operant conditioning is a behavior modification approach that centers on the belief that behavior is modified more by its consequences than its causes. Therefore, if one wishes to increase a particular behavior or cause it to continue, one provides a **positive reinforcer**, some immediate reward. For example, suppose some students were not doing their homework well. If those students were given a piece of candy every time their homework was done well, and they began to do their homework well more often, then the candy would be functioning as a positive reinforcer.[10]

Negative reinforcement occurs when something a student does not want, such as nagging or the revocation of the right to park in the student parking lot, is withdrawn, and the desired behavior increases. If you continually ask certain students about their homework, or lack of it, and they start doing the homework simply to "get you off their backs," the principle of negative reinforcement is at work.

Punishment occurs when the presentation of a stimulus results in a decrease in the undesired behavior. If students are required to stay after school if they forget to do their homework, and they do their homework in order to avoid staying after school, then staying after school is a punishment.

Care must be taken not to make assumptions about reinforcers or punishments. For example, if some students were particularly conscious of their weight, candy would probably not function as a positive reinforcer. In fact, it might even be seen as a form of sarcasm or punishment. In the case of negative reinforcement, some students, such as those who receive little if any attention, might feel that the nagging was better than no attention at all. In the case of punishment, if the student was scheduled for some activity that was disliked even more than school, a detention might function as a positive reinforcer rather than as punishment. The point here is that the only way to determine whether an action is a positive reinforcer, a negative reinforcer, or a punishment is to see its effect on the target behavior.

Use

One can use operant conditioning to initiate or continue desirable behaviors. All that is necessary is to find something that the individual(s) value and make attainment of that thing contingent on achieving some desired behavior. Pizza Hut® conducts a nationwide program known as Book It.© This program is designed to encourage reading among elementary school students. Each teacher who chooses to participate sets reading goals for each student. Every month that the students reach their individual goals they are rewarded with a coupon for an individual pizza at a Pizza Hut® restaurant. If all the students in the class reach their goals, the class gets a pizza party from Pizza Hut®.

When used to end undesirable behaviors, operant conditioning usually involves the following steps:

1. *The teacher identifies the behavior to be changed.*

   Care needs to be taken here. Behaviors, by themselves, are neutral. They become misbehaviors when someone decides the behavior was inappropriate for the time and place it was demonstrated. Since you decide what constitutes a misbehavior, you have the option of considering every glance out the window and every whisper to be worthy of immediate intervention on your part or of choosing to overlook behaviors that are not truly disruptive.

2. *Devise and Try Countermeasures.*

   Countermeasures will depend on the misbehavior. For example, if a student, Tom, whispers only occasionally, ignoring it might be appropriate. However, while this option might work, it might also result in other students misinterpreting your lack of action for approval.

   A second option would be to move Tom to a different seat where neighbors would be unlikely to whisper back. This option might work, but it may be less desirable than other possibilities because it is unlikely to bring about a lasting modification in Tom's behavior.

   A third option would be to try to determine why Tom was whispering. For example, it may be that he frequently fails to prepare adequately and whispers prior to discussions in an attempt to acquire needed information. In this case, you could wait for a time when Tom is able to participate in a discussion of homework and then praise him for his good work and valuable contributions.

If the praise or other positive reinforcement is forthcoming each time he contributes to discussions without whispering beforehand, the whispering might soon cease. This procedure, while effective, depends on waiting until the student is adequately prepared, so it could turn out to be a long-term approach.

A fourth option to speed up the reinforcement process could be initiated. The teacher could

a. Make specific homework assignments for each student.
b. Privately encourage Tom to do the assignment.
c. Call on some students to discuss their homework but call on Tom the first day only if he has done his homework, and ignore whispering if it occurs.
d. Again, make specific assignments and privately encourage Tom to do his.
e. As soon as Tom has made an effort to do the assignment even if it came only as the result of heavy prompting, call on him during the discussion and praise his contribution. Again, ignore his whispering if it occurs.
f. Repeat steps d and e each day, praising Tom's contributions and ignoring his whispering. The whispering should decrease and disappear within a few days. If it does not, the analysis must be reexamined for alternative explanations for the behavior.

The point of the operant conditioning process is to focus attention on desired behavior and to provide an incentive for students to engage in that behavior. The incentive may be praise, points, or any other reward valued by the student, and the expectation is that the desired behavior will soon become self-reinforcing and will replace the undesirable behavior, which is never reinforced.

Keep in mind that sometimes the removal or withholding of a stimulus (for example, the denying of an opportunity to receive attention and reinforcement from peers) is as effective as the presentation of a stimulus (for example, the giving of praise or rewards). Once the right stimulus is found for any individual, a procedure can be established to help bring about lasting behavioral changes via operant conditioning.

Reservations about Operant Conditioning

This emphasis on rewards rather than causes seems superficial to many educators and has caused many to express reservations about using operant conditioning techniques. Among the arguments used by opponents of operant conditioning is that the process may cause as many problems as it solves. When teachers use operant conditioning, the basic process is to identify the specific behaviors they wish to increase and reward the student when the desired behavior is demonstrated. It is usually not long until other students observe that one way to get extra attention or rewards from the teacher is to misbehave and then behave properly on cue. If this happens, operant conditioning techniques can be unfair to those students who behave properly.

Still another concern of many educators is that operant conditioning techniques imply that appropriate behavior should be demonstrated only because such behavior will generate an **extrinsic reward** such as praise, candy, money, or free time. They maintain that the use of rewards for appropriate behavior obscures the fact that such behavior has its own **intrinsic rewards**, such as the feeling of having done the right thing, and will not, in fact, bring extrinsic rewards in the "real" world. They claim, therefore, that operant conditioning techniques mislead students by giving them a false impression of reality.

There are other reservations concerning operant conditioning, including where to draw the line between creativity and exuberance, and the need for an environment conducive to learning. However, most of the attacks on operant conditioning have been prompted by aversion to its abuses by individual teachers who use it indiscriminately and without regard for its ramifications. When used properly, the rewards often pertain to student fulfillment of basic needs, such as the needs for esteem and self-actualization. Further, when teachers fully understand the ramifications of the technique, they are quick to point out to students the intrinsic rewards of the desired behavior and thus lead students away from continued dependence on extrinsic rewards.

BEHAVIOR MODIFICATION: REALITY THERAPY

Reality therapy is a behavior modification technique pioneered by Dr. William Glasser in his work as a psychiatrist.[11] It utilizes student needs, but its philosophical orientation is significantly different from that of operant conditioning. In operant conditioning, individuals undergoing the conditioning are often unaware that their behavior is being manipulated. No attempt is made to treat individuals as responsible people, to make them partners in a joint effort to modify behavior, or to help them see the cause-effect relationships between their behavior and its long-term consequences.

Reality therapy, on the other hand, makes individuals the prime movers in the modification of their own behavior. Reality therapy is predicated on the idea that people engage in those behaviors they believe will satisfy one or more perceived or unperceived needs but that some individuals have either a distorted idea of what their goals are or a distorted idea of how to achieve them. Reality therapists see their role as a "perception sharpener"—one who attempts to help the individual perceive the reality of the situation. The assumption is made that the students know right from wrong.

Reality therapy begins with the current situation. Although reality therapists are well aware that many problems have roots in past events, they are not willing to allow those past events to become excuses for future actions. The individual's attention is focused on the behavior to be modified, not on the root causes of that behavior, and the individual is helped to see the consequences of continuing the undesirable behavior as well as the consequences of modified behavior. The basic reasoning is not to dwell on the past since the past cannot be changed. Instead, think about the future; you *can* shape that. The following step-by-step procedure is illustrative of how a teacher might use reality therapy to deal with Tom's whispering.

1. *Help the Student Identify the Undesirable Behavior.*

   In this case, the teacher would arrange to see Tom privately. The teacher would first get Tom to identify the problem. It is important that Tom identifies problem, because then he is taking the first step toward its solution. If the teacher makes the identification, Tom is likely to look to the teacher for the solution rather than to seek that solution for himself.

   Care is exercised not to ask Tom why he is engaging in the undesired behavior (whispering). To do so would provide him with an opportunity to offer an excuse for his actions and to focus attention on the excuse rather than the action. The reality therapist does not deny that there may be legitimate reasons for inappropriate behavior; he or she simply insists on beginning with the inappropriate behavior rather than with a series of antecedent events. Nothing can be done about the past, but something can be done about the future.

2. *Help the Student Identify the Consequences of Undesirable Behavior.*

   It is important that the consequences identified be real and logical. If the environment is manipulated so the consequences of a particular action are unreasonably harsh or virtually meaningless, the situation becomes contrived and irrelevant to the real world. In such a situation, no technique in likely to be effective. In this case, for example, telling Tom that he will be suspended from school if whispering continues is unreasonable. Similarly, it would be unreasonable to tell him that inappropriate behavior will have no consequences. It is appropriate, however, to point out that consequences are often cumulative and tend to get more and more severe.

3. *Help the Student Make a Value Judgment about the Consequences.*

   The purpose of this step is to help the student see that the inappropriate behavior is contributing more to eventual unhappiness than to immediate or long-range happiness. The student is likely to have inaccurate perceptions about the effects of the behavior and may need help in making a value judgment about its desirability or undesirability. In this case, continued whispering will, because it interferes with the learning of others, cause Tom to be removed from the room and possibly miss so much work that he will fail the course. If Tom says that he understands all that and has no problem with it, the discussion is at an end. The student may have made a terribly unwise choice in your opinion, but you must respect his right to make the choice. Hopefully, however, Tom will decide that the consequences are undesirable. Everyone has the right to live their life as they see fit, providing they do not interfere with the lives of others.

4. *Have the Student Formulate a Plan for Changing the Behavior.*

Once Tom has concluded that the behavior is not, in fact, in his own best interests, the next step is for him to suggest alternatives to that behavior. If possible, he should be encouraged to propose an alternative behavior, for example, that he will:

a. Simply stop whispering.
b. Admit to not knowing an answer or not doing his homework, rather than trying to acquire last-minute information via whispering.
c. Tell the teacher before class when he is not prepared and then he will not be called on to answer questions.

Of these three alternatives, the last is the least acceptable, and the teacher should reject it if Tom does not see its inappropriateness, because it forces the teacher to share responsibility for his actions when, in fact, that responsibility belongs to him alone. It is important that Tom recognize that: (1) the current situation is a result of his own behavior, and (2) he can extract himself from the situation by engaging in behaviors that are both socially acceptable and conducive to achievement of his own, and other people's, success and happiness.

5. *Have the Student Select and Implement a Specific Plan.*

After Tom (perhaps with the teacher's help) has generated alternatives, he should decide which one to implement. At this point, the teacher's role is to monitor Tom's behavior, to see how well he is following the plan, and to provide appropriate reinforcement.

The differences between the operant conditioning approach to behavior modification, and the reality therapy approach, are many and significant. It is unlikely that both approaches will appeal to all teachers, or that all teachers will be able to use both with equal effectiveness. It is suggested, therefore, that before either approach is decided on, teachers assess their own philosophical position concerning classroom control and behavior modification. Haphazard or indiscriminate use of either or both of these procedures can not only be frustrating and futile, it can harm a teacher's rapport with students. Used properly, however, these procedures may bring about lasting behavioral changes.

BEHAVIOR MODIFICATION: THE "LET'S KEEP IT SMALL" APPROACH

In the mind of every teacher is a conceptual model of an "ideal" teaching-learning environment. You may prefer a highly structured environment and someone else, a loosely structured environment, or just the opposite may be true. Similarly, you may be willing to tolerate a much broader range of deviant student behaviors than other teachers. Nonetheless, regardless of how carefully you plan and how skillfully you conduct your classes, there may still be minor disruptions that can develop into major classroom management problems. The best way to deal with such problems is to keep them small.

Jacob S. Kounin reports that teacher-initiated disciplinary acts (he and his associates labeled them "desists") can have significant effects on the other students in the class who are not the target of discipline. These effects have been called "ripple effects." In one study it was found that teachers who use angry or punitive desists often cause other students in the room to refocus their attention from the work at hand to the disturbance and the teacher's reaction to it. On the other hand, simple reprimands tend to have a smaller ripple effect.[12] Kounin also reported that interviews with high school students indicate that, for a teacher viewed as fair and generally liked by the students, desist actions are less likely to cause ripple effects destructive to the teaching-learning environment.[13]

One could conclude, therefore, that to deal successfully with most discipline problems, teachers should establish good rapport with their students and should use simple reprimands to deal with occasional deviant behavior. Mild desists can include actions such as moving toward disruptive students, standing by them, glancing at them, and directing questions at them, as well as direct reprimands. Further, reprimands should be in the form of direct statements rather than questions. "Please stop talking" is more desirable than "Would you please stop talking?" because it does not invite a verbal response from the student.

If mild desists are not effective, and the previously discussed preventive measures are being used, or if reality therapy or operant conditioning techniques have failed, the teacher needs a plan of action. In some schools, teachers are told exactly what disciplinary procedure to use. If such a policy exists, it should be followed precisely. If no policy exists, the teacher should develop one based on whatever policies do exist. The following procedure is based on the belief that most people already have more problems than they want and that they will not choose to complicate their own lives if they can avoid doing so. It is called the "Let's Keep It Small" approach because the idea is to solve the problem with the involvement of as few people as possible. Here are the steps.

1. If a student engages in behavior that interferes with the teaching-learning process, politely tell the student to stop.
2. If the deviant behavior persists, tell the student to remain in the room for a short meeting after the class is dismissed. Keep the meeting brief, businesslike, and to the point. Explain to the student that such behavior is unacceptable. At the very least, it was keeping other students from learning because it was

taking your time and attention away from helping those students. Try to get a commitment from the student that such misbehavior will not reoccur. Most importantly, have a note card at hand and let the student see you noting the problem, who was involved, and the date. Ask the student to initial the entry. The purpose of the anecdotal record is to help convince the student that you are serious and intend to follow through. You want the student to realize that cooperation will be far less troublesome than non-cooperation.

3. If the offending student continues the disruptive behavior, schedule a mutually convenient time for a longer meeting with the student. The reason for ensuring that the time for the meeting is mutually agreeable is that students will find reasons why they cannot meet at teacher-decided times. You should be willing to meet before, after, or at an appropriate time during the school day. Make sure that the student understands the commitment to meet. If there is any doubt about the student's showing up, make two copies of the time and place and mutually initial each copy.

    It should be made clear to the student that such a meeting is not synonymous with detention. The purpose of the meeting is to review the student's offenses and to outline the consequences of future offenses. The teacher should explain why the offenses cannot be tolerated (because they disrupt the teaching-learning process and keep other students from learning). The focus of the meeting should be on identifying and eliminating the misbehavior, not on excuses, and not on the student personally. A record of the meeting, offense, date, and so forth should be added to the anecdotal record card and the student should be asked to initial the entry.

    At this point, even the slowest student should begin to feel that the procedure and meetings are a bother (or even a little embarrassing) and will also realize that you mean what you say and that you intend to see the problem ended. Notice that no punitive action has been taken. The emphasis is on changing the behavior of the students, not punishing the students. Students should be told that further problems will result in your contacting their parents; the choice of involving others is theirs.

4. If the problem persists, enlist the aid of the student's parents. This step may or may not help, but taking it is important in any case. At the next offense, as the student is leaving the room, note that you will be contacting the student's parents. Once this step is announced, it is important that the contact with the parents be made as soon as possible, preferably before the end of the school day. If this is not done, the student may arrive home before the teacher's call and set a stage that is difficult or impossible to cope with. Once the contact is made, go through the anecdotal record explaining the actions taken, enlist

parental support, and explain that if the problem continues you will need to refer the student to the school administration. A record of the home contact should be made on the anecdotal record card.

5.   If the problem persists, refer the student to the school disciplinarian but, before making the referral, contact the disciplinarian and discuss the anecdotal record with the list of offenses and corrective efforts. This is important because the disciplinarian must understand that you have tried to deal with the problem professionally. You had a minimum of two conferences with the student, you talked with the parents, and you are now hoping that the disciplinarian can help resolve the problem. Once the disciplinarian understands that the problem is not superficial, work with the student can be attempted by this new party. If the disciplinarian decides on some punitive action, the choice will not be yours.

6.   In most cases, if you have made a professional, but unsuccessful, attempt to deal with a disruptive student, the administration will be willing to help. Administrators will be less willing to help if you charge into the principal's office screaming that student X is impossible, incorrigible, and ought to be thrown out of school immediately, preferably minus a head. Typically, the administrator will try essentially the same steps you tried. However, the administrator might also impose detentions and suspensions and might even go so far as to recommend that the Board of Education expel the student.

One advantage of the "Let's Keep It Small" approach is that you are, at no point, threatening punitive action. You are simply trying to get students to control their own behavior so that teaching and learning can take place effectively in the room. Others may impose punishments, but you do not. In fact, you are doing all you can to keep the student from reaching the point at which punishment might be administered.

Another advantage is that you are acknowledging that only the student can solve the problem. You can steadily involve more people, which will probably make things increasingly unpleasant for the student, but only the student can choose to end the problem. This is the true state of affairs and you want the student to know that you know it.

POTENTIALLY DANGEROUS SITUATIONS

At some point, you may face a potentially dangerous situation. Some of the more obvious examples include students who are armed, verbally abusing you or other students, drunk, high on drugs, overtly defying authority, or maliciously destroying property. In such situations your first obligation is to do what you can to keep students from harming themselves or others. This does not mean that you are expected to throw yourself between a drunk student's gun and the class. It does mean that you will remain calm, that you will notify the administration of the problem either by intercom or by sending a student to the main office, and that you will try to contain the situation until help arrives. Keep in mind that you are responsible for all of the other students in the class. If you send them from the room or leave them alone, perhaps in order to escort the offending student to the main office, some provision must be made for their supervision.

Special Cases

Hyperactivity, Attention Deficit Hyperactivity Disorder (ADHD), and Attention Deficit Disorder (ADD)

Sometimes when teachers see a student who is continually restless, given to sudden outbursts, or unable to concentrate on the work at hand, they attribute it to **hyperactivity**, or **attention deficit hyperactivity disorder** (ADHD), as it now called. Without hyperactivity, the problem is called **attention deficit disorder** (ADD). Hyperactivity was, at one time, thought to be caused by the inability of an individual to assign priorities to the many sensory inputs constantly bombarding the brain. Then it was thought to be caused by a chemical imbalance in the brain. Today, doctors are still not sure just how to define or treat hyperactivity or attention deficit disorder, but experts believe that as many as 3.5 million students under the age of eighteen suffer from it.[14] However, one thing is certain. You, as a classroom teacher, are not qualified to diagnose such problems and attempting to do so may cause harm. What occasionally happens is that a teacher mistakes lapses of attention, restlessness, or even the normal exuberance of youth for hyperactivity or attention deficit disorder. Having "diagnosed" the problem, the uninformed teacher may call the student's parents (or have the school nurse call them) and suggest that they take the student to a physician and "have the doctor give him something."

Unfortunately, some physicians will accept the teacher's "diagnosis" and prescribe a treatment on that basis after only a cursory examination. The typical treatment for hyperactivity is the prescription of amphetamines such as Ritalin and Dexedrine. Although these drugs act as stimulants for adults, they act as depressants for children. It is difficult to predict accurately the exact effect of any specific drug on any specific child, and many children are being adversely affected by such treatment. Even worse, because of the increasing instances in which drugs are prescribed for students based on inadequate diagnoses, many students are exposed to drugs who do not need to be.

If you suspect that a student may be hyperactive or suffering from attention deficit disorder, the initial step should be to double-check the basis for the suspicion. The procedure is to keep a written record of the frequency of each "hyperactive" act, check with other teachers to see if the student is demonstrating similar behavior in other classes, and engage in discussions with the school nurse and guidance personnel to see if they have been told of any specific problems the student may be having.

Dyslexia

Dyslexia is a medical problem that hinders one's ability to learn to read and it is estimated to affect between five and ten percent of the US population.[15] In some cases, dyslexia causes people to see certain letters or words transposed. In 1994, it was discovered dyslexia is not so much a vision problem as it is a hearing problem. People with dyslexia cannot process sounds properly. If students cannot hear what sounds certain letters make, they cannot sound out words. This, in turn, hinders their ability to learn to read.[16] As is sometimes the case with hyperactivity and attention deficit disorder, students with dyslexia may, mistakenly, be thought to be lazy, obstinate, or simply misbehaving.

If the suspected behaviors are persistent and not just isolated examples, the collected data should be discussed with the guidance department and nurse. If the results of this conference indicate that an examination by a physician is in order, then the parents should be involved in a separate conference in which such an examination is recommended. At this conference, the parents should be provided with a copy of the list of incidents without any diagnosis of the source of the problem. The *doctor alone* should diagnose the problem and prescribe any treatment.

Assuming that the teacher is informed of treatment, it is then the teacher's responsibility to continue to monitor the student's behavior. In this way, the effectiveness of the treatment can be determined, and its eventual elimination hastened.

It should be noted that differentiating between real and imagined problems is not easy. Sometimes students will, in fact, have medical or psychological problems that account for their problems at school. More often, however, students and parents will look for, and accept, any rationale to excuse disruptive behavior or poor performance. Citing a medical or psychological problem makes a particularly good excuse because it tends to generate sympathy, but claims that "the devil made me do it" have also been heard. In any case, it is best to avoid diagnosing a problem or labeling a student. Your diagnosis may be incorrect, and a label does not help. It may, in fact, be used as an excuse.

LEGAL TERMS AND ISSUES

In most cases, teachers are able to resolve classroom management problems quickly and easily. Few problems require the involvement of parents and even fewer require the involvement of school administrators. Nonetheless, situations that have legal ramifications may arise, so it is useful to know some of the legal terms that might be encountered.

In loco parentis is Latin for "in place of the parent." Courts of law generally recognize that a teacher acts in place of a parent during school activities. If a question is raised about the propriety of a given action, such as breaking up a fight or detaining a student to prevent a harmful act, the question that is most likely to be asked is whether the teacher acted as a *reasonable and prudent* parent would have acted. A judge or jury would answer that question on a case-by-case basis (case law) because each situation is likely to be unique.

In loco parentis offers you some protection as you go about the task of helping students, but it does not offer immunity to bad judgment. For example, if a student mentions taking drugs, you are placed in an uncomfortable position. A reasonable and prudent person would be expected to try to get help for the student, perhaps by notifying parents, a counselor, or a school administrator. If you do not do this, and the student dies from a drug overdose, how would you feel? Your active intervention might have saved a life. If it is school policy to report such situations, and you do not do so, you might be charged with **negligence**: "the omission to do something which a reasonable man, guided by those ordinary considerations which ordinarily regulate human affairs, would do, or the doing of something which a reasonable and prudent man would not do."[17] On the other hand, if you do notify someone, students might perceive that action as a betrayal of trust, and that perception would seriously weaken your rapport with all students. The choices are not always easy.

Sometimes teachers witness illegal acts. For example, if a student is forced or frightened into giving his lunch money to another student, that action is not just "a shame," it is **extortion**: "the obtaining of property from another induced by wrongful use of actual or threatened force, violence, or fear, or under color of official right."[18] A student might also **menace** someone by showing a "disposition to inflict an evil or injury upon another."[19] Some teachers, if menaced, immediately report the situation, and many administrators immediately notify the police, choosing to be safe rather than sorry.

A more serious threat is an **assault**: "any willful attempt or threat to inflict injury upon another, when coupled with an apparent present ability to do so (or) any intentional display of force such as would give the victim reason to fear or expect immediate bodily harm."[20] If the student actually carries out the threat and makes bodily contact, the offense of **battery** has been committed.

Teachers are sometimes the victims of slander. **Slander** is "the speaking of base and defamatory words tending to prejudice another in his reputation, office, trade, business, or means of livelihood."[21] Students sometimes say things about teachers that are not true. To the extent that such comments do not go beyond one or two students, they may be no cause for concern. However, if such comments or rumors become widespread, they may result in a formal or informal inquiry about the teacher. Depending on how much trouble the comments or rumors cause, the teacher might consider filing charges of slander against the perpetrators. **Libel** is essentially slander in writing.

Sometimes, despite the best efforts of a teacher, it is necessary to remove a student from the classroom. A teacher usually has the right to remove a student for part or all of a class period by having the student go to some other supervised place in the school such as a detention room or the main office. A principal usually has the right to suspend a student from all activities for up to a week. The suspension may be an in-school suspension (the student comes to school, but spends the time in a detention area usually away from other students) or an out-of-school suspension (the student is not allowed into the school during the suspension period). In-school suspensions are most often used when there is doubt as to who would be supervising the out-of-school student.

Students who commit serious breaches of school rules are sometimes expelled. Expulsion is such a serious matter that it is usually left to school boards to impose that penalty. When a school board expels a student, it generally bans the student from attending school or school functions for a specified period of time and establishes the conditions under which the student may then return to school.

LAWSUITS

Historically, laws have been passed to ensure the greatest happiness for the greatest number. The laws provide a structure and element of stability that is analogous to a curriculum in schools. At the same time, laws must also be applied so as to ensure that everyone has equal rights and protection. Sometimes the two goals conflict as, when in a school, a teacher claims the right, as part of academic freedom, to deviate extensively from the established curriculum. It is from conflicts such as these that lawsuits arise.

Student Suspensions

In January of 1975, the US Supreme Court ruled in *Coss v. Lopez* that if a student is to be suspended from school for more than a week (this varies from state to state), school administrators are obligated to (1) inform the student that a hearing will be conducted at a particular time and place, (2) explain what the charges will be, (3) show or explain the evidence used to justify the suspension, and (4) listen to the student's side of the story.

In February of 1975, the US Supreme Court, in *Wood v. Strickland*, held that if students were to be expelled from school, they were entitled to face their accusers, cross-examine witnesses, introduce witnesses of their own, be represented by counsel, and to appeal. The court also ruled that individual teachers could be held personally liable in monetary damages if they knowingly, or reasonably should have known, that what they were doing would deprive an individual of a civil right.

Teacher Negligence

Cases involving allegations of teacher negligence are most often associated with situations in which students suffer physical harm. In deciding such cases, the court generally uses a three-point test. The first point that the plaintiff (the person bringing the complaint) must demonstrate is that the defendant (in this case, the teacher) had a legal obligation to perform a particular duty, such as to provide adequate supervision. The second point that the plaintiff must demonstrate is that the defendant willfully failed to carry out that obligation. The third point is that the defendant's failure to carry out this legal responsibility was the proximate cause of the student's injury.

Suppose, for example, that a teacher spent four or five minutes writing something on the blackboard, and during this time John and Sam were silently sword-fighting with their pencils and John's pencil ended up in Sam's eye. It is quite possible that a court would rule that the teacher had a legal obligation to provide adequate supervision, that such supervision was not provided because the teacher's back was to the students for so long, and that the teacher's failure to provide adequate supervision was therefore the proximate cause of the injury. If the teacher had been watching the students, the "sword fight" would never have taken place. Is the use of overhead projectors beginning to sound better and better to you?

Generally, teachers have little to fear from the courts, but being the litigious society that we are, it pays to take precautions. Read your teacher's handbook carefully and follow its rules. Further, although you are unlikely to ever need it, consider the benefits of the malpractice insurance offered as part of membership in both the National Education Association (NEA), and the American Federation of Teachers (AFT).

SUMMARY

The goal of classroom management procedures should be to help students develop self-control. This development is facilitated by freeing students from as many restraints as possible and expecting them to think about, and control, their own behavior rather than mindlessly following rules. Some teachers find that they can extend student freedom to the point of needing only one classroom rule: You may do whatever you like as long as you do not disturb anyone else.

The key to helping students develop self-control is to help them be successful. The first step in this process is to recognize basic human needs and plan the instructional program so that students can satisfy as many of those basic needs as possible. Abraham Maslow identified the following basic human needs: physiological, safety, love, self-esteem, and self-actualization. Physiological needs refer to the maintenance of life and may be reflected in a classroom by a student's need for a drink, for sleep, or to visit a restroom. Physiological needs are powerful enough to override other needs and often must be met immediately. Students sometimes use these same needs as excuses to avoid work or to disrupt class. In these cases, the teacher may speak privately to the student, expressing concern over the student's repeated need for water or the bathroom, and offer to refer the student to the school nurse (or a similar staff member) for a checkup.

Safety needs refer to physical safety. Concern over physical safety may surface in a class where a student refuses to participate in a particular activity, or it may relate to a fear of physical abuse from peers. It is important to remember that regardless of whether a student's fear is real or imaginary, it is real to the student. Students are often embarrassed about being afraid. The teacher should minimize the potential for embarrassment by working privately with the student to help overcome the fear, step by step. If fear keeps a student from completing a required objective, however, the student cannot be given credit for achieving that objective. With respect to safety, students should know, by the words and actions of the teacher, that they are safe both physically and psychologically in the classroom. Teachers can help students meet safety needs by establishing a routine and treating students as people with feelings.

Love needs refer to the kind of love shared by parents and children and as such has little relevance to the classroom. There is, however, at least one point of relevance. With the increasing amount of violence, the high number of divorces, and the high mobility of the population, the classroom may be the only social unit in which the student can be safe from both physical and psychological abuse.

The need for self-esteem refers to the development of a positive self-concept, and teachers are in an ideal position to help students meet that need. Self-esteem is founded on a sense of satisfaction about oneself. Teachers can help students achieve this sense of satisfaction by conveying to students that the work they are doing is serious and worthwhile. This can be done by developing a course syllabus that contains relevant objectives; setting up a calendar showing when various topics will be covered, due dates for papers, and test dates; and selecting appropriate grading criteria. On the first day of class this syllabus should be distributed to students and discussed. This approach lets students know that the teacher has given serious thought to the course and has outlined a reasonable plan for helping them achieve the objectives.

A student's sense of achievement is fostered by internal and external recognition of achievement, premised upon the student's attainment of some significant goal. The teacher, therefore, must be sure that the objectives of the course are set at a reasonably high level. If students feel they are improving their skills, abilities, or knowledge in ways that seem valuable to them, they receive the internal recognition of achievement necessary for meeting self-esteem needs. External recognition refers to having others (such as parents, peers, or authority figures) acknowledge a student's achievement. Favorable grades, phone calls to parents (giving good news), and the sharing of students' work are ways of attending to the need for external recognition.

The highest need, self-actualization, refers to lifelong continual growth and improvement. Once again, the course objectives play a central role. If those objectives were formulated with long-term utility in mind, they will be seen as contributing to the satisfaction of the need for self-actualization.

Regardless of how diligently a teacher tries to help students meet their needs, classroom disruptions may still occur. Operant conditioning is one way to deal with disruptive students, but it puts the teacher rather than the student in control of solving the problem. Another approach, reality therapy, puts the student in control, but works only if the student wants to change the behavior.

A third way to deal with such problems is to use the "Let's Keep It Small" approach. To use this approach, explain to students why disruptions will not be tolerated and explain the procedure that will be used to handle them. That procedure consists of first telling a student to stop the undesired behavior. If the behavior continues, the teacher begins an anecdotal record, which will document the student's name, the date, the problem, and what was done. The student may be asked to initial the entry to show that awareness of it. If the problem persists after two or three private meetings with the teacher (each with its own entry in the anecdotal record), the student's parents will be contacted. If the problem persists after that, the school administration will be brought in. This course of action demonstrates to the students that the teacher means business, it enables the teacher to follow a consistent, nonpunitive procedure, and it documents the history of the problem and the attempts made to solve it.

With respect to legal issues, teachers will find that if they fulfill the responsibilities assigned to them and act as reasonable and prudent parents would act, they have little to fear from the courts. For example, the usual test applied in negligence suits is whether the teacher had a clear responsibility to the student, whether the teacher willfully failed to fulfill that responsibility, and whether the student suffered actual harm as a consequence of the teacher's failure to fulfill the responsibility. Teachers should not utilize corporal punishment because it is educationally unsound even if it is legal in their school district.

If teachers are humane and recognize that students have basic human needs that must be at least partly fulfilled, and if they establish and maintain a classroom management program aimed at helping students learn to control their own behavior so they can function as effective citizens in a democratic society, they will have few, if any, classroom management problems.

SO HOW DOES THIS AFFECT MY TEACHING?

Each of us should have the right to live our lives as we see fit. However, since we are social animals and interact with others, we sometimes have to control our first impulses and desires in order for the larger group to function. Your job, with respect to classroom management, is to help students recognize these truths. Further, you will have all you can do to live your own life successfully; do not try to live your students' lives for them. Help them learn to take responsibility for their own actions. If they learn nothing else from you other than that, they will have learned something of incalculable value. Further, if they learn that, they are also likely to achieve the other course objectives and, for the last time, their success is your success.

KEY TERMS, PEOPLE, AND IDEAS

Self-Control

You may do whatever you like as long as you do not disturb anyone else

Natural Consequences

Maslow's Hierarchy of Needs

　Physiological—air, food, water, using the bathroom, sleep, interest in the opposite sex

　Safety—other students, the curriculum, corporal punishment

　Love

　Self-Esteem—internal and external

　Self-Actualization

Behavior Modification

Operant Conditioning—B. F. Skinner—teacher is the primary mover

Positive and Negative reinforcement

Punishment

Intrinsic and Extrinsic Rewards

Reality Therapy—William Glasser—student is the primary mover

Let's Keep It Small

Hyperactivity, Attention Deficit Hyperactivity Disorder, Dyslexia

In loco parentis—In place of the parent

Negligence, Extortion, Menace, Assault, Battery, Slander, Libel

QUESTIONS FOR CONSIDERATION

1. To what extent do you think it would be useful to establish a grading scale for student behavior and to report that separately along with the student's academic grade?

2. Aside from the need to maintain a classroom environment conducive to teaching and learning, to what extent should teachers concern themselves with student behavior?

ENDNOTES

1　A. H. Maslow, "A Theory of Human Motivation," *Psychological Review 50* (1943): 370–96.

2　Linda Lantieri, "Waging Peace in Our School," *Phi Delta Kappan* 76, no. 5 (January 1995): 386.

3　Chancellor's Working Group on School-Based Violence Prevention, "Draft Report" (New York City Board of Education, July 1994), as cited in Lantieri, 386.

4　"20th Annual Gallup Poll of the Public's Attitudes Toward the Public Schools," *Phi Delta Kappan* 70, no. 1 (September 1988): 32–46.

5　Ingraham et al. v. Wright et al., United States Reports, Cases Adjudged in The Supreme Court at October Term, 1976, Vol. 430 (Washington, DC: US Government Printing Office, 1979), 651.

6　Robert Farnighetti, *The World Almanac and Book of Facts, 1994* (New Jersey: World Almanac, an imprint of Funk and Wagnalls, 1993), 957.

7   Robert Farnighetti, *The World Almanac and Book of Facts, 1995* (New Jersey: World Almanac, an imprint of Funk and Wagnalls, 1994), 960.

8   Maslow, "A Theory of Human Motivation," 382.

9   Anne Flowers and Edward C. Bolmeier, *Law and Pupil Control* (Cincinnati: W. H. Anderson, 1964).

10   B. F. Skinner, "The Evolution of Behavior," *Journal of Experimental Analysis of Behavior* (March 1984): 217–221.

11   William Glasser, *Reality Therapy—A New Approach to Psychiatry* (New York: Harper and Row, 1965).

12   Jacob Kounin, *Discipline and Group Management in Classrooms* (New York: Holt, Rinehart and Winston, 1970), 49.

13   Kounin, *Discipline and Group Management in Classrooms*, 142.

14   Claudia Wallis, "Life in Overdrive," *Time* 144, no. 3 (July 18, 1994): 43.

15   Sharon Begley, "Why Johnny and Joani Can't Read," *Time* 144, no. 9 (August 29, 1994): 52

16   Begley, "Why Johnny and Joani Can't Read," 52.

17   Henry Campbell Black, *Black's Law Dictionary*, 5th ed. (St. Paul: West, 1979), 930.

18   Black, *Black's Law Dictionary*, 525.

19   Black, *Black's Law Dictionary*, 1137.

20   Black, *Black's Law Dictionary*, 105.

21   Black, *Black's Law Dictionary*, 1244.

CHAPTER 12

Educational Technology

INTRODUCTION

With the advent of the computer, instruction and learning in the classroom changed forever. From research and essays to spreadsheets and calculations, technology has greatly enhanced teacher preparation, instruction, and assessment. Technology today makes it possible to transform traditional lecture style, teacher-centered classrooms into project-centered, inquiry based, student-oriented learning centers.

For many educators, it is somehow unsettling to realize that in a technologically advanced country such as ours, instruction is carried out much as it was 2,400 years ago in the days of Socrates, Plato, and Aristotle. While there is nothing wrong with telling, asking, and discussing, there are other tools that teachers can use to supplement and, in some cases, to replace these basic instructional activities. Some of the tools, such as the Internet, computer simulations and platforms, and DVDs, make it possible to give students experiences that were impossible or impractical just a few years ago.

There is an ancient proverb that says, "A picture is worth a thousand words." One wonders what the "exchange rate" would be for a time-lapse motion picture that enables students to watch a rosebud as it unfolds into full bloom or a film that gives students an idea of the drama and mindless passions aroused by one of Hitler's torchlight parades. How does one calculate an "exchange rate" when a student experiences an accident in an auto simulator rather than in a real car? Without the use of mediated instruction, many valuable and interesting learning experiences would be either impossible or impractical, and the students' education would be that much poorer.

Furthermore, when computers were first being used in public schools, there were predictions that many teachers would soon be replaced by computers. The prediction was made for a number of reasons: Computer-assisted instruction could be available to students 24-hours a day, seven days a week; it consisted of continually updated instructional content; computers never demand pay raises, and they never call in sick. While all of these things are true, teachers are not likely to be replaced by computers any time soon. Nonetheless, there are still concerns about technology in education and one of the purposes of this chapter is to familiarize you with some of these concerns. The most important purpose of this chapter, however, is to provide you with some insights, techniques and current uses of technology that are likely to save you time, help you do your work in and out of class faster and more effectively, and help your students learn. The more tools you can use to enhance and enrich learning experiences, the more successful your students are likely to be and, the more successful they are, the more successful you will be.

Specifically, this chapter will define technology integration, what it consists of, and barriers to its implementation. Moreover, it will discuss twenty-first-century learning goals and skills and how technology can assist in their implementation. Finally, it will examine new cutting-edge technologies available for teachers to use in their classrooms.

LEARNING OUTCOMES

You will be able, in writing, to:

1. Define and exemplify terms such as technology, hardware, software, word processors, spreadsheet, database, online instruction, and technology integration.
2. Describe six steps that lead to effective utilization of instructional media.
3. After writing a precise instructional objective, describe two sequences of instructional activities, including the use of mediated instruction, which could help students achieve the objective, and explain one advantage of each sequence.
4. Using cause-effect reasoning, explain four advantages and four disadvantages of online instruction with respect to traditional classroom instruction.
5. Explain the difference between technology of instruction and technology in instruction.
6. Describe six steps that lead to effective utilization of instructional media.
7. After writing a precise instructional objective, describe two sequences of instructional activities, including the use of mediated instruction, which could help students achieve the objective, and explain one advantage of each sequence.

8. Shown two PowerPoint presentations, determine which one is technically the best and defend your determination by orally citing at least two advantages of the selected presentation.

9. Explain at least four ways to integrate technology into teaching.

TECHNOLOGY IN AND OF INSTRUCTION

When people talk about technology in education, they generally have in mind the use of devices such as overhead projectors, document cameras, smart boards, and computers. This meaning is workable, and for the purpose of this discussion, it refers to **technology in instruction.** The word "technology," stems from the Greek *tekhne*, which meant a blending of science and art. The *American Heritage Dictionary* definition of 'technology' is: "a. The application of science, especially to industrial and commercial objectives. b. The entire body of methods and materials used to achieve such objectives."[1] Behaviorists, with their work with stimulus-response learning, provided strong evidence that the idea of dividing complex tasks into smaller, less complex tasks, and using an appropriate reward structure was an effective learning strategy. This approach is the essence of the **technology of instruction.**

To the extent that teachers communicate expected learning outcomes in terms that are observable and measurable, they are following behaviorist principles. They have determined what the student should be able to do at the end of the course and their plans reflect their best thinking about how to divide the complex behaviors expected, so that students can master them efficiently. To this extent, these teachers use a technological approach, whether they do or do not use technological devices. With this beginning point, we can turn our attention to the selection and use of a variety of teaching aids.

General Utilization Factors

Mediated instruction, by definition, includes any instruction that makes use of some device (mechanical or otherwise) to facilitate learning. Although there is tremendous variety in the forms of mediated instruction available, some utilization procedures apply to all forms. Among these are the following.

1. *Select mediated instruction for specific instructional objectives.* To be most effective, mediated instruction should be an integral part of the instructional procedures. Its use should not be an afterthought. Further, in many schools it is necessary to reserve equipment well in advance. Planning on your part is crucial. If mediated instruction is used on the spur of the moment, without relationship to specific objectives, students will realize that it is being used as a time-filler or diversion. The clear message the teacher will be sending is, "I did not have anything else planned, so let's do this." This is clearly a major problem in the

utilization of the Internet in classroom. If the use of the Internet is not carefully planned, it becomes an aimless activity.

2. *Become familiar with the material or device prior to using it with students.* Depending on the form of mediated instruction being considered, the teacher should read it, view it, handle it, and otherwise use it prior to exposing students to it. This will not only provide assurance that the instructional aid is exactly what was expected, but it will also enable the teacher to estimate how much time to allow for correct use, pinpoint specific strengths and weaknesses, and thus better prepare students. When mechanical devices are involved, the teacher will become more proficient in the operation of the device and thus avoid the distraction (and embarrassment) that accompanies the misuse of equipment.

3. *Prepare the students.* If students are to derive the full benefit of mediated instruction, if they are to know what to look for, they should be given some idea of its general content or purpose beforehand. Usually a brief description is sufficient to orient students, but it may be useful to provide guide questions for students to answer. This helps to further focus student attention on important points.

4. *Use the mediated instruction correctly.* There is little value in attempting to use mediated instruction if there is insufficient time for its proper use or if other conditions are not appropriate. Common sense will provide good guidance in the use of most mediated instruction. For example, if a device has a volume control, remember that it controls only the volume of the machine, not the students. If students are noisy, raising the volume on the device will not necessarily cause them to quiet down. In fact, it may have just the opposite effect. They may talk louder, so they can hear each other more easily.

5. *For visual aids, lighting may be a problem.* In most classrooms, there is sufficient light for most activities, but in some rooms it may be difficult or impossible to darken the room enough to effectively use devices such as film projectors. In others, glare from windows may be a problem. It is a good idea to see if lighting will be a problem before reserving equipment.

6. *Conduct follow-up activities.* Follow-up activities provide an opportunity to clarify confusing points, answer questions, discuss interesting points, and integrate the new information with previous learning. Follow-up activities also allow the teacher to point out subtle points that may have been missed, to correct misconceptions, and tie up loose ends.

7. *Evaluate the mediated instruction.* After using any form of mediated instruction, it is helpful to write a short evaluation of how effectively it helped students achieve the specified objectives. As these evaluations accumulate, they can be used to help select the most appropriate and effective form of mediated instruction for each type of objective.

Reading Materials

Textbooks

In 1454, **Johann Gutenberg** (c. 1398–1468) used movable metal type to print the *Bible* of 42 lines, so called because each of the 1,282 pages had forty-two lines.[2] In 1658, **Johann Comenius** (1592–1670) published *Orbus pictus* (*The World in Pictures*). It was the world's first illustrated textbook specifically written for children. Since that time, educators have made increasing use of books as instructional aids. Today, books are the most common instructional aid available, and they can also be one of the most powerful. Textbooks have a number of sometimes forgotten advantages. For example, they can provide students with a common body of information arranged in a logical order. This facilitates discussions and can help students see cause-effect relationships. Most high school texts also include chapter summaries, questions to be answered, and associated learning activities that provide guides for studying the information. Considering that most textbooks can be used repeatedly and that most contain pictures, charts, graphs, and/or maps, they are relatively inexpensive. Finally, textbooks can be adapted to individual needs and interests and to self-pacing.

As with any instructional tool, textbooks can be misused, and most of the disadvantages associated with them stem from such misuses. Perhaps the greatest misuse is to allow them to dictate what is taught. To be marketable, textbooks must contain accurate, up-to-date information deemed important to educators nationwide. However, this does not mean that the information is, by itself, automatically relevant to your students or to your objectives. Further, unless there is a school rule to the contrary, it is not necessary to cover the entire book or to devote equal time to each chapter or unit. The course objectives, written with consideration of the needs and abilities of your students, should dictate the direction and pace of instruction. A textbook is a foundation, a beginning point. Teachers should build on the content of the textbook to help make the content relevant to students.

A good first step in using a textbook is to review it. Although you will know most, if not all, of the material, the author's approach may be unique. After reviewing the book, you will be able to make students aware of the author's perspective and of new information developed since the book was published. There might also be unintentional biases that should be discussed.

The next steps are to explain to students why that particular text is being used and to give them an overview of it. Taking time to do these things, like taking time to go over the course syllabus, lets students know that you recognize that they are real live people who appreciate seeing "the big picture." Most students can also benefit from a short review on using a textbook: A survey of the table of contents, with comments concerning what will be emphasized; a discussion of the author's perspective; an explanation of how the index is organized; and a survey of a representative chapter will help make students aware that you are trying to help them be successful.

When surveying the representative chapter, point out that it is helpful to convert the chapter title and headings into questions and then to read to find the answers. It is also helpful, before reading the chapter, to look at the chapter summary and the questions at the end of the chapter. Paying attention to words in boldface and italics, to captions, and to pictures, maps, and charts, often makes it easier to understand major points. Having students write answers to questions posed by the teacher or the author is another way to focus student attention on important points in each chapter.

Audio Aids

Radios, Record, Tape, and CD Players

Radios, record, audiotape, and compact disk (CD) players all utilize a single sensory input, sound. With the advent of films, television, and videotapes, purely auditory devices are being used less frequently, but they still have their place. Radios, for example, because they are less expensive and cumbersome than televisions, are a convenient means for getting up-to-the-minute news reports for class analysis. Records, audio tape, and CD players make it possible to conveniently listen to plays, operas, concerts, and speeches, while tape recorders make it possible to record broadcast material, guest speakers (with their permission), class debates, and other activities for later use and analysis. These forms of mediated instruction are also used extensively as audio models for students. Audio tape recorders provide an added dimension by enabling students to record, and then listen to, their own voices for diagnostic or developmental purposes.

One problem with the use of audio-only aids is that they lack a visual attention point. Students, used to watching a teacher, a TV, or computer monitor screen; may literally not know what to look at while listening to an audio-only aid. Unless part of the reason for using such an aid is to help students learn to listen, it may be helpful to provide visual focal points, such as pictures or maps, which relate to what the students are listening to.

Research in the area of listening is enlightening. For example, one study revealed that approximately forty-five percent of the average adult's working day is spent listening and that this figure rises to sixty percent for elementary school students and ninety percent for high school and college students.[3] Unfortunately, the same study showed that even if students are concentrating on what they hear, they retain only about fifty percent and within two months will be able to recall less than half of that.[4] In another study, it was estimated that about forty-five percent of all classroom communication time is spent listening.[5] With so much time spent listening, students might well profit from instruction and practice in effective listening.

Telephones

Telephones represent yet another purely auditory form of mediated instruction. Although the telephone was invented in 1876, and the radio in 1895, the telephone's nineteen-year advantage has not been reflected in its greater use by educators. This is unfortunate, because the telephone companies have much to offer, and they are generally quite willing to work with educators.

One use of telephones is **teleconferencing**. Many phones have a conference mode that makes two-way communication possible between a whole class and a speaker at some distant point. Teleconferencing is more convenient than asking a speaker to come to a class but has many of the advantages of actually having the speaker there. All students can listen at the same time, ask questions, and receive answers.

Although student preparation is important with all forms of mediated instruction, it is particularly important with teleconferencing, because phone charges are calculated according to the time the telephone line is in use. Adequate preparation includes letting the speaker know, in advance, the objective of the teleconference and some of the key information students are seeking. Preparation of the students would include formulating specific questions to ask the speaker.

In 1971, the American Telephone & Telegraph Company developed a device called a **Variable Speech Control** (VSC). The purpose of the VSC is to change the rate at which speech can be understood by omitting pauses and shortening vowel sounds. The practical applications of the device include enabling blind people to listen to and comprehend spoken words nearly as quickly as sighted people can read and comprehend written words and enabling teachers and students to make greater use of taped materials by allowing them to listen to recorded tapes in shorter periods of time. Heinich et al. suggest that "research has shown that learning time can be cut (as much as 50 percent and an average of 32 percent) and comprehension increased (as much as 9.3 percent and an average of 4.2 percent) by using compressed and variable-speed audio tapes."[6]

Today, many students have cell phones. While there is no doubt that each student who has one feels that it is absolutely necessary to be available twenty-four- hours a day, seven days a week, it is recommended that you remind students, orally and in writing, that having class time interrupted by cell phone calls, incoming or outgoing, is not acceptable. Ask that all cell phones be turned off before class begins. There may be a school policy regarding cell phones. If so, be sure to follow it.

Visual Aids

Still and Motion Pictures

Still pictures, whether in the form of paintings, magazine clippings, photographs, slides, or filmstrips, have unique properties that make them extremely valuable as instructional aids. Among these properties are their abilities to (1) convey abstractions powerfully without depending on verbal descriptions; (2) focus attention on a characteristic situation or on a particular step in a process; and (3) allow students to study an image at length, to refer back to it conveniently, and to make side-by-side comparisons.

Pictures, from sources such as magazines, travel bureaus, and commercial concerns, are one of the easiest to acquire and least expensive forms of mediated instruction. The instructional value of pictures will be increased if they are selected for use in particular instructional units. Complex or "busy" pictures may cause some students to miss important points. Pictures in color usually attract and hold attention better than those in black and white, and all pictures must be large enough to be seen easily. Ensuring that the picture does not present a biased view (unless such a view is intended) is important.

Different photography techniques can provide unique pictures in either still or motion form. Chief among these techniques are **time-lapse** (showing events in condensed time), **micro** (pictures taken through a microscope), **long-range** (magnifying distant objects), **X-ray** (looking below the object's surface to show internal structures, **infrared** (showing heat patterns), and **slow-motion** (slowing events down). Students may watch as a flower unfolds into full bloom or as a single cell divides. They can see the Earth as astronauts see it or gain an understanding of the phenomenon of nuclear fission. **Animation** is a technique in which a sequence of still pictures, when seen in quick succession (typically twenty-four frames per second), gives the impression of movement because each picture is drawn so that it differs from the one before it by only a small incremental change.

If a picture seems particularly useful, you may want to save it for repeated use. In such cases, it is a good idea to protect the picture by mounting it on poster board and laminating it.

Slides and Filmstrips

Slides and filmstrips have all the advantages of pictures and the added advantage of increased realism. Because slides are actual photographs and are shown via a bright light source, colors appear more brilliant, and scenes appear more real than in printed pictures. In addition, it is much easier to store a set of slides than a set of large, mounted pictures.

A more significant advantage associated with slides is the opportunity they provide for teachers to create their own instructional aids. Many teachers make it a point to take along a camera and slide film (rather than print film) when vacationing or traveling. Consequently, these teachers are able to build up an impressive set of slides that are useful in stimulating and maintaining student interest. Many teachers have also initiated class projects wherein students organize a slide program complete with an accompanying tape recording. Such projects have the dual advantages of being useful, interesting learning activities, and increasing the teacher's store of instructional aids.

A filmstrip is essentially a series of connected slides. Most filmstrips are prepared commercially, and many have brief captions printed on each frame. Some filmstrip projectors are sprocketless, thus prolonging filmstrip life. Typically, as the filmstrip is advanced, the caption is read by the teacher or by students and the frame is discussed. Some filmstrips have recorded captions that are played back via a tape recorder.

Bulletin Boards

Bulletin boards are ideally suited for the display of visual materials such as pictures, cartoons, postcards, newspaper clippings, outstanding papers, and student-made **collages** (an artistic composition of objects pasted over a surface) and **montages** (a pictorial composition made from many pictures or designs closely arranged or superimposed on each other). Bulletin boards promote learning best when they concern a single idea or topic. They should be neat and uncluttered, make use of bright colors and attention-getting materials such as colored yarn and plastics, and they should be pictorially, rather than verbally, oriented. The instructional value of bulletin boards is usually increased if viewer participation is encouraged. Ways to do this include manipulative devices and questions with answers covered by flaps.

A bulletin board's instructional value lasts a relatively short time, in some cases not more than a few days. Having gone to the trouble of constructing an exceptional bulletin board, there is no reason to take it down as long as students continue to find it useful. However, once students stop paying attention to the display or the class moves on to some other topic, the bulletin board should be replaced.

Teachers can, and should, encourage groups of students to put up new bulletin boards throughout the year. This helps increase student interest in the associated units and is likely to result in increased learning as students do the research and creative work needed to produce an attractive and interesting display. The teacher can provide advice and assistance in the form of suggesting sources for, and providing, actual materials.

Maps, Globes, Charts, and Graphs

Maps, globes, charts, and graphs are grouped together because these forms of mediated instruction are heavily emphasized in the new national standards in mathematics, history, and geography. Students may have had little practice in interpreting maps, globes, charts, and graphs, so specific instruction in these skills may be needed.

Maps and globes are used to show portions of the Earth's surface on a smaller scale. Cartographers construct maps and globes to emphasize political, geographic, and climatic divisions, and have developed different map projections. It is helpful to draw students' attention to the particular projection being used and to discuss the way it distorts the real size and shape of particular geographic features. Without an understanding of projection, students may have misconceptions about maps.

Students' attention should be drawn to the legend of the map or globe. It is here that the cartographer explains the meanings of the symbols used, gives the scale to which features are drawn, and provides additional information such as the meanings of particular colors.

The teacher should study maps and globes before using them. In today's world, political boundaries and the names of cities and countries change more often than one might suspect, so it is common for maps and globes to be out of date. When this happens, students' attention should be drawn to the inaccuracy and correct information provided.

Charts differ from graphs and diagrams in that they may include a wider variety of pictorial forms. The most common kinds of charts are flow charts (showing sequential steps), process charts (showing some process from start to finish), and time charts (showing developments over a period of time). The instructional value of charts is maximized when time is taken to be sure that students can read and interpret the data.

Graphs and diagrams generally have only simple lines or bars. Graphs are used primarily to condense and convey numerical data into visual, iconic, form. The most common kinds of graphs are circle and pie graphs (used to show the relationship of parts to the whole), bar graphs (used to show comparative data such as the changes in unemployment from year to year), and line graphs (used to plot profiles of patterns).

Although students should be given special instruction in the use of maps, globes, charts, and graphs, teachers should use the least complicated aid that will serve the immediate purpose. Trying to select an aid that can be used in a variety of lessons will be a false economy if students have difficulty interpreting the aid or are confused by it.

Chalk or Whiteboards

Chalk or whiteboards are available in almost every classroom and most teachers use them frequently to display instructions, diagrams, examples, and other information that is subject to frequent change. Board work also gives students the chance to demonstrate their abilities and allows active student participation.

There are a number of ways the teacher can use chalkboards to make them more valuable to students. Printing is often easier for students to read than cursive writing and characters at least two inches high can be read easily from a distance of about thirty feet (the length of an average classroom). It is difficult for students to understand teachers who face the board and talk at the same time, so when you write on the board, stop talking. As a point of information, having your back to students for more than a minute or two is unwise. If an accident occurs while you are writing on the board for an extended time, it might be argued that you are partly to blame since you failed to provide adequate supervision.

The use of templates to facilitate the drawing of frequently used shapes saves time and results in greater consistency. An inexpensive template can be made by simply tracing a design and punching holes along the traced lines. Tapping a dusty chalk eraser along the template while it is held to the board will create a dotted outline. Pictures can also be traced on the board from projected images.

When using the chalkboard, avoid cluttering. Once an item on the board has served its purpose, it should be erased so students will not be distracted by it. It is a good idea, however, to reserve one area of the board for announcements and homework and to leave that information on the board throughout the period. Some teachers also leave the objective(s) for the lesson on the board. Certain types of colored chalk (those containing oil) are intended for use on paper, not on chalkboards. If that kind of chalk is used on a chalkboard, it may stain the board permanently.

Overhead Projectors

Of the types of projectors available to teachers, overhead projectors are the most commonly used. Overhead projectors project images drawn, written, or printed on transparent film (usually acetate). They are often used instead of the chalk or whiteboard because they allow a teacher to write so that everyone can see and, at the same time, continue monitoring what is going on in the room and maintain eye contact with students. Another advantage is that the overhead projector can be used without darkening the room. This facilitates notetaking and student interaction.

Using an overhead projector requires only a grease pencil, china marker, crayon, or special felt-tipped pen and a sheet of clear plastic to protect the glass projection plate from stains. Grease pencils, crayons, and china markers contain a wax-based material that blocks light. What is drawn or written with them will appear black regardless of their color. Color makes projections more eye-catching and interesting and can be easily achieved using special felt-tipped pens filled with a water-based, non-beading, transparent ink. The ink can be removed with a damp paper towel or by holding the sheet under running water.

Some overheads come equipped with a roll of acetate. The teacher writes on the acetate and then simply rolls up the used surface to expose an unused portion. This temporarily eliminates the need to erase. Teachers can simply write or draw on blank transparencies, but preparing transparencies beforehand results in more professional-looking projections that are easier for students to read. Further, such transparencies subtly communicate to students the fact that you took the time to prepare appropriate materials.

Transparencies are easy to make. Use a word processor or presentation program, such as Microsoft's *PowerPoint*™, for the creative work. Then, instead of using a laser printer to print the work on paper, print it on a blank transparency specifically designed for that purpose. This same special transparency can be used in a copier so a written, typed, or traced page, or a page from a book or magazine, can also be made into a transparency. A word of caution. If an ordinary transparency is run through a laser printer or copier it is likely to melt and ruin the equipment (along with your whole day). Use only transparency material specifically designed for use in laser printers and copiers.

Readability is important. Characters about this size project clearly. Crowding, either horizontally or vertically, makes the transparency hard to read. Allow more than the usual amount of space between lines and between words in large type, and print no more than twenty lines on a transparency.

Overlays are sheets of acetate laid over a base transparency. A typical overlay sequence might consist of a base transparency showing an outline map of the United States. Over this, the teacher might place a transparency showing major river systems. A third overlay might depict major cities so students could see their proximity to rivers, and a fourth transparency might be used to show railroad development.

It is often possible to acquire commercially prepared transparencies and overlays made by experts who have a wealth of materials with which to work. Such transparencies are usually more polished than teacher-made materials, but they cost more.

Most overhead projectors have a thermostatically controlled switch that permits the fan to continue operating until the interior of the projector is cool. If the machine does not stop when turned off, do not pull the plug. It will stop automatically when it has cooled down.

Document Cameras

Document cameras combine the best features of opaque and overhead projectors. As do opaque projectors, document cameras project the image of any document, transparent or not, in its original color(s). The advantage of the document camera is that the room does not have to be darkened.

Real Things

Real things, such as specimens, can be used to help students learn. Depending on what is being taught, teachers and students may display models, mock-ups, pets, coin collections, insects, or dozens of other objects. The list is as limitless and as varied as there are real things in the world that may be displayed without danger or great expense. Modified representations of real things, such as cut-away or "exploded" models, are also helpful. In the latter, the whole is broken into segments and each segment is held apart from the others, while the pieces maintain the same relative positions as in the unexploded model. Other good teaching tools are models that students can assemble and disassemble, and **dioramas** (three-dimensional scenes that students construct).

Audio-Visual Combinations

Multimedia Kits

As more educators adopt the systems approach to education, more are finding multimedia kits helpful. Multimedia kits are compilations of instructional materials that include a variety of mediated instruction forms. These materials are designed to help students achieve specific instructional objectives by exposing them to different types of closely integrated educational experiences.

A typical multimedia kit may contain booklets, filmstrips, audio tapes, and artifacts. All the components are selected with a single purpose in mind—to generate and maintain students' interest in a particular topic or subject while, at the same time, providing them with as much pertinent information as possible.

Multimedia kits can be used well with groups, but they can also be useful as self-instructional aids that students use at their own convenience and at their own rates. As with most other forms of mediated instruction, multimedia kits may be prepared by teachers themselves or purchased ready-made.

Film, Television, and Video Tapes

Films, television, and video tapes provide students with more of a "you are there" feeling than do most other forms of mediated instruction. They also enable students to view demonstrations (both scientific and social), experiments, natural phenomena, and other events that would be too difficult, dangerous, or even impossible to view otherwise (for instance, moon walks and erupting volcanoes).

Proper preparation of students and good planning in the use of films and video tapes can enhance learning. Providing questions to be answered or study guides, and explaining new words, will help. Further, films and tapes can be stopped at crucial points in order to focus students' attention on a particular point, and they do not need to be shown from start to finish. These are tools; it is up to the teacher to use them wisely.

Most schools, universities, and libraries maintain film and/or tape libraries and most media center people and librarians are willing to help familiarize teachers with their holdings and to help in ordering or reserving materials.

Educational television, or ETV, programming is often of particular value to teachers. The Public Broadcasting Service (PBS), for example, often carries instructional programming aimed at high school and college audiences. Some PBS programs, such as *Sesame Street, Masterpiece Theatre,* and *Nova,* have won awards for their high quality.

The Discovery channel and The Learning Channel (TLC) are other sources of programs suitable to a wide variety of subject areas.

One of the newer applications of broadcast television is **Channel One**, a creation of Whittle Communications. With *Channel One*, schools are given the equipment needed to receive the satellite transmissions and record and play back the program. In exchange, students watch a daily twelve-minute news program that includes two minutes of commercial advertising.[7] *CNN Newsroom* is a program similar to *Channel One*.

Another way to use television is for **distance learning**. In this application, students at different sites are able to see and hear each other. Students get the benefit of interacting with other students, speakers, or teachers in distant places without the need to travel. The idea is excellent, and it opens up new possibilities for teaching and learning.[8]

Closed-circuit television is still another way to use the medium. In closed-circuit television, only TV sets connected directly to a transmitter, or adapted to receive the 2,500 MHz (megahertz) wavelength reserved for closed-circuit television, can receive the programs. Closed-circuit television is most often used on an "in-house" basis to televise meetings and debates, demonstrations and experiments, and even regular classes. Because it is an in-house operation, students can participate in the actual program development and televising, thus adding yet another dimension to their educational experience.

Video tape recorders and players are replacing film projectors and becoming a major instructional tool. Schools are acquiring VCR equipment, not only for taping and saving lectures, demonstrations, and theatrical presentations, but also for use in everyday teaching situations. They enable teachers and students to see themselves as others see them. Coaches, for instance, have found VCR equipment invaluable for instant feedback of student psychomotor skills and teachers tape their own lessons in order to analyze their strengths and weaknesses.

CD-WORM, or compact disk-write once read many times, is an emerging technology that enables users to create their own compact disks. Since the disk cannot be erased, its utility is somewhat limited.

Programmed Instruction

Programmed instruction is one of the clearest examples of the behaviorist teaching strategy. Teachers have long wished for a way to ensure that students mastered one point before moving on to the next and in 1925, **Sidney L. Pressey** demonstrated a "teaching machine," which helped ensure that this happened. Pressey's machine was more of a testing machine than a teaching machine. It presented the learner with a question and a choice of four answers. The student answered the question by pressing one of four keys, but the next question was revealed only if the answer was correct. Pressey's device not only kept a record of student's answers, but also could function as a reinforcer by keeping track of points earned.[9]

Programmed instruction did not gain wide attention until 1954, when B. F. Skinner published an article titled, "The Science of Learning and the Art of Teaching." In this article, Skinner explained how the principles of operant conditioning were relevant to the teaching-learning process.[10]

In programming material, the author takes information and breaks it into a series of small, carefully sequenced, steps. As students move from step to step, they receive immediate feedback concerning their learning progress. One of the major differences between programmed and traditional texts is that with programmed materials, students are actively participating in the learning process (they must construct or select responses), whereas with traditional texts, students are passive readers. A second difference is that the formation of misconceptions is reduced (or eliminated entirely) because the sequential nature of the program carefully relates each new piece of information to the one immediately preceding it. Such texts may be particularly useful with students with some special needs.

There are two basic strategies for all programmed materials, whether they are presented via programmed texts, teaching machines, or computers. **Linear programming** is most closely associated with the work of **B. F. Skinner**.[11] In linear programs, each student goes through an identical series of small instructional blocks or "frames," usually less than six sentences in length. Students' attention is drawn to key information by **cues** such as **bold face** type, *italics*, or underlining, and the student is then presented with a question calling for the key information. The student constructs or selects a response and, in a programmed text, turns a page or uncovers an "answer area" and sees if the answer is correct. If a "teaching machine" is used, the student cannot move on until the right answer is selected. This ensures that the last thing the student sees with respect to that question is the correct answer. Linear programs are designed to ensure a **high success rate**. If designed properly, students should be able to answer at least ninety percent of the questions on the first try.[12]

Nonlinear (branching, or intrinsic) programming is associated most closely with **Norman A. Crowder**.[13] In nonlinear programs, students are presented with larger blocks of information sometimes as long as a page. As in linear programs, each block is followed by a question, but in branching programs there is no use of cues to ensure a correct answer. Each of the possible answers is keyed to additional information. The author anticipates wrong responses so, when students select a wrong answer, they are referred to pages or parts of the program containing remedial information. They are then referred back to the original question or to new information. When students answer correctly, they move on to the next block of new information. Since the path that any one student takes through the program is dependent on his or her answers to individual questions, it is possible for every student to take a different path. While the paths and rates of progress may differ, all students acquire the same basic information.

One characteristic of all programmed materials is that they must, by their very nature, eliminate student creativity. All acceptable responses are programmed, and divergent thinking is, in terms of the program, incorrect thinking. There are some who believe that for the basic content that makes up much of our needed knowledgebase, programmed materials will eventually replace traditional kinds of instruction. They believe that it is in the integration and application of knowledge that human teachers are most needed.

Computer-Assisted Instruction (CAI)

The first large-scale computer, the Electronic Numerical Integrator and Computer (ENIAC), was put into operation in 1946. Its main function was to help scientists and engineers work on problems related to military needs. The first commercially available computer, the UNIVersal Automatic Computer 1 (UNIVAC 1), was introduced in 1951.

Advantages of CAI

Educators were not far behind the scientists, engineers, and businessmen with respect to computer use. Although not designed as such, it soon became clear that the interaction possible with computers could make them powerful instructional tools. In 1963, **Patrick Suppes** implemented large-scale CAI projects in schools in East Palo Alto, California, and in McComb, Mississippi. The Computer Curriculum Corporation (CCC) was formed shortly thereafter to market the materials.[14] These efforts were followed in the early 1970s with large time-sharing projects such as the PLATO (Programmed Logic for Automated Teaching Operations) project at the University of Illinois, and the TICCIT (Time-Shared Interactive Computer-Controlled Information Television) project at Brigham Young University. The time-sharing in these projects consisted of having the CAI programs in a large mainframe computer with hundreds of computer terminals connected to it via telecommunication lines. Since most of the time in CAI is spent waiting for the student to read and respond to computer output, the mainframes could provide virtually instantaneous feedback to all the students connected to them.

CAI held many promises. For example, students would be able work at their own rates. Overworked teachers would be able to devote more of their time to helping those students who most needed their help, and students would be more actively engaged in learning since they had the full attention of the "teacher." Further, other forms of mediated instruction, such as books, videotapes, and television, are one-way communicators. Information goes from them to students. Computers are two-way communicators. Information, questions, and other stimuli go from them to students, but then the students provide input that shapes the next output from the computer. This interaction makes it possible for computers to approximate some of the individualization typically associated with tutoring.

For all its advantages, the delivery of CAI via time-shared systems depended on linking distant terminals, via telecommunication lines, to central computers, and this was costly. In 1977, Tandy/Radio Shack introduced the TRS-80, Model 1; Apple Computer introduced the Apple II; and Commodore, Ltd. introduced the Commodore Personal Electronic Transactor (PET). These were the first, fully assembled, commercially available microcomputers and they solved the problem of telecommunication costs. For all intents and purposes, microcomputers launched the "computer revolution" by making the power of computers available to virtually everyone.

By 1981, about 42.7 percent of all high schools used microcomputers. By 1990, the figure was about 98.8 percent.[15] Hundreds of research studies have been conducted comparing the effectiveness of CAI v. traditional instruction. Almost universally, these studies show that while instructional time is typically reduced, there is no significant difference in achievement scores.[16] These studies also show that elementary students are more likely than secondary students to profit from CAI.[17]

Most educators are now well aware of the existence of CAI and many have the opportunity to select software (the actual programs, usually on a disk). They make their choices from among the following categories of programs.

Drill and Practice Programs

As the name implies, drill and practice programs provide drill and practice over skills and knowledge already learned and, due to their purpose, most focus on low-level skills. These programs can help students because (1) each student is able to progress at his or her own rate, (2) such programs often automatically adjust the complexity of the content to the abilities of the student, (3) students receive immediate feedback concerning the appropriateness of each response, and (4) the interaction is fast, so the learner is directly involved with the work (on task) all the time. There is some evidence that students gain the most from the use of drill and practice programs during the first fifteen minutes of use. After that, the fast interaction seems to tire students, resulting in diminishing returns.[18]

Tutorial Programs

As the name implies, tutorial programs function like a tutor presenting new (primary) information. These programs can help students because they provide information, ask a question about the content and, depending on the student's response, either go on to the next block of new information or branch to remedial information designed to clarify misconceptions. The branching in most tutorial programs is relatively limited, with students typically choosing from among three or four answers to each question. The sophistication and cost of the program is largely dependent on the extent of the branching.

Tutorial programs are most useful for remediation or enrichment. Remediation is called for when a student either misses a lesson or does not understand a lesson. If an appropriate tutorial program is available, it may provide the additional help such a student needs to progress. Enrichment is called for when a student already possesses the skills and knowledge to be taught to the class as a whole. Such a student should be encouraged to acquire new skills or knowledge and for this, the use of a tutorial program might be appropriate.

Usually, tutorial programs are *not* the best tool for teaching a whole class a particular skill or piece of information. When a teacher is presenting new information to a whole group, often a student will ask a question or make a comment that will help clarify things for other students. That kind of interaction is missing from CAI. For the most part, people teach people at least as well as machines teach people. Therefore, for whole-class instruction, teachers would be wise to do the job themselves.

Simulation Programs

Simulation programs present approximations of real-life situations. A student may simulate a pioneer traveling the Oregon Trail, the ruler of a country, or a chemist with a laboratory full of dangerous chemicals, but in all cases, the student is safe and in charge. Simulation programs can help students because they remove the danger or inconvenience of the real-life situations but still require the student to decide what to do next and to deal with the consequences of that decision. Without a computer, it would not be possible for each student to make his or her own decision and to have the next event be consistent with his or her choice. Since recognition of cause-effect relationships is essential to the maturation process, simulation programs can be said to help students mature.

Simulation programs also help students integrate knowledge and learn from mistakes. These features combine to make simulation programs among the most valuable that students can use. By enabling students to engage in activities that would be impossible, impractical, or too dangerous to engage in otherwise, simulation programs provide learning opportunities that are unique and invaluable.

Simulation programs are the most time-consuming to write because the programmer must provide sequences of choices consistent with each decision by each student. To enable each student to experience the cumulative consequences of each of his or her choices, the programmer must develop extensive branches, which can require thousands of hours of programming time.

Despite the fact that good simulation programs seem to put the learner in full control of the direction of the program, that control is an illusion. All programs, regardless of how extensive their branching may be, are closed systems. The student can only select choices from among those presented by the programmer so although it might appear otherwise, there is no room for creativity on the part of the student. There is only one end result for each possible path, and it has already been written by the programmer.

There is an additional downside to simulations. Because they are so effective in capturing and maintaining students' interest, it is difficult to use them within regular class periods. Students get involved and want to see the consequences of their decisions and to follow their plans through to the end. Typical class periods often make this impossible, so conventional divisions in the school day actually hinder the most effective use of simulation programs.

Gaming Programs

Gaming programs capitalize on fast action, graphics, and all too often, violence. These programs typically have little relation to instructional objectives and their use in the classroom can rarely be justified. One possible justification might be to help beginning students gain confidence in their ability to use computers.

Developments in CAI

When microcomputers became popular in the early 1980s, thousands of instructional programs were put on the market. Most of those programs were (and most new programs still are) **stand-alone** programs. They "stand alone" in that they focus on isolated skills or information. They are not designed to relate to other programs or to units of study. This makes it difficult for teachers to integrate them into instructional plans.

Some vendors responded to this problem by marketing sequences of programs that built on each other (for example, programs that deal, sequentially, with nouns, pronouns, and other parts of speech) or had some common element, typically a record-keeping system that kept track of students' achievements as they went from program to program. These **computer-managed instruction** (CMI) programs are somewhat easier to build into a curriculum, because they can help students develop a sequence of skills. Further, because they typically keep track of the student's performance through more than one program, they enable the teacher to see if any performance pattern is evident that might point to particular areas of strength or weakness. These programs are also easier for teachers to learn to use than stand-alone programs because all programs in the series use the same commands.

The most complete form of CMI is the **integrated computer curriculum**. An integrated computer curriculum is one in which some subject area such as math or reading is dealt with through a series of grade levels such as 4–6 or 6–12. Some programs deal with two or more subject areas as well as two or more grade levels. The most sophisticated of these integrated computer curriculums include a series of precise instructional objectives, a variety of program types (tutorial, drill and practice, and simulation) to help each student achieve the objectives, and a sophisticated record-keeping system that tracks each student. Two of the largest companies that market such integrated computer curriculums are the Computer Curriculum Corporation, and WICAT (World Institute of Computer Assisted Teaching).

Disadvantages of CAI

Individualization in a Group Instruction Setting

At the same time that CAI opens up new possibilities for individualizing instruction and for having students achieve objectives that were impractical or impossible before CAI, it also poses some serious problems. Perhaps the most fundamental of these is that most schools are set up to provide instruction to groups, not to individuals. For example, while most teachers try to work with individuals as much as possible, the main thrust of their planning, teaching, and evaluating is geared to working with groups. Computers, however, like pens, pencils, and hand-held calculators, are tools best used by individuals as they work at their own rates. CAI simply does not fit very well into a system set up for group instruction.

This basic problem generates other problems. For example, lesson planning is complicated because teachers plan lessons for whole classes. If you direct some students to engage in activities other than those planned for the class, you must have separate plans for those students. The plans might not be as extensive as complete lesson plans but if some students are going to be working at computers, you must be able to explain to a parent or to a principal how the computer work will help those students achieve specific course objectives. Many teachers find that they do not have enough time or energy to make additional plans, so they avoid activities, such as CAI, that require them.

Aside from the problem of extra planning, a related problem is that while students are using computers they are missing all or part of the planned lesson. When it is time to use the information they missed, those students who were using the computers will, in effect, be penalized. It is unfair to ask students to use information or skills presented while they were directed to engage in some other activity. To be fair, some adjustment would have to be made in evaluating these students and this, again, would mean more work for the teacher.

Inadequate Teacher Preparation

Another problem hindering the use of CAI in schools is the fact that relatively few prospective teachers receive adequate instruction in how and when to use CAI effectively. Many teacher education programs help students learn how to design web pages and how to use word processors and spreadsheets, but fewer help their students learn how to use computer-assisted instruction programs effectively.

Differing Expectations

Most teachers go into teaching to work with students, and each intends to do the best possible job. It is not likely, however, that many teachers envision their students spending a great deal of time sitting eighteen inches from a computer monitor and interacting with a computer program that is providing stimuli visually via the monitor and aurally via headphones. In this situation, the teacher is not needed. This reduced or non-role differs significantly from the role teachers expect to play and from the role that administrators and parents expect them to play. Even though students may be learning, the teacher may not be seen as teaching.

Hardware and Software Problems

Computers have few moving parts so, with reasonable care, they last a long time. However, about every three years hardware advances, particularly advances in the speed and power of central processing units (CPUs), make it possible for software writers to develop more powerful programs that make use of the new hardware. Changes also occur with respect to software, but few schools can afford to replace their computer hardware or software as often as some teachers would like.

Interactive Video

Another CAI development is interactive video. This technology links the interactive capability of computers with material stored on videotape or disks. Instead of calling up just words or still pictures, the computer can start a videotape or disk player and make use of action materials such as a segment of a political speech or an actual demonstration. This technology mates two sophisticated learning tools, computers and television. Interactive video provides somewhat less intense interaction than regular CAI because students spend part of their time watching the video portion of the program. The ability to build into the program full-motion events, however, more than compensates for the decrease in interaction.

In 1992, about 2,000 high schools, or fourteen percent, had interactive videodisk players. By 1994, the number had grown to about 4,500 or twenty-seven percent.[19]

Networking

Networking refers to linking one computer with others. If the network links computers in a relatively small geographic area, such as a school or suburban school district, it is referred to as a local area network or (LAN). The largest network is the worldwide

Internet. Via the Internet, you and your students can access libraries, art galleries, and databases throughout the world and can share ideas via electronic mail (e-mail) with people worldwide. As of 2020, the number of internet users worldwide is estimated to be 4,833,521,806. Asia holds the first place in the world with an estimated 2,525,033,874 million users. Europe comes in second place with an estimated 727,848,547 million users. Africa holds the third place with an estimated number of 566,138,772 million users. Latin America/Caribbean holds fourth place with an estimated 467,817,332 million users. North America comes in fifth place with an estimated 332,908,868 million users. The Middle East holds sixth place with an estimated 260,991,690 million users.[20] According to EducationData.org, it is estimated that in 2017, a total of 19.7 million students enrolled in courses at degree-granting postsecondary institutions.[21] Of these, 6.6 million students enrolled in some form of distance education/online learning courses.

1. 5.5 million undergraduate students
   - 3.2 million (19.5 percent) students took least one but not all of their courses online
   - 2.2 million (13.3 percent) students enrolled in exclusively distance education/online courses
2. 1 million post-baccalaureate students
   - 274,211 (9.1 percent) students took at least one but not all of their courses online
   - 868,708 (28.9 percent) students enrolled in exclusively distance education/online courses.[22]

The idea of networking and all that it entails, particularly in e-mail and user groups, poses some interesting questions for educators. For example, it is now possible for teachers to make things such as syllabi, assignments, study questions, and one-on-one conversations available to students via LANs or Internet. There is a question, however, of whether teachers really want to be available to students twenty-four hours a day, seven days a week. Further, there is a question of whether it is equitable to make some things, even one-on-one conversations, available to students who have ready access to computers while putting those same things out of the reach of students who do not have ready access to computers.

THE INTERNET

It can be said that the Internet was first started in 1858 with the laying of the first trans-atlantic cable. However, this was a failure because the cable was only in service for a few days. It was not until 1866 when a more successful cable was laid that remained in service for almost one hundred years. The predecessor to the Internet was the Advanced

Research Projects Agency Network (ARPANET), which was formed in 1962 by the US Department of Defense. The Internet as we know it today was not started until 1969 when an Interface Message Processor (IMP) was sent to UCLA. This was the first known transmission on the Internet. That particular system was only connected to four other sites, so communication was limited to those sites only and the system was primitive. The public did not actually see the Internet until 1972 when a public demonstration was held, and it did not begin to make a public impact until two years after the demonstration that was held in 1972.[23]

Even though the Internet has only been in use since the mid-1970s, it has impacted everyone. Millions of users log on everyday all over the world to pay bills, chat with friends and strangers, and conduct business. Teachers have an unlimited resource at their fingertips. Many teachers use WebQuest programs to teach students certain material. Even if teachers do not use the Internet as a way to teach students its benefits for research and planning lessons are enormous. There are hundreds of websites dedicated to helping teachers improve their lesson plans or even classroom management.

TECHNOLOGY IN THE CLASSROOM

What is technology integration, and what does that imply for today's twenty-first-century classroom? The International Technology Education Association (ITEA) broadly defined technology in the *Standards for Technological Literacy and Content for the Study of Technology* as "how people modify the natural world to suit their own purposes. From the Greek word techne, meaning art or artifice or craft, technology literally means the act of making or crafting, but more generally it refers to the diverse collection of processes and knowledge that people use to extend human abilities and to satisfy human needs and wants."[24] Implicit in this understanding of technology education is its ever-changing and evolving nature. This applies both to its implementation and its integration. Teachers, however, cannot implement twenty-first-century technological skills in their classrooms without the necessary knowledge, training, and time, much less integrate those skills in a successful, cohesive manner into their curriculum.[25] However, that is exactly what the technology standards in No Child Left Behind (NCLB) mandate. The specific NCLB goals for Title II, Part D, Enhancing Education through Technology are the following:

- To improve student academic achievement through the use of technology in elementary and secondary schools;
- To assist every student in crossing the digital divide by ensuring that every student is technologically literate by the time the student finishes the eighth grade regardless of race, ethnicity, gender, family income, location, or disability;

- To encourage the effective integration of technology resources and systems with teacher training and curriculum development to establish research-based instructional methods that can be widely implemented as best practices by state education agencies and local education agencies.[26]

In his article "Technology's Potential Promise for Enhancing Student Learning," Michael Golden wrote, "Effective teachers who are attentive to the goal of quality instruction are using technology as a tool to get there."[27] However, incorporating technology in the classroom today runs the gamut from those teachers and schools who have changed very little in their curriculum since the advent of computers in their schools to those elite few teachers and schools who are using the very latest Web 2.0 technologies ranging from blogs, wikis, and podcasts to smartboards. Unfortunately, with respect to technology use and integration, many schools' practices seem to fluctuate.

At issue is the need for teachers to avoid stagnation and keep abreast of current trends in technology, and this requires intervention strategies from the district level, such as in-service workshops, technology classes for teachers, and a dedicated technology budget, which requires a healthy district budget and a supportive administration and school board.[28]

Nowadays, students are often more technology literate than the instructors who are teaching them. Dubbed "millennial" students, these new students are comfortable multi-taskers who listen to the TV while talking on their cell phones, downloading songs on their iPods, and IMing their friends on the computer all at the same time. According to Taylor and MacNeil, "Technology and multitasking are a way of life for the new millennial students, and trial and error (Nintendo logic) is the key learning strategy. They are used to bits and bytes, flash and color, and there is zero tolerance for delays".[29] In an article titled "Engage Me or Enrage Me," Prensky warns of the digital divide not between the underprivileged, inner city school students and suburban middle-class students, but today's millennial students who have outpaced their technologically "illiterate" teachers and schools who are still teaching in classrooms their grandparents would be have been comfortable attending.[30]

According to the Partnership for 21st Century Skills, in an article titled "Learning for the 21st Century and MILE Guide," there is a profound gap between the knowledge and skills most students learn in schools and the skills students will need in typical twenty-first-century communities and workplaces. They conclude that we need education today that connects to students' lives, reflects how people learn, and emphasizes core subjects and learning skills.[31]

Golden stated, "Technology is a tool that has the potential to improve educational leaders at all levels … and to redefine what education means in the 21st century."[32] To do this, we need to use twenty-first-century tools and technology to develop twenty-first-century skills that can be translated into careers and jobs in the marketplace upon graduation from high school and college.

Technology Integration

Technology integration is not only a process but also a resource that enables teachers to create learning experiences that actively and meaningfully engage students. The use of technology allows teachers to adjust curriculum based on students' needs and/or learning styles. Okojie and Olinzock stated that through the use of technology integration, learning, as well as teaching, becomes active, engaging, and meaningful.[33] It is important that technology is not an add-on that is attached to a lesson but rather that technology is integrated during the planning of the lesson. "During the integration phase, the technology becomes an integral part of the course in terms of delivery, learning, management, or other aspects of the class."[34]

Technology integration is not simply acquiring skills in the use of technology. Professional development is also important. Professional development offers teachers the knowledge and skills to implement technology into their curriculum in a cohesive and comprehensive manner. It is imperative that professional development be ongoing and current so teachers will be able to access and incorporate these exciting new technologies. Too often professional development consists of abbreviated workshops where teachers are given a "shot-gun" basic introduction to some aspect of technology currently in vogue for classroom or professional use. However, teachers are frequently not provided with the next step, which is instruction on how to integrate this technical skill into their curriculum. When teachers are not given examples or shown suggestions for using technology in their specific subject areas, their actual instructional practices remain traditional, and technology may not be used at all or may become simply an add-on activity to a particular lesson. Short-term instruction on how to use a piece of technology does not lead to its long-term adoption into the curriculum. A major misconception is that knowing how to use a piece of technology will automatically lead to using it to improve the curriculum.

Matzen and Edmunds state the following:

> When teachers are provided with technology professional development focusing primarily on technical skills, they may fall back on technology uses consistent with their existing instructional practices simply because they have not been provided with an alternative vision for the use of technology.[35]

This lack of practical application, then, is a major barrier to technology integration and implementation.

Technology Integration Barriers

Researchers have investigated the barriers to integrating technology into their lessons. It is a recognized fact that teachers need some kind of support as they implement technology in the classroom.[36]

Initially, some basic barriers have been consistently identified in teacher preparation programs. These barriers include time, support, teaching models, infrastructure, and culture/tradition. Faculty at the college level preparing preservice teachers for the classroom identify lack of time as a major barrier to integrating technology into their curriculum. Some faculty members perceive the demand to use more technology as an attack on their academic freedom and their personal time. Job demands limit their available time for rewriting curriculum to include technology.[37] Gaytan (2002) points to a survey taken at the College of Business Administration at the University of Texas at El Paso, which reports "that the lack of time and incentives to become trained were the two main barriers to the effective integration of multimedia technology into their instructional practices."[38] University faculty need to see specific examples of integrated technology so that they can provide future teachers with the tools to implement technology in their own disciplines.[39] Teacher preparation programs must include integrated technology. Teachers often teach as they were taught. One study indicated that methods courses that include technology integration instruction were most helpful in assisting teachers to integrate technology into their own classroom.[40]

When teachers leave the university and enter their own classrooms, they face some of the same barriers as the instructors in their pre-service programs. As Franklin concluded from her research, some barriers that elementary educators are facing include lack of time, the amount of curriculum expected to be covered in the school year, and the added pressures to perform well on federal and state mandated tests.[41]

Insecurity with technology is a frequent barrier to technology integration. Many educators find comfort using traditional teaching methods and resist integrating technology due to lack of familiarity with technology. Pressure to integrate technology can cause anxiety in individuals who have little knowledge of twenty-first- century technology. Having a support staff that offers confidential and on-going aid reduces this anxiety and promotes change. Assistance in preparing materials and setting up hardware reduces concerns.[42] Four components that signify comfort with technology are as follows: understanding its capabilities, knowing how it functions, using it to create simple applications, and identifying support services.[43]

The infrastructure must support the use of technology. There must be adequate access to supported resources, and faculty members must have opportunities to use these facilities. Instructors must have confidence that planned activities can be carried out because labs are available for use and in working order.[44]

All these factors must be addressed in order to encourage and empower teachers to continue updating and integrating technology into their classrooms. Time, preparation, instruction models, support, infrastructure, and knowledge about the technology are all key elements teachers need before implementing technology into their classroom and integrating it into their curriculum.

Current Uses of Technology

Amid the flurry of formulating lesson plans, scoring projects, and preparing students for mandated testing, teachers are expected to engage students in meaningful learning activities—but meaningful to whom? Lesson delivery in today's classroom is a far cry from the early beginnings of education that originated in the one room schoolhouse. Today, kaleidoscopes of colors, cacophonies of sounds, and montages of images bombard the young learners even before they initially enter a classroom. At an early age they are physically engaged at home through the use of preparatory educational software provided by concerned parents. Why should they expect anything different when they enter the classroom? It is delegated to their formal academic instructors to continue this active learning engagement upon entering the realm of mandated education.

However, this is often not the case. The use of technology in today's classroom is often at the discretion of the instructor. While instructors are reluctant to use technology, classrooms seem to have utilized many aspects of technology tools. Calculators are so commonplace that one neglects to list them as a form of technology. Becoming standards in classrooms are the usage of basic word processing and spreadsheet bundles provided by computer manufacturers. Not surprisingly, new teachers do not remember the invigorating odor of "hot off the press" dittos. Computer word processing programs and desktop printers have saved thousands of teacher preparation hours. Word processing programs have enabled teachers to create and edit project instructions, rubrics and worksheets. The tedious steps of correcting an error on mimeograph stencils have been replaced by the delete and insert buttons of the computer keyboard. Cut and paste commands have become favorites among teachers and students alike. Fax machines and scanners have replaced the laborious process of duplicating records, worksheets, and illustrations for the masses. Gone are the smeared blue letters and indistinct diagram details. Clear legible copies are reproduced rapidly with the use of multi-tasking copy machines.

PowerPoint delivery of lessons is becoming the norm for the next teaching generation while the "old guard" clings to more traditional lesson deliveries. Instead of using technology as an innovative teaching tool, they regard technology as a means to gather and manage information.[45] Due to lack of time and training, many teachers are reluctant to try exciting, novel technologies. Therefore, many classrooms remain stagnant, lecture-based, teacher-controlled, and passive student enclaves. Technology is interjected as an afterthought not an integral part of the curriculum. Computers are used for basic keyboarding skills and drills or for word processing such as typing book reports and essays, and the Internet is used for conducting research. Teachers still cling to their overhead projectors like comfort food.

The problem with this is that technology in the classroom really is not up to the teacher anymore. No Child Left Behind changed all that with their technology goals. If we are really going to take NCLB seriously, then we have to improve student academic achievement through the use of technology. We must assist students across the digital divide regardless of race, ethnicity, or poverty, and we need to encourage the integration of technology resources and systems with curriculum development to establish research based instructional methods.[46] It is not an option anymore; it is the law.

Twenty-First-Century Goals

If we are going to be effective teachers in this new century, then we must teach twenty-first-century goals. "Accelerating technological change, rapidly accumulating knowledge, increasing global competition, and rising workforce capabilities around the world make 21st century skills essential.[47] So, what are twenty-first- century goals and how can technology facilitate this process? According to the *Partnership for 21st Century Skills in Learning and the MILE Guide*, the following are key goals for twenty-first-century literacy:

- Emphasizing core subjects
- Emphasizing learning skills such as information and communication skills, thinking and problem-solving skills, and interpersonal and self-directional skills
- Using 21st century tools to develop learning skills
- Teaching and learning in a 21st century context
- Teaching and learning 21st century content including global awareness, financial economic, business, and civic literacy
- Using 21st century assessments[48]

Technology integration is a valuable tool to help achieve these goals. By using technology in the classroom, the teacher creates a learning environment that is student-centered, problem-solving oriented, inquiry-based, and project-centered.[49] It also adds in key components such as communication, collaboration, and differentiation so lessons can be tailored to individual students' needs. Technology, in short, can create the digital learning environment needed to develop twenty-first-century skills.

Technology can help strengthen and reinforce literacy in basic core subjects such as math and writing. Eleven percent of West Virginia's gain in basic skills was directly related to education technology. PUMP Algebra and Project Explore, which was used for writing, helped raise literacy scores in Union City, New Jersey.[50] As showcased in the

Peoria Journal Star, junior students at Princeville High School in Illinois showed marked improvement on their state mandated tests and ACT preparatory exams after completing several school sponsored sessions of KeyTrain software.[51]

Technology is perfect for teaching communication and information. Project based instruction and collaboration builds interpersonal and self-directed skills, which are needed in the twenty-first-century workforce. The vast resources of information on the internet are powerful tools for research. Students can access more information about different cultures, scientific data, or global awareness in one hour on the internet than they could find in the library in days. Google Earth uses satellite images to allow students to literally view images anywhere in the world.

Technology can also improve inventive thinking skills such as problem solving, critical thinking, and creativity, which are definitely twenty-first-century goals. Because of the customized content of technology (CEO Forum, 2003), it challenges students to develop a more effective way to search for information and solve their problems.[52] Students have to search and access the information and have more than one source at their fingertips, instead of relying on the traditional textbook for all their answers.

By implementing technology and integrating it into their curriculum, teachers can create the twenty-first-century context for learning in their classrooms. Students need a twenty-first-century learning environment that will reflect the work environment they will one day be entering. Using authentic assessments from student portfolios, online journals and writings, blogs, and video clips are just a few ways to use twenty-first-century assessments to measure these new skills.

Finally, technology can help improve effectiveness for teachers as well by improving professionalism, instructional practices, communication, collaboration, efficiency, and constructive time spent on administrative tasks.[53] However, in order for the best results, school districts need to invest the money and time for teacher inservice, training, and collaboration.

The Millennial Student

There has been a revolution taking place while our backs have been turned. It centers around technology, and the key players are the students, the new millennial students. Exactly who are these millennial students? According to Taylor and MacNeil, the millennial students are the children of Baby Boomers and early GenXers.[54] They are children who were born after 1982. Their lives have been shaped by technology. They are the "planned for" children who have been raised on Nickelodeon, dressed by Baby Gap, and enrolled in the right preschool in preparation for the right college. They are plugged in and connected 24/7.

Millennial children are achievers. They have been raised to have a positive self-esteem, be practical, and optimistic. Therefore, they have strong connections to their parents who tend to be overprotective. Baby-on-Board signs, child restraint laws, movie ratings, and campus security were all created with their welfare in mind.[55] Millennial children tend to be team-oriented, pressured, and conventional, as opposed to their more independent, free-living, hippie-generation parents.

Millennial children are pushed to study hard in order to get into the right college. They are pushed to succeed and find careers with a satisfactory income.[56] They are pushed to participate in any number of activities from soccer to special "teams" above and beyond the school's sports programs. Add in music lessons, dance lessons, and whatever else will round out their education, and it is no wonder these children are overextended, over-whelmed, and over-achievers. This is precisely why they are the ultimate multitaskers! They must be in order to survive.

The millennial students are the smartest group yet with rising scores in math, science, and standardized tests. They are absolutely fearless around technology, whereas many of their instructors are scared to death they will break something. They are accustomed to keyboards and websites; many of them started out on computers before attending kinder-garten. They want everything right now, and they have absolutely zero tolerance for delay.

Millennial students are definitely visual learners. According to the American Academy of Pediatrics, students watch an average of four hours of television a day and twenty-six percent of those same children spend one to two hours online a day. They want the "world at their fingertips" and they want it now, preferably in some excitingly digitized platform. In order to reach these students, teachers must engage them on their level.[57]

Instant gratification could have been invented for them. These are the same children who are texting each other and tuning out the teacher during another boring lesson taught in the same old lecture style. If we do not engage them, then we will truly lose them.[58]

What are the best ways to engage a millennial student? Taylor and MacNeil urge that to reach these students, information needs to be individually tailored and porta-ble.[59] Content must be dynamically generated and interactive. Students are engaged with technology, they are comfortable with technology, it is their preferred modus operandi, and if we are to reach this new generation of student, it better become ours. It is time to introduce some cutting-edge technologies into the classroom.

Cutting-Edge Technologies

In order to reach the millennial students in today's classrooms, teachers need to incor-porate cutting-edge technologies to teach the twenty-first-century skills these students are going to need to compete in tomorrow's marketplace.

Some of the exciting new classroom tools available include interactive whiteboards. One example such as SMART Boards, designed by SMART Technologies, allow the teacher to write, erase, and perform mouse functions with a finger or pen. Anyone can write in digital ink over applications, websites, or videos.[60] Work can be saved directly into different software applications, which means teachers can create and prepare lessons at home and students can work and review lessons from home. Another type of whiteboard is the "pencentric" whiteboard from the Numonics Corporation. The teacher touches the whiteboard with an electronic pen and all the program functions are automatically transferred to the pen. The company has licensed a clip-art library with about three thousand images, which is incorporated into its whiteboard.[61] PolyVision also has created a whiteboard with some innovative and exciting characteristics. They are mobile and self-calibrating and come with remote controls so teachers can navigate around the classroom as they use the whiteboard. In addition, teachers can also write, print, stream their cable TV, access the Internet, display PowerPoint presentations, and project from a DVD/VCR. The CEO of PolyVision, Michael Dunn, insists that "how we teach, and not what we teach, must change in the US if we are to have our students compete in a global economy."[62]

Another cutting-edge tool to use in the classroom is a tablet PC. Lenovo makes one called the ThinkPad X-4. Teachers who use these say they find the tablet much better than laptops because there is no screen barrier between the student and the teacher, which makes communication much easier.[63] At the end of the day, everything is saved and can be posted so if students are sick or absent, notes can be posted and reviewed from home.

MEMS, or micro-electro-mechanical systems, is a new technology developed by Cornell researchers that will soon allow teachers to teach lessons by projecting images from personal digital assistants.[64] This new technology may actually turn a cell phone into a projector! Another type of new projector is the PowerLite 82c digital projector from Epson. It was released in 2005 and can be used to deliver presentations in different types of settings. It features automatic focus, a five-watt audio system, and a four second startup. Teachers are able to hook it up to almost anything.

From projecting to producing, some new products from NewTek (https://www.newtek.com/) allow teachers to build lessons to master the art of broadcasting, which include both technology and journalism.[65] The product is called TriCaster and is a "simplified live switching and audio mixing device with real-time output to video, and the VT(4), a software tool that offers web streaming, real time keying, titling, editing, two-dimensional video painting, three-dimensional modeling, and animation."[66]

These innovative new tools and gadgets to use in the classroom are costly, and most public schools today face budget restrictions while school board members try to apportion the tax dollar in a fiscally responsible manner and stretch it to meet its optimum potential. That does not always translate into new technologies, especially if that district is still struggling to come up with a viable computer lab with thirty computers and a printer. However, there are state and federal grants available and private sectors can be solicited to form partnerships with the schools. Universities and community colleges can also become valuable allies to help with a technology program. For example, Illinois Central College, a neighboring community college in Peoria, Illinois, has a waiting list of schools who have signed up for their "outdated" computers and printers when the college upgrades their writing labs. Businesses such as Caterpillar and State Farm are also often willing to help schools with technology funds or equipment.

Other less expensive "cutting edge" technologies include not the gadgets, but the software applications, which can be much more cost effective if not free. Dubbed the Web 2.0 technologies, these applications include online blogging, podcasting, and wikis. Most students are already blogging, which is like an online diary, and using multiple social networking sites such as MySpace or Facebook, so the concept is already familiar and fun for the students. Many blogging accounts are free, such as 21Classes.com (www.21classes.com), and easy to apply to a classroom setting. The possibilities are endless. In a literature class students can use blogs as online journals to write poetry or literature essays, journal responses to literature questions, or keep an online diary response to novels they have read. Blogs can be written and edited collaboratively between students of different ages and different schools such as the Talkback Project.[67] This project began as collaboration between preservice teachers at Indiana University and middle school students who read novels and responded weekly in their blogs.

Another 2.0 application in the classroom is the use of wikis. Wikis are interactive databases which visitors can edit live. In fact, their building blocks are the comments from the visitors to the site. They can be added onto by anyone who has new information to share. The only problem is since the information is edited by anyone; it needs to be verified for accuracy. There is free software available to build classroom wikis such as www.wiki.com. Again, the applications are endless. Students in a social studies class can create maps in wikimapia to share with other students or science students can build a wiki to share how to build a volcano in wikihow. A wiki makes it easy to share ideas and information and literally get everyone on the same page in real time. Additional features can include calendar sharing, live AV conferencing, and RSS feeds. Possible problems to be considered include privacy and security issues if the wiki is published to the web. These problems can be mitigated by locking some pages or moderating the wiki so only registered users can view the pages.[68]

Taken from the combination of iPod and broadcast, podcasting is an audio recording that is posted on the web and can be downloaded and played later. Again, like blogs and wikis there are a plethora of free podcasting sites and tutorials available, such as PodBean.com. Podcasts are engaging students because they provide an easy way to disperse multimedia content to a large group of people.[69] Most students have iPods glued to their ears and like to be able to listen to music whenever and wherever they like. So why not give them lessons in the same format? Podcasts have many attractive features. They address different learning styles, plus are highly mobile. Teachers can use their cell phones to create a podcast of daily or weekly homework assignments, which parents can then download so they can stay current on their child's activities. Teachers can also create PowerPoint podcasts with step-by-step instructions for various projects. Additionally, students can create podcasts to showcase their projects and share what they have learned, and even take a virtual tour through a soundseeing tour podcast. Podcasts are especially suited for music or foreign language classes. They are also extremely mobile. Apple has now introduced enhanced podcasts that allow listeners to see pictures on their photo iPods.[70]

Video podcasting, or vodcasting, is another exciting cutting-edge tool that is a spinoff of podcasting, and is still in its infancy. It is basically the same as a podcast, but the video clips are fed through RSS 2.0 enclosures instead of audio clips.[71] In order to use vodcasting, the computer needs to be powerful enough to edit material and files can be much larger than podcasts, but vodcasting would be a great medium for collaborative projects.

Another way to engage students is through the use of WebQuests, which are inquiry-oriented activities that use web resources to solve a problem.[72] These can be created in a Word document with hyperlinks connected directly to the websites teachers want the students to research. There are also several virtual tours, which can be accessed and connected to the WebQuest via hyperlinks, also. Therefore, a teacher whose students are reading the novel *The Adventures of Tom Sawyer* can create a WebQuest about Mark Twain with hyperlinks to different questions about his life including a virtual tour of Tom Sawyer's house and cave in Hannibal, Missouri. Voila! What an exciting way to learn more information about the topic!

Current technology extends beyond the boundaries of the classroom walls. Access to the Internet empowers the learner to communicate and share their findings locally, nationally, and globally. Primary students can document shapes in their physical environment during "shape walks" while middle school students analyze through digital documentation how geometric form dictates function.[73] This enables students to "show me what you know" in terms of alternative assessments to standard paper tests.[74] Their findings and images may be posted to a webpage with a contact email for any possible queries or responses. Through the use of digital videography, students in Indiana produced interstitials (short videos that fill time between programming) of interviews with local World War II veterans.[75] These vignettes were aired by the local public broadcast station. Students were provided the opportunity to compile an oral history of the veterans' experiences. As technology advances and costs decrease, digital photography is becoming available to more children of all ages. Digital photography incorporates real-world skills into academic studies.[76] Any student can participate in the SETI@home project. The Search for Extra Terrestrial Intelligence (SETI) provides budding astronomers the opportunity to participate in the analysis of data collected from the world's largest telescope located in Puerto Rico. Free SETI@home software is downloaded that will set the home computer to work analyzing data downloads while the computer is idle. Any significant information is forwarded to the University of California, Berkeley, for further examination.[77]

Historically, technology has brought about revolutions in transportation, agriculture, manufacturing, sanitation, and the art of war. Its applications are numerous. Geographic Information Systems (GIS) and Global Positioning Systems (GPS) bring new meaning to longitude and latitude bearings in the classrooms. Modern day orienteering has moved away from the use of traditional magnetic compasses to handheld GPS units that can map routes to identified waypoints. Complacency in classroom is replaced by activity in the field. Geocaching, the new wave of orienteering, engages the novice geoexplorer to share experiences while employing inquiry and critical thinking skills.[78] This learning can transcend itself to the use of mobile navigation systems that are currently being touted as a must have accessory by the transportation industry.

Technology advancements naturally enhance scientific studies. Airport security cameras have been adapted to fit onto the eyepiece of microscopes. Instructors can then project microscopic images through a video recorder onto a television screen enabling fledgling biologists a preview of what they are to observe. The life cycles of living organisms can be recorded and later slowed to analyze their methods of locomotion and reproduction. Digital microscopy has supplemented this experience by sending the images to a computer where the images may be captured for inclusion into laboratory reports.[79] Digital balances and pH meters have erased margins of errors in laboratory measurements.[80] Portable calculator-based laboratory (CBL) probeware capable of interfacing with graphing calculators enable students to design problem-based learning scenarios while selecting their own experimental parameters. Similar handheld data collection units such as data loggers and ecologgers are creating microcomputer-based laboratories (MBL) in the classroom, making data collecting more precise with less errors in recording results.[81] Immediate feedback is available providing students with the opportunity to devise new variables to test.

In the quest for information students have other options besides the words scrolling across the monitors. Visual libraries are available with interactive tutorials, simulated virtual dissections, and archived historical video clips. Simulcast programs enable students to experience the moment in real-time. For example, students could witness the Kennedy/Nixon presidential debate and *virtually* watch the beads of sweat drip from Richard Nixon's face. In this way students have a more interactive, realistic way of experiencing history and drawing their own conclusions.

Many instructional publishers (e.g., Holt, Rinehart and Winston, www.hrw.com) make online editions of their textbook accessible with a password. The excuse "I forgot my textbook at school" no longer has validity in an Internet wired home. These publishers also have made available the capability of creating, storing, and grading online assessments. Teachers, using an LCD projector, can project actual textbook illustrations eliminating the dual usage of the bulky overhead projectors.

Computers have enhanced students' abilities to record, store, organize, and analyze data with greater accuracy.[82] As tools for special needs students, computer devices deliver assistive technology with the use of touch screens, track balls, micromice, and alternative keyboards. With these tools special needs students should be able to have the same freedom that regular division students experience in the computer laboratory.[83]

Cutting-edge technologies offer a dazzling and, sometimes, overwhelming array of choices to assist teachers with technology integration. Some technology such as smartboards, tablet PCs, and MEMs are expensive and will require board approval or grant money to implement, while software applications are more affordable and can be just as exciting. Many internet Web 2.0 applications such as blogs, wikis, and podcasts can be integrated into a teacher's curriculum for free. Either way, time and preparation are needed but well worth the effort.

SUMMARY

Technology is ever changing and evolving. New applications and hardware appear on the market at an alarming rate. By the time the requisition sheet has been approved, something newer and better has replaced it. Many teachers are daunted by the task, and due to lack of time, training, support, and cold hard cash rely on the tried and true methods their parents would have been comfortable using. However, technology integration is no longer an option in today's classroom. No Child Left Behind demands we assist students, all students, regardless of race, ethnicity, financial status, or disability across the digital divide. Student achievement must be improved through the use of technology, and effective integration of technology resources and systems needs to be encouraged through teacher training and curriculum development. Teachers today must employ twenty-first-century goals to teach these new century skills to their students. These goals emphasize core subjects, communication skills, problem-solving skills, interpersonal, and self-directional skills. Global awareness, financial, economic, business and civic literacy are also key twenty-first-century content areas.[84] Without these skills, students will not be equipped to compete in tomorrow's workforce. This is the digital age, and we are teaching a new breed of students, the millennial students. These millennial students are plugged in and connected 24/7 and expect their learning space to be like MySpace. They want their learning to be portable, interactive, and dynamic.[85] In order to engage them and meet their needs for the new century, we owe it to our students, our schools, and ourselves to integrate and implement technology into our classrooms in order to give our students the necessary twenty-first-century skills to compete in tomorrow's global marketplace.

Technology integration and implementation in the twenty-first-century classroom cannot be ignored. As teachers of the millennial student, we must all stand at the forefront and be the leaders of tomorrow with the tools of today. Technology usage should not be limited to any single curriculum topic but integrated into all subjects no matter what grade level or aspect of learning. Time and commitment are barriers that can be surmounted one step at a time. The key is to start slowly and use resources already available on the internet. Many websites have free resources for teachers that are easy to integrate into any curriculum such as wikis, blogs, and podcasts. There are free webpage templates available to build classroom homepages, which will help keep both students and parents informed about what is happening in the classroom. WebQuests can be created in a Word document with links to relevant websites to enhance any subject. PowerPoint podcast presentations are an excellent way to create an oral presentation along with PhotoStory. Brochures created in Microsoft Publisher or Word are an exciting alternative to boring book reports. No matter what the format, technology can be that extra ingredient that makes a classroom snap, crackle, and pop! With technology integration and implementation into the curriculum, teachers can engage the millennial students and teach them twenty-first-century skills to prepare them for the future.

Online Instruction

Over the past several years, the Internet has become a major resource for both teachers and students. During the early stage of its development, approximately during the mid-1990s, the Internet was limited in use and capability. It was mainly used to search for information. Since the 1960s however, the Internet has evolved into more than a database. It has become a significant communication tool. The new technology makes it possible for educators to offer courses online.

What Is Online Instruction?

Online instruction involves the use of the Internet to either replace a traditional classroom with a virtual classroom, or to complement the traditional classroom with additional opportunities for learning. According to McCormack and Jones, "[a] Web-based classroom is an environment created on the World Wide Web in which students and educators can perform learning-related tasks."[86] This definition implies that the Internet can be used in a variety of ways such as delivering instruction, conducting instructional activities, assessing, and communicating with students.

Online and **distance learning** enables students at different sites to interact and, depending on the equipment available, to see and hear each other. Students get the benefit of interacting with other students, speakers, or teachers in distant places without the need to travel. The idea is excellent, and it opens up new possibilities for teaching and learning.[87]

During the 2017–18 school year, about twenty-one percent of public schools and thirteen percent of private schools offered any courses entirely online. Among public schools, a higher percentage of charter schools (thirty percent) offered any courses entirely online, compared to traditional public schools (twenty percent).[88]

The Internet also provides educators with a variety of online learning models. The first type is informal learning in which the learner is using a particular website to find information. The second type is self-paced learning where the learners complete certain tasks and activities within a given period of time. Students move from one stage to another based on their ability. The third type is leader-led. Here, the learner is led through online discussions or workshops. Performance support tools are the fourth online learning type in which the learner is lead through a series of steps with the use of online materials. An example of this type is the development of lesson plans or instructional activities by following specific established criteria or rubrics and the use of multimedia or the Internet as a resource.

These four types of online learning can also be blended together to form more effective learning opportunities for students. Given the number of online learning possibilities, teachers can choose the type of online learning that will best suit their students' needs.[89]

Components of Online Instruction

When choosing to implement any type of online instruction, you must consider what will be involved. Online instruction includes the same components as traditional teaching, but these components now have to be mediated with technology. The major components of online instruction are the outside world, the course, the students, the educators, and technical factors.[90] Before putting an online system into effect, you must consider all of these components.

The first component to consider is outside factors such as the educational institution and society. For example, you must make sure that the institution has sufficient funding and other resources to enable you to implement the kind of online system that you have in mind.[91] Further, you need to make sure that your students will have enough opportunities to access the Internet while in school and, perhaps, at home.

The second component to consider is the subject matter itself. You need to decide what material will be covered in the class. In addition, you need to select the mode of delivery for the material.[92] The mode of delivery can be decided by considering one of the four online learning types discussed earlier. You must choose a style that will be effective in helping the students achieve the course objectives. It might be necessary to combine two or more of the online learning types to build the most effective program.

The students are the third component to consider. Since the online classroom is supposed to enable students to learn, the classroom should be designed to meet each student's needs and characteristics. This involves taking into account a number of different factors including, age, cultural background, prior knowledge, physical abilities and disabilities, individual learning styles, and students' motivation.[93]

The fourth component to online teaching is you. This is important to consider because you are one half of the teacher-learner partnership. The design of the online classroom must closely reflect your characteristics, preferences, and abilities.[94] Since you will be designing and implementing the whole process, it is important that your preferences are taken into consideration.

Technical factors are the fifth component to online instruction. Technical factors include anything in the web-based program that involves some sort of technology. The teacher must find out what types of software or hardware will be needed in their class. This component also includes identifying the means of communication. You must make sure that students will be able to communicate with you (i.e., do they have ready access to the Internet and e-mail?). You must also consider any training or other technical support that may be needed to implement the program.[95] Once you have considered all of these components, you can possibly begin to implement the program and then judge whether or not it is working to your expectations.

Advantages and Disadvantages of Online Instruction

Online instruction is a controversial topic. There are many educators who are in favor of it while others are unsure of its benefits. Those who oppose online instruction argue that online instruction limits the contact and communication between students and teachers.[96] The lack of face-to-face meetings gives the feeling that the class void and impersonal.

Supporters of online instruction would disagree with this because in an online setting, the teacher can be as involved in the learning process. Online instruction allows for many levels of involvement. In addition, if a teacher wishes to meet face to face with a student, the teacher can request such a meeting. However, face-to-face meetings should be built into the course goals and expectations.

Others believe that online instruction reduces the interaction and communication between students and teachers. People in this camp argue that the lack of face-to-face meeting makes it harder for teachers and students to communicate.[97] This, however, may not be true because online classes can include chat rooms, group discussions, message boards, and e-mail.[98] The fact that online instruction could possibly have all of these modes of communication, leads one to believe that there will be more opportunities for the students to interact and communicate with not only the teacher but also with other students in class. Increased interaction and communication between teachers and students is a step in the right direction for improving any kind of instruction.

Yet another concern about online instruction is the idea that students will not learn as much as they would via traditional instruction. The literature suggests that online students typically learn the same content as they would via traditional instruction, but that they will also have "increased knowledge of computing and the Internet".[99] To the extent that this is true, online instruction can truly help to improve education because greater use of technology is one of the goals in many school improvement plans. You need to weigh the advantages and disadvantages of online instruction for you and your students, and reach your own conclusion.

Positive Outcomes

There has been some research done dealing with online instruction that point out an array of benefits. One of these positive outcomes is the idea that online classroom promotes more flexibility.[100] With online classes, the student can choose when and where they learn the material and can do the online work whenever it is convenient for them. Online instruction clearly provides students with more flexibility than traditional classes.

Another positive outcome of online instruction is increased motivation and enjoyment. Students that were taking an online course, when compared with students that were taking the same traditional course, showed much more motivation and enjoyment.[101] Students enjoy the Internet classes more because it is a different learning method than in a traditional class. They get to control the learning process more and they find this more enjoyable than being lectured at in a traditional classroom. Student motivation is more likely to increase as a result of students' engagement and continued participation.

Increased participation is often a positive factor that is associated with online instruction. Students are more likely to participate in the online classroom than they would in the traditional classroom.[102] This point is also made in the discussion of CAI where we point out that the computer's speed means that it is always waiting for the student's response thus fostering high on-task time. In an online classroom students are forced to participate because they cannot get through the class without going the through the material and doing the assignments. They have to be active learners, but in a traditional class, a student could possibly sit through the whole class without participating in any of the discussions. Online instruction requires that students participate more than in a traditional classroom, therefore resulting in increased participation.

Online instruction is still in its early stages of development. While it provides students with many benefits such as flexibility, enjoyment, and active participation and engagement, it has not shown to increase students' knowledge and skill. Its effectiveness in this regard will still undergo further scrutiny.

The Computer as a Tool

The first large-scale computer, the Electronic Numerical Integrator and Computer (**ENIAC**), was put into operation in 1946. It weighed about thirty tons and its main function was to help scientists and engineers calculate the trajectories of artillery shells. The first commercially available computer, the UNIVersal Automatic Computer 1 (**UNIVAC 1**), was introduced in 1951. It weighed about thirteen tons and its main function was to help process ballots for the 1952 presidential election. With a sample of just one percent of the voting population it predicted that Eisenhower would win.[103] Since the time of the ENIAC, computers have gotten smaller and faster. In 2006, scientists began building a computer able to perform one quadrillion (1,000,000,000,000,000) operations per second.[104] It is interesting to note that while computers have gone from thirty tons to less than six pounds and are now able to operate in terms too fast for most of us to comprehend, no computer now, and no computer likely to be developed in the foreseeable future, comes close to handling the variety of data that the three-pound human brain handles so well.

Application Programs

Unlike CAI programs, which help students learn or practice skills or information, usually for specific subject areas, application programs are tools used to do particular kinds of tasks. There are four major types.

Word Processors

Word processors are to typewriters what typewriters were to pens and pencils. They facilitate the transfer of ideas from your head to paper. Teachers use word processors, such as Microsoft's *Word*® and Novell's *Word Perfect*®, to generate all kinds of documents including syllabi, handouts, and tests. Students use them to develop writing skills and complete written assignments.

The use of word processors can save users countless hours of typing and retyping and they make it more likely that users will correct their own work, but there is one troublesome point. Prior to word processors, students did their original thinking and writing at home. Class time was used to analyze what they had written. When word processors are used in schools, time that had been used for analysis must now be used for doing the original writing. The advantages of having students work at word processors must be weighed against the loss of instructional time.

Advantages

Word processors help users generate better quality work because error correction is quick and easy. We can delete or replace unwanted words or sentences and use cut and paste functions to restructure whole sections of a paper. Further, most word processors come with built-in spell checkers and will also check for simple punctuation and grammar errors. Finally, after a short time, most users find they can type faster, and more legibly, than they can write. All of these factors make it possible for you and your students to generate more polished products more quickly than was typical with pen and paper or with typewriters.

Disadvantages

With all of the help that word processors can provide, it is still necessary for the user to take the time to proofread, but some students simply do not do that. Some students forget that the spell checker will not differentiate between words such as "hear" and "here," and "their" and "there," and that while most word processors will identify a misspelled word, it is still up to the user to make the correction.

Another concern is time usage. Prior to word processors, students did their most of their writing at home, and class time was used to discuss or analyze what they had written. However, although computers are increasingly common, some students may not have access to a computer at home. Therefore, if a word processing assignment is given, class time must be allocated for it. This, in turn, means that time that might have been used for discussion or analysis must now be used for doing the original writing. The advantages of having students use word processors must be weighed against the loss of instructional time.

Tips for You

If students use a word processor, they may be able to submit papers electronically and, if they can, consider the advantages of having them do so. You may, for example, find it easier to read something on a screen than on paper, and you may find it easier to insert a typed comment rather than writing one out by hand. Also, the problem of poor penmanship is eliminated, but this is counterbalanced by the fact that word processors do nothing to help students develop better penmanship.

It is recommended that you establish some simple formatting rules such as the size of margins and fonts. Doing this will help keep some students from submitting a paper with quarter-inch margins and a font size of 8 in order to fit a too-long paper into the space allowed or, conversely, getting a paper with two-inch margins and a font size of 14.

You are likely to see a decrease in the number of spelling, punctuation, and grammatical errors if you begin deducting points for such errors. Typically, students can write better than they sometimes do, and knowing that poor proofreading may cost them points is often enough of an incentive to prompt the extra care.

If you choose to have students submit work electronically, it is recommended that you set up a file on your computer for each class (e.g., US History, 9:00 a.m.) and within that folder, set up another folder labeled "Student Work." As students submit work, have them label the file with their last name, course, and date (e.g., Smith, Paper 1, 01-25-2020). Then, you can put comments on the work, grade it, and then save it in the Student Work folder, changing the date in the filename if needed. If you give students the option of submitting a rewrite, after grading it you can save it with a different date (e.g., Smith, Paper 1, 02-08-2020). This provides you with a chronological record of the work submitted and graded, including the comments and suggestions that you put on each paper.

Most word processors enable you to create tables and you could use this function to maintain a record of such things as pictures for bulletin boards or displays. For example:

Course	Subject	Date
US History	Gettysburg Battlefield	April 2020
US History	Lincoln Memorial, Wash. DC	April 2020

Spreadsheets

Spreadsheets are programs used to keep track of, and manipulate, data arranged in rows and columns. Programs, such as *Excel*®, and *Lotus 1,2,3*® and derivatives of them, greatly simplify grade keeping.

Advantages

Once you enter column headings for students' names and for work to be graded, all that remains is to enter the scores for each assignment or test. Built-in functions enable the program to calculate the average of each column of scores; the total points earned by each student; the number of points needed for an A, B, C, and D; and the number of scores falling in each category. All of the calculations, such as the class mean and each student's total points can be automatically updated each time a new grade is entered and, while computers may have their faults, making computational errors is not one of them; if you enter the correct grades, the calculations will be fast and correct.

Many schools have purchased grading software that all teachers are expected to use. This step is taken for a number of reasons. One reason is that it enables teachers to save time in recording grades. Another reason is that it helps ensure that all teachers use a common format for grade reporting, and still another reason is that it enables administrators to set up a system by which they, parents, and students can have online access to relevant grade information.

Although spreadsheets are designed to handle numeric data, they can be used, to some extent, as databases. For example, if you used a spreadsheet instead of a table to maintain your picture file, it would be easy to resort your pictures as needed using the column headings as your sort fields (e.g., course, subject, etc.).

Disadvantages

If you choose to put your grades online on your own website you must be very much aware of confidentiality issues. It is crucial that you double check the spreadsheet to be sure that names have been replaced with student ID numbers.

Tips for You

If you keep grades on your own spreadsheet or on your school's gradebook program, it is important to have students be able to continually check the accuracy of those grades. What sometimes happens is that you grade a paper, but forget to record the grade on the spreadsheet or gradebook program. Students can, and will, help to find those errors if you ask them to.

Databases

Databases such as *Access*® and *Paradox*® enable teachers to build, maintain, and easily manipulate banks of data such as test items and portfolios of student work. There are also professionally developed databases containing demographic, geographic, and other data. A prospective teacher's knowledge of, and ability to use, such tools will be a point in his or her favor during a job interview.

One database that you may find particularly useful is the one maintained by Phi Delta Kappa. Among other things, it contains online copies of each of the Phi Delta Kappa/Gallup Polls of the Public's Attitudes Toward the public Schools from 1969 to the present. The URL is https://pdkpoll.org/. Other useful databases are maintained by the National Center for Educational Statistics. The URL is http://nces.ed.gov/. Your state department of education also maintains a database and it focuses on issues and data particularly relevant to educators in your state.

Advantages

Existing databases can provide you with a wealth of current and accurate information to share with your students. Databases that you build yourself allow greater flexibility in labeling and sorting materials than either tables or spreadsheets.

Disadvantages

Developing your own database is a somewhat more complex undertaking than using tables or spreadsheets.

Tips for You

Check websites before sending students to them to ensure that they are still functioning and that they contain correct information. Governmental agencies and large organizations are most likely to maintain their websites properly.

Presentation Tools

Programs such as *PowerPoint*® and *Freelance*® are computer programs that enable users to make professional-looking slides that can enhance oral presentations. Built-in features such as choices of templates and choice of using animation and sound make presentation programs ideal instructional tools. If the appropriate hardware is available, documents generated with such programs can be displayed on a large screen monitor in addition to being displayed on the computer's regular monitor.

Advantages

Presentation programs are ideally suited for the presentation of graphs, charts, pictures, and short blocks of information such as a sequence of main points or facts. When used in this way, each slide or part of a slide serves as a jumping off point for a discussion. Putting more than eight lines on a slide is not recommended because if the material is on the screen, you are tempted to turn away from the students and read the material to them. If this happens, it reduces your eye contact with students, and if it happens often, it may cause your students to question your credibility.

Disadvantages

One disadvantage of presentation software is that some people spend a huge amount of time adding features such as animation and sound even though those features do not help convey the message more effectively. In fact, unless such features are relevant to the main point(s), they act as distractions and hinder effective communication of the message. It is important to impress upon your students that the shorter and simpler the presentation is, the more effective it is.

Tips for You

Use a non-serif font such as Arial or Tahoma. Serifs are the small curls or lines at the end of a letter and, while they make it easier to read text on a printed page, they make it more difficult to read text on a screen. This is Times New Roman, font size 10, and this is Arial, font size 10. Note the difference in the shape of the letters.

Choose a background for slides that is plain. If a slide background has any significant texture to it or designs on it, those factors make it more difficult to read the text.

When presenting a series of points on one slide, present a point and then dim it before presenting the next point. This enables students to see the previous point without having that point be distracting. When dimming previous points, it is recommended that you use a less intense shade of the same color as the text. "Dimming" a point by using a sharply contrasting color defeats the purpose.

Make the first slide an introductory slide with your name, school, and topic. Number each slide (e.g., 3 out of 10); so that students have an idea of how far through the presentation you are at any given point.

Including graphics such as charts or graphs is a good idea, but be sure that they are large enough for students to read easily. Also, be aware that if shading is used to differentiating part of graph, that the colors may look different when projected.

When making any presentation (with our without PowerPoint), maintain eye contact with your audience as opposed to reading material from a screen or notes, remember to speak loudly and clearly enough to be easily heard and understood at the back of the room, and keep your hands out of your pockets and out of your hair.

Some Computer-Related Devices

CD-ROM and CD-I

A CD-ROM (Compact Disk-Read Only Memory) contains a large amount of digitized information. For example, whole encyclopedias, complete with text, pictures, and sound, can be recorded on CD-ROMs and easily accessed by students. Using an encyclopedia on CD-ROM, for example, students can gain information about a topic, be referred to further information related to that topic, and then, without moving from their chairs and with just a few keystrokes, get that related information. In 1992 about twenty-five hundred high schools, or about fifteen percent, had CD-ROMs. In 1994, the number was about sixty-seven hundred, or forty percent.[105]

A CD-I (Compact Disk-Interactive) contains visual and audio data typically found on a CD-ROM, with computer-assisted instruction programming. It will provide for more flexibility than traditional CD-ROMs and more realism than traditional CAI.

Hardware and Software Problems

Computers have few moving parts so, with reasonable care, they last a long time. However, about every three years hardware advances, particularly advances in the speed and power of central processing units (CPU), make it possible for software writers to develop more powerful programs that make use of the new hardware. The older hardware and software become obsolete, few schools can afford to replace their computers with new ones every three years.

Further complicating matters are incompatible operating systems. A **disk operating system (DOS)** is the program that tells the computer how to access and use the programs stored on the hard and floppy disks. When microcomputers first became available, each company (Tandy/Radio Shack, Apple, and Commodore) wrote its own DOS. For example, Tandy/Radio Shack used the Tandy/Radio Shack Disk Operating System (TRSDOS), and Apple used the Apple Disk Operating System (Apple DOS).

When IBM entered the microcomputer market in 1981, it contracted with a company named Microsoft to write the DOS for the new IBM personal computers (PCs), and the result was the **Microsoft Disk Operating System (MS-DOS)**. As the microcomputer market expanded, other companies began producing computers and, in order to capitalize on the power of IBM in the business world, they made their computers IBM compatible—they made them to operate with MS-DOS.

Today, most software comes in versions designed for either IBM compatible or Apple Macintosh computers, but there are programs that enable IBM compatibles and Macintoshes to exchange information. Further, vendors produce parallel versions of programs, such as Microsoft's *Word*® and *Excel*®, to run on IBM compatibles and Macintoshes and this helps reduce conversion problems. Nonetheless, the problems with hardware and software obsolescence and incompatibility hinder the more rapid expansion of CAI.

Still further, many older buildings lack appropriate wiring and appropriate workspace for CAI. Problems such as these are expensive to correct.

Scanners
Scanner or optical character readers "read" the words on a page and save them in a computer's memory, just as if they had been entered from a keyboard. The file created can be saved as a word processing file or simply as data. The capability of scanners enables teachers to take any typed or printed page and convert it to a computer file. There is no longer a need to enter printed data via a keyboard.

Voice Synthesizers
Voice synthesizers can be used in conjunction with scanners to facilitate learning for the visually handicapped. One or more pages can be scanned into a computer's memory and then a voice synthesizer can be used to orally read the material. Students who have difficulty reading can listen.

DVDs
The on-line dictionary Webopedia defines DVDs as *digital versatile disc or digital video disc*, a type of optical disk technology similar to the CD-ROM. A DVD holds a minimum of 4.7GB of data, enough for a full-length movie. DVDs are commonly used as a medium

for digital representation of movies and other multimedia presentations that combine sound with graphics.

The DVD specification supports disks with capacities of from 4.7GB to 17GB and access rates of 600KBps to 1.3MBps. One of the best features of DVD drives is that they are backward-compatible with CD-ROMs, meaning they can play old CD-ROMs, CD-I disks, and video CDs, as well as new DVD-ROMs. Newer DVD players can also read CD-R disks. DVD uses MPEG-2 to compress video data.[106]

DVDs can be used in different areas and can achieve different purposes. Teachers can use them in the classroom as part of presentations. Also, DVD programs can be placed on reserve at the library. Students can view those programs at their convenience. Teachers also can use DVDs to supplement information that cannot be found in the textbook. Also, they can be used to reinforce concepts and ideas that are difficult to grasp. It also can be effective for students who might miss class due to unexpected absence.

Smart Boards (Interactive Whiteboards)
Nowadays, several digital technology tools (e.g., interactive whiteboards, tablets, handheld devices such as e-readers) are becoming a part of the instructional technology utilized in K–12 institutions. An interactive whiteboard is a touch screen device that works in conjunction with a computer and a projector. Teachers use whiteboards so they can use multimedia in their lesson plans. Utilizing whiteboards aims at improving and maximizing student learning. Using whiteboards helps students' engagement, active participation, and it helps create and promote an environment for differentiated instruction, thus meeting the needs of diverse learners.

SUMMARY

Two reasons instructional media are used are to (1) help vary the stimuli by which students learn, thus helping to capture and maintain interest, and (2) expose students to stimuli and experiences that might not otherwise be available, safe, or practical. Regardless of the kind of media being considered, there are certain steps that a teacher can take to help ensure that the media are selected and used properly. These steps include (1) selecting media that will help students achieve specific instructional objectives; (2) becoming familiar with the content of the material or the operation of the device before using it with students; (3) preparing the students so they can focus on specific elements or ideas; (4) maximizing the utility of the media by properly adjusting volume, brightness, size, or clarity; (5) conducting follow-up activities in order to clarify confusing points and to bring about closure; and (6) evaluate the experience to determine to what extent it contributed to students' achievement of the specified objective.

Many forms of mediated instruction are available to teachers, including older forms such as textbooks, films and filmstrips, overhead transparencies, maps and charts, bulletin boards, real things, audio and video tapes, television, and computers. Although each form of media has specific advantages and disadvantages, only computers have the advantage of being two-way communicators. The ability to respond to the input of individual students makes computers among the most powerful instructional tools that a teacher can use.

The expansion of computer utilization in the schools makes it possible for teachers to help students acquire skills that are highly relevant to our increasingly technological society. Two of these skills are the ability to use computers for word processing and to search large databases for specific information. Computers are also used to provide different forms of computer-assisted instruction, including drill and practice, tutorials, and simulations.

The use of CAI is hampered by the fact that schools are currently set up to provide group instruction, whereas computers are best used by individuals. This basic conflict generates problems for teachers with respect to planning, teaching, and evaluating. Other problems concern hardware and software incompatibility.

The Internet has dramatically changed education. We spend a good deal of time teaching students to use Internet-related resources and many of those resources are, without doubt, valuable. At the same time, some educators argue that the time spent teaching students to use the Internet comes at the expense of time previously used to teach content-related concepts and skills.

One of the most rapidly growing areas is that of online instruction. For those who like the idea it is a way of making instruction available to students while reducing or eliminating travel time and costs. It also reduces the need for traditional campuses.

For those who are less enthusiastic, online instruction is troubling because the instructor is not always sure who is at the other end of the communication line. Is it the students or a knowledgeable friend? From the student's perspective, who is actually teaching the course? The use of instructors from other countries to provide online tutoring and instruction is already happening, so it is not far-fetched to see that online courses offered by US institutions might actually be taught by adjunct faculty outside the United States. This is not necessarily bad, but it is something to think about.

SO HOW DOES THIS AFFECT MY TEACHING?

You cannot build a house with just a hammer or just a saw. You need a variety of tools, and the same is true of teaching and learning. No single procedure or tool can be used to help students achieve the variety of skills and knowledge that should be called for in your instructional objectives. There is a rich variety of tools available and the only factor limiting the use of most of them is the desire and/or creativity of the teacher. You can just lecture or lecture and discuss, but tools are readily available with which you can do much more. The most successful teachers use them.

Computers present serious challenges and great possibilities. Few schools are designed, and relatively few teachers are prepared, to capitalize on the potential of computer technology. Taken to its extreme, CAI could enable students to stay at home and learn much of what they now learn in school settings. The socialization factor would be missing, but its importance is a matter of philosophic position. What is most important is that you recognize that variety is important in capturing and maintaining student interest and that as you use new tools and teach students how to use them, you are helping to expand possibilities for them. Not only will the appropriate use of instructional tools help students achieve the objectives of the course, it will also make them aware of tools that they might use in other contexts. Use media. It will help you and your students be successful. At the same time, think about the truly revolutionary changes that computers can make in the way students are educated. Are you, for example, prepared to respond on your own time and via e-mail to each and every student who wants to ask a question or debate a point? Think about it. Just because a thing can be done does not necessarily mean that it is wise to do it.

KEY TERMS, PEOPLE, AND IDEAS

Technology

Mediated Instruction

Audio Aids—Radios, Record, Tape and CD Players

Telephones, Teleconferencing, Variable Speech Control

Opaque, Slide and Filmstrip Projectors

Bulletin boards, interaction

Overhead Projectors, transparencies, overlays

Document Cameras

Multimedia Kits

ETV, Whittle Communications, *Channel One*

Distance Learning

Closed-circuit television

Video tape recorders and players

Programmed Instruction

Sidney Pressey—teaching machine

B. F. Skinner, Linear programs—identical small steps, cues, high success rate

Norman Crowder, Branching programs—larger blocks of information, no cues, remediation, different paths

Computer Assisted Instruction (CAI), Computer Managed Instruction (CMI)

Patrick Suppes—Computer Curriculum Corporation

Time-sharing—PLATO, TICCIT

Microcomputers, 1979

CAI types: Drill and Practice, Tutorial, Simulation, Games

Stand-alone, computer managed, and integrated curriculum programs

Interactive video

Networking, LAN, Internet, e-mail

Online instruction

Technology integration

Disk Operating System (DOS), Central Processing Unit (CPU)

Application Programs—Word Processors, Spreadsheets, Databases, Presentation

CD-ROM, CD-I, Scanners, Voice Synthesizers, SMART boards

QUESTIONS FOR CONSIDERATION

1. Educational technology has changed rapidly during the twentieth and twenty-first centuries. To what extent do you agree or disagree that educational technology such as computers, the Internet, etc., help students learn?
2. Which of those educational technologies do think is more helpful to students' learning and why?
3. Explain at least five computer-related applications and how they can be integrated into instruction.
4. To what extent do you agree or disagree with the idea that online instruction helps promote students' learning?

ENDNOTES

1   *The American Heritage Dictionary*, 2nd ed., (Boston: Houghton Mifflin Co., 1985), 1248.

2   *Encyclopedia Britannica*, "Johann Gutenberg," 1960 ed., 12.

3   J. W. Brown, R. B. Lewis, and F. H. Fred, *A. V. Instruction—Media and Methods*, 3rd ed. (New York: McGrawHill, 1969).

4   Brown, Lewis, and Fred, *A. V. Instruction—Media and Methods*, 327.

5   D. B. Strother, "On Listening," *Phi Delta Kappan 68*, no. 8 (April 1987): 625–28.

6   R. Heinich, M. Molenda, and J. D. Russell, *Instructional Media*, 4th ed. (New York: Macmillan, 1993), 181.

7   E. A. Yeager and E. A. Pandiscio, "Newscasts in the Classroom," *Educational Leadership 50*, no. 8 (1993): 52–53.

8   L. H. Rutherford and S. Grana, "Fully Activating Interactive TV: Creating a Blended Family," *T.H.E Journal 22*, no. 3 (October 1994): 86–90.

9   S. L. Pressey, "A Machine for Automatic Teaching of Drill Material," *School and Society 25*, no. 645 (May 1927): 549–92.

10   B. F. Skinner, "The Science of Learning and the Art of Teaching," *The Harvard Educational Review 24* (Spring 1954): 86–97.

11   B. F. Skinner, *The Technology of Teaching* (Englewood Cliffs: Prentice Hall, 1968).

12   P. Saettler, *The Evolution of American Educational Technology* (Englewood: Libraries Unlimited, 1990), 295–96.

13   N. A. Crowder, "Automatic Tutoring by Means of Intrinsic Programming," in *Automatic Teaching: The State of the Art*, ed. Eugene Gatanter (New York: John Wiley, 1959), 109–10.

14   R. P. Niemiec and H. J. Walberg, "From Teaching Machines to Microcomputers: Some Milestones in the History of Computer-Based Instruction," *Journal of Research on Computing in Education* 21, no. 3 (Spring 1989): 272.

15   *The World Almanac Book and Book of Facts*, (New Jersey: Funk and Wagnalls, 1994), 196.

16   J. A. Kulik, R. L. Bangert, and G. W. Williams, "Effects of Computer-Based Teaching on Secondary School Students," *Journal of Educational Psychology* 75, no. 1 (1983): 19–26.

17   R. Niemiec et al., "The Effectiveness of Computer-based Instruction at the Elementary School Level: A Quantitative Synthesis," *AEDS Journal* 3 (1985): 19–37.

18   G. Poulson and E. Macken, *Evaluation Studies of CCC Elementary School Curriculums, 1975–1977* (Palo Alto: Computer Curriculum Corp., 1978).

19   *The World Almanac Book and Book of Facts 1995*, 221.

20   Internet World Stats: Usage and Population Statistics, accessed September 10, 2020, http://www.internetworldstats.com/stats.htm.

21   EducationData.Org, Online Education Statistics, accessed September 12, 2020, https://educationdata.org/online-education-statistics/.

22   EducationData.Org, Online Education Statistics.

23   G. Gromov, Internet pre-History: Ancient Roads of Telecommunications & Computers (1995), accessed September 14, 2020, http://www.netvalley.com/intval_intr.html.

24   International Technology Education Association (ITEA), Standards for Technological Literacy: Content for the Study of Technology. (2007). Retrieved from https://www.iteea.org/File.aspx?id=67767&v=b26b7852, March 20, 2021.

25   M. Golden, "Technology's potential, promise for enhancing student learning," *T.H.E Journal* 31, no. 12 (2004): 42, 44.

26   US Department of Education, No Child Left Behind. (Public Law 107-110), (Washington, DC: US Government Printing Office, 2001,) accessed December 2, 2020, https://www2.ed.gov/nclb/landing.jhtml.

27   Golden, "Technology's potential, promise for enhancing student learning," 44.

28   C. J. Shields and G. Rogers, "Incorporating experimental technologies in the middle level technology education classroom," *Journal of Industrial Teacher Education* 41, no. 4 (2005): 72–80.

29   S. Taylor and N. MacNeil, Understanding the millennial student, May 2005, slide 21, accessed December 2, 2020, https://www.powershow.com/view/a9ba3-Y2VkO/Understanding_the_Millennial_Student_powerpoint_ppt_presentation?varnishcache=1.

30   M. Prensky, "Engage me or enrage me: What today's learners demand," *Educause Review* (Sep–Oct 2005): 61–64.

31   US Department of Education, Learning for the 21st Century: A Report and MILE Guide for 21st Century Skills (Washington, DC, 2002), accessed December 2, 2020, https://files.eric.ed.gov/fulltext/ED480035.pdf.

32 Golden, "Technology's potential, promise for enhancing student learning," 42.

33 M. Okojie, and A. Olinzock, "Developing a positive mind-set toward the use of technology for classroom instruction," *International Journal of Instructional Media* 33, no. 1 (2006): 33–39.

34 V. Otero et al., "Integrating technology into teacher education," *Journal of Teacher Education* 56, no. 1 (2005): 10.

35 N. Matzen and J. Edmunds, "Technology as a catalyst for change: The role of professional development," *Journal of Research on Technology in Education* 39, no. 4 (2007): 418.

36 Okojie and Olinzock, "Developing a positive mind-set toward the use of technology for classroom instruction," 33–39.

37 D. Brzycki and K. Dudt, "Overcoming barriers to technology use in teacher preparation programs," *Journal of Technology and Teacher Education* 13, no. 4 (2005): 619–41.

38 J. Gaytan, "Multimedia technology integration and instructional practices in teaching business," *Delta Pi Epsilon* 44, no. 3 (2002): 216.

39 Brzycki and Dudt, "Overcoming barriers to technology use in teacher preparation programs," 619–41.

40 C. Franklin, "Factors that influence elementary teachers' use of computers," *Journal of Technology and Teacher Education* 15, no. 2 (2007): 267–93.

41 Franklin, "Factors that influence elementary teachers' use of computers," 267–93.

42 Gaytan, "Multimedia technology integration and instructional practices in teaching business," 205–20.

43 L. Liu, and D. L. Johnson, "Assessing student learning in instructional technology: Dimensions of a learning model," *Computers in the Schools* 18, no. 2/3 (2001): 79–95.

44 S. Dexter, A. H. Doering, and E. S. Riedel, "Content area specific technology integration: A model for educating teachers," *Journal of Technology and Teacher Education* 14, no. 2 (2006): 325–45.

45 S. Nussbaum-Beach, "No limits," *Technology & Learning* 28, no. 7 (2008): 15–18.

46 US Department of Education, Learning for the 21st Century: A Report and MILE Guide for 21st Century Skills, (Washington, DC, 2002), accessed December 2, 2020, https://files.eric.ed.gov/fulltext/ED480035.pdf.

47 S. Cramer, "Update your classroom with learning objects and twenty-first century skills," *The Clearing House* 89, no. 3 (2007): 126–32.

48 Cramer, "Update your classroom with learning objects and twenty-first century skills."

49 CEO Forum, Key building blocks for student achievement in the 21st century: Assessment, alignment, accountability, access, analysis, school technology, and readiness report, 2001, accessed December 2, 2020, http://www.cckln.edu.hk/libweb/Search%20Subject/All%20teachers/21st%20century%20learning/sch%20technology%20report.pdf.

50 CEO Forum, Key building blocks for student achievement in the 21st century.

51   C. Jellick, "Princeville: Becoming a 'model school,'" *Peoria Journal Star*, November 4, 2007, A17.

52   CEO Forum, Key building blocks for student achievement in the 21st century.

53   CEO Forum, Key building blocks for student achievement in the 21st century.

54   Taylor and MacNeil, Understanding the millennial student.

55   Taylor and MacNeil, Understanding the millennial student.

56   Taylor and MacNeil, Understanding the millennial student.

57   M. Villano, "Display technology: Picture this!" *T.H.E. Journal* 33, no. 16 (2006): 16–20.

58   Prensky M. (2005, Sept/Oct) Engage me or enrage me: What today's learners demand. *Educause Review*, 61–64.

59   Taylor and MacNeil, Understanding the millennial student.

60   N. Starkman, "The wonders of interactive whiteboards," *T.H.E. Journal* 33, no. 11 (May 2006): 1–3.

61   Starkman, "The wonders of interactive whiteboards."

62   Starkman, "The wonders of interactive whiteboards," 3.

63   V. Rivero, "The secrets of their success," *T.H.E. Journal* 23, no. 11 (June 2006): 41–46, 48, 50.

64   Villano "Display technology: Picture this!"

65   Villano "Display technology: Picture this!"

66   Villano "Display technology: Picture this!" 5.

67   Witte S. (2007, Oct.). That's online writing, not boring school writing: Writing with blogs and the Talkback Project. *Journal of Adolescent and Adult Literacy* 51, no. 2 (October 2007): 92–96.

68   Wikipedia. UNIVAC 1, http://en.wikipedia.org/wiki/UNIVAC_I, retrieved September 21, 2020.

69   Podcasting-k-12 Handhelds. (2007). Retrieved December 2, 2020, from Podcasting-k-12 handhelds website: https://dklaus79.blogspot.com/2007/01/podcasting-k12-handhelds.html.

70   B. Flanagan and B. Calandra, "Podcasting in the classroom," *Learning and Leading with Technology* 33, no. 3 (2005): 20–25.

71   Flanagan and Calandra, "Podcasting in the classroom."

72   Cramer, "Update your classroom with learning objects and twenty-first century skills."

73   H. Clark, A. Hosticka, and J. Bedell, "Digital cameras in the K–12 classroom," Proceedings of SITE 2000, San Diego, CA, 150, 1169–74.

74   M. Bowerman, "Technology for all: Successful strategies for meeting the needs of diverse learners," *T.H.E. Journal* 32, no. 10 (2005): 20.

75   S. McLester et al., "Making history," *Technology & Learning* 28, no. 7 (2008): 26.

76   Nussbaum-Beach, "No limits."

77   M. Schack, "Joining the search for extraterrestrial intelligence," *Science Teacher* 73, no. 7 (2006): 56–62.

78   E. Shaunessy and C. Page, "Promoting inquiry in the gifted classroom through GPS and GIS technologies," *Gifted Child Today* 29, no. 4 (2006): 42–53.

79   M. Travaille and S. D. Adams, "Using Digital Microscopy," *Science Teacher* 73, no. 4 (2006): 50–54.

80   E. Christmann and A. Holy, "Testing the pH of soft drinks," *Science Scope* 28, no. 8 (2005): 54–55.

81   M. Millar, "Technology in the lab; part I: What research says about using probeware in the science classroom," *Science Teacher* 72, no. 7 (2005): 34.

82   American Association for the Advancement of Science, *Benchmarks for science literacy* (New York: Oxford Press, 1993).

83   M. Horejsi, "Making technology inclusive," *Science and Children* 40, no. 3 (2003): 20–24.

84   CEO Forum, Key building blocks for student achievement in the 21st century.

85   Taylor and MacNeil, Understanding the millennial student.

86   McCormack and Jones, *Building a Web-Based Education System*, 1.

87   Rutherford and Grana, "Fully Activating Interactive TV: Creating a Blended Family."

88   Institute of Educational Sciences: National Center for Education Statistics. What percentage of elementary and secondary schools offer distance education? 2019, accessed September 14, 2020, https://nces.ed.gov/fastfacts/display.asp?id=79.

89   B. Broadbent, *ABCs of e-Learning: Reaping the Benefits and Avoiding the Pitfalls* (San Francisco: Jossey-Bass/Pfeiffer, 2002), 10–16.

90   C. McCormack and D. Jones, *Building a Web-Based Education System* (New York: Wiley Computer Publishing, 1998), 30.

91   McCormack and Jones, *Building a Web-Based Education System*, 31.

92   McCormack and Jones, *Building a Web-Based Education System*, 39.

93   McCormack and Jones, *Building a Web-Based Education System*, 44.

94   McCormack and Jones, *Building a Web-Based Education System*, 43.

95   McCormack and Jones, *Building a Web-Based Education System*, 45–51.

96   M. H. Partee, *Cyberteaching: Instructional Technology on the Modern Campus* (New York: University Press of America, Inc., 2002), 55.

97   J. Stephenson, *Teaching & Learning Online: Pedagogies for New Technologies* (London: Kogan Page Limited, 2001), 1–224.

98   F. Gillespie, "Instructional Design for the New Technologies," in *The Impact of Technology on Faculty Development, Life, and Work*, ed. K. H. Gillespie (San Francisco: Jossey-Bass, 1998), 39–52.

99   J. W. Schofield and A. L. Davidson, *Bringing the Internet to School: Lessons from an Urban District* (San Francisco, CA, Jossey-Bass, 2002): 207–55.

100   McCormack and Jones, *Building a Web-Based Education System*, 20–21.

101   Schofield and Davidson, *Bringing the Internet to School: Lessons from an Urban District*, 207–55.

102   Partee, *Cyberteaching: Instructional Technology on the Modern Campus*, 55.

103   Wikipedia, UNIVAC 1, http://en.wikipedia.org/wiki/UNIVAC_I, accessed September 21, 2020.

104   Petaflop, http://www.petaflop.info/, 2020, accessed September 22, 2020.

105   *The World Almanac Book and Book of Facts* (1995), 221.

106   Webopedia, http://www.webopedia.com/TERM/D/DVD.html, accessed September 24, 2020.

Index